Renewal of Business Tenancies

RENEWAL OF BUSINESS TENANCIES

A Practical Guide

Michael Haley

The Law Society

© Michael Haley 2006

Crown copyright material is reproduced with the permission of the Controller of Her Majesty's Stationery Office

ISBN-10: 1-85328-993-0
ISBN-13: 978-1-85328-993-4

Published in 2006 by the Law Society Publishing
113 Chancery Lane, London WC2A 1PL

Typeset by J&L Composition, Filey, North Yorkshire
Printed by MPG Books Ltd, Bodmin, Cornwall

Contents

Preface

The law of landlord and tenant is undoubtedly complex and abstruse. This is particularly so in the context of business leases and the operation of Part II of the Landlord and Tenant Act 1954, as revamped by the Regulatory Reform (Business Tenancies) (England and Wales) Order 2003. The purpose of this book is to shed light on the intricate workings of this important statutory scheme and to guide the reader through the mass of case law that it has generated in its wake. Perhaps sad, but true, it is a product of many years of research and writing on the 1954 Act. It also reflects distant memories of my life as a practising solicitor.

The law is stated as at 1 June 2006.

Michael Haley
Professor of Law
Keele University

Table of cases

Table of statutes

Table of statutory instruments

CHAPTER 1

Past and present

Contents

- Introduction
- The Landlord and Tenant Act 1927
- Part II of the Landlord and Tenant Act 1954
- The Regulatory Reform (Business Tenancies) (England and Wales) Order 2003

1.1 INTRODUCTION

Since *Pepper* v. *Hart* [1993] 1 All ER 42, the courts are willing and able to consider Hansard, government Green and White Papers and other official publications (such as Law Commission Reports) in the interpretation of legislative provisions. As Lord Griffiths put it, 'The courts now adopt a purposive approach which seeks to give effect to the true purpose of legislation and are prepared to look at much extraneous material that bears upon the background against which the legislation was enacted'. Nevertheless, the luxury of investigating the antecedents of Part II of the Landlord and Tenant Act 1954 (1954 Act) is one which is rarely afforded to the busy practitioner. It is however important to have some understanding of the background to the 1954 Act and its underlying policy. Perhaps inconveniently, in order to understand the present it has become necessary to negotiate the past. This chapter is designed to trace the origins of the present system and to follow its development up to and including the Regulatory Reform (Business Tenancies) (England and Wales) Order 2003, SI 2003/3096 (2003 Order).

1.1.1 Shortened history

As early as 1889, the Select Committee on Town Holdings accepted the need for legislation to protect business tenants from exploitation by their landlords. The Committee acknowledged that some landlords were demanding high rents as a condition of a lease renewal and that, if these demands remained unmet, their tenants would be evicted at the end of the contractual term. In addition to the loss of the premises, the tenant would sacrifice the value of any improvements made and, of course, whatever goodwill had been established. In order to eradicate this mischief, the Committee recommended that tenants should, on quitting the premises, be entitled to compensation for improvements and goodwill. Although it was not suggested that business tenants be given security of tenure, it was anticipated that an effective compensation scheme would encourage many landlords to grant a lease renewal as an alternative to digging deep into their pockets. The emphasis was upon safeguarding the financial interests of the tenant rather than ensuring the continuation of that tenant's business.

It was to take a further 38 years before Parliament made any serious effort to curtail the exploitation of business tenants. The first piece of permanent legislation, designed to regulate the relationship between the parties to a commercial lease, emerged in the form of Part I of the Landlord and Tenant Act 1927. The emphasis remained upon safeguarding the tenant's goodwill and improvements. While the intentions of the legislature were well meaning, the principle of compensation was woefully deficient in satisfying the needs of the business community. The imposition of financial sanctions as a deterrent was a mere second-best and it was clear that security of tenure was the only vehicle through which the tenant's interests could be effectively safeguarded.

1.1.2 Traditional resistance

The history leading up to the Landlord and Tenant Act 1927 provides a striking example of Parliamentary hesitancy and slowness. This is in contrast to the pioneering legislation which had already imposed controls over agricultural lettings and residential tenancies. Indeed, by 1918, most European countries had in place a statutory code for the protection of tenants of business premises. Tenant militancy, particularly on the part of small shopkeepers, was to stimulate reform. It was their protests and activism which meant that they (unlike other business tenants) would fall within the Rent Restrictions Act 1915 and later benefit exclusively from the Leasehold Property (Temporary Provisions) Act 1951. Although it was of more general application, the Rent Restrictions Act 1920 also emerged in order to quell the fear of discontent among shopkeepers.

In the view of Parliament, there appeared little justification for imposing controls over all landlords merely to curtail the activities of a small minority and, thereby, threaten future investment and building. It is, therefore, no coincidence that reforms eventually came about in the post-war periods when, on both occasions, it was felt strongly that the law had to be modernised to suit the needs of a commercialised, industrial nation. The movement for change gathered momentum because of extreme market distortions, an anti-profiteering ethos and the need to maintain economic recovery. Those opposed to change however continued to exert a restraining influence upon the development and form of legal controls. Until the Landlord and Tenant Act 1954, caution prevailed to the extent that reforms were both modest and limited.

Despite effective resistance from the landlord lobby, the calls for legislative intervention did not disappear. As a result of growing urbanisation and the increased population in cities and towns, the pressure for reform became heightened. In 1906, the Town Tenants' League was established and political lobbying for change began in earnest. Subsequently, the cause was championed also by the Leasehold Reform Association and the National Chamber of Trade. From 1908 onwards, the proposal of a Town Tenants Bill (usually dealing with both residential and business premises) became a regular feature of the House of Commons order paper. None however was destined to reach the statute book. By 1920, the case for reform was more vital. A post-war shortage of new building and the revival of trade and commerce ensured that competition for business premises was great. This abnormal demand and inadequacy of supply created a seller's market in which landlords were able to abuse their superior bargaining power. The potential for exploitation now assumed a much higher profile. It was feared that unscrupulous landlords were keen to capitalise on the distorted market and to raise rents to extortionate levels. In the background, entrepreneurs and multiple shopkeepers lurked waiting for the opportunity to buy leases with established goodwill over the heads of sitting tenants. The spectre of the profiteering landlord loomed large over the commercial rented sector.

The national interest introduced a new dynamic into the case for reform. It had become clear that, in order to facilitate a post-war economic recovery, existing businesses and premises had to be preserved while new buildings were constructed to cater for business expansion. Without the prospect of recompense at the end of their terms, tenants would be reluctant to sink money into development schemes and, thereby, enhance the value of the demised premises. Undue increases in rents were likely to lead to business closures and higher levels of unemployment, or to be passed on to the consumer and, thereby, stimulate inflation. The difficulty, of course, was to devise a regulatory system which prevented landlords from taking undue advantage of the abnormal demand for business accommodation and yet did not discourage new investment in property development. Unfortunately, there was no consensus as to what form that control should adopt.

1.1.3 Temporary expediencies

Prior to the Landlord and Tenant Act 1927, there existed two experimental provisions which extended limited rights to the business tenant. First, under the Increase of Rent and Mortgage Interest (War Restrictions) Act 1915

3

protection was offered to single lettings of small dwellings which had a mixed business and residential user. In a time of housing shortage, the protection of business premises was, therefore, by a side wind. Such protection as was offered took the form of a non-assignable prolongation of the tenancy beyond its contractual term and a system of rent control designed to maintain rents at the 1914 level. This was a mechanism clearly unsuited to the needs of business tenants.

Secondly, Rent and Mortgage Restrictions Act 1920, s.13 exclusively related to leases of business premises which fell within prescribed rateable values. For the first time, protection was extended to tenants of business premises without the need to establish an element of residential user. Although it had been the intention of the government to exclude business tenancies entirely from the Act, pressure from all political parties ensured the inclusion of this special and temporary provision. The immediate concern was to ensure that the hybrid class of tenants, which had fallen within the 1915 Act, would not face immediate eviction when that Act was repealed. The protection operated on two levels: it prevented the landlord from increasing the rent by more than 35 per cent and inhibited the recovery of possession at the end of the contractual tenancy. This control was designed only to last for a period of one year and lapsed on 24 June 1921. Accordingly, and until the Landlord and Tenant Act 1927, market forces were again allowed to prevail and, excepting mixed tenancies, commercial tenants were compelled to rely solely upon their contractual rights.

In 1920, the Select Committee on Business Premises recommended a further short-term remedy. Although this was to be ignored, it does contain the seeds of what was to develop into Part II of the Landlord and Tenant Act 1954. The proposal was to offer business tenants the right, on the expiry of the contractual term, to apply to a tribunal for the continuation of their tenancies (akin to the statutory tenancy already available to residential tenants). The landlord would be given the ability to oppose the application on strictly delimited grounds and, if successful, the tribunal would have the power to award compensation to the tenant. The Committee believed that these controls were necessary only as a temporary measure (they were intended to last only for a period of two-and-a-half years) to cater for the immediate post-war shortage of premises.

Contrary to the expectations of the Select Committee and many politicians however the problems experienced by business tenants did not disappear. An increased demand for retail outlets ensured that speculation in properties with established goodwill persisted. Tenants now complained of the additional abuse that, in order to obtain consent to make improvements, some lessors demanded the payment of a fine and/or increased rent. Rumours were rife that, in large cities, many tenants had been ruined by the operation of the present system.

4

When permanent reform came, it was primarily a political ploy which, at a time when public support was slipping away from the government, was designed to keep on board the votes of the disgruntled trading and shop-keeping community. With one year to go before the next election, the government clearly saw profit in placating a growing sense of injustice. The government stance was that, when worked by an ideal landlord, the leasehold system operated perfectly well to the benefit of both parties and the general community. By necessity however it had to be acknowledged that there were unscrupulous landlords who did take unfair advantage of their tenants, particularly when the time came to make an improvement or to obtain a renewal. It followed that legislative controls would merely serve as a code of practice designed to put all landlords in the same category as the good landlord. Hence, the reasonable lessor would have nothing to fear from an enactment framed to shield the tenant against the action of a harsh and unconscionable landlord. Although the Landlord and Tenant Bill 1927 had a stormy ride through the Commons, it was rushed through the House of Lords and received Royal Assent on 22 December 1927.

1.2 THE LANDLORD AND TENANT ACT 1927

Part I of the Landlord and Tenant Act 1927 was modelled on the general recommendations of the Select Committee on Town Holdings 1889. The scheme was to echo legislation which was thought to operate well in both Eire and France. The protection of the business tenant's interests was, therefore, to be achieved by a system which offered compensation for loss of goodwill and improvements. The theory was simple: if the landlord gained through the presence of the tenant then compensation must be paid or a renewal granted. It was a measure which appeared to go some way both in redressing the inequality of bargaining power and in tackling the mischief of which business tenants had long complained. Business tenants were, at least in the short term, satisfied by the fact that some protective legislation was in place and the hope that it would facilitate reasonable security of tenure.

In reality, the scheme was defective and provided little assistance to the business community. It was thought of as a timid measure which simply did not go far enough. The failure to offer security of tenure as a direct right was its major deficiency. In addition, the key goodwill provisions were ill-thought out, largely unworkable and easily sidestepped by a well advised landlord. Although the 1927 Act may validly be viewed as a wasted opportunity, it did recognise the necessity that business tenancies be subject to permanent statutory regulation. From there on, the principle was unchallengeable and there could be no retreat. Indeed, the abject failure of the statutory scheme encouraged the later adoption of more radical solutions to the problems faced by the business community. Unarguably, the most significant aspect of Part I

5

was the machinery whereby, in admittedly rare circumstances, the tenant could be awarded a new lease. For the first time, the court was given the jurisdiction to order the grant of a new tenancy of business premises. This was to set a broader precedent for future reforms.

As regards business tenancies, the 1927 Act addressed the mischief of bad landlordism in several discrete ways:

- the general attempt was made to minimise the effect of leasehold covenants which prohibited the alienation, development or improvement of premises. This was achieved by s.19 which implies into qualified covenants (those which expressly require the consent of the landlord) the proviso that this consent cannot be unreasonably withheld. With some minor amendment, these measures remain in force to the present day;
- the business tenant was entitled to claim compensation for approved structural improvements (which cannot be removed as tenant's fixtures) at the end of the lease;
- the business tenant was allowed to claim compensation for goodwill at the end of the contractual term. As goodwill is an intangible form of personal property which can be assigned and/or protected against unlawful interference, it was a logical progression to allow a tenant to be recompensed for its loss;
- the business tenant was entitled to the grant of a new lease in circumstances where the lessee was entitled to compensation for goodwill, but the sum to be awarded (based on landlord's gain) would be insufficient to compensate the tenant. If the tenant's claim was successful there could only be one renewal and its term could not exceed 14 years. The rent was to be fixed by the court on the basis of what a willing lessee would pay to a willing lessor, disregarding any value attributable to goodwill and tenant's improvements.

1.2.1 Momentum continued

It was only in the aftermath of the Second World War that concern for the business tenant again became a pressing issue. For almost a decade there had been no new building, and bombing had seriously depleted the stock of pre-existing premises, particularly in the larger cities. Since 1945, there had been a major revival and expansion of commercial activity, and existing businesses now found themselves in fierce competition with new firms seeking premises from which to trade. As in 1918, this increased demand created a seller's market in which landlords were able to take advantage of their sitting tenants. It became clear that the Landlord and Tenant Act 1927 had failed to achieve its purpose, and that business tenants remained vulnerable to exploitation. Accordingly, in December 1948 the government set up the Leasehold Committee with the remit to determine whether business tenants should be given security of tenure and/or enhanced rights to compensation for improvements at the expiry of their tenancies. The Committee published two reports, that is, an Interim Report (1949) and a Final Report (1950). The Reports contained fundamentally divergent approaches and made very different recommendations.

1.2.2 Interim recommendations

The Interim Report based its recommendations on the assumption that business tenants did not want rent control, rather they sought security of tenure and the ability to carry on trade without interruption. Compensation was viewed as being insufficient to achieve this stability. The Committee felt that there was an immediate need to secure the sitting tenant against the risk of unreasonable disturbance by the landlord. This enabled it to make the crucial leap and recommend that a general entitlement to security of tenure for existing tenants was the only way to ensure fair dealing. A simple, predictable and easily enforced renewal scheme would obviate the need for any system of rent control and largely overcome the defects associated with the goodwill provisions contained in the 1927 Act. The Interim Report advocated a sweeping system whereby sitting tenants, excepting those in new buildings, would be given the *prima facie* right to a new lease. This renewal could not exceed seven years, but the tenant would then be able to apply for further renewals. Only in special circumstances would the landlord be able to defeat the tenant's claim. The right to renewal was to extend to all types of business and professional activity and was not to be limited according to size of the premises or rateable values. There was also to be no minimum period of occupation as a condition of entitlement. The scheme was to interlock with the Landlord and Tenant Act 1927 to the extent that a failure to secure renewal would not deprive the tenant of any claim for compensation for goodwill and improvements and that a notice of a claim for a new lease would operate also as notice of an alternative claim to compensation.

1.2.3 Recommendations of the Final Report

The Committee (now under a different chairman) drew final conclusions that varied greatly, both in principle and in detail, from the Committee's interim recommendations. It was felt that the business tenant's predicament had been overstated in the Interim Report and did not justify placing drastic restrictions on the contractual rights of all landlords of commercial premises. As its chairman, Jenkins L.J. explained, 'If abuse is the exception rather than the rule, I do not see how it can be right in principle to subject the whole business community to a new system of control . . . merely for the purpose of preventing the relatively few cases of unfair dealing which might otherwise occur'.

7

The Final Report was however to favour renewal rights over compensation and took the view that, if the tenant's claim was successful, a new lease not exceeding 14 years could be ordered. The tenant would be entitled to apply for a further renewal at a later date. The rent payable under the renewed lease was to be a fair market rent, disregarding any goodwill and tenants' improvements. The other terms of the new lease, subject to the discretion of the tribunal, were to mirror those in the original tenancy. If the claim for renewal was refused, compensation would remain as the alternative. Nevertheless, the Final Report did not advocate a *prima facie* right to security of tenure. Instead, it proposed a scheme under which the tenant had to establish special circumstances in order to justify a new lease. This reflected the basic tenet of the Final Report that the landlord's right of property should not be overridden in any fundamental fashion. In marked contrast to its interim recommendations, the Committee now sought to protect the legitimate claims of the landlords and to avoid unduly favouring tenants. The Committee resolved that the existing machinery contained in the Landlord and Tenant Act 1927 should be modified to allow the tenant to apply for a new lease without first proving the case for compensation. This was subject to what the Committee described as 'just exceptions' whereby the tenant's claim would be debarred. It was intended that the tenant would have to show that:

- it had carried on a trade, business or profession from the premises for a minimum period of three years;
- no suitable alternative accommodation was available;
- it was reasonable for a new tenancy to be ordered against the wishes of the landlord.

1.2.4 New deal for tenants

Although it was apparent that further legislative controls were necessary to protect business tenants, the irreconcilable differences, in both tone and content, between the Interim and Final Reports of the Leasehold Committee obscured the way forward. Hence, it was to take a further four years before a revamped code for commercial premises was introduced. Although many of the Committee's recommendations were never to be followed, within the two reports can be found the basic framework of what was to become the Landlord and Tenant Act 1954. The enduring legacy of these protracted and divergent deliberations was, undoubtedly, the shift of emphasis from compensation towards renewal rights. It meant that security of tenure was to become the hallmark of subsequent legislation. The outstanding difficulty, of course, was to design a scheme which, while derogating from the landlord's common law rights, would operate fairly and effectively.

In the aftermath of the publication of the Final Report however the Leasehold Property (Temporary Provisions) Act 1951 was passed through

Parliament. This was destined to have a life span of only three years, and Part II of the 1951 Act gave tenants (of retail shop premises only) the ability to apply to the county court for a new tenancy, not exceeding one year, at a reasonable rent. Further applications could be made later and, in theory at least, a series of extensions built up. The temporary scheme, albeit popular with shop tenants, was merely a stop-gap measure until Parliament could decide on a permanent and generally applicable system. It did however provide a valuable opportunity for experimentation with a system which afforded security of tenure as a *prima facie* right. It was an experiment which appeared to work well.

In January 1953, the government produced a White Paper which accepted the general proposition that improved security of tenure should be made available as a permanent measure to business and professional tenants. It admitted that rent control and the concept of a statutory tenancy should not feature in the regulation of business tenancies. Nevertheless, the White Paper concluded that neither scheme put forward by the Leasehold Committee was wholly satisfactory and that 'a new approach' was required. The tenant was to be offered the automatic right to a new lease on fair market terms, defeasible only on limited grounds. The twin tenets of this new deal for commercial lessees were as follows. First, a tenant in occupation had a greater right than any alternative tenant to the premises. Secondly, if the landlord successfully opposed renewal, the tenant should (in defined circumstances) be entitled to claim compensation for disturbance. The new deal for business tenants was finally to materialise.

1.3 PART II OF THE LANDLORD AND TENANT ACT 1954

The central strand of policy underlying the Part II provisions is that the business tenant is to be given legal rights sufficient to enforce the standards expected from a reasonable landlord. The 1954 Act, moreover, was framed so that the poor tenant (i.e. one in breach of covenant) would not be entitled to renewal or compensation. By these means, the disturbance of business premises was to be reduced to a minimum and the parties encouraged to settle by agreement without recourse to the courts. The key features of the statutory scheme are as follows:

- the 1954 Act applies to a tenancy of premises occupied by the tenant for business purposes which are not otherwise excluded from the statutory scheme;
- until the contractual tenancy is terminated, the 1954 Act lies dormant. Accordingly, it does nothing to affect the rights of the parties at this stage and to prevent the original lease being brought to an end by any method provided by the contract (e.g. by the exercise of a break clause);

9

- on the termination of the contractual tenancy however the status quo is preserved through the mechanism of a continuation tenancy. This continuation tenancy allows the tenant to remain in possession, essentially on the same terms as before. The continuation tenancy is designed to operate during the continuation period until final disposal of any renewal application;
- the continuation tenancy may only be terminated by one of the methods permitted by the 1954 Act. These are forfeiture, notice to quit by a periodic tenant, consensual surrender, landlord's statutory termination notice, tenant's statutory request for a new lease and a fixed-term tenant's notice;
- the tenant is afforded the right to a new lease on terms agreed with the landlord or ordered by the court. The landlord can defeat the tenant's right to a renewal only on strictly delimited grounds;
- in certain circumstances, the tenant can claim compensation for the loss of the right to obtain a new lease (commonly known as disturbance). The availability of compensation depends upon what grounds of opposition the landlord successfully defeated the tenant's renewal right.

1.3.1 Maintaining a balance

Although the landlord's ability to let the premises is severely impeded by the tenant's rights, the 1954 Act should not be viewed as a tenant's charter. The Act takes pains to preserve the core advantages of landlordism. This is achieved in the following ways:

- there is no rental subsidy for the tenant on renewal and the landlord can oppose the claim for a new lease in the interests of good estate management;
- the 1954 Act does not freeze the terms of the original lease, and gives the court the discretion to redefine, where deemed appropriate and reasonable, the contractual relationship between the parties;
- the compensation provisions may also work favourably in the landlord's interest as the amount to be awarded reflects neither the tenant's loss nor the landlord's gain. Instead, it is based on an arbitrary formula of a sum equal to the rateable value of the premises, multiplied by one if the tenant had been in occupation for less than 14 years, or by two if occupation was for more than 14 years. Undoubtedly, this 'rough and ready' measure can work unfairly for tenants and lead to substantial injustice;
- lease renewal is not automatic. Instead, being the subject of a highly technical procedure, the new lease has to be earned by the tenant through time-consuming form filling and process serving.

1.3.2 From principle to detail

As part of its first programme of reform, the Law Commission considered the operation of Part II of the Landlord and Tenant Act 1954. In 1967 it produced a Working Paper and in 1969 published a Final Report. The Commission adopted the stance that the 1954 Act worked quite successfully and had proved advantageous both to the landlord and to the tenant. Although there was no attempt to redefine principle or policy, the Report accepted that certain anomalies and failings had emerged during the preceding 15 years. Nevertheless, the Commission declined to investigate all known shortcomings and a number of issues were left over for future consideration. The neglected problem areas included the definition of the term 'business'; the complexity, timing and service of the statutory notices and counter notices; and the lack of sanctions for the failure by landlords and tenants to provide information as required by the 1954 Act. Ironically, it was to take a further 20 years before these issues were aired again.

As a result of its survey, the Law Commission recommended a number of changes and these were to form the basis of the Law of Property Act 1969. The Commission sought to make the provisions more certain, workable and just. The reforms were designed to ensure that both parties to the lease obtained fair treatment. The Law of Property Act 1969 was, therefore, no more than an exercise in fine-tuning and clarification. The landlord's position was however strengthened in several substantive ways and these included:

- the introduction of an interim rent procedure, whereby the landlord could apply for a new rent to cover the period of the tenant's continuation tenancy, was designed purely to improve the landlord's income stream from the premises;
- enabling the court to include a rent review clause within the new lease;
- giving the court the power to sanction 'contracting out' and extending the scope for temporary lettings to fall outside the statutory provisions.

From the tenant's perspective, the Law of Property Act 1969 contained three benefits. First, the disregard of tenant's improvements in setting the new rent was, subject to conditions, to embrace improvements made during previous tenancies. Secondly, the condition precedent that a formal application for a new lease must precede a claim for compensation for disturbance was abandoned. Thirdly, where the landlord claimed possession on the basis of redevelopment, the court was authorised to grant the tenant a new lease of part of the original holding (e.g. where possession of only part of the tenant's holding was reasonably required to carry out the works).

Little further development occurred until 1984, when the Department of the Environment undertook a review of the workings of the statutory scheme. This review concluded that no legislative changes were required. It was accepted that the 1954 Act operated satisfactorily and maintained an even balance between the rights of both landlord and tenant. Nevertheless, there remained areas of detail which were widely held to be in need of reform. Subsequently, the cause was again championed by the Law Commission. In 1988, a Working Paper was published which focused attention upon a number of technical defects evident in the statutory scheme, but did not propose any fundamental reform. In 1992, a Law Commission Report embodied an extensive catalogue of detailed reforms with the intention of producing a more streamlined and fair procedure. Significantly, the Commission again stressed that no fundamental changes were necessary and accepted that the objectives of the 1954 Act had stood the test of time.

In 2001, the Department of the Environment, Transport and the Regions published a Consultation Paper which again emphasised that no basic changes to the existing system were required. The Consultation Paper put forward a number of reform proposals, largely based upon the recommendations of the Law Commission, in order to modernise the detailed operation of the law. The governmental aims were to remove a number of anomalies from the current system and to engineer a more streamlined, fair and effective renewal process. They were not however designed to mark any major shift in policy or to alter fundamentally the 'philosophically sound' legislative framework imposed by the 1954 Act.

1.4 THE REGULATORY REFORM (BUSINESS TENANCIES) (ENGLAND AND WALES) ORDER 2003

The 2003 Order has implemented many of the recommendations put forward in the Consultation Paper. The changes to Part II of the Landlord and Tenant Act 1954 came into effect on 1 June 2004. This reform package was introduced in a novel fashion through a relatively new Parliamentary procedure, i.e. a regulatory reform order under the Regulatory Reform Act 2001. Although the 2003 Order has made various and major changes to the renewal scheme, there was to be no fundamental shift in policy. Instead, as the Deputy Prime Minister explained in his published commentary on the reform proposals, the 2003 Order seeks, 'to make the renewal or termination of business tenancies quicker, easier, fairer and cheaper. It would remove certain traps for the unwary. This is particularly important for small business tenants without access to in-house professional advice'. The primary changes introduced in the wake of the 2003 Order include:

- abolishing court involvement with contracting out;
- extending the meaning of occupation by lifting the corporate veil that exists between companies and the people that control them;
- prescribing new *pro forma* notices (to be found in the Landlord and Tenant Act 1954, Part 2 (Notices) Regulations 2004, SI 2004/1005);

- increasing the information that one party can require from the other and widening the availability of redress for a failure to provide such information;
- abolishing the tenant's counter notice (in both its negative and positive forms);
- allowing landlords to apply for renewal on behalf of their tenants;
- altering the time limits for court applications as well as permitting their extension by agreement;
- allowing the landlord to apply for a termination order which will end the continuation tenancy;
- making changes relating to the timing of a fixed-term tenant's notice to terminate a continuation tenancy;
- promoting new rules as to the calculation of the interim rent when the landlord does not oppose renewal and extending to the tenant the right to apply for an interim rent;
- amending the provisions concerning compensation for disturbance and misrepresentation;
- promoting a more sensible operation of the Part II machinery when a split or divided reversion is in existence.

CHAPTER 2

Statutory scheme

Contents

2.1   INTRODUCTION

As demonstrated in the preceding chapter, the fundamental aim of Part II of the Landlord and Tenant Act 1954 is to confer on business tenants security of tenure without otherwise interfering with market forces. Provided that the tenant complies, within prescribed time limits, with a series of complex and technical statutory formalities, and on the understanding that the landlord cannot establish a ground of opposition as listed in s.30(1)(*a*)–(*g*), the entitlement is to a new lease at a market rent. If the tenant is unable to obtain a renewal, flat rate compensation for disturbance may be available under s.37(1). Until the contractual tenancy is terminated however the relationship between landlord and tenant remains regulated by the general law. Although the 1954 Act does nothing to prevent the original lease being brought to an end by any method provided by the contract (e.g. the exercise of a break clause), termination of the contractual term serves to activate its protective provisions. Provided that the lease is not contracted out of the Act, a s.24(1) continuation tenancy arises immediately and the relationship between landlord and tenant indefinitely maintained.

The continuation tenancy, moreover, may only be terminated by one of the methods permitted by the Act. Of these methods, the landlord's s.25 termination notice and the tenant's s.26 request for a new tenancy have a dual function and serve also to engage the renewal procedure. These latter notices however may only be served by and on a limited class of landlord or tenant, as appropriate. It is with the adaptation of the common law and the mechanisms, concepts and characters pivotal to the statutory scheme that this chapter is concerned.

2.2 CONTRACTING OUT: THE NEW RULES

In its original form, the 1954 Act contained a blanket prohibition on contracting out. As a result of the Law of Property Act 1969, a radical facility was introduced into s.38 under which the parties were able to make a joint application to the court, requesting the approval for the grant of a fixed-term lease to which ss.24–28 of the 1954 Act did not apply. Other agreements purporting to exclude or to modify the tenant's renewal rights were rendered void by s.38(1). As the contracting out of a head lease ensures that any later sub-tenancies granted will also fall outside the statutory scheme, the facility effectively guarantees that the landlord can recover possession at the end of the contractual term.

The ambition of the legislature in 1969 was merely to offer contracting out as an encouragement for landlords to grant short-lets of properties which would otherwise stand empty. Nevertheless, contracting out quickly became the primary method by which landlords sidestep the security of tenure provisions. The facility has, therefore, been utilised much more widely than was originally envisaged and is employed regardless of the length of the lease to be granted. The general availability of contracting out, and the ease by which it can be engineered, has potentially rendered the statutory scheme optional at the behest of the parties.

This is particularly so in light of the changes introduced by the Regulatory Reform (Business Tenancies) (England and Wales) Order 2003, SI 2003/3096.

The original s.38 has been overhauled by the insertion of a new s.38A into the 1954 Act. This has had the effect of abandoning the court's involvement with contracting out and has left the matter now solely in the hands of the parties. The parties enjoy an exclusively statutory jurisdiction to make the order and therefore there can be no contracting out beyond that permitted by s.38A. As demonstrated in *Nicholls* v. *Kinsey* [1994] 2 WLR 622, no additional power is available. Hence, a departure from the procedure laid down by Parliament will make the agreement inherently invalid and always a nullity.

Not all leases can however be taken outside the ambit of the 1954 Act and there are still formalities that need to be attended to before a contracting out is valid.

2.2.1 A term of years certain

Only a tenancy granted for 'a term of years certain' can be contracted out of the 1954 Act. For more than 20 years it has been the conventional wisdom that, for these purposes, the expression 'a term of years certain' includes any fixed term (including a term for a year and for less than a year). It does not matter, moreover, whether the lease contains an option to surrender before its term ends or a break clause (*Scholl Manufacturing Co Ltd* v. *Clifton (Slimline) Ltd* [1967] 1 Ch 41). Although it can be regarded as a term of years, a periodic tenancy falls outside the 1954 Act because such tenancies are not certain. In *Re Land & Premises at Liss, Hants* [1971] 3 All ER 380, for example, Goulding J. recognised that a six-month tenancy fell within the ambit of the contracting-out provisions. In the light that they do not apply to a periodic tenancy, he explained, 'But it seems very unlikely that having decided to permit contracting out with regard to fixed terms, the legislature should think it was inappropriate where the fixed term was very short although appropriate where the fixed term was long. One would have thought that if a distinction had been made it would have been much more likely to be the other way'. In *Nicholls* v. *Kinsey* [1994] 2 WLR 622 however a 12-month term to be followed by a yearly tenancy was held to fall outside the scope of the provisions. While it could be properly regarded as a term of years, the yearly tenancy arising at the end of the fixed term prevented it from being 'certain'. It could not, moreover, be construed as a fixed term of at least two years' duration (*EWP Ltd* v. *Moore* [1992] QB 460). If the rider of the periodic tenancy had not been added, the tenancy in the *Nicholls* case would have been validly contracted out.

2.2.2 Subsisting lease

As the facility is available only in relation to a proposed lease however there can be no contracting out of a subsisting lease. A tenancy granted unconditionally cannot later be brought before the court for approval (*Essexcrest Ltd* v. *Evenlex Ltd* [1988] 1 EG 56). Although the drafting of the contracting-out provisions did not anticipate that the landlord and tenant would already have an existing relationship, in *Tottenham Hotspur Football & Athletic Co Ltd* v. *Princegrove Publishers Ltd* [1974] 1 All ER 17 Lawson J. concluded, 'The language is apt to cover – and, clearly, in my judgment, the sub-section does cover – a situation in which an existing landlord and tenant agree that there shall be a new lease of the demised premises, to come into existence between them at some future date'. This means that, at the end of a current lease, any new lease between the parties can be contracted out of the 1954 Act.

2.2.3 Procedure

As mentioned, contracting out no longer has to be approved and ordered by the court. Although the involvement of the court was traditionally viewed as a safeguard to prevent wholesale avoidance of the 1954 Act, the judiciary most certainly did not adopt an interventionist stance. In reality, the former procedure offered little more than bringing the significance of exclusion formally to the attention of the tenant. In order to minimise expense and delay, in 1992 the Law Commission recommended the introduction of a new system under which contracting out will be a matter solely for agreement. It is this system that is embodied within s.38A.

The new procedure depends upon the landlord serving a notice on the tenant and the tenant, following a period of reflection, declaring that the lease is to be contracted out. The process unfolds as follows:

- the landlord must serve on the tenant a notice in the form, or substantially in the form, set out in Schedule 1 to the 2003 Order;
- the landlord has obtained a signed declaration from the tenant. If the notice is given at least 14 days prior to the contracting out, the declaration is a simple, signed acknowledgement by the tenant. If the 14 days' advance warning is waived, the tenant must make a formal statutory declaration;
- by virtue of Schedule 2 to the 2003 Order, the agreement must be contained in (or endorsed upon) the lease. It is thought that, if it is an oral, fixed-term tenancy, the agreement must be noted in any other document as specified by the court. In *Tottenham Hotspur Football & Athletic Co Ltd* v. *Princegrove Publishers Ltd* [1974] 1 All ER 17, Lawson J. explained the purpose behind this requirement, 'these procedural devices were introduced in order that third parties, prospective assignees, or prospective mortgagees of the tenant's interest under a lease should know . . . that this is a lease which . . . has a special restriction'. Although the Law Commission proposed that the contracting out of oral leases should be prevented, this has not been implemented. Accordingly, there may still be the trap for a future assignee of an oral lease. Contracting out may have occurred, but the assignee may remain unaware.

2.2.4 Landlord's notice

The contracting-out notice is highly stylised and set out in Schedule 1 to the 2003 Order. Understandably, it requires the name and address of both parties to be set out. It also contains an important 'health' warning which tells the tenant that the lease will not carry security of tenure and that the tenant should not enter the lease without recourse to a professional adviser. The notice goes on to explain in laymen's terms what are the consequences of sacrificing security of tenure. The message even when paraphrased is stark:

- you will have no right to stay in the premises when the lease ends;
- you will need to leave the premises unless the landlord offers you a new lease;
- you will be unable to obtain statutory compensation for loss of the premises;
- you will have no right to ask the court to set the rent under any new lease offered by the landlord;
- you should seek legal advice before giving up these rights, particularly so if you wish to stay in the premises at the end of the lease.

The notice also states that if the notice gives a 14-day cooling off period, the tenant will need only to sign a simple declaration that the notice has been received and its consequences accepted. The tenant is advised that, unless there are special reasons for taking the lease sooner, it is appropriate to ask the landlord for at least a 14-day cooling off period within which the tenant can consider whether to give up its statutory rights. It would also avoid a separate visit to a solicitor. This saving occurs because, if a lesser period is offered by the landlord, the tenant will have to visit an independent solicitor in order to sign a statutory declaration that the notice has been received and its contents are understood.

2.2.5 Agreement and declaration

Schedule 2 to the 2003 Order stipulates the requirements for a valid contracting-out agreement. It makes clear that the general rule is that the notice must be served on the tenant not less than 14 days before the tenant enters the tenancy or, if earlier, any contract to take the tenancy. In such a case, the tenant or its agent must make a declaration before entry into the lease/contract in the form, or substantially in the form, as set out in paragraph 7. This simple declaration must include the name and address of the declarant, the address of the premises to be demised, the commencement date of the proposed lease and a statement that the consequences of the notice are accepted. It also contains a prominent warning that the tenant will be giving up key legal rights and should not sign without taking legal advice.

If the requirement as to 14 days' notice is not met, the notice must still be served on the tenant before the tenant takes the lease or, if earlier, enters any contract to take the tenancy. The tenant or its agent must before that time make a statutory declaration in the form, or substantially in the form, set out in paragraph 8. The form of statutory declaration to be used here contains information similar to the paragraph 7 notice (above), except of course it requires a solemn and sincere declaration in front of a solicitor and the solicitor is required to sign the declaration.

2.2.6   Post-notice changes

There is no requirement that the draft lease be sent to the tenant along with the landlord's notice. Indeed, the notice need only disclose the parties to the proposed lease. The tenant's declaration, moreover, only needs to contain in addition a statement of the address of the premises and the commencement date of the lease on the tenant's declaration. No further details of the terms are explicitly referred to in either the notice or declaration. It is however inconceivable that the tenant would not have seen a draft lease before agreeing to contract out of the 1954 Act.

It remains to be seen whether, as under the old law, a major change in the terms of the lease between the time when the landlord's notice is served and the making of the tenant's declaration will invalidate the contracting out. Similarly, the question must be posed in circumstances where the substantial changes occur after the declaration, but (of course) prior to the grant. The issue turns upon the relevance to the revamped scheme of the reasoning of the Court of Appeal in *Receiver for the Metropolitan Police District* v. *Palacegate Properties Ltd* [2000] 3 All ER 663.

2.2.7   The *Palacegate* point

The disputed lease in favour of Palacegate Properties Ltd was for five years, subject to a break clause, and allowed the tenant to use the land as a car park and storage area. The parties made their joint application to court and put a draft of the lease before the district judge. The court order was issued and the lease was later granted. The tenant later argued that the contracting out was void on the basis that the lease contracted out made no reference to how the annual rent was to be paid and, hence, the presumption at common law was that it was payable in arrears. The lease as later executed required the rent to be payable in advance. It was submitted by the tenant that, as the implied term of the lease as approved by the court had been altered by an express term of the later grant, the tenancy was brought back within the scope of the 1954 Act.

The tenant relied on the expression 'in relation to a tenancy to be granted' (which is a phrase still used in s.38(1) and s.38A(1)). It was contended that contracting out can occur only when the tenant knows what is being given up in relation to the whole of a specific tenancy. The landlord countered that, as the tenant knows that statutory protection is being given up with respect to the proposed tenancy, the parties should thereafter be free to agree such terms as they see fit. Pill L.J. saw some force in this contention, but felt that the words 'in relation to that tenancy' could not simply be ignored. The difficulty was what effect should be given to that expression. Most certainly, the parties could not have total freedom to contract new terms. As Pill L.J. concluded, 'I do not consider that a section which provides that an agreement to waive protection ... gives a green light to a landlord to make wholesale changes to the draft tenancy'. Consequently, the words 'that tenancy' require the terms of the actual grant to bear a substantial similarity to the draft put before the tenant when contracting out occurs. Pill L.J. however drew a distinction between those changes that were deemed so substantial as to undermine the freedom of consent and those that were not. The mere fact that the draft version is different from the terms of the lease as granted does not therefore automatically invalidate the agreement to contract out. The court is concerned with whether the tenant understands it is giving up protection. As Pill L.J. acknowledged, 'Whether the rent is payable in advance or in arrears has in present circumstances no bearing whatever upon that function'. The precise identity of the landlord appears also to be insufficiently material to taint the contracting out (*Brighton & Hove City Council* v. *Collinson* [2004] EWCA Civ 678).

As the new notice and declaration procedure does require the prospective tenant to confirm that it knows what is being given up, the tenant's consent must in some way be premised upon the terms of the proposed grant. Hence a major change could well be material to the tenant's giving of informed consent to the sacrifice of statutory protection. For example, the duration of the lease would be a material consideration in the case of a lease which contemplated substantial capital expenditure by the tenant. As Pill L.J. accepted, a change which substantially shortens the term would therefore be material and cast doubt upon the validity of the tenant's agreement. Under the old scheme, it would operate to nullify the contracting out. By analogy, if the terms of the draft lease are subsequently varied by the insertion of a break clause, this change would under the old law take the tenancy outside the scope of the order.

Owing to the emphasis upon consent, recourse to legal advice and time for reflection, the same reasoning must apply under the new scheme. This is particularly as the revamped provisions still employ the phrase 'in relation to that tenancy' which had proved so significant in *Receiver for the Metropolitan Police District* v. *Palacegate Properties Ltd* [2000] 3 All ER 663. It follows that a major change in the terms may be a relevant factor for the purposes of s.38A and remain material to the tenant's giving of informed consent.

2.3 COMPETENT LANDLORD

The 1954 Act draws an important distinction between the 'immediate' landlord and the 'competent' landlord. Although the same landlord may embody both characteristics (e.g. where the freeholder is the tenant's landlord), this is not necessarily the case where sub-tenancies have been created. The immediate landlord, simply put, is the landlord who grants the interest to the tenant (or sub-tenant). The competent landlord is however a more difficult concept as it is a term of art which is subject to a complex statutory definition in s.44 of and Schedule 6 to the 1954 Act. To satisfy the standard of competency, the landlord's interest must:

- be an interest in reversion expectant (whether immediately or otherwise) on the termination of the relevant tenancy;
- be either the fee simple or, where sub-tenancies exist, a tenancy which will not end within 14 months or any further time by which it may be continued under either s.64 (to cater for court proceedings) or s.36(2) (time allowed for the revocation of an order for a new tenancy).

If the reversion has been severed, it is the owners of the severed parts who collectively constitute the competent landlord (s.44(1A)). Severance most certainly does not create a separate tenancy in respect of each severed part. In this type of case, notices must be served either by (whether comprising a joint notice or separate notices operating at the same time) or on all the relevant landlords (*M&P Enterprises (London) Ltd* v. *Norfolk Square Hotels Ltd* [1994] 1 EGLR 129).

A mesne landlord holding by virtue of a tenancy by estoppel (i.e. where it is presumed that the landlord has a title which in reality it does not have), may qualify as the competent landlord. The effect of the doctrine of estoppel is to require the parties and the court to treat an imaginary state of affairs as real (that is, that the landlord was entitled to a freehold or leasehold interest) (see *Bell* v. *General Accident Fire & Life Assurance Corporation Ltd* [1998] 17 EG 144). Similarly, a mesne landlord holding under a periodic tenancy may satisfy the definition, provided that no common law notice to quit has been served by either party. A mesne landlord with a fixed term however will cease to be the competent landlord once that tenant exercises a break clause designed to terminate the head lease within 14 months.

Reduced to its basics, therefore, the term 'competent landlord' means either the freeholder or a tenant whose leasehold interest will not end for at least 14 months. The latter requirement aims to ensure that the competent landlord, having more than a nominal reversion, will have a sufficient interest and incentive to take proper action in relation to the termination and renewal of sub-tenancies. It is however necessary that the competent landlord hold under a legal estate and not by virtue of an equitable estate. In *Pearson* v. *Alyo* (1990) 60 P & CR 56, Nourse L.J. admitted that, 'The subsection is concerned only with legal owners. The Act would be unworkable if it were otherwise'.

2.3.1 Where sub-tenancies exist

The definition of a competent landlord means that, where there is a fixed-term head lease and a sub-lease (which is within the scope of the 1954 Act), the competent landlord will be the head lessee until the last 14 months of the head lease. If this lease has less than 14 months to run, the competent landlord will be the freeholder and not the sub-tenant's immediate landlord. Differences emerge however according to whether the sub-tenancy is of the whole or merely part only of the holding comprised in the head lease. If the whole is sub-let, the matter is relatively straightforward. The head lessee will no longer occupy any part of the holding and, therefore, will not be protected by the provisions of Part II (*Graysim Holdings Ltd* v. *P & O Property Holdings Ltd* [1995] 4 All ER 831). Hence, the head lease will terminate by effluxion of time. As soon as the head lease enters its final 14 months, the head lessee will cease to be the competent landlord. The next superior landlord who satisfies the statutory definition will then be the appropriate landlord for renewal purposes (s.44(1)(*b*)). As Lord Reid explained in *Bowes-Lyon* v. *Green* [1963] AC 420, 'If the interest of the tenant's immediate landlord does not fulfil the ... conditions then you go back until you find someone whose interest does fulfil them'.

When the head lessee sub-lets only part of the premises and continues to occupy the remainder for the purposes of a business, the head lease remains within the protection of the 1954 Act. If the head tenant seeks a renewal however the new lease may only relate to those parts of the holding which are still occupied by that tenant. This is subject to the contrary insistence of the head lessor under s.32(2). The other parts may be the subject of a potential renewal application brought by the sub-tenant. The head lease will not be ended by expiry of the contractual term and it is necessary that the statutory procedures be employed. Unless and until a statutory notice is served to bring the head lease to an end, the immediate landlord continues to be the competent landlord of the sub-tenant. If such notice is served, and regardless of when it will expire, the immediate landlord is then not entitled to serve any statutory notice on the sub-tenant. The head landlord is then enabled to serve a s.25 notice directly on the sub-tenant. In the *Bowes-Lyon* v. *Green* [1963] AC 420, Lord Reid described this innovation as 'a radical method by-passing the immediate landlord'.

2.3.2 Importance of distinction between landlords

This distinction between landlords is vital because for some purposes the involvement of the 'immediate' landlord is necessary, whereas for the majority of procedures, the participation of the 'competent' landlord is required. Although the immediate landlord has a more limited role to play in the renewal procedure, it is this landlord who must, by virtue of s.24(2): receive service of a notice to quit given by a periodic tenant; accept any surrender from the tenant; serve a s.24(3) notice on a non-occupying tenant; and instigate forfeiture proceedings. The immediate landlord must also receive service of any s.27 notice given by the tenant to end a fixed-term lease.

Excepting the above procedures, a tenancy to which Part II extends can be terminated or renewed only with the participation of the competent landlord.

It is the competent landlord who must serve a s.25 notice and it is on this landlord that a s.26 request must be served. The involvement of the competent landlord is also necessary concerning the s.24A interim rent procedure, the agreement of a new tenancy, the resistance of the tenant's application for a new lease and the application for a termination order.

2.3.3 Changes in identity

Although there may only be one competent landlord at any given time, changes of identity may occur during the period when renewal or termination is sought. For example, in *XL Fisheries* v. *Leeds Corporation* [1955] 2 QB 636, a change of landlord came after the service of the tenant's s.26 request. The material times for adjudging who is the competent landlord are at the service of the renewal documentation and, later, at the date of the hearing. As the new competent landlord steps into the shoes of the predecessor, it is necessary that this new party be joined to any existing renewal proceedings. As Jenkins L.J. explained in *Piper* v. *Muggleton* [1956] 2 QB 569, 'it is necessary that at every stage of the proceedings down to final judgment the person claiming to be or joined as being "the landlord" should in fact answer that description according to the statutory definition'.

Accordingly, in *Rene Claro (Haute Coiffure) Ltd* v. *Halle Concerts Society* [1969] 2 All ER 842 where the tenant requested a new tenancy, but omitted to make the new competent landlord a party to the action, the proceedings failed. The issue concerned the identity of the competent landlord when the sub-tenant's renewal application was heard. As the mesne landlord had dropped from the picture and the new competent landlord had not been joined to the proceedings, the sub-tenant's action was not properly constituted. This illustrates that the problem of correctly identifying the competent landlord is particularly acute where sub-underleases have been created. In this scenario the sub-underlessee may experience different parties becoming the competent landlord within rapid succession.

In the situation where the interest of the competent landlord is subject to a mortgage, under which either the mortgagee is in possession or a receiver has been appointed by the mortgagee or by the court, s.67 deems the mortgagee to be the competent landlord. The mortgagee is as Upjohn L.J. commented in *Meah* v. *Mouskos* [1968] 2 QB 23, 'putting it quite generally, virtually substituted for the landlord'. This deeming rule applies for all purposes, except as regards receiving a tenant's s.40(3) notice for particulars which expressly deals with mortgagees and the service of information notices. The mortgagee in possession must give and receive relevant notices under the 1954 Act, grant any new lease and, of course, be joined to the tenant's renewal proceedings. The purpose of s.67 is as described by Russell L.J., 'to apply the position which obtains at law in general in relation to the [mortgagees's] ability to grant leases and extensions of leases, to the grant of leases or extensions of leases under the Act of 1954'.

In the scenario where, after the tenant has commenced proceedings, the landlord's mortgagee takes possession or appoints a receiver, the court will normally allow the existing proceedings to be amended or, if necessary, order a rehearing.

2.3.4   Relationship with other landlords

The 1954 Act contains a complex series of rules which govern the relationship between the competent landlord and any other landlords. These rules concern the ability of the competent landlord to take action which will bind either a mesne landlord or a superior landlord. Not surprisingly, the ability to bind a superior landlord is particularly restricted.

Mesne landlords

Under para. 3(1) of Sched. 6, a notice served by the competent landlord can bind all mesne landlords. This rule extends to any notice given to terminate the lease and to any agreement made with the tenant as to the grant and terms of a new tenancy. The competent landlord is empowered by para. 3(2) to execute a new lease, and this takes effect as if the mesne landlord was a party to it. It is of no consequence that the competent landlord will not be the tenant's immediate landlord when the new lease commences. There is no requirement that the consent of a mesne landlord be obtained because a landlord who stands between the competent landlord and the relevant tenant has no role to play in the renewal scheme.

If the competent landlord acts without the consent of the mesne landlord, there may be liability on the former to pay the latter compensation for any consequential loss (para. 4(1)). There is however the proviso that the mesne landlord's consent cannot unreasonably be withheld, but may be given subject to reasonable conditions. Such conditions might include the payment of compensation or the modification of any notice to be served on, or agreement to be reached with, the tenant. Questions of reasonableness are to be decided by the court. Liability to pay compensation does not arise where consent has been sought, but the mesne landlord has unreasonably withheld that consent.

Superior landlords

Any agreement which the competent landlord proposes to enter may have an effect on the interest of a superior landlord. Accordingly, the consent of every superior landlord who will become the immediate landlord of the sub-tenant during any part of the period covered by the agreement is necessary before the agreement can be effective (Sched. 6, para. 5). Accordingly, the competent landlord cannot unilaterally bind either a superior landlord or the freeholder where the agreement with the sub-tenant is to run beyond the end of the competent landlord's lease. A superior landlord who has a reversionary term upon which any new lease ordered by the court may encroach, therefore, should be made a party to the proceedings. If not, the court will not be able to order a reversionary tenancy (*Birch (A&W)* v. *PB (Sloane) & Cadogan Settled Estates Co.* (1956) 106 LJ 204).

Additional rules

Two further rules are relevant and both were introduced as a result of amendments by the Law of Property Act 1969. The first rule applies when the competent landlord's contractual tenancy is one which can or will be brought to an end within 16 months or any further time by which the tenancy may be continued under either s.36(2) (revocation of new lease) or s.64 (final disposal of unsuccessful renewal application). Following the service of a s.25 notice or a s.26 request, such a competent landlord must send a copy of the relevant documentation to the landlord next in the chain (Sched. 6, para. 7(a)). The underlying rationale is that, if a change of competent landlord is to occur within the near future, the next competent landlord should have full information concerning what acts have been taken by the predecessor. The process, once initiated, must then be continued up the chain until notification reaches the freeholder (Sched. 6, para. 7(b)). For some less than apparent reason the documentation must still be forwarded to other landlords higher in the chain, even when the superior landlord's lease will endure beyond any lease that could be granted to the tenant by the court.

The second rule applies if the competent landlord serves a s.25 notice and a superior landlord later becomes the competent landlord, that notice may be withdrawn by the replacement landlord (Sched. 6, para. 6). A prescribed form of withdrawal (Form 6) must be adopted and it is without prejudice to any future notices given by the new landlord. It is necessary however that the superior landlord becomes the competent landlord and withdraws the notice within two months of it being served. This facility does not extend to a landlord's counter notice served in response to a tenant's s.26 request.

2.4 PROVISIONS AS TO REVERSIONS

By virtue of s.69(1), the protection of the 1954 Act extends to a sub-tenant as to any other tenant. It is, therefore, possible that under the Act a sub-tenancy can be continued beyond, or a reversionary lease granted to the sub-tenant which subsists beyond, the termination of the immediate landlord's tenancy. At common law, this would be impossible because the sub-tenancy would fall with the head lease (*Sherwood (Baron)* v. *Moody* [1952] 1 All ER 389) and, in any event, the rules of privity of contract and estate would render the covenants in the sub-tenancy unenforceable by or against the head lessor. Accordingly, s.65 was innovated so as to regulate the rights and obligations of the parties where a reversionary lease is created. Although the statutory provision is detailed and complex, it is fortunate that its effect may be described more simply. The general consequence is to ensure that, when the interest of the intermediate landlord runs out, the interest of the superior landlord will be deemed to be the reversion. This result is engineered in a variety of ways. First, and for as long as it subsists, the immediate superior tenancy is preserved and deemed to be an interest in reversion expectant (immediately expectant if no intermediate tenancy exists) upon the termination of the inferior tenancy. This is so even though the inferior tenancy will continue beyond it (s.65(1)). As a result of this fiction, and while the head tenancy and the sub-tenancy exist, both parties to the underlease remain able to sue and to be sued on the covenants.

Secondly, when the immediate superior tenancy ends, the 'continuing' sub-tenancy becomes a tenancy held directly under the superior landlord next in the chain (s.65(2)). This landlord has no option other than to accept this, perhaps unwanted, change of status and, of course, will now be bound by the terms of a sub-lease negotiated by others. This simply could not occur at common law.

Thirdly, if a continuation tenancy extends beyond the date on which a lease of the reversion, granted by the landlord, is to commence, the latter takes effect subject to the former, including the tenant's renewal rights (s.65(3)).

Fourthly, if the statutory renewal is to commence after a landlord's lease of the reversion will take effect, the reversionary lease takes subject to the new tenancy and the new tenant enjoys the right to possession (s.65(4)). Such a reversionary lease is an interest expectant on the termination of the renewed tenancy.

2.4.1 Order of reversionary leases

The court is given the express power to order reversionary leases. Under Sched. 6, para. 2, the court is able to grant a new tenancy under the renewal scheme which, whether by agreement or otherwise, can extend beyond the date that the immediate landlord's interest comes to an end. This is achieved by creating such reversionary tenancies as may be necessary to secure the grant of the new lease and to ensure that what the 1954 Act refers to as the 'inferior tenancy' may be prolonged beyond the term of a superior tenancy. An example of this arising would be where the head tenant has three years remaining under a head lease not protected by the Act and the sub-tenant has obtained a renewal for a 15-year term. The court must order two leases: one for three years to be granted immediately by the current competent landlord; and one for 12 years to be granted when the first lease ends by the next landlord able to grant such a term. These two leases are however deemed to comprise a single 15-year term and no continuation rights emerge at the end of the first tenancy.

2.5 TERMINATING THE CONTRACTUAL TENANCY

Understandably, the 1954 Act draws a distinction between the termination of the contractual relationship between the parties and the termination of the continuation tenancy which arises under s.24(1). As previously mentioned, the contract can be determined by any of the established common law methods (expiry of time and notice to quit, for example). The relevance of the 1954 Act however is that the tenancy continues notwithstanding that the contract which previously underpinned it has been brought to an end. The central tenet of the statutory scheme is that a tenancy within its ambit can, by virtue of s.24(1), be terminated only by one of the methods prescribed in the Act itself. Unfortunately, the interaction between the common law rites of termination and the statutory provisions which potentially override them may sometimes prove obscure. The complexity of the Part II machinery tends to defy a ready understanding of its operation and this is particularly evident when put to the test in an abnormal context. For example, in *Bentley & Skinner (Bond St. Jewellers) Ltd* v. *Searchmap Ltd* [2003] EWHC 1621 (Ch) the tenant argued that the landlord had, in order to exercise an option to break and to prevent the order of a new lease, disguised its true intentions. Although the tenant later took a negotiated lease of the same premises, on appeal it sought to challenge the validity of the landlord's actions and, thereby, rekindle its renewal rights. This case is considered below in the context of surrender.

As the legislative design is to prevent the landlord from exercising common law rights to refuse a renewal or to offer a new lease on a 'take it or leave it' basis, not surprisingly it is the landlord's rights that are primarily curtailed. Nevertheless, the 1954 Act throughout attempts to strike a compromise between the conflicting interests of the parties. The landlord's rights of ownership are preserved to the extent that if he requires the premises for his own use or for redevelopment, the tenant will not be granted a renewal. In like vein, the landlord's powers of forfeiture are preserved so that possession may be recovered from a defaulting tenant at any time. Alternatively, the landlord might rely on the tenant's breach of covenant as a ground for opposing renewal under the Act.

The permitted methods of termination represent an amalgam of conventional modes of termination (albeit sometimes with minor modification) and novel, statutory rights exclusively fashioned for the renewal scheme. The majority depend upon the action or inaction of the tenant; the others can be activated only by the landlord or with the joint agreement of the parties. In contrast to the retained common law methods under which the tenant is denied any rights under the 1954 Act, the key statutory methods (that is, termination by a landlord's s.25 notice and tenant's s.26 request) operate both to preserve renewal rights and to activate the renewal procedure. The termination rights that fall to be considered are:

- tenant's notice to quit;
- tenant's s.26 request;
- tenant's cessation of occupation;
- forfeiture by the landlord;
- landlord's s.25 notice;
- merger and agreement; and
- surrender.

2.5.1 Tenant's notice to quit

The 1954 Act does not oblige the tenant to seek a renewal nor does it aim to tie the tenant to an unwanted continuation. Instead, it exists to benefit the tenant and not to act as a restriction. Accordingly, there is express provision enabling the tenant, by service of a notice to quit on the immediate landlord, to prevent a continuation tenancy arising or to terminate one that has arisen. The term 'notice to quit' is defined in s.69(1) as being a notice to terminate the lease given in accordance with its terms (e.g. a notice served in the exercise of a break clause). This definition does not however include the s.25 notice or the s.26 request. In all cases however the effectiveness of the tenant's notice is subject to the qualification in s.24(2)(*a*) and s.27(1), (2) that the tenant must have been in occupation under the tenancy for at least one month. This is designed to prevent any device whereby the tenant is persuaded to give a notice to quit at the commencement of the tenancy thereby bringing the tenancy to an end at the expiry of the notice. In addition, a notice to quit cannot be served by the tenant after the service of a s.26 request for a new lease (s.26(4)). As these procedures are mutually exclusive, the first to be served in time prevails (*Long Acre Securities Ltd* v. *Electro Acoustic Industries Ltd* [1990] 1 EGLR 91).

Nothing in the 1954 Act allows termination on a date earlier than that on which the lease could or would have ended at common law. As Sellers J. explained in *Castle Laundry (London) Ltd* v. *Read* [1955] 1 QB 586, 'the date on which the tenancy could be determined by a notice under the Act can be no earlier than that which the contract itself specifies'. The precise means to be employed depend upon whether the tenancy is periodic or fixed term.

In the case of a periodic tenancy the process is simple. Section 24(2) allows the tenant to serve on the immediate landlord an ordinary notice to quit in accordance with the terms of the lease. This will terminate the tenancy in the ordinary way whether or not it is already being continued under the 1954 Act. Although at common law the notice would normally also terminate a sub-tenancy, as will become clear an underlease protected by the 1954 Act will be continued.

As regards a fixed term, and with the exception of a break clause, the tenant is unable unilaterally to terminate the lease early. Nevertheless, the tenant is entitled to serve a s.27(1) notice on the immediate landlord so as to prevent a continuation tenancy automatically arising at the end of the contractual term. This leaves unaffected any protected sub-tenancies. Although no special form of notice is required, and it has never been keyed in to quarter days, it must be served not less than three months before the contractual date of expiry. If the tenant serves a notice of lesser duration, it will not prevent a continuation tenancy arising at the end of the contractual lease. It is now simpler to move out of possession before the end of the contractual term (s.27(1A)).

If a continuation tenancy is in existence, the continuation can be brought to an end on any day by not less than three months' written notice. The major change here is that it is no longer necessary for this notice to be timed to expire on a quarter day. Section 27(2) goes on to state that it does not matter whether the three months' notice is given after the contractual term date or before it. Section 27(3) provides that, where a continuation tenancy is termi-nated in this way, any rent payable in respect of a period which begins before and ends after the tenancy is terminated shall be apportioned. Any rent paid by the tenant that is in excess of the apportioned amount is recoverable by the tenant. The s.27 notices are particularly useful where the landlord refuses to accept a surrender and shows no sign of issuing a s.25 termination notice.

It is arguable from the wording of s.27(2) that a notice which is given, say, two months before the end of the contractual term, but which is timed to expire more than one month into the continuation tenancy, will operate to terminate the continuation tenancy. Support for this view can be found in the admission in s.27(2) that it does not matter whether the notice is served before or after the continuation has arisen. This conclusion is however open to doubt. First, if this was the intended outcome of s.27, then why bother main-taining two distinct provisions (i.e. s.27(1) and (2))? If the intention was that a notice served during the contractual term should operate to terminate the continuation tenancy within its initial three months, this could have been easily done within one subsection.

Secondly, the allowance that the notice may be served either before or after the contractual term date does not necessarily mean that a notice which lapses within the first three months of the continuation is effective. Section 27(2) speaks of a 'tenancy which is continuing' and requires that this tenancy cannot be brought to an end by less than three months' notice. It is logical to conclude that, as a notice cannot terminate a tenancy which does not yet exist, a notice that lapses before a full three months into the continuation period will be ineffectual.

For example, the tenant serves six months' notice on the landlord. Service occurs two months before the end of the contractual lease. This notice will not prevent a continuation tenancy arising, but it will be effective to terminate the continuation tenancy at its expiry. It clearly gives more than three months' notice running within the continuation period. In contrast, if the notice instead had given four months' notice, this would (it is submitted) have failed to terminate the continuation. It enjoyed a life span within the continuation period of less than three months. Whether this interpretation will be shared by the court is uncertain, but the moral is clear: make sure that the tenant's notice is timed so as to achieve without doubt the intended outcome.

2.5.2 Tenant's section 26 request

The tenant who seeks a renewal may terminate the contractual tenancy by the service of a request for a new tenancy upon the competent landlord. The tenant is prevented under s.26(4) from serving a request if the tenant has already served a notice to quit or the landlord has served a s.25 notice. Not every tenant is empowered to serve such a request. To qualify for this entitlement, the tenancy had to be granted for a term of years exceeding one year (whether or not continued under the 1954 Act) or be a term of years and thereafter from year to year (s.26(6)). Subject to the latter exception, periodic tenants are unable to serve a request for a new tenancy. The request must, moreover, adhere to a prescribed form (Form 3), set out the tenant's proposals for a new lease and specify a date, not less than six and not more than 12 months from its service, on which the lease is to terminate and the new lease to begin. If the timing of the s.26 request is synchronised to match the end date of the contractual term, the contractual lease will end automatically on the stipulated date. The landlord has two months within which to serve a s.26(6) counter notice stating opposition and the ground(s) upon which the opposition is based. A landlord who does not serve an effective counter notice loses the right to object to the new lease.

If the tenant or landlord applies to the court for a renewal before the date specified for the commencement of the new lease in the request, a continuation tenancy will subsist until final disposal as defined in s.64. If neither party makes a timely application, the tenancy will end on the date set out in the request.

2.5.3 Tenant's cessation of occupation

It was decided in *Esselte AB & British Sugar Plc* v. *Pearl Assurance Plc* [1997] 1 WLR 891 that, where the tenant has ceased to occupy the premises by the end of the contractual lease, no continuation tenancy can arise. This is because the tenancy is no longer one to which the 1954 Act applies. The Act, as Morritt L.J. concluded, 'cannot be construed so as to include the past'. There the tenant was granted a five-year lease which was due to expire on 14 February 1993. By December 1992, it was accepted that the tenant had ceased to occupy the premises for the purposes of its business. On 16 January 1993, the tenant served a s.27(2) notice on the landlord with the intention of terminating the lease on 24 June 1993. Rent was paid up to 14 February 1993 (that is, the contractual end date of the lease), but the landlords argued that the tenant's liability extended until 24 June (that is, the date the notice to quit expired). The thrust of the tenant's argument was that, for a continuation tenancy to arise, the statutory conditions contained in s.23 had to be satisfied at the time the contractual term ended. Accordingly, as it had ceased to occupy for business purposes before that time, a continuation was no longer possible. Section 24 is expressed in the present tense so that the restrictions upon termination did not affect a tenancy which, when it terminated at common law, was outside the ambit of the 1954 Act.

This principle has now been given statutory recognition in s.27(1A), which provides that the 1954 Act will not apply 'to a tenancy for a term of years certain where the tenant is not in occupation of the property' at the end of the contractual term. This statutory provision only applies to fixed-term leases and, somewhat surprisingly, leaves periodic tenancies still to be governed by the decision in the *Esselte* case.

As regards fixed-term tenancies, if the tenant is not in occupation when the lease expires or when a break clause is exercised, the tenancy falls outside the provisions of Part II. This approach, moreover, is not disturbed by the fact that the tenant has already served a s.27 notice which has yet to expire. It also means that, if the landlord serves a s.25 notice after the tenant has quit occupation, the notice will be invalid and cannot prolong the tenancy until the stated termination date. A different approach is taken as regards a fixed term that is being continued under the auspices of s.24. Section 27(2) makes it clear that a continuation tenancy will not end merely by the tenant ceasing to occupy the premises. The tenant may then have to serve a s.27(2) notice to bring the continuation to an end in three months' time. Alternatively, the landlord is offered the opportunity to terminate the continuation tenancy by service of a notice under s.24(3)(*a*). The period for this notice is between three and six months. In this situation, the tenant might seek to shorten the notice period by serving a s.27(2) notice of three months.

As regards a periodic tenancy, s.27(1A) has no application. Following the *Esselte* case, the landlord is able to serve an effective common law notice to quit on the tenant who has ceased to occupy. The notice will be effective even if the tenant subsequently resumes occupation (s.24(3)(*b*)). This protects the landlord from a post-notice change of tactics by the tenant.

2.5.4 Landlord's forfeiture

The 1954 Act ensures that forfeiture of the lease (including the forfeiture of a superior lease) remains unaffected (s.24(2)). Forfeiture therefore precludes a tenant from claiming security of tenure. The tenant however has the right to claim relief and, if relief is sought, the Act continues to apply to the tenancy. Termination occurs only when the forfeiture is absolute and not while relief can still be granted by the court. As Megarry V.C. made clear in *Meadows* v. *Clerical Medical & General Life Assurance Society* [1981] Ch 70, s.24(2) contemplates the situation where the tenancy has truly come to an end and the forfeiture process completed. This is so even if the contractual term has already expired by effluxion of time. Accordingly, until the matter of relief is disposed of, the tenant remains able to apply for a new tenancy or to pursue any ongoing application.

Clearly, there is some overlap between forfeiture for breach of covenant and the landlord's ability to oppose the grant of a new lease. The grounds for forfeiture are likely also to constitute grounds of opposition under s.30(1). This means that, if the lease is drawing to a close, the landlord may decide to forego forfeiture proceedings and concentrate upon defeating the tenant's claim for renewal. It is however open for the landlord to pursue both courses of action. In *Norton* v. *Charles Deane Productions Ltd* (1969) 214 EG 559, for example, the landlord's forfeiture action failed, but the tenant was still denied a new lease under the 1954 Act.

As regards sub-tenancies, at common law they fall with the head lease: the rule is that forfeiture ends all inferior interests. The sub-tenant may apply to the court for relief in order that, as Kekewich J. put it in *Ewart* v. *Fryer* [1901] 1 Ch 499, 'injustice may not be done to an innocent man, who for no fault of his own has been deprived of that which he had contracted to acquire'. If successful, the relief granted to a sub-tenant can comprise the order of a new lease, but for a term no longer than the original sub-tenancy. The court, otherwise, enjoys an extremely wide discretion as to the form relief may take.

Where the sub-tenancy is already being continued under the 1954 Act, a different scenario emerges within which the sub-tenant is entitled in the normal way to a new lease on terms (including duration) as agreed or determined by the court (s.65(2)). The forfeiture of the superior interest will, in this latter instance, leave the sub-tenancy totally unaffected. In addition, the mesne landlord will not be liable for failing to deliver up vacant possession.

When the contractual term has some years to run, forfeiture has its attractions. It represents the only means by which the landlord can terminate a fixed-term lease prematurely and rid itself of a problematic tenant. Always providing that the lease contains a re-entry clause, forfeiture might well be the most desirable option. As forfeiture is concerned with the termination of the original contractual tenancy (whether or not being continued), it not only ends the existing contractual lease, but also deprives the tenant of any renewal rights. It should be appreciated however that relief from forfeiture is routinely granted to the tenant, for example on the payment of rent arrears and the remedy of other breach of covenant. The danger therefore is that a forfeiture action may merely ensure the performance of covenants without enabling the landlord to retake possession. This might also steal the landlord's thunder if any resistance to the tenant having a new lease was to be based upon those breaches.

Matters are somewhat different therefore when the lease is drawing to a close. If the motive of the landlord is solely to recover possession, the most effective course is usually to employ the machinery of the 1954 Act:

- as a breach of covenant is a prerequisite of a forfeiture action, that breach is likely also to fall within one of the fault-based grounds of opposition;
- unlike forfeiture, the court enjoys at best a discretion and is under no obligation to grant relief to the tenant;
- although breaches of covenant for the purposes of forfeiture can be waived (often inadvertently) by the landlord, waiver is relevant only to those statutory grounds which invoke the court's discretion and even then only to the extent that it can influence the exercise of that discretion;
- until any forfeiture proceedings are concluded the 1954 Act continues to apply to the tenancy and renewal proceedings are kept in abeyance. This potential for delay is magnified as the forfeiture is not complete when the writ is served. Such delay and uncertainty can only work to the disadvantage of the landlord who has a good case to regain possession under the 1954 Act.

2.5.5 Landlord's statutory notice

The landlord is able to serve a notice to quit as reserved in the lease, but as regards tenancies protected by the 1954 Act the notice will only sever the contractual relationship between the parties. Even if accepted by the head tenant, the notice cannot affect any protected sub-tenancy. Accordingly, in *Scholl Manufacturing Co Ltd* v. *Clifton (Slimline) Ltd* [1967] 1 Ch 41 the exercise of a break clause in the lease ended the contractual tenancy, but the landlord still needed to serve the special statutory notice under s.25 in order to regain possession. Similarly, the service of a landlord's notice to quit on a periodic tenant would not prevent a continuation tenancy coming into existence (*Wheeler* v. *Mercer* [1955] 3 WLR 714).

It is possible that, say, the notice of break and the statutory notice could be framed within one document and timed so as to satisfy both the contractual and the statutory requirements. Such occurred in *Keith Bayley Rogers & Co* v. *Cubes Ltd* (1975) 31 P & CR 412. In deciding whether the notice will operate for the purposes of s.25, the document must be construed in a commonsense way and the court must not adopt an over-technical approach in the face of clear language. The landlord should make clear (e.g. in a covering letter) that the notice is designed to achieve this dual purpose. It should also not be overlooked that, for a dual notice to be effective, the immediate landlord must also be the tenant's competent landlord. While the severance of contractual ties is to be undertaken by the immediate landlord, the termination of the 1954 Act protected tenancy falls within the remit of the competent landlord. It is however generally to be recommended that the documentation be kept distinct so as to minimise the impact of error. This, of course, is inevitable when the immediate landlord and the competent landlord are not one and the same person.

The form and content of a valid s.25 notice are closely prescribed. The two major forms are Form 1 (where the landlord is not opposed to renewal) and Form 2 (where the landlord is opposed to renewal). If the notice does not follow this prescription, it is likely to be invalid. It then becomes necessary for the landlord to serve a further and effective s.25 notice. The notice, which must state a termination date not less than six and not more than 12 months in the future, operates on various levels:

- when the termination date is reached, an existing contractual tenancy ends and is replaced by a continuation tenancy;
- it engages the renewal procedure and places the onus upon the tenant to apply to the court within strict time limits;
- the notice must disclose whether the landlord opposes a new lease and, if so, upon what grounds and,
- if there is no opposition, the landlord must propose the terms of the new lease.

2.5.6 Merger and agreement

Although merger (that is, the tenant buying out the landlord's interest) is not specified in s.24(2) as being an approved method of termination, it is an inevitable conclusion that there can be no statutory continuation of a lease which is no longer legally in existence. Merger does not however arise automatically; it must be intended to occur. If merger is intended by the tenant, the lease will end and be absorbed by the superior interest. Merger of a head lease does not however affect the interests of a sub-tenant (s.65(2)).

As regards other agreements, the emphasis of the 1954 Act is to encourage settlement between the tenant and the competent landlord as to both the grant and the terms of a renewal. A full agreement between the parties, therefore, ousts the jurisdiction of the court. Indeed, if agreement is reached after an application for a new tenancy is lodged, that application (if not withdrawn) is automatically invalidated by s.28 (*Hancock & Willis* v. *GMS Syndicate Ltd* (1983) 265 EG 473). Once a binding agreement is reached, the

STATUTORY SCHEME

tenant cannot have a change of mind and apply for a new lease under the Part II machinery. Not surprisingly, where the landlord and tenant agree in writing to a new lease, the original tenancy (whether or not already being continued under the 1954 Act) will subsist until the commencement date for the new term. This is so even when the new tenancy is timed to commence during the existence of the contractual term. Common practice however is for the commencement of the agreed lease to occur on the day after the original one has terminated.

If a continuation has arisen, the tenancy comes to an end on the date specified in the agreement and, during the intervening period, is not protected by the 1954 Act. If agreement for a renewal is not achieved by the parties, the matter must be resolved by the court. In that situation, the court is empowered to reject the tenant's right to a new lease only on the grounds specified in s.30(1)(a)–(g). The tenancy will however be continued under s.64 until three months after 'final disposal', that is, until all proceedings including appeals have come to an end. This rule gives way where final disposal occurs earlier than the termination date specified in the statutory notice or request. In such a case, the tenancy will end at the later date.

2.5.7 Surrender

Surrender is the yielding of the leasehold estate to the immediate landlord and the causing of the lease to be extinguished by the reversion. Surrender can never be unilateral as it requires the agreement of both parties. As regards joint tenants, and unlike with a notice to quit, the rule is that all of them must join in or acquiesce in the surrender (*Hounslow London Borough Council* v. *Pilling* [1994] 1 All ER 432). Surrender can occur expressly only by deed. A surrender of the legal estate by letter will be ineffective (*Tarjomani* v. *Panther Securities Ltd* (1983) 46 P & CR 32).

Surrender can however be implied by operation of law (without writing) from the conduct of the parties (Law of Property Act 1925, s.54(2)(c)). As the doctrine of estoppel forms the foundation of surrender by operation of law, there must be conduct by the tenant unequivocally amounting to an acceptance that the tenancy has been terminated. As Peter Gibson L.J. explained in *Gibbs Mew Plc* v. *Gemmell* [1998] 1 EG 117, 'That conduct can be relinquishment by the tenant of possession and its acceptance by the landlord or other conduct by the tenant inconsistent with the continuation of the tenancy, and in addition the circumstances must be such as to render it inequitable for the tenant to dispute that the tenancy has ceased'. There the original lease was surrendered by the tenant accepting a tenancy at will intended to supersede the former lease and granted on more advantageous terms. Similarly, in *Bentley & Skinner (Bond St. Jewellers) Ltd* v. *Searchmap Ltd* [2003] EWHC 1621 (HC), the landlord served a s.25 notice and subsequently the tenant accepted a privately negotiated new lease on different

35

terms. Such conduct unequivocally amounted to an acceptance that the former tenancy had been terminated and, in the circumstances, made it unconscionable for the tenant to dispute that the tenancy had ceased. In other words, a surrender by operation of law occurred when the new lease was taken. The tenant was, therefore, unable to argue that the original lease was still in existence. The motivation for this challenge was that the new lease had been contracted out of the 1954 Act and granted on terms less advantageous to the tenant than if renewal had been ordered by the court.

The retention of this common law method of termination means that, following a valid surrender, there is no need for the landlord to follow the 1954 Act procedure (*Lansdowne Tutors Ltd* v. *Younger* (2000) 79 P & CR D36. The requirement that the tenant must have been in occupation under the tenancy for at least one month before the instrument of surrender is executed has been abandoned by the introduction of the 2003 Order. Immediate surrenders are now effective regardless of occupation.

Agreements to surrender

An actual surrender must be contrasted with an agreement to surrender (whether immediately or at a future date) which is governed by the contracting-out provisions in s.38A(2). The distinction however applies only to express surrenders and has no resonance as regards surrender by operation of law. In *Gibbs Mew Plc* v. *Gemmell* [1998] 1 EG 117, the tenant unsuccessfully argued that the acceptance of a tenancy at will amounted merely to an agreement to surrender which was void under s.38(1). The tenant was estopped from denying that the prior tenancy had been surrendered by conduct.

The reason why actual surrenders are treated differently from agreements to surrender was explained clearly by the Law Commission in its (1988) Working Paper:

> To prevent the tenant surrendering the property to his landlord would be an encroachment on his freedom which is not necessary to defend the statutory right of renewal. On the other hand, to obtain from a tenant an undertaking in advance that he will surrender the lease sometime later is to invite him to forego those rights before he is in a position to judge how matters will stand at the date in question. The Act, therefore, limits the parties' freedom of contract when the tenant might be susceptible to undue persuasion by the landlord, without unnecessarily limiting their freedom to bargain.

By way of illustration, a deed of surrender which the tenant executes as a condition of the grant of a new lease would clearly be viewed as an agreement to surrender and, thereby, remain unenforceable unless it satisfied s.38A(2). Conversely, and as in *Tarjomani* v. *Panther Securities Ltd* (1983) 46 P & CR 32, a letter purporting to effect immediate surrender could not be viewed either as an immediate surrender or as an agreement to surrender. In addition, since the Law of Property (Miscellaneous Provisions) Act 1989, an agreement to surrender (being a bilateral contract relating to an interest in land) must be in writing and signed by both parties. If not, and subject to estoppel, the agreement can have no legal consequence. Although agreements to surrender are not common, a s.38A(2) agreement might prove helpful where, for example, one tenant seeks to move out, a new tenant wishes to move in and the parties prefer a new lease instead of the assignment of the existing tenancy. The Working Paper concluded that the 1954 Act should not continue to invalidate agreements to surrender which are intended to take effect immediately, but this amendment was never adopted.

Section 38A(2), (3) allows for the parties to agree to surrender a lease, on a set date or on the occurrence of a specified event, provided that the landlord has served a notice on the tenant in the form (or substantially in the form) prescribed in Schedule 3 to the 2003 Order. In addition, the requirements specified in Schedule 4 must be satisfied.

The form of the notice that an agreement to surrender is to be made contains a warning to the tenant as to the effects of a surrender and cautions the tenant to seek legal advice. If the notice is received at least 14 days before the agreement is to be entered into, the tenant need only sign a simple declaration that the notice has been received and its consequences accepted. If the tenant does not receive at least 14 days' notice, the tenant will have to visit a solicitor and make a statutory declaration. The forms of declaration are set out in Schedule 4 and contain the relevant details as to the parties and the tenancy to be surrendered. Again, the forms contain a warning to the tenant of the legal consequences, such as loss of renewal rights and any entitlement to statutory compensation. The declaration must then be contained in or endorsed on the contract.

Offer-back clauses

A further related area concerns the so-called 'offer-back clause' which, traditionally, is attached to a covenant against assignment and provides that, on an intended assignment, the tenant must first offer to surrender the lease. This offer back may be without consideration or in consideration of a payment (often referable to the premium value of the unexpired term). The landlord has the option to accept the tenant's surrender and, if surrender occurs, this will terminate the tenant's lease. If the landlord declines the offer, the tenant can only assign the lease with the landlord's consent (which cannot be unreasonably withheld). The reliance upon the offer-back clause does not render the landlord's objections unreasonable.

A problem arises where the landlord accepts the tenant's obligatory offer, but the tenant does not actually wish to surrender. Even if committed to writing, the agreement to surrender remains unenforceable by virtue of s.38A(2) unless the notice and declaration procedure has been adopted prior to the creation of the lease (see *Stevenson & Rush (Holdings) Ltd* v. *Langdon* (1978) 38 P & CR 208). Nevertheless, as the right to assign has been made dependent on the landlord rejecting the offer, the tenant will be unable to assign without being in breach of covenant, resulting in an unsatisfactory stalemate. Although the Law Commission Working Paper provisionally recommended that reform was necessary, no reform was to emerge. The fear is that, by favouring one party at the other's expense, the balance of the 1954 Act would be disturbed. In addition, it was concluded that such contracts would now be invalidated by the Law of Property (Miscellaneous Provisions) Act 1989 and, hence, no further action was necessary. Nevertheless, the 1989 Act does not facilitate lawful assignment which will remain dependent upon the landlord's refusal of the tenant's offer. The potential stalemate therefore continues unabated.

2.6 CONTINUATION TENANCY

It is not necessary that a new tenancy come into being as soon as the contractual tenancy ends. This is because of the 'continuation tenancy' which arises at the end of the contractual term and operates to keep the relationship of landlord and tenant alive beyond that time. By virtue of s.65 the continuation of a head lease will also support an underlease for a longer term than would otherwise be possible. Owing to this mechanism, the time between the determination of the original lease and the grant of a new tenancy may often be measured in years. The continuation is however not to be treated as a holding over at common law nor, as was made clear in *Lewis* v. *MTC (Cars) Ltd* [1975] 1 All ER 874, can any periodic tenancy be implied by reason of continued occupation and the payment of rent. Being of an uncertain duration, the continuation tenancy simply has no equivalent under the common law.

The continuation allows the tenant to remain in possession, essentially on the same terms as before. As Fox L.J. explained in *Cadogan* v. *Dimovic* [1984] 2 All ER 168, 'There are not two terms, one created by the original grant, and on the expiry of that, a new one created by statute'. The only departures from this rule concern the ability of the landlord or tenant to apply to the court for an interim rent under s.24A and the additional restrictions placed upon the termination of a continuation tenancy. It follows, therefore, that the tenant is entitled to the same premises as under the original lease. This means that, although the tenant may only occupy part of the demised premises at the end of the contractual lease, it is the whole of the tenancy that is continued under s.24. The statutory continuation moreover ensures that both parties remain liable on their leasehold covenants and that rights of way (and other incorporeal hereditaments) enjoyed under the original tenancy remain enforceable.

Any guarantor of the tenant will however normally be released from prospective liability. The continuing liability of a guarantor can be expressly catered for in the guarantee (*Junction Estates* v. *Cope* (1974) 27 P & CR 482). A right to remove tenant's fixtures will also persist during the continuation period.

2.6.1 Assignment of a continuation tenancy

Although described by Sellers J. in *Castle Laundry (London)* v. *Read* [1955] 1 QB 586 as 'a business statutory tenancy', this epithet is misleading. Unlike a statutory tenancy under the Rent Act 1977, a continuation tenancy confers an estate in land which can be assigned or forfeited for breach of covenant. As Lord Denning M.R. acknowledged in *Cheryl Investments Ltd* v. *Saldanha* [1979] 1 All ER 5: 'This "continuation tenancy" is nothing like a statutory tenancy. It is not a personal privilege of the tenant. It is a piece of property which he can assign or dispose of to a third person, provided that it was not prohibited by the terms of the contract'.

Before such an assignment takes place, there are a number of practical considerations to be taken on board:

- the assignee must be aware of the possibility the landlord might oppose a renewal on grounds concerning which the assignee has no knowledge and no defence;
- the assignee must ensure that the assignor has satisfied the requirements concerning, say, an application to the court and the service of proceedings on the landlord;
- the assignee will often be unsure as to what the terms of any renewal will be and this will mean that few assignees will offer more than a nominal premium for the assignment.

2.7 NOTICE FOR PARTICULARS

As demonstrated, the Part II procedures require that certain steps be taken by the correct person at the correct time. Central to the statutory machinery is that both parties are able to identify each other and to ascertain the nature and extent of their respective interests. It is an important preliminary step that the parties should have all the necessary information in order to exercise their statutory rights. This is of paramount importance where sub-letting has occurred. The tenant will need to know the identity of the competent landlord and the competent landlord will need to know whether the tenant is still in occupation and (where relevant) the details of any sub-tenancy. Hence, the facility exists within s.40 whereby either party may serve notice on the other so as to acquire the requisite information.

It is to be appreciated however that a s.40 notice cannot be served by or on a tenant more than two years before the date on which (discounting the statutory renewal provisions) the lease is either due to expire or can be brought to an end by a landlord's notice to quit (s.40(6)). This restriction is intended to avoid purposeless and vexatious notices being served by either party.

2.7.1   Tenant's notice

A tenant can serve a notice (Form 5) provided that the tenancy is of premises used wholly or partly for the purposes of a business and is either for a term certain exceeding one year or for any term certain and thereafter from year to year (s.40(3)). There is no requirement that the tenant be in occupation nor that it is the tenant's business which is carried on at the premises. The notice may be served on the immediate landlord and any person having a superior interest, including any mortgagee in possession of such an interest (s.40(3)). Following service, it is the duty of the recipient to respond in writing within one month (s.40(5)(a)) providing certain key information. This information, listed in s.40(4)(a)–(d) is as follows:

- whether the recipient is the freeholder or a mortgagee in possession;
- if not, the tenant must be notified, to the best of the recipient's knowledge and belief, of the name and address of the person who is the recipient's immediate landlord (or, where relevant, the mortgagor's immediate landlord); the term of the recipient's tenancy; and the earliest date (if any) at which that tenancy is terminable by notice to quit given by the relevant landlord. The recipient must state also whether a notice has been given under s.25 or a request made under s.26 in relation to the recipient's tenancy and, if so, must provide details of such documentation;
- the recipient must state, to the best of his knowledge and belief, the name and address of any other person who owns an interest in reversion in any part of the premises;
- if the recipient is a reversioner, he must state whether there is a mortgagee in possession of his interest in the premises and, if so, provide to the best of his knowledge (and belief) the name and address of the mortgagee.

2.7.2   Landlord's notice

Similarly, the immediate or a superior landlord can serve a notice (Form 4) on the tenant requiring the tenant to respond in writing (s.40(1)). The recipient must respond within one month (s.40(5)(a)). The information to be supplied by the tenant is stipulated in s.40(2)(a)–(c) as follows:

- whether the tenant occupies the premises or part of them wholly or partly for the purposes of a business carried on by him;

- if not, the recipient must provide the details of any sub-tenancy granted. These details are general in scope and relate to the premises comprised in the sub-tenancy, its term (including the provisions for termination by notice to quit), the rent and the name of the sub-tenant. There is no duty to provide any further details of the sub-tenancy (e.g. as to any user clause);
- the recipient must state to the best of his knowledge and belief whether the sub-tenant is in occupation of the premises and, if not, the sub-tenant's address is to be supplied. There is no provision requiring the tenant to reveal whether or not the sub-tenant is carrying on a business at the premises;
- whether the sub-tenancy has been contracted out of the 1954 Act;
- whether a notice has been given under s.25 or a request made under s.26 in relation to the sub-tenancy and, if so, details must be furnished;
- the recipient must provide to the best of his knowledge and belief the name and address of any other person who owns an interest in reversion in any part of the premises. As the above information is limited to an immediate sub-tenancy, if further underleases have been created then it is advisable for the landlord to serve additional notices on all tenants.

The information as to occupation assumes obvious importance as it will disclose whether, at the time of response, the tenancy is protected by the 1954 Act. The landlord should be aware however that the tenant may at some time resume occupation and, thereby, regain the protection of the Part II provisions. It may be necessary to serve a further s.40(1) notice before attempting to engage the renewal provisions. There is no doubt that the present system is under-used. Much of the information sought by the landlord can, indeed, be gained from a physical inspection of the holding. The service of a s.40 notice moreover alerts the other party that a termination notice or request for a new tenancy is in prospect. In addition, either party can later be estopped from denying any representation made in response to a s.40 notice. Any replies should therefore be careful and accurate.

2.7.3 Sanctions

A criticism levied against the old law was that, although s.40 imposed duties, it provided no redress for their non-observance. The absence of any specified penalty clearly undermined the effectiveness of this important safeguard for those who seek to exercise their statutory rights. Section 40B now makes it explicit that a person who has broken any duty imposed by s.40 may be the subject of civil proceedings for breach of statutory duty. The section goes on to make clear that in such proceedings a court may order the person to comply with the statutory duty and may make an award of damages. It was determined that there should not be criminal sanctions for a breach of the s.40 duties.

41

2.7.4 Updating

A further criticism of the old law was that, once the information was provided by a party, there was no obligation to keep it up to date. This is now dealt with by s.40(5)(*b*) which provides that the recipient is under an ongoing duty to ensure that the information remains accurate for a period of six months from the service of the request. If, within that period, the recipient becomes aware that the information provided is not, or is no longer, correct the correct information must be provided within one month of the recipient becoming so aware.

2.7.5 Transfer cases

Once served a s.40 notice cannot be withdrawn or cancelled. The duty to respond therefore persists despite any assignment of the serving party's estate. Section 40A(1) deals with the scenario where a person who has been served with a s.40 notice transfers his interest in the property to another and facilitates the curtailment of the recipient's responsibilities under s.40. On communicating in writing the fact of the transfer and the name and address of the assignee to the serving party, the recipient ceases to be subject to the s.40 duties.

A corresponding provision is found in s.40A(2) which deals with the scenario where the person who serves a s.40 notice transfers his interest in the premises to another. If the transferor or transferee provides the recipient with written details of the transfer and the name and address of the transferee, the recipient's s.40 response is to be made to the transferee. Where the transfer has occurred, but the details of it are not given to the recipient, the information required under s.40 may be given to either the transferor or the transferee.

2.8 KEY TIME LIMITS

It is necessary for the parties and their legal advisers to take the necessary procedural steps within the tightly prescribed time limits. As the statutory rights are only exercisable in accordance with the procedures set out in the 1954 Act, where the time requirements are not satisfied the landlord may lose the right to oppose a new lease, the tenant may face eviction and the adviser be subjected to a claim in negligence. These time limits are strict and the court has no jurisdiction to extend them. The following table depicts the major time limits that must be satisfied.

Section	Purpose	Time limit
40(6)	notice for information	no more than 24 months before end of tenant's lease
25	landlord's termination notice	between six and 12 months' notice
26	tenant's request for new tenancy	between six and 12 months' notice
26(6)	landlord's counter notice	within two months of service of s.26 request
27	fixed-term tenant's notice to quit	at least three months before tenancy will expire
29A	application to court	**earliest time:** any time after service of s.25 notice or, unless landlord's counter notice served earlier, two months after service of s.26 request **latest time:** subject to agreement, the action must be commenced before the termination date specified in the landlord's s.25 notice or tenant's s.26 request
36(2)	revocation	within 14 days of order. Tenancy continues thereafter for a reasonable period
64	final disposal	three months after cessation of proceedings, including time for any appeal

2.8.1 Corresponding date rule

As shown above, the 1954 Act imposes a variety of time limits within which, for example, notices and counter notices are to be served and court proceedings commenced. The majority of these time limits are measured in months which, for the purposes of the Act, means calendar months. Hence, as Lord Diplock calculated in *Dodds* v. *Walker* [1981] 2 All ER 609: 'one month's notice given in a 30-day month is one day shorter than one month's notice given in a 31-day month and is three days shorter if it is given in February'.

In this context it is important to appreciate the workings of the so-called 'corresponding date rule'. This means that a period of months calculated from a specified date will end on the corresponding date in the appropriate subsequent month. As Lord Diplock further explained, 'The corresponding

43

date rule is simple. It is easy of application . . . all that the calculator has to do is mark in his diary the corresponding date in the appropriate subsequent month'. Lord Russell provided the following example, 'in a four month period, when service of the relevant notice was on 28th September; time would begin to run at midnight on 28th–29th September and would end at midnight on 28th–29th January, a period embracing four calendar months'. In *Hogg Bullimore & Co* v. *Co-operative Insurance Society* (1985) 50 P & CR 105, a s.25 notice served on 2 April was effective to terminate the tenancy on 2 October. The notice therefore specified a termination date of 'not less than' six months in the future.

Accordingly, the 1954 Act does not require 'clear' months for, as Fox L.J. concluded in *Riley (EJ) Investments Ltd* v. *Eurostile Holdings Ltd* [1985] 3 All ER 181, 'just as there are dates which are less than two months . . . there are dates which are more than two months . . . there must be a date which is simply two months, no more and no less'. It also follows that, for the landlord in the *Hogg Bullimore* case to have specified a date 'not more than' 12 months in the future, the notice must, at the latest, have been timed to expire on 2 April of the following year. Where the month does not have a corresponding date (e.g. where one month's notice is served on 31 March), the period will end on the last day on the appropriate month in which it expires (that is, 30 April). The expressions 'not less than' and 'not more than' therefore result in the period allowed, in which the action is to occur, being taken to include both the date of service and the corresponding date on which the notice expires. There is however some doubt as to the application of the corresponding date rule where the action is to be taken 'within' a specified number of months. In *Lester* v. *Garland* (1808) 15 Ves Jr 248, it was held that, in calculating the period which has elapsed since the occurrence of a stated event, the day on which the event occurred is to be discounted. If correct, this would give the landlord an extra day within which to comply, say, with the service of a counter notice.

CHAPTER 3

Scope of the Act

Contents

- Introduction
- Leases and licences
- Premises
- Occupation
- For the purposes of a business
- Excluded tenancies
- The Crown and government departments: special provisions

3.1 INTRODUCTION

Subject to a number of common law and statutory exceptions, s.23(1) extends the protection of the Landlord and Tenant Act 1954 to 'any tenancy where the property comprised in the tenancy is or includes premises which are occupied by the tenant and are so occupied for the purposes of a business carried on by him or for those and other purposes'. Almost every phrase of that provision has been subject to judicial discussion and interpretation. The requirements are that:

- a tenancy exists. This is defined in s.69(1) to include leases, sub-tenancies and agreements for a lease, but excludes a demise by way of mortgage. Tenancies by estoppel fall within the 1954 Act (*Bell* v. *General Accident Fire & Life Assurance Corporation Ltd* [1998] 1 EGLR 69);
- the tenancy must be of premises which are occupied by the tenant;
- this occupation must be wholly or partly attributable to the tenant's business; and
- the tenancy must not be otherwise excluded from the ambit of statutory protection.

Each of these conditions is to be examined in depth in the course of this chapter and attention also focused on the special provisions that relate to public bodies.

3.2 LEASES AND LICENCES

As the 1954 Act applies only to tenancies, licence agreements necessarily fall outside its ambit (*Shell-Mex & BP Ltd* v. *Manchester Garages Ltd* [1971] 1 All ER 841). The relationship between licensor and licensee is too fleeting and precarious to be the subject of renewal rights. A landlord who wishes to side-step the protective provisions might therefore attempt to do so by creating a licence instead of a tenancy. The employment of this tactic is not against public policy and it does constitute a valid avoidance measure. As Buckley L.J. emphasised in *Shell-Mex & BP Ltd* v. *Manchester Garages Ltd*: 'One should not approach the problem with a tendency to attempt to find a tenancy because unless there is a tenancy the case will escape the effects of the statute'.

It is to be appreciated that a licence is fundamentally different from a lease in that it cannot confer a legal estate and, at best, bestows only a personal privilege on the licensee. The classic exposition is that of Vaughan C.J. in *Thomas* v. *Sorrell* (1673) Vaugh 330, 'a dispensation or licence properly passeth no interest, nor alters or transfers property in any thing, but only makes an action lawful which without it had been unlawful'. As evident from the mass of associated case law however the distinction between a lease and licence is, traditionally, difficult to draw. In order to impose a test which would make identification of a tenancy more effective, in *Street* v. *Mountford* [1985] AC 809 Lord Templeman promoted the working rule that where, 'accommodation is granted for a term at a rent with exclusive possession, the landlord providing neither attendance or services, the grant is a tenancy . . .'. This rule is somewhat easier to state than it is to apply and, being subject to a variety of qualifications, is apt to be misleading.

3.2.1 Certainty of term

The 'term' must be certain in that the lease must have an ascertainable and certain duration (i.e. a defined beginning and a defined end). This is no new rule and was recognised as early as *Say* v. *Smith* (1563) Plowd 269. If the lease does not state a commencement date, none will be implied. By way of illustration, in *Lace* v. *Chantler* [1944] 1 KB 368 a lease granted for the duration of the War was held to be void for uncertainty. In its place however the court was able to find a weekly, implied periodic tenancy arising from the tenant's taking of possession and the landlord's acceptance of a weekly rent. As Lord Greene explained, 'A term created by a leasehold tenancy agreement must be expressed either with certainty and specifically or by reference to something which can, at the time when the lease takes effect, be looked at as a certain ascertainment of what the term was meant to be. In the present case, when this tenancy agreement took effect the term was completely uncertain'.

Some uncertainty existed as to whether the *Lace* v. *Chantler* rule applied to periodic tenancies. The Court of Appeal in *Canadian Imperial Bank of Commerce* v. *Bello* (1992) 64 P & CR 48 (a lease until the payment of a debt upheld), for example, held that the rule applied exclusively to fixed terms and only then when the determining event was outside the control of the parties. This argument was abandoned by the House of Lords in *Prudential Assurance Co. Ltd* v. *London Residuary Body* [1992] 2 AC 386 where it was concluded that the rule applied even-handedly to both fixed terms and periodic tenancies. It also was not affected by whether the event was in or out of the control of the parties. Although the House of Lords did not seize the opportunity to overrule its previous decision, Lord Browne-Wilkinson was at a loss to understand why the rule existed. He commented, 'This bizarre outcome results from the application of an ancient and technical rule of law . . . No one has produced any satisfactory rationale for the genesis of this rule. No one has been able to point to any useful purpose that it serves at the present day'.

3.2.2   Rent

The reservation of a rent (albeit normally present) is not an essential feature of a lease. Accordingly, a 'no rent–no tenancy' principle does not exist. This was demonstrated in *Ashburn Anstalt* v. *Arnold* [1988] 2 All ER 147 where the tenant occupied a shop rent-free prior to redevelopment. Indeed, s.205(1)(xxvii) of the Law of Property Act 1925 defines a term of years absolute 'whether or not at a rent'. Unlike the Rent Act 1977 moreover there is no requirement that any rent be payable before a tenancy can be protected by the Part II provisions of the 1954 Act. The payment of 'rent' however remains indicative that a lease has been created, whereas the absence of any payment whatsoever may support the proposition that a licence has been entered into. Hence, the tendency for purported licence agreements is to describe payments as 'licence fees' or 'accommodation charges'.

3.2.3   Exclusive possession

Exclusive possession is the touchstone of a lease and is the legal right to exclude all others from the demised property. As Lord Templeman concluded in *Street* v. *Mountford* [1985] AC 809, 'A tenant armed with exclusive possession can keep out strangers and keep out the landlord unless the landlord is exercising limited rights reserved to him by the tenancy agreement to enter and view and repair'. Exclusive possession however must be distinguished from exclusive occupation which is, essentially, an issue of fact and physical use. The distinction is of importance as an occupier can have the sole occupation of premises without having exclusive possession.

Although exclusive possession is a prerequisite of a tenancy, it offers no guarantee that a tenancy has been created. As accepted in *Street* v. *Mountford*, the grant of exclusive possession may, in exceptional circumstances, be consistent with a licence agreement. These exceptions include where there is a lack of intention to create legal relations (e.g. when the arrangement is an act of friendship or charity) and where possession is referable to some other legal relationship (e.g. employer and employee or vendor and purchaser). In these and similar circumstances it is open to the court to conclude that occupation is referable to a relationship other than a tenancy. Although the list is not exhaustive, the courts appear reluctant to extend the already approved categories.

Exclusive possession and its denial

Exclusive possession has become the crucial factor in marking the distinction between a lease and a licence. Accordingly, in *Smith* v. *Northside Developments* (1988) 55 P & CR 164 the Court of Appeal admitted that, when in doubt, the court should look for exclusive possession with particular emphasis upon whether the landlord can be excluded. This might be difficult to discern where the agreement calls itself a licence and purports to deny the occupier exclusive possession by reserving a degree of control over the premises for the grantor. For example, in *Shell-Mex & BP Ltd* v. *Manchester Garages Ltd* a licence was upheld in circumstances where the possession and control retained by the licensor (particularly concerning the products that could be sold) ran contrary to the grant of exclusive possession. While such tactics alone are insufficient to guarantee the creation of a licence, it is an inescapable conclusion that, if exclusive possession is denied both at law and in fact, there can be no tenancy. Nevertheless, the court must be concerned with the true bargain, as opposed to the apparent bargain, struck between the parties and it is this which must be examined. Hence, it is the objective intentions of the parties and their real rights under the agreement which must be identified. Each case will, therefore, turn upon its own facts and be examined in the light of all the surrounding circumstances.

In order to create a licence, there will normally be a written agreement which expressly denies the existence of exclusive possession. As regards such agreements, the court must approach the document in an even-handed manner and apply the usual rules of construction. The descriptive label attached by the parties to the transaction is not conclusive. As Lord Templeman put it in *Street* v. *Mountford*: 'If the agreement satisfied all the requirements of a tenancy, then the agreement produced a tenancy and the parties cannot alter the effect of the agreement by insisting that they only created a licence'. The court's function moreover is to detect any sham or pretence agreements and misleading labels. All depends on the interaction between the wording of the agreement and the factual matrix in which the agreement exists. As *Street* v. *Mountford* demonstrates, where the language of the licence contradicts the reality of the lease, the facts are to prevail. Unrealistic provisions in the contract can, therefore, be disregarded. It remains for the occupier to show that the agreement is a sham or pretence and, if this burden is not discharged, the contract must be construed as it stands. As Millett J. explained in *Camden LBC* v. *Shortlife Community Housing Ltd* (1993) 25 HLR 330, 'Unless the parties' professed intentions differed from their true intention, or failed to reflect the true substance of the real transaction, this is conclusive'.

Where there is no written agreement, there is of course nothing for the courts to construe. A different approach is to be adopted and the decision of the court based purely upon the surrounding circumstances, for example, the relationship between the parties, the nature and extent of the accommodation, and the intended and actual mode of occupation. The judge's task, as Sir John Arnold explained in *Smith* v. *Northside Developments* (1988) 55 P & CR 164, is to determine 'whether there was or was not exclusive possession from the circumstances and the facts of the case in order to see whether the proper inference is that such a term was intended by means of and derived from a history of such a right being recognised'. There the evidence of a particular conversation indicated that exclusive possession had not been granted.

3.2.4 Licences of business premises

As the decision of *Street* v. *Mountford* is confined to residential premises, doubt has been expressed as to whether it applies fully in the commercial sector. As Glidewell L.J. admitted in *Dresden Estates Ltd* v. *Collinson* (1988) 55 P & CR 47, 'the indicia, which may make it more apparent in the case of a residential tenant or a residential occupier that he is indeed a tenant, may be less applicable or be less likely to have that effect in the case of business tenancies'. Although subsequent cases have stressed that Lord Templeman's approach applies equally to all forms of tenancies, it is undeniable that commercial arrangements lend themselves to the creation of licences more readily than their residential counterparts. So, for example, in *Venus Investments Ltd* v. *Stocktop Ltd* [1996] EGCS 173 it was held that, as the agreement contained neither a forfeiture clause nor a right for the grantor to enter and inspect the premises, it did not resemble a commercial lease and therefore must be a licence. It was held that the presence of exclusive possession was not to be inferred in the case of commercial property as readily as with residential premises. This distinction is logical in view of the fact that the attributes of commercial property are usually completely different from those of residential premises and the premises themselves are open to a far wider range of potential uses. Accordingly, *Street* v. *Mountford* is capable of being distinguished when the court deems it appropriate. The exercise, as Hutchison L.J. accepted in *Hunts Refuse Disposals Ltd* v. *Norfolk Environmental Waste Services Ltd* [1997] 1 EGLR 16 'is not to be undertaken in a vacuum, but rather with a proper regard to the context in which the issue arises ... while one would ordinarily expect that someone in occupation of a small house for a fixed term at a rent had exclusive possession, one would I suggest have no such preconceptions about a person given the right to tip rubbish in the excavated parts of a large plot of land, on other parts of which, it seems, quarrying was continuing'.

Some remaining potential for licences of business premises can be identified in the following areas:

- where there is genuinely no grant of exclusive possession. This could arise where there is a sharing of floor space, as in *Smith* v. *Northside Developments* (1988) 55 P & CR 164 where market traders moved into joint occupation of part of a shop unit. As the others who used the premises could gain access only via the part occupied by the market traders, there could be no exclusive possession;
- where there is a trade concession agreement, for example to sell refreshments in a theatre (*Clore* v. *Theatrical Properties Ltd* [1936] 3 All ER 483) or to sell petrol on a garage forecourt (*Shell-Mex & BP Ltd* v. *Manchester Garages Ltd* [1971] 1 All ER 841);
- where occupation is limited to only part of the day or week (*Manchester City Council* v. *NCP Ltd* [1982] 1 EGLR 94);
- where the right is to occupy part of the premises for storage and the licensor has the right to vary which part can be used (*Dresden Estates Ltd* v. *Collinson* (1988) 55 P & CR 47);
- where there is occupation of a lock-up market stall (*Gloucester City Council* v. *Williams* (1990) *The Times*, 15 May);
- where a prospective tenant is allowed into occupation pending the grant of a lease (*Isaac* v. *Hotel de Paris Ltd* [1960] 1 WLR 239). For a licence to be produced it has to be genuinely intended that the transaction will actually take place;
- where the term granted is uncertain (e.g. 'until the landlord requires the premises for other purposes'), the agreement expressly denies that any tenancy is to be implied and the rent is set to vary from, say, month to month. Although untested, this could prevent a periodic tenancy occurring by implication and, at worst, give rise to a tenancy at will which, as will be shown, is itself outside the 1954 Act.

A new approach

In *National Car Parks Ltd* v. *Trinity Development Company (Banbury) Ltd* [2001] EWCA Civ 1686, the Court of Appeal upheld a licence agreement of a shoppers' car park in circumstances where there was very little control by the landlord over the conduct of the tenant's business. The agreement carefully avoided reference to the granting of exclusive possession and moreover expressly stated that it was not intended to give any proprietary interest to the licensee. Not surprisingly, Arden L.J. acknowledged that her sole task was to determine whether or not the agreement granted exclusive possession of the car park. As drafted, the agreement was, undoubtedly, redolent with the flavour of a licence: it employed language consistent with a licence, denied exclusive possession and deliberately avoided terms which might indicate a tenancy. Arden L.J. rightly accepted that the proper approach to construction was to look at the substance of the agreement as a whole rather than to concentrate merely upon its outward appearance. She explained, 'The fact that the parties describe their agreement as a tenancy does not prevent it from being a licence, or vice versa'. Arden L.J. was clearly influenced by the fact that the present agreement was modelled upon the precedent upheld as a licence by the Court of Appeal in *Shell-Mex & BP Ltd* v. *Manchester Garages* [1971] 1 All ER 841. The rights and control retained there by the licensor were, when viewed cumulatively, utterly inconsistent with the occupier having exclusive possession of the premises. As in the *Shell-Mex* case, the licensor here had not reserved a right of entry. Arden L.J. felt that the omission of this term was a key signifier of a licence agreement.

While accepting that a declaration that exclusive possession was not given will not prevent a tenancy arising if that relationship represents the true effect of the agreement, Arden L.J. believed that the labels attached by the parties could not be ignored, 'It would in my judgment be a strong thing for the law to disregard totally the parties' choice of wording and to do so would be inconsistent with the general principle of freedom of contract and the principle that documents should be interpreted as a whole . . . it does not give rise to any presumption. At most it is relevant as a pointer'. Buxton L.J. agreed that it would, indeed, be an 'extreme' response to exclude from the construction process those parts of the agreement which stated the intention of the parties. Both felt that an examination of the agreement as a whole necessarily included a consideration what the parties had indicated they intended to do. Arden L.J. acknowledged also that the weight to be given to the parties' declaration of intentions might vary according to the respective circumstances of the parties, 'it must be approached with healthy scepticism, particularly, for instance, if the parties' bargaining positions are asymmetrical . . .'. Here it was significant that it was an arm's length agreement between two commercial parties who, having been legally advised, could be taken to have appreciated the implications of creating a licence instead of a tenancy.

Arden L.J. found it to be significant that the agreement was framed as a series of obligations on the tenant and did not start, as a tenancy would, with a conferral of an express right of occupation. As the agreement was not challenged on the basis of it being a sham or a pretence, it fell to be construed as

51

it stood. Accordingly, the absences of a covenant for quiet enjoyment and an express right of re-entry, being terms characteristically found in a tenancy agreement, were viewed as significant omissions.

In *Clear Channel UK Ltd* v. *Manchester City Council* [2005] EWCA Civ 1304, the claimant erected and maintained 13 large advertising signs at various sites owned by the Council. Clear Channel asserted that it had a tenancy whereas the Council countered that the agreement gave rise to a licence. The Court of Appeal concluded that, for exclusive possession to exist, the area(s) of land over which the right is said to exist must be capable of precise definition at the date when the right is said to have been created. Here the Council contended successfully that the agreement referred to larger undefined areas of land owned by it and that this indicated only the general location of the displays. Hence, it was not possible to spell out the grant of exclusive possession over specific areas of land occupied by the displays.

While that is not a controversial line of reasoning, Jonathan Parker L.J. went on to echo the sentiments expressed in *National Car Parks Ltd* v. *Trinity Development Company (Banbury) Ltd* [2001] EWCA Civ 1686. He considered that the form of the contract could not be ignored:

> the fact remains that this was a contract negotiated between two substantial parties of equal bargaining power and with the benefit of full legal advice. Where the contract so negotiated contains not merely a label but a clause which sets out in unequivocal terms the parties' intention as to its legal effect, I would in any event have taken some persuading that its true effect was directly contrary to that expressed intention.

Jonathan Parker L.J. admitted surprise that Clear Channel now sought to renege on the agreement which had been expressly and deliberately framed as a licence.

3.3 PREMISES

For the 1954 Act to apply there must be a letting of property which is or includes 'premises'. Although the Act does not define 'premises', what falls within the scope of the term is usually self-evident: offices, warehouses, shops and factories, for example. Nevertheless, the expression is construed widely as embracing land and any buildings on it. There is however no need for any building whatsoever because bare land can constitute premises. An example of this is *Bracey* v. *Read* [1963] Ch 88 where gallops used for the purposes of training and exercising horses were held to be premises. Other illustrations include *Harley Queen* v. *Forsyte Kerman* (1983) 6 CLY 2077 where the protection of the Act extended to open land used as a car park and *Botterill* v. *Bedfordshire CC* [1985] 1 EGLR 82 where the tenancy of land used for a gun club was protected.

3.3.1 Incorporeal hereditaments

Part II of the 1954 Act does not extend to tenancies of incorporeal hereditaments such as a right of way, a right to fish or a lease of chattels. The rationale is that, although these rights and easements can be enjoyed, they do not constitute premises and cannot be occupied (*Nevill Long & Co (Boards) Ltd* v. *Firmenich & Co* (1984) 47 P & CR 59). They do however qualify for protection if granted as ancillary rights under a lease of corporeal premises.

The Law Commission, in its 1988 Working Paper, provisionally concluded that this distinction was untenable and that, for the purposes of the Act, leases of incorporeal hereditaments should be classified as 'premises'. The suggestion was that the word 'occupy' currently employed within s.23(1) should be replaced by the term 'use'. It is arguable however that this change would fail to achieve its objective. An analogous provision requiring the premises to be used for the purposes of a business can be found in Part I of the Landlord and Tenant Act 1927, but incorporeal hereditaments still remain outside its scope. Of course, if the Act embraced incorporeal hereditaments, because such hereditaments have no rateable value, the present compensation scheme for disturbance would need to be radically reformed. Although the subsequent Law Commission Report (1992) concluded that change was unjustified, it did acknowledge that, 'There will be some circumstances in which the renewal of such a lease is just as important to protect the goodwill and future of a business as the renewal of a normal lease of business premises'. This change is unlikely to ever make the statute book.

3.4 OCCUPATION

The premises must be occupied by the tenant or the tenant's employee before the statutory provisions can apply. In this sense, the concept of occupation attributes eligibility. Once within the ambit of the 1954 Act, the tenant is entitled to a grant of a new lease, but only of the holding as it exists at the time of the hearing. Under s.23(3), the tenant's holding comprises all the property demised under the original lease, excepting any part which is no longer occupied by the tenant or the tenant's employees. Accordingly, the parcels of the new lease might not necessarily correspond with those under the previous tenancy. The use of 'occupation' in this context is determinative of the property (if any) which will be the subject matter of the new lease, that is, it prescribes entitlement. As Lord Nicholls explained in *Graysim Holdings Ltd* v. *P&O Property Holdings Ltd* [1995] 4 All ER 831, 'Although a business tenancy may include property not occupied by the tenant, property not occupied by him or his employees is excluded from the holding and, accordingly, it is not property in respect of which the tenant is entitled to obtain a new tenancy or to recover compensation'. As the design of the 1954 Act is to protect the continuing use of the premises for business purposes, occupation must exist not only at the end of the contractual term, it must also persist throughout any proceedings for a new lease (*Domer* v. *Gulf Oil (Great Britain) Ltd* (1975) 119 SJ 392). Accordingly, if the condition ceases to be fulfilled while proceedings are ongoing, the competent landlord can apply to have the tenant's application dismissed for a lack of *locus standi* (*Demetriou* v. *Poolaction* (1991) 63 P & CR 536).

3.4.1 Occupation in context

Although the notion of 'occupation' is crucial within the renewal process, it remains undefined in the Act. It is however well established that occupation turns upon issues of fact, must be real and genuine and is to be given an ordinary and commonsense meaning. As Ralph Gibson L.J. put it in *Wandsworth LBC* v. *Singh* (1991) 62 P & CR 219, the issue is whether it was likely that, 'an observer knowing the facts and applying the ordinary and popular meaning of the phrase "occupation for the purposes of a business or activity", would hold that tenant to be in occupation'. This notion was pursued by Lord Nicholls in *Graysim Holdings Ltd* v. *P&O Property Holdings Ltd* [1995] 4 All ER 831 where he explained that 'occupation' was not a term of art and was incapable of having a precise meaning applicable in all circumstances:

> The circumstances of two cases are never identical, and seldom close enough to make comparisons of much value. The types of property, and the possible uses of property, vary so widely that there can be no hard and fast rules. The degree of presence and exclusion required to constitute occupation, and the acts needed to evince presence and exclusion, must always depend on the nature of the premises, the use to which they are being put, and the rights enjoyed or exercised by the persons in question.

Lord Nicholls recognised that there are various shades of possible interpretation according to the statutory context in which the term is employed. Accordingly, in difficult cases the decision will be reached with close regard to the purpose for which the concept of 'occupation' is employed and the consequences flowing from the presence or absence of occupation. As the interpretation must be one which best suits the spirit and intention of the 1954 Act, it is unsafe to rely on decisions concerning, for example, the Rent Act 1977 or rating law. In *Wandsworth LBC* v. *Singh* (1991) 62 P & CR 219, for example, the local authority took a tenancy of some 500 square metres of public open space which they and their sub-contractors visited periodically. As the authority's activity was more than mere passive management of the land, it was held sufficient to constitute occupation.

3.4.2 Effect of sub-letting

Within the context of the 1954 Act, the term 'occupation' requires some business activity to be carried on by the tenant on the demised property. In circumstances where the tenant has not parted with possession of the premises, the position is straightforward. The court adopts a liberal approach and both 'business' and 'occupation' are readily discernible. This is because the attention of the court is focused upon the legal right to occupy and the control and user which is attendant upon that right.

A very different approach is adopted where it is clear that the premises are occupied, but it is uncertain who the occupier is for the purposes of the Act. This situation arose in *Graysim Holdings Ltd* v. *P&O Property Holdings Ltd* [1995] 4 All ER 831 where, following the sub-letting of stalls in the tenant's market, more than one party claimed to exercise rights and control over the same premises and all had a potential claim to the status of occupier. The issue is further complicated, as in the *Graysim* case, where it is the business of the tenant to permit others, in return for payment, to use the property for their own business purposes. Lord Nicholls did acknowledge that a tenant can remain in occupation of the premises even though others have been permitted to come on to the property and to use it temporarily for their business purposes. He provided the examples of a hotel company which provides rooms and facilities once a month for an antiques fair and a farmer who permits his field to be used periodically for a car boot sale. Nevertheless, he realised that it is an entirely different matter when the tenant has allowed another to carry on a business on the premises in circumstances where the tenant is entirely excluded from the property. Hence, in *Latif* v. *Hillside Estates (Swansea) Ltd* [1992] EGCS 75 the tenant, following the sub-lease of a shop, was held not to be in occupation. By way of illustration, Lord Nicholls considered the position of a tenant who carries on the business of letting office accommodation, 'He acquires a lease of the property, which he sub-lets. Under the sublease he has the usual right as landlord to enter the sublet property for various purposes, and he derives financial profit from the property in the form of rent, but plainly he would not occupy the property'.

It is to be accepted that there is no clear dividing line between the two extremes: the difference is one of degree, not of kind. Although the decision as to who occupies is a question of fact heavily dependent upon the circumstances of any given case, Lord Nicholls was able to offer some general guidance. He felt that, if the premises are sub-let, there would usually be little difficulty. The sub-tenant would have exclusive possession of the premises; the tenant would cease to be in occupation of them and would thereby lose all renewal rights. In the *Graysim* case, for example, the tenant retained occupation only of the common parts and service rooms in the market hall. Once the head lease ended the tenant could no longer be said to occupy those parts for business purposes. It is the sub-tenant who will have a sufficient degree of sole use of the property so as to enable the business to be carried on at the premises to the exclusion of everyone else. For example, in *Bassari Ltd* v. *London Borough of Camden* [1998] EGCS 27 it was held that the letting of furnished apartments took the mesne landlord outside the protection of the 1954 Act once all the flats had been let.

Where however the permission takes the form of a licence, there is more scope for debate. As the rights granted to a licensee are usually less extensive than those granted to a tenant (in particular, licences rarely afford exclusive possession), the licensor will clearly have a stronger claim to occupation. A sufficiency of control could be evidenced by, for example, the provision of services, continued presence through the medium of a manager, and the amount of time and resources allocated to management of the premises. A clear example of this would usually emerge when the premises are a boarding house or hotel.

3.4.3 The myth of coextensive occupation

A number of authorities lend support to the proposition that occupation under the 1954 Act can be shared. For example, in *William Boyer & Sons* v. *Adams* (1975) 32 P & CR 89 the court recognised the coexistence of both the tenant's and the sub-tenant's business occupancies. Any belief that occupation is not unitary and indivisible promotes the conclusion that the sub-tenant can occupy part of the building while, simultaneously, the tenant occupies the whole. In *Graysim Holdings Ltd* v. *P&O Property Holdings Ltd* [1995] 4 All ER 831 however Lord Nicholls rejected this argument and felt that such an approach was untenable, 'I am unable to accept that a tenant of a business tenancy can sub-let part of the property to a business subtenant on terms which would have the legal result that thereafter the sublet property would form the holding of the subtenant's business tenancy and yet, at the same time, remain part of the holding of the tenant's business tenancy'. Lord Nicholls concluded that the notion of dual occupation was inconsistent with the wording of s.23(3) which excludes from the tenant's holding those parts not occupied by the tenant. This provision necessarily means that property occupied by some other party must be excluded, 'One would not expect to find that two persons, other than persons acting jointly, could each be in occupation of the same property for this purpose'. If it were otherwise, somewhat curious results would ensue.

First, if the sub-let part formed part of the holding of both the tenant and the sub-tenant, each would *prima facie* be entitled to the grant of a new lease from the same landlord in respect of the same property.

Secondly, if the landlord successfully opposed the grant, both the tenant and the sub-tenant might be entitled to recover compensation for disturbance. Not surprisingly, Lord Nicholls adopted the view that such repercussions ran contrary to the scheme and policy of the Act, 'The Act looks through to the occupying tenants, here the traders, and affords them statutory protection, not their landlord. Intermediate landlords, not themselves in occupation, are not within the class of persons the Act was seeking to protect'.

3.4.4 Vicarious occupation

Occupation of premises through an agent, representative (including a company) or employee will suffice for the purposes of the Act (*Pegler* v. *Craven* [1952] 2 QB 69). The occupier must however genuinely be acting on behalf of the tenant and this will be evidenced by the tenant's degree of control, financial interest in the business and the right to resort to the premises. In *Teasdale* v. *Walker* [1958] 3 All ER 307, the new occupier was allowed in, purportedly, under a management agreement, but the court held that there had, in reality, been the grant of a sub-tenancy. Hence the occupation was not vicarious. Where there is doubt, the agreement must be construed to determine whether the respective rights and obligations of the tenant and the *de facto* occupier show that the occupier is conducting the tenant's business or an entirely different business.

Companies

Traditionally, problems arose when the premises were occupied, and the business run, by a separate legal entity from the tenant. As this clearly cannot be regarded as representative occupation, the rule was that, where the tenant runs a business through a company, it is the company that is the occupier and not the tenant who controls it. As Wilmer L.J. pointed out in *Tunstall* v. *Steigmann* [1962] 2 QB 593, 'There is no escape from the fact that a company is a legal entity separate from its corporators . . . This is no matter of form; it is a matter of substance and realty'. There would, of course, have been no difficulty had the lease been assigned to the company because then the company would be both tenant and occupier.

In order to overcome this potential trap for the tenant who decides to incorporate the business, s.23(1A) now provides that the corporate veil be lifted and that, for these purposes, companies should be equated with those individuals who control them. This will mean that a tenant would still be able to claim renewal even though its corporate *alter ego* is in occupation. This change merely gives statutory recognition to a commercial reality.

Groups of companies

Where the tenant is a company, representative occupation through an employee, manager or agent is clearly essential. It is possible moreover that one company can manage another company's business. The general rule is that the representative must occupy in the sense that it has control and use of the premises on behalf of the tenant. In *Trans-Britannia Properties Ltd v. Darby Properties Ltd* [1986] 1 EGLR 151, following the sub-letting of lock-up garages, the tenant's representative only had nominal control over the premises. The very nature of the business amounted to parting with occupation and control.

By virtue of s.42(2) however a special rule applies in relation to a group of companies. This provides that the occupation and carrying on business by one company within the group shall be treated as occupation and carrying on business by the tenant company. For these purposes s.42(1) provides that two bodies corporate are members of a group only when one is a subsidiary of the other or both are subsidiaries of a third company. The 1992 Law Commission Report advocated that this definition of a group of companies be extended to include pyramid companies controlled by the same individual, notwithstanding that there may be lacking any connected share holding. This recommendation was not taken forward.

Trusts

Where a tenancy is held on an express or implied trust, s.41(1) provides that occupation by any or all of the beneficiaries is to be treated as occupation by the tenant trustee(s). This is of great practical importance because trustees are not usually given a power to trade. A change in the identity of the trustee moreover is not to be treated as a change in the person of the tenant. The provisions as to trusts necessarily apply to property which is co-owned regardless of whether the co-owners are, in equity, joint tenants or tenants in common. It is to be appreciated however that any statutory notices must still be served by and on the tenant and proceedings commenced by the tenant trustee (*Sevenarts Ltd v. Busvine* [1968] 1 WLR 1929). The ambit of s.41(1) was explained by Lord Evershed M.R. in *Frish Ltd v. Barclays Bank* [1955] 2 QB 541 as:

> dealing only, with the case where, although the tenancy is vested in someone who is properly described as the tenant, nevertheless it is found that the tenant himself happens to be a trustee and the premises are actually occupied by, and the business is actually being carried on, not by the tenant trustee himself but by the beneficiary or beneficiaries, or one of them, for whom the tenant is a trustee.

For the trustees to take advantage of this special provision, the occupier must be a beneficiary entitled to occupy by virtue of the equitable interest under the trust and must not be in occupation under some independent contractual relationship. For example, in *Frish v. Barclays Bank* [1955] 2 QB 541 the trustees could not take advantage of this provision where the beneficiary occupied *qua* sub-tenant and not under the terms of the trust. The terms of the trust moreover must either give the beneficiaries the right to occupy or be such that it is proper to allow the beneficiaries into occupation. In the *Frish* case, the property was held under a trust for sale with the income to be held on discretionary trusts for the beneficiaries. It was held that none of the beneficiaries had a right to occupy under this discretionary trust. Similarly, the trustees cannot allow a non-beneficiary to occupy and still claim the benefit of the statutory provision. This is illustrated by *Methodist Secondary Schools Trust Deed Trustees* v. *O'Leary* [1993] 1 EGLR 105 where the management board of a school occupied the property, but were not entitled to any personal benefit under the trust. The provision also does not cater for occupation under a charitable purpose trust.

3.4.5 Ceasing occupation

There is no obligation on the tenant physically to occupy throughout the entirety of the contractual term and, in the situation where the tenant resumes occupation while the contractual lease is in existence, the renewal right will generally be rekindled. A lack of occupation may prove crucial at two key stages: first, when the contractual term ends; and, secondly, when the application for a new lease is made and heard. Although an absence of *de facto* occupation at any of these times is potentially fatal to the tenant's statutory entitlement, it is not in itself decisive. If the tenant has abandoned the premises, the protection of the 1954 Act will clearly cease. Temporary absence or intermittent use however will not usually produce such drastic consequences. For example, in *Bell* v. *Alfred Franks & Bartlett & Co Ltd* [1980] 1 All ER 356, the tenant still occupied premises which were sometimes (but not always) used for storage purposes. Similarly, in *Pulleng* v. *Curran* (1982) 44 P & CR 58 it was made clear that the tenancy will remain within the 1954 Act where the premises are temporarily unoccupied due to illness, bankruptcy or economic recession. The distinction between occupation and non-occupation is therefore one of fact and degree.

A number of influential factors were identified in *Bacchiocchi* v. *Academic Agency Ltd* [1998] 2 All ER 241:

- the extent of the tenant's physical presence on, use of, and control over the premises. In this context even a small amount of business use would suffice to show that the business has not ceased (*Flairline Properties Ltd* v. *Aziz Hassan* [1999] 1 EGLR 138);
- whether the tenant vacated the premises voluntarily or involuntarily, in the sense of leaving for reasons beyond the tenant's control. In the *Flairline Properties* case, for example, the fact that the tenant's restaurant had been damaged by fire was significant;

- whether having vacated, the tenant evinced an intention to return. This would embrace 'live' evidence of the tenant and others about the tenant's intention to return and any relevant correspondence. It does not require that the landlord be informed of this intention. In the *Flairline Properties* case, it was held that the tenant is not required to establish a reasonable prospect of bringing about re-occupancy within the near or reasonable future. The court also made it clear that there was no need even for the tenant to show a genuine, firm and settled intention to occupy; and
- whether the thread of continuity of occupation was broken.

Continuity of occupation

In *I&H Caplan Ltd* v. *Caplan (No. 2)* [1963] 1 WLR 1247, the tenant voluntarily moved out for seven months while the renewal application was on-going. Cross J. regarded this as a borderline case, but held that the thread of continuity of occupation was not broken. He said:

> I think it is quite clear that a tenant does not lose the protection of this Act simply by ceasing physically to occupy the premises. They may well continue to be occupied for the purposes of a business although they are *de facto* empty for some period of time. One rather obvious example would be if there was a need for urgent structural repairs and the tenant had to go out of physical occupation in order to enable them to be effected . . . On the other hand . . . a mere intention to resume occupation if you get a new tenancy will not preserve the continuity of the business user if the thread has once been definitely broken.

A similar justification would arise where the interruption of business user was, say, due to seasonal closure (*Artemiou* v. *Procopiou* [1966] 1 QB 878). In *Morrisons Holdings Ltd* v. *Manders Property (Wolverhampton) Ltd* [1976] 1 WLR 533, the tenants ceased trading as a result of a fire in an adjoining property, but required the landlords to reinstate so that they could continue trading as soon as possible. It was held that, in order to obtain a renewal, the tenant must show that there is continuing occupation or, if events beyond the tenant's control have caused the tenant to vacate, that the tenant continues to exert and claim the right of occupancy. Although no longer in physical occupation, the tenants were, therefore, entitled to a new lease. This is to be contrasted with the situation where the premises are rendered uninhabitable by reason of disrepair, the landlord is under no obligation to repair, and the tenant cannot afford to effect the works. It would then be impracticable for the tenant to continue in business at those premises and, regardless of the professed intentions of the tenant, occupation will have ceased.

Conversely, in *Hancock & Willis* v. *GMS Syndicate Ltd* (1983) 265 EG 473, the tenants moved to larger premises for six months and licensed their former premises to others, reserving a wine cellar and the right to use the dining room twice a month. The tenants' furniture, carpets and files remained at the premises, but this could not constitute constructive occupation as the tenants reserved no right to enter and they were not in the business of storage. The thread of continuity on these facts was, therefore, clearly broken. Eveleigh L.J. concluded:

> The words with which we are concerned import, in my judgment an element of control and user and they involve the notion of physical occupation. That does not mean physical occupation every minute of the day, provided the right to occupy continues. But it is necessary for the judge trying the case to assess the whole situation where the element of control and use may exist in variable degrees. At the end of the day it is a question of fact for the tribunal to decide, treating the words as ordinary words in the way in which I have referred to them.

3.5 FOR THE PURPOSES OF A BUSINESS

The tenant must not merely occupy the premises; the occupation must be (in whole or part) for the purposes of a business carried on by the tenant. There is no requirement that the tenant's business actually be conducted on the premises as ancillary use will suffice provided that it is in the furtherance of the tenant's business. Occupation preparatory to the operation of a business might however be insufficient. As Megaw L.J. commented in *Hillil Property & Investment Co* v. *Naraine Pharmacy Ltd* (1979) 39 P & CR 67 at 73, 'It is not a question of whether the building at which one is looking is the main seat of the business, but whether it is occupied for the purposes of the business'.

In *Bell* v. *Alfred Franks & Bartlett & Co Ltd* [1980] 1 All ER 356, for example, the passive storage of cartons in a lock-up garage was held to constitute occupation for business purposes. This is to be contrasted with *Chapman* v. *Freeman* [1978] 3 All ER 878 where it was held that an employer's tenancy of a nearby cottage, for the purpose of housing hotel staff, fell outside the Act. There the Court of Appeal held that the tenant was in (vicarious) occupation, but that the occupation was not for business purposes. As Lord Denning M.R. explained, 'Speaking generally, the test is whether it is necessary for any of the staff to live in this cottage for the better performance of their duties. It is no doubt highly convenient that they should live there, but that is not enough'. He added, 'it is a dwelling house simply for the convenience of the person carrying on the business. It is not a business tenancy'. He likened it to a barrister who rented a flat near chambers which would be used for residential rather than business purposes. As Geoffrey Lane L.J. acknowledged, the conclusion would be different if the employee had been required to be on hand at all times to perform the duties. This does not impose a 'necessity test' and, instead, the requirement is that the occupation be for business reasons and not merely for the convenience of the person carrying on the business. Accordingly, a car park for customers and visitors would qualify as ancillary use (*Hunt* v. *Decca Navigator* [1972] EGD 331). A car park solely for staff away from the place of business would however not be regarded as furthering the tenant's business.

3.5.1 Mixed user

For the purposes of s.32(1) there is no requirement that the property demised under a new lease be occupied solely for the purposes of a business. Wholly residential tenancies however automatically fall outside the scope of the business tenancy legislation. Nevertheless, it is permissible that the premises be used for a mixture of business and residential purposes. In the conjoined appeals in *Cheryl Investments Ltd* v. *Saldanha; Royal Life Savings Society* v. *Page* [1979] 1 All ER 5, the premises concerned were used as residences and also for business purposes, that is, respectively, an accountant's business and a doctor's surgery. As a rule of thumb, it might be argued that, when there is more than a nominal authorised business user, the *prima facie* presumption is that the 1954 Act applies. The threshold is therefore low in that the business user does not have to be the predominant, main or principal purpose. All that is necessary is that the commercial use be of some significant degree. Hence, the tenancy will not fall within the 1954 Act if the business use is shown to be incidental. For example, in *Wright* v. *Mortimer* (1996) 28 HLR 719, a residential flat in which an art historian carried out a third of his work and used part of his sitting room as an office did not constitute business premises.

The determination turns primarily upon issues of fact (including the nature of the business) and degree. As Waite L.J. admitted in *Wright* v. *Mortimer* (1996) 28 HLR 719, 'issues involving a fine balance . . . may depend in the last analysis upon the general impression created in the mind of the judge by the evidence'. Accordingly, in *Gurton* v. *Parrott* [1991] 1 EGLR 98 where the tenant resided and carried out a dog breeding and kennelling business at the premises, it was held that the commercial use (there akin to a hobby) was insufficiently substantial and that the tenancy fell outside the 1954 Act. Similarly, in *Royal Life Saving Society* v. *Page* [1979] 1 All ER 5 the tenant (a doctor who had consulting rooms elsewhere) made professional use of his maisonette once or twice a year, but the tenancy was held to fall outside the 1954 Act.

It should be appreciated that protection under the 1954 Act ousts any protection that could otherwise be afforded to the tenant under the Rent Act 1977 or the Housing Act 1988. It is however possible that changes in use during the currency of the lease might take the tenancy from one statutory code to another. This is so even if the landlord is not aware of the change of use (*Cheryl Investments* v. *Saldanha* [1979] 1 All ER 5). Although a cessation of business will take the tenancy outside the 1954 Act, the persistence of some residential use will not automatically engage the provisions of, say, the Housing Act 1988. A new tenancy agreement would, therefore, be necessary. A wholly residential tenancy, which later develops a substantial, authorised business user will, it seems, transfer more readily to the business code. This is particularly so when the change of user is expressly permitted by the landlord (*Henry Smith's Charity Trustees* v. *Wagle & Tippet* [1990] 1 QB 42).

3.5.2 Business

Within s.23(2) the term 'business' is defined as including 'a trade, profession or employment and includes any activity carried on by a body of persons whether corporate or unincorporate'. This definition applies throughout the Part II provisions. Accordingly, the 1954 Act draws a distinction between those tenants who are individuals and those that are bodies (e.g. trade unions and friendly societies) or corporations (e.g. local authorities, statutory under-takers and private companies). It is only for bodies and corporations that the extension to 'any activity' is made. The activities of a government department are expressly included within this provision (s.56(3)).

For other tenants the business must constitute a trade, profession or employment. As the 1954 Act was designed to regulate a wide range of tenan-cies and to embrace a wide range of commercial activity, the understanding of the term 'business' is, not surprisingly, broad based. Lindley L.J. in *Rolls* v. *Miller* (1884) LR 27 Ch D 71 described it as including, 'almost anything which is an occupation, as distinguished from a pleasure – anything which is an occupation or a duty which requires attention is a business'. The term therefore connotes some commercial activity with the ambition of making a gain or a profit. The actual making of a profit is not however essential, nor does payment itself necessarily indicate a business. In *Abernethie* v. *AM & J Kleiman* [1970] 1 QB 10, for example, the running of a Sunday school without reward was not a business. As Widgery L.J. admitted:

> It certainly does not follow . . . that Parliament intended to push the tentacles of the Act . . . into domestic lettings and the activities which a man carries out in his private rooms as part of his hobby or recreation . . . what a man does with his spare time in his home is most unlikely to qualify for the description 'business' unless it has some direct commercial involvement in it, whether it be a hobby or a recreation or the performance of a social duty . . .

Similarly, in *Secretary for State for Transport* v. *Jenkins* (30 October 1997) the tenants ran a community farm as a non-commercial enterprise and this prompted Millett L.J. to conclude: 'Not only is the enterprise not carried on with a view to profit, it is not carried on as a trading activity, but rather in the spirit of public benevolence. As such it is not a trade, profession or employment, nor is it any kind of business'.

Trade, profession and employment

The term 'trade' is viewed as being of narrower meaning than the general expression 'business'. It connotes the activity of buying and selling and will normally involve a profit-making aspect. A guest house run on a non-profit basis was however held to be a trade in *Ireland* v. *Taylor* [1949] 1 KB 300. In *Brighton College* v. *Marriott (Inspector of Taxes)* [1926] AC 192, a college was carrying on a trade even though it was a charitable institution. This case also made it clear that a given activity might be classified both as a trade and as a business.

The concept of a 'profession' enjoys a scope less certain than a 'business' or a 'trade'. In *IRC* v. *Maxse* [1919] 1 KB 647, Scrutton L.J. provided the working definition of a profession as, 'an occupation requiring either purely intellectual skill or manual skill controlled, as in painting, sculpture or surgery, by the intellectual skill of the operator, as distinguished from an occupation which is substantially the production or sale or arrangement for production and sale of commodities'. Accordingly, the category of professionals is wide and includes clergy, lawyers, doctors, accountants, surveyors, architects and the like. If in doubt, the court will adopt a commonsense interpretation. This is illustrated in *Abernethie* v. *AM & J Kleiman* [1970] 1 QB 10 where Harman L.J. said of a voluntary Sunday school, 'It is not carried on professionally: it is carried on amateurishly, just the opposite to "professionally"'.

In the context of the 1954 Act, the term 'employment' is used as meaning a calling and is broad enough to cover most business occupations. This is in recognition that profits may be earned in many ways. The term 'employment' has, therefore, included the occupation of a lecturer (*Lecture League Ltd* v. *LCC* (1913) 108 LT 924) and the carrying on of a teaching hospital (*Hills (Patents) Ltd* v. *University College Hospital Board of Governors* [1956] 1 QB 90). In *Abernethie* v. *AM & J Kleiman Ltd* [1970] 1 QB 10, the tenant gratuitously ran a weekly Sunday school from his premises (previously a shop). This was clearly neither a trade nor a profession and, in considering whether it was an employment, Harman L.J. added, 'In my view, it clearly is not. "Employment" in that sense must mean something much more regular than that. It means, I should have thought, either employing somebody else or being employed by someone else'.

Activity by a body of persons

This expression has been given a liberal interpretation by the courts:

- in *Addiscombe Garden Estates Ltd* v. *Crabbe* [1958] 1 QB 513, the meaning embraced the 'activity' of a member's tennis club;
- in *Wandsworth LBC* v. *Singh* (1991) 62 P & CR 219, the activity of the local authority was providing a public park;

- in *Hills (Patents) Ltd* v. *University College Hospital Board of Governors* [1956] 1 QB 90, the activity was the running of an NHS hospital;
- in *Parkes* v. *Westminster Roman Catholic Diocese Trustee* (1978) 36 P & CR 22, the provision of a community centre sufficed;
- in *Ye Olde Cheshire Cheese Ltd* v. *Daily Telegraph plc* [1988] 3 All ER 217, it was held to extend to the running of a restaurant and the use of storage areas for restaurant purposes; and
- in *Lee-Verhulst (Investments) Ltd* v. *Harwood Trust* [1973] 1 QB 204, the supply of residential accommodation for staff was regarded as an activity.

One limitation however was imposed by the Court of Appeal in *Hillil Property & Investment Co* v. *Naraine Pharmacy* (1979) 39 P & CR 67 where Megaw L.J. concluded that, although different from a trade, profession or employment, 'an activity for this purpose ... must be something which is correlative to the conceptions involved in those words'. There the casual dumping of waste building materials on empty shop premises was held not to be an activity on those premises. A similar approach was adopted in *Abernethie* v. *AM & J Kleiman* [1970] 1 QB 10 where the Court of Appeal was sceptical as to whether the running of a Sunday school for one hour per week could amount to an activity for these purposes. Hence, there has to be a business element to the activity for it to qualify for protection under the Act.

As regards 'a body of persons' a generous meaning is to be given. In *Secretary of State for Transport* v. *Jenkins* (30 October 1997), for example, Millett L.J. recognised that a very loose and informal farming collective might suffice for these purposes. This was so even though there was no evidence of any membership list, constitution or rules, or of any membership fee being charged. Nevertheless, he acknowledged that joint tenants are not *ipso facto* a body of persons, 'The expression must connote some involvement or participation in a common activity other than the mere joint ownership of the property'. Although there need not be a precise identity between the persons who are in occupation as tenants and those who carry on the activity, it remains necessary that the activity carried on there is the tenants' business activity.

3.5.3 Unauthorised business user

There unfortunately is no straightforward rule which entails that a tenant who carries on a business which constitutes a breach of a user covenant is outside the protection of the 1954 Act. Instead, there is a somewhat elaborate provision within s.23(4) which deals with use unauthorised by the current tenancy. This provides that a business carried on in breach of only certain types of covenant does not qualify for protection. This rule of non-protection applies where there is a blanket prohibition against business use (e.g. 'not to use the premises for business purposes' or 'to use the premises for the purposes of a dwelling only') or a covenant prohibiting the general carrying on of a trade, profession and/or employment (e.g. 'not to use the premises for the purposes of any trade').

The deprivation of protection does not, therefore, arise in the following situations: first where the prohibition relates only to part of the premises (e.g. a covenant which requires that only the upper floor of the demised premises be used only for residential purposes). Secondly, where the covenant is directed against use for the purposes of a specified business (e.g. 'not to use the premises as a solicitors' office'). Thirdly, where it restricts use to a particular business (e.g. 'to use the premises only as a solicitors' office').

Consent and acquiescence

This limited rule of non-protection gives way either where the tenant's immediate landlord (or the landlord's predecessor in title) consented to the breach or where the immediate landlord (but not a predecessor in title) acquiesced in it (s.23(4)). The difference in approach concerning the predecessor in title reflects the fact that the current landlord could not be aware of a predecessor's state of mind.

For these purposes 'consent' connotes a positive act of acceptance and requires more than a mere absence of objection. 'Acquiescence' however is the passive failure to take steps concerning a known breach. Hence, an acceptance of rent by a landlord who has a full knowledge of the facts could amount to an acquiescence in the breach. Conversely, the absence of actual knowledge that a business is being carried on at the premises necessitates that there can be no acquiescence. For example, in *Brown* v. *Myerson* (21 July 1998) the tenant conducted the business of a licensed conveyancer from home. Although the business was advertised at the front of the house, the landlord had no actual knowledge that the user covenant was breached. There could be no acquiescence.

In its 1988 Working Paper, the Law Commission expressed the view that, 'The way in which the position is at present expressed provides the opportunity for evading the Act'. This could occur where a landlord has acquiesced in the establishment of an unauthorised business, but now wishes to escape the security of tenure provisions. The landlord can potentially achieve this by assigning the freehold to an associate who, having neither consented nor acquiesced in the user, can terminate the tenancy without going through the statutory machinery. To avoid this happening, the Working Paper concluded provisionally that the same test for both the current and former landlords be used, 'so that ownership of the reversion is not critical to whether the tenant enjoys renewal rights'. This suggestion was not to be pursued further.

3.6 EXCLUDED TENANCIES

There are a variety of exclusions from the scope of Part II of the 1954 Act and invariably this withholding of protection is based upon sound reasoning, for example where the tenancy is protected by another statutory code or as an encouragement to grant temporary lettings. Most are expressly listed in s.43, some arise under other statutory provisions and one is derived from the common law. These exceptions to the general availability of security of tenure now fall to be considered.

3.6.1 Agricultural holdings and farm business tenancies

Section 43(1)(*a*), (*aa*) excludes leases governed by the Agricultural Holdings Act 1986 or the Agricultural Tenancies Act 1995, respectively, from the protection of the 1954 Act. The Agricultural Tenancies Act 1995 replaces the 1986 Act as regards tenancies created after 1 September 1995. Instead of an agricultural holding, new lettings will give rise to a farm business tenancy. This exemption extends also to lettings which, if they had not been excluded by s.2(3) of the 1986 Act, would have been within the agricultural code and to tenancies of agricultural land which have been taken outside that code with the approval of the relevant minister. Where the letting is for a business with an agricultural aspect however a potential difficulty arises concerning which statutory code is applicable. The resolution turns upon which is the substantial or dominant user. If however the tenancy *prima facie* satisfies both codes, then it will be excluded from the 1954 Act (*Short* v. *Greeves* [1988] 8 EG 109).

On any subsequent change of user, the test of dominant purpose may again be invoked and could result in a former agricultural holding/farm business tenancy becoming a business lease governed by the 1954 Act. This possibility was considered in *Russell* v. *Booker* (1982) 5 HLR 10 where the Court of Appeal laid down helpful guidance:

- the purpose as expressed in, or contemplated by, the agreement is the essential factor;
- where the original agreement has been superseded by a new contract, the purpose may be considered in the light of that new contract;
- a new contract may be inferred by the court from user known to the landlord;
- a mere unilateral change cannot of itself bring the tenancy within the protection of a different statutory regime; and
- where no particular user has been provided for in, or contemplated by, the agreement, actual and subsequent user will determine which code is to apply.

3.6.2 Mining leases

By virtue of s.43(1)(*b*), tenancies created by mining leases do not attract renewal rights under the 1954 Act. Mining leases are excluded because the tenant's business involves the depletion of the land's mineral resources and it is important for the landlord to regain possession at the end of the contractual tenancy. A mining lease is one granted for a mining or related purpose and is defined in s.25 of the Landlord and Tenant Act 1927 as extending to mines and minerals and thereby includes all solid substances that can be obtained from beneath the surface of the earth for the purpose of profit. The definition does not, therefore, exclude from the Act a tenancy for the drilling of oil and gas.

3.6.3 Service tenancies

Part II of the 1954 Act does not apply to a tenancy granted to the tenant as the holder of an office, appointment or employment when the tenancy will end (or becomes liable to end) on the termination of that service or employment. If, as is likely, the tenancy was granted after 1 October 1954, the additional requirement imposed by s.43(2) is that the tenancy must be in writing and must express the purpose of the grant. The court is left to ascertain whether the alleged service agreement is genuine or a sham (*Teasdale* v. *Walker* [1958] 3 All ER 307).

3.6.4 Short tenancies

By virtue of s.43(3), the Act does not apply to a lease for a term of years certain not exceeding six months, unless there is provision for renewal or extension beyond six months or the tenant (and/or a predecessor in business) has been in occupation for more than 12 months. This provision allows for consecutive tenancies to be granted for a period totalling 12 months provided that there is no provision in the tenancy relating to the grant of a further term. This facility is useful as it encourages such transactions as, for example, the letting of shop premises to charities and retail outlets over the seasonal periods. The 'occupation' limitation is designed to restrict the use of short leases to new tenants and to new businesses. It should be emphasised that the exemption extends only to fixed-term tenancies.

This exception was considered by Neuberger J. in *Cricket Ltd* v. *Shaftesbury Plc* [1999] 28 EG 127 where the tenant held over after two successive tenancies (of five months' duration each). The holding over was as a tenant at will and this final period of occupation took the total period beyond the 12-month ceiling. The court held that the period of occupation as a tenant at will (or licensee or trespasser) could not enter into the calculation. The basic notion was that such relationships fall entirely outside the definition of 'tenancy' for the purposes of the 1954 Act. After the end of the second fixed term, and in the context of s.43(3), the claimant in the view of Neuberger J., 'was not the tenant: he was not a tenant because the word "tenant" in the 1954 Act does not extend to a tenant at will'. The approach of Neuberger J. is understandable in that it prevents a tenant, who has occupied under two six-month tenancies, holding over at the end of the last tenancy and claiming that the excess period of occupation takes the tenancies outside the exception in s.43(3).

3.6.5 Tenancies at will

Unlike in the residential sector, it has been determined that a business tenancy at will falls outside the ambit of statutory protection. It would be, as Lord Morton admitted in *Wheeler* v. *Mercer* [1957] AC 416, 'surprising if the legislation had intended to bring within the scope of the Act a relationship so personal and so fleeting as a tenancy at will'. This is so regardless of whether the tenancy arises expressly or by implication of law (*Manfield & Sons Ltd* v. *Botchin* [1970] 2 QB 612). The rationale underlying this exclusion is that the Act applies only to tenancies that can be brought to an end by notice to quit or by effluxion of time.

For a tenancy at will to arise the arrangement must be expressly or impliedly made terminable at the will of either party and must not contain any terms that are inconsistent with a tenancy at will (e.g. relating to re-entry and forfeiture). The safest use of such a tenancy occurs where the tenant is holding over at the end of the lease or has moved into possession pending negotiation of the terms of the lease. In other situations, a tenant might be reluctant to accept such an uncertain letting.

Of course, the primary difficulty experienced by the court is distinguishing a genuine tenancy at will from a periodic tenancy or a licence agreement. As Nicholls L.J. advised in *Javad* v. *Aqil* [1991] 1 WLR 1007:

> Of course, when one party permits another to enter or remain on his land on payment of a sum of money, and that other has no statutory entitlement to be there, almost inevitably there will be some consensual relationship between them. It may be no more than a licence determinable at any time, or a tenancy at will. But when and so long as the parties are in the throes of negotiating larger terms, caution must be exercised before inferring or imputing to the parties an intention to give to the occupant more than a very limited interest, be it licence or tenancy. Otherwise the court would be in danger of inferring or imputing from conduct, such as the payment of rent and the carrying out of repairs, whose explanation lies in the parties' expectation that they will be able to reach agreement on the larger terms, an intention to grant a lesser interest, such as a periodic tenancy, which the parties never had in contemplation at all.

3.7 THE CROWN AND GOVERNMENT DEPARTMENTS: SPECIAL PROVISIONS

3.7.1 Crown as landlord

Subject to certain qualifications, s.56(1) ensures that the Crown falls within the classification of a competent landlord for the purposes of the Part II provisions. Without this express inclusion, the Crown would not be bound by the security of tenure provisions (*Wirral Estates Ltd* v. *Shaw* [1932] 2 KB 247). The Act provides that where the landlord's interest is held by Her Majesty in right of the Crown or the Duchy of Lancaster, or is held by the Duchy of Cornwall, the tenant (who otherwise qualifies for protection under the statutory scheme) is entitled to the full benefit of the Act. Subject to some exceptions, s.56(1) applies the same general rule when the landlord's interest is held by a government department. For the purposes of the Act, when an interest belongs to Her Majesty in right of the Duchy of Lancaster, the Chancellor of the Duchy represents Her Majesty and is deemed to own the interest. As regards the Duchy of Cornwall, such person as the Duke appoints shall be deemed to own the interest.

3.7.2 Crown as tenant

As a result of s.56(1), the Crown may also, in certain circumstances, take advantage of the protection of Part II in the capacity of a tenant. For such protection to exist, the premises must be occupied for the purposes of a business (not necessarily the business of the Crown) and fall within the general ambit of s.23. One modification of this rule exists in s.56(3) and exclusively relates to tenancies held by, or on behalf of, a government department. This departure is that premises occupied for the purposes of a government department are, whether or not it is in reality the case, deemed to be occupied for the purposes of a business. As Scott J. explained in *Linden* v. *DHSS* [1986] 1 All ER 691, 'In my judgment s.56(3) brings within Part II of the 1954 Act any tenancy held by a government department if the premises are being occupied for any purpose of any government department'. Even if the premises are not occupied for the purposes of a government department, the department is protected by Part II provided that no rent is payable by any other occupier (s.56(4)). The government department is thereby deemed to still occupy for its own purposes.

In addition, any provisions that require the premises to have been occupied for the purposes of a tenant's business for a period of time or that, on a change of tenant, the new occupier should have succeeded to the business of the predecessor are subject to a further deeming provision. The occupation condition is automatically deemed to be satisfied where the government department has occupied during that period. As regards a succession condition, one government department is deemed to be in the same business as another (s.56(3)(*a*), (*b*)).

3.7.3   Modification of tenant's rights in the public interest

Although the fact that the landlord's interest is held by a government department does not in itself prevent a tenant from claiming security of tenure, there are a series of provisions which, on the basis of public interest or national security, can modify the tenant's right to a new tenancy. These special rights are in addition to the landlord's ordinary rights enjoyed under Part II of the 1954 Act. By way of some safeguard, s.59 ensures that the tenant will normally be entitled to compensation for disturbance. The public interest ground applies when the interest of the competent landlord (or any superior landlord) belongs to, or is held for the purposes of, either a government department or any local authority, health authority or special health authority, development corporation, statutory undertaker or the National Trust (s.57(1)). For these purposes however the Commissioners of Crown Lands do not constitute a government department (s.57(8)).

Certification

The Minister (or Board) in charge of the appropriate government department or other body may issue a certificate to the effect that the use or occupation of the demised property (or any part of it) will be changed from a specified date and that the property is required for the purposes of the relevant public body (s.57(1)). Certification excludes the tenant's right to renew. There is moreover no obligation that the proposed change be essential and it suffices that it is required in the circumstances.

A further alternative which is open to the landlord allows a different type of certificate to be issued (a certificate for break clause) where the tenant's renewal application is already under way and no order has yet been made. This certificate is to the effect that it is necessary, in the public interest, that the court must include in the new lease a break clause, determinable on six months' notice by the landlord (s.57(5)).

Preliminary notice

It is provided by s.57(2) that none of these certificates may be issued unless the tenant has been given preliminary notice (no form is prescribed) that the Minister (or Board) is contemplating the issue of the document. The tenant then has 21 days in which to make written representations to the Minister (or Board) concerning the matter. Account must be taken of the representations of the tenant before any decision to issue the certificate is made. There is no appeal from the giving of a certificate, but it is subject to judicial review. Such scrutiny is essential for, as Dunn L.J. explained in *R* v. *Secretary of State for the Environment, ex p. Powis* [1981] 1 All ER 788:

> The result of these provisions is that business tenants of local authorities and other public bodies may be deprived . . . of the rights which they would otherwise have had of applying to the county court for a new tenancy. They are deprived of the opportunity of testing in court any objection by the landlord under s.30 of the Act to a grant of a new tenancy, with the advantages of a public hearing, discovery of documents and cross examination of witnesses.

Legal consequences

The consequences of certification hinge primarily upon whether the landlord has served a s.25 notice or the tenant has served a s.26 request. If the landlord has served a termination notice, the specified date of termination becomes significant. It also dictates what form of s.25 notice is to be served. Section 57(3) provides that, if the date specified is not earlier than the date set out in the certificate (and the notice contains a copy of the certificate), the tenant can make no application for a new lease. When the date of termination is earlier than the date specified in the certificate (and, again, provided that a copy of the certificate is included with the notice), the court can grant a renewal, but only for a term expiring no later than the certified date. The new tenancy will be outside the protection of the 1954 Act and there can be no further renewal (s.57(3)(*b*)).

Where the tenant has served a request for a new lease, much depends upon whether the request was served after or before the issue of the certificate. If the s.26 request is served after the certificate, the landlord can serve a counter notice, within two months, containing a copy of the certificate. When the termination date specified in the request is later than the date specified in that certificate, s.57(4) disentitles the tenant from making an application for renewal. Where the termination date is earlier than the date contained in the certificate, a new tenancy can be granted, but for a duration no longer than the date set out in the certificate. The new tenancy falls outside the Part II machinery. If the tenant's request precedes the issue of the certificate, the request is invalid if either the preliminary certification notice has been given by the Minister (or Board) or is given within two months of the s.26 request. The provisions as to certification apply even where the authority using them acquired the reversion after the tenant served a s.26 request. The consequence is that the current tenancy continues with the proviso that, once the decision as to whether to issue a certificate is taken, the tenant can make a fresh request for a new lease.

3.7.4   National security

Where the landlord's interest belongs to, or is held for the purposes of a government department, s.58(1)(*a*), (*b*) provides that the tenancy may be terminated on the grounds of national security. This special provision prevents the operation of the Part II machinery. The procedure involved requires a certificate from the Minister of the government department to the effect that, for reasons of national security, it is necessary that the use or occupation of the demised premises shall be discontinued or changed. Unlike the other type of certification discussed above, there is no requirement for any preliminary notice to be given to the tenant. The issue of a certificate does however have implications as regards the service of renewal documentation.

Implications

Where the landlord, after the issue of the certificate, serves a s.25 notice which contains a copy of the certificate the tenant is unable to apply for a new lease. If the tenant makes a s.26 request for a new tenancy the landlord has two months within which to issue a certificate (if it has not already done so) and serve a counter notice (containing a copy of the certificate) so as to preclude the tenant's renewal application. The counter notice should set a date on which the tenancy is to come to an end. If it precedes the termination date specified in the tenant's request, and is at least six months from the giving of the counter notice (and not earlier than the date the tenancy could be terminated at common law), the current tenancy will end on the date set out in the counter notice. In all other cases, the lease will terminate on the date specified in the tenant's request. As regards prospective certification, s.58 expressly validates any agreement between the parties that, on the giving of such certification, the tenancy may be terminated by notice to quit of such duration as agreed, provided that the notice concerns a copy of the certificate (s.58(2)(*a*)). If no agreement is achieved, and the tenant has applied for a new lease, the court shall, at the behest of the landlord, make this provision for early termination a term of any new lease (58(4)(*a*), (*b*)).

3.7.5   Other official bodies

Further provisions apply when the Secretary of State or the Urban Regeneration Agency is the landlord and the demised property is located within a specified development area or an intermediate area. Under the auspices of s.60(1), the Secretary of State may certify that a change of use or occupation is necessary or expedient for the purposes of Sched. 2 to the Industrial Development Act 1982. Section 58(1)(*a*), (*b*) of the 1954 Act applies in the same manner as it does to government departments.

In addition, the Secretary of State for Wales may issue a similar certificate, concerning property leased by the Welsh Development Agency, for the purpose of providing employment appropriate to the needs of the area (s.60A(1)). If the court makes an order for the grant of a new lease, and the Secretary of State certifies that it is necessary or expedient, the court must include a covenant against alienation (s.60A(2)).

CHAPTER 4

Landlord's section 25 notice

Contents

- Introduction
- Multiple notices: *Barclays Bank Plc* v. *Bee*
- Who can serve a section 25 notice?
- Person to be served
- Formalities
- Form and content
- Defects and omissions
- General rules of service

4.1 INTRODUCTION

The operation of the Landlord and Tenant Act 1954, Part II machinery depends heavily on the service of appropriate notices on the correct parties. In the absence of agreement or legislative provision, notices must be served in a way that they can be proved to have been received by the intended recipient. Accordingly, it is convenient within this chapter to consider the general rules of service as they apply to any document to be served under the Landlord and Tenant Acts 1927 and 1954. In addition, the special rules relating to partnerships will be discussed. Nevertheless, the primary focus is upon the landlord's s.25 notice which is, arguably, the most important notice within the renewal process. This notice represents the usual method by which the renewal machinery is engaged and invokes the statutory jurisdiction of the court. The s.25 notice is highly functional in that it not only terminates the existing contractual lease, but also brings into being a s.24 continuation tenancy and furnishes the tenant with both a record of the landlord's identity and intentions and a general catalogue of statutory rights. The service of this termination notice does not however necessarily mean that the landlord seeks to regain possession. It is common for the landlord to initiate proceedings so

75

as to ensure the negotiation of, or court order for, a new lease at a market rent.

Owing to its technical nature and role, the form of the s.25 notice is heavily stylised and its contents closely prescribed by the Landlord and Tenant 1954, Part 2 (Notices) Regulations 2004, SI 2004/1005. The working rule is that, due to the mandatory tone both of the Act and the ancillary Notices Regulations, a notice which does not comply with the statutory and extra-statutory prescription will not activate the renewal process (*Weinbergs Weatherproofs* v. *Radcliffe Paper Mill Co.* [1957] 3 All ER 663). There is however nothing to prevent a landlord from subsequently serving a further notice which complies with the statutory provisions (*Whelton Sinclair* v. *Hyland* [1992] 41 EG 112). As Dillon L.J. concluded in *Smith* v. *Draper* (1990) 60 P & CR 252, 'I cannot see any reason why, if the tenant does not agree to treating an apparently invalid notice as valid, the landlord should not immediately serve an unquestionably valid notice'.

The tenant who is faced with a notice which appears invalid is in a partic-ularly acute dilemma because for the lessee there is no second chance. As Paull J. admitted in *Craddock* v. *Fieldman* (1960) 175 EG 1149, 'the tenant is always in an unfortunate position when he receives . . . a notice to quit under the Landlord and Tenant Act. If he takes no step at all then if that notice is a good one he may find himself without any power of asking for a new lease. He must therefore protect his position'. Leaving arguments as to validity for a later date therefore the lessee should always respond to each notice served by the landlord. This means where necessary making multiple court applica-tions to ensure that no application is made after the termination date stated in any potentially valid s.25 notice. This will ensure that the tenant does not sacrifice renewal rights through procedural inaction. In order to prevent waiver of the defect, these procedural steps should be taken 'without preju-dice' to any contention as to invalidity. To avoid an estoppel, the tenant must make no representation to the landlord, act without delay and, where appro-priate, add a plea to the application for a new lease that the notice is invalid and that this should be decided as a preliminary issue.

4.2 MULTIPLE NOTICES: *BARCLAYS BANK PLC* V. *BEE*

Where multiple notices are served the extent of the tenant's entitlement may turn upon the particular notice to be upheld. Such was demonstrated in *Barclays Bank Plc* v. *Bee* [2002] 1 WLR 332 where three termination notices were served on the tenant. The landlord's solicitors purported to serve an initial s.25 termination notice on the tenant. The covering letter stated that it enclosed a termination notice and suggested that there was a copy to be returned. Unfortunately, appended to this letter were two s.25 notices which were similar, but not identical, in content. Although both were in the appropriate *pro forma* version, the crucial difference was that one notice (document A) stated that the landlord would oppose any renewal application whereas the other (document B) declared that there would be no such opposition. As Aldous L.J. appreciated, 'Clearly either document A or document B should not have been sent . . . one document was meant to be sent as the notice with a copy to be returned'. Document A moreover did not specify any of the grounds of opposition as listed in s.30(1) and consequently was irredeemably flawed. The tenant acknowledged receipt, but reserved the right to challenge the validity of document A. The landlord then served a further s.25 notice (document C) which stated opposition on the basis of redevelopment (ground (f)) and owner occupation (ground (g)).

The tenant, Barclays Bank, took the view that document B constituted an effective s.25 notice which could not be withdrawn by the landlord. It followed that document C was an invalid notice. The tenant commenced renewal proceedings and the landlord opposed the application on the understanding that the notice last served was effective. In the Court of Appeal, Aldous L.J. acknowledged that the forms used in documents A, B and C were in the prescribed version provided that they were completed correctly. Document A was clearly incorrectly completed and, as it did not specify any statutory ground of opposition, was ineffective. If standing alone however either of the documents B and C could constitute a valid s.25 notice. The difficulty was that there can only be one valid termination notice for, as Aldous L.J. explained, 'a valid s.25 notice, once served, cannot be amended nor can it be withdrawn. It follows that if document B constituted a valid notice then document C could not be a valid notice'. At first blush therefore the argument that document B was the valid notice appeared likely to succeed. As Aldous L.J. continued, 'Of course that is correct if the notice that was served with the letter . . . was the only notice'. It would however be artificial to consider document B in isolation.

Aldous L.J. took the stance that, where a tenant serves two inconsistent notices, both notices will be bad because of the ensuing uncertainty as to the intention of the serving party. He reasoned:

> In this case, the landlord stated that he was sending a notice. He in fact sent two documents. On the face of them they are inconsistent. One of them stated that he would not be opposing the grant of a new tenancy, while in the other he stated that he would. No doubt one complied with the terms of the Act and would be an effective notice, and the other was not because it contained none of the grounds contained in s.30 of the Act. If the principles of contract are to be applied . . . I cannot see that there could be a valid contract if Barclays Bank had said 'I accept your notice'. The terms of such a contract would in my view be unclear.

Aldous L.J. considered his approach to be in line with that advocated by the House of Lords in *Mannai Investment Co. Ltd* v. *Eagle Star Life Assurance Co. Ltd* [1997] 2 WLR 945. He felt that the *Mannai* case offered a curative only when there is an absence of ambiguity. As Lord Steyn had put it in *Mannai*, 'does the notice construed against its contextual setting unambiguously inform a reasonable recipient how and when the notice is to operate under the right reserved?' As on the present facts, Barclays Bank knew that the landlord had future development plans for the property, and had received two documents which read together were inconsistent, the reasonable recipient would have a reasonable doubt as to whether the landlord intended to oppose renewal. As Arden L.J. commented, 'How then, I ask, could it be plain to the tenant that the landlord would not oppose when he had served on the tenant a document stating that that was his intention?' Once ambiguity is identified, Arden L.J. felt that the conclusion was inevitable 'if there is a doubt it is resolved in favour of the conclusion that the notice is ineffective'.

Although that doubt is normally to the benefit of the tenant, here it is was the landlord who sought to minimise the impact of his solicitor's carelessness. Nevertheless, Arden L.J. could not accept that the *Mannai* approach entailed that an effective notice could only be rendered ineffective by another effective notice. She believed that her approach was consistent with good commercial sense, that is, a tenant who is in receipt of a s.25 notice may have to take an urgent decision as to whether or not to take over some other premises.

The tenant argued that the court could have no regard to document A because it was, by virtue of s.25(6), fatally flawed and was to 'have no effect'. This submission was roundly rejected. Arden L.J. felt that, 'the fact that the notice, document A, is ineffective for the purposes of s.25 does not mean that it is a complete non-event. It makes a statement as much as a covering letter would do'. Wilson J. agreed that the invalidity of the notice, 'does not disentitle it from being part of the context necessary to the construction of document B'. Arden L.J. also held that document A could not be ignored because the reasonable recipient would not be aware that the landlord could not add new grounds of opposition (or amend existing ones) at a later date. As she explained, 'Neither the notice, nor the notes on it, nor s.25 itself, says that the notice cannot be amended, although that is established by the case law'. This assertion was pivotal to her decision because it entailed that the objective recipient could not be expected to know that document A was inherently invalid. Hence, it could not be ignored.

It is clear that the decision of the Court of Appeal was greatly influenced by the contextual analysis propounded by the House of Lords in *Mannai Investment Co. Ltd* v. *Eagle Star Life Assurance Co. Ltd* [1997] 2 WLR 945. There Lord Steyn admitted that, 'in respect of contracts and contractual notices the contextual scene is always relevant'. The movement away from a strict construction towards a commercial construction of documents is undoubtedly attractive in that it prevents the triumph of technicality over justice. Indeed, this type of approach is widely used when, for example, the court has to determine the meaning of words employed within a notice.

The use of a liberal construction however is much more contentious when its effect is to invalidate what would otherwise be valid. This must be particularly so when the invalidity works to the benefit of the party making the initial mistake. There is much to commend the attitude of Lord Jauncey who, in his dissenting speech in *Mannai* said, 'There will, of course, be cases where an unintended slip in the drafting of a notice will result in hardship to the giver thereof but he will only have himself to blame for not complying with the terms of the empowering provision'. The House of Lords simply could not have envisaged its contextual approach being applied in the circumstances arising in *Barclays Bank Plc* v. *Bee*. To apply it in this way therefore condones careless drafting, overlooks the clearest statutory language of s.25(6) and instils uncertainty into the renewal process. It is indeed a major irony that, if the tenant had failed to respond to document C by a timely court application, it would (despite the confusion caused by the landlord) have lost all renewal rights. As the tenant only has the one chance to respond, any major doubt as to validity of the landlord's notice should, where possible, be resolved in the tenant's favour. In these circumstances, it is hardly unreasonable to expect a landlord to ensure that his notice satisfies the statutory requirements.

4.3   WHO CAN SERVE A SECTION 25 NOTICE?

The s.25 notice may be served only by, or on behalf of, the competent landlord. The competent landlord is either the owner of the fee simple or, where underleases have been created, the landlord next above the tenant in the chain who holds a reversion of at least 14 months' duration. As regards the service of a s.25 notice, the relevant time for ascertaining the correct identity of the competent landlord is at the date the notice is served and it is from this date that the 14-month time limit is to be measured. The competent landlord and a sub-tenant's immediate landlord need not therefore be one and the same person. This distinction assumes importance because, as demonstrated in *Yamaha-Kemble Music (UK) Ltd* v. *ARC Properties Ltd* [1990] 1 EGLR 261, a notice served by the wrong landlord is invalid. The notice may however be signed by an authorised agent of the competent landlord or be signed in the landlord's name by someone with due authority *per procurationem*.

There can, of course, be joint landlords who, because they are entitled to the entirety of the land comprised in the relevant reversion, together will constitute the competent landlord (*M&P Enterprises (London) Ltd* v. *Norfolk Square Hotels Ltd* [1994] 1 EGLR 129). In that scenario, and although preferably all should join in the giving of the notice, it has been held that one of them alone may serve the statutory notice (*Leckhampton Dairies Ltd* v. *Artus Whitfield Ltd* (1986) 130 SJ 225). To be effective however such a notice must state the name(s) of the other joint landlord(s) (*Pearson* v. *Alyo* (1990) 60 P & CR 50).

Although there can only be one competent landlord at any given time, the landlord's identity can change during the course of proceedings. If the landlord ceases to be 'competent' subsequent to the service of a s.25 notice, the tenant should be informed. Otherwise, as recognised in *Shelley* v. *United Artists Corporation Ltd* [1990] 1 EGLR 103, an estoppel might arise which will defeat any assertion that the tenant's proceedings have been pursued against the wrong landlord. The landlord's successor may, of course, adopt the notice and, where relevant, the grounds of opposition stated therein. Conversely, the 1954 Act provides that the notice can be withdrawn by the new landlord, but only within two months of its service (Sched. 6, para. 6). To effect withdrawal, the new competent landlord must serve on the tenant a notice in the prescribed form.

4.3.1   Split reversions

A split or divided reversion arises where different landlords hold the reversions of separate parts of the demised property. This fragmentation can occur in a variety of ways, for example:

- a landlord may dispose of part(s) only of the reversion of the property demised to the tenant;
- a tenant who has two leases with different landlords may sub-let both properties under a single tenancy; and
- a tenant who holds two or more properties from the same landlord, under separate leases and for different terms, may sub-let both properties under a single lease. As occurred in *Dodson Bull Carpet Co. Ltd* v. *City of London Corporation* [1975] 1 WLR 781, the sub-tenant may end up with a different landlord for each property.

Traditionally, the problem with split reversions is that, although an ordinary notice to quit can be validly served in relation to part of the holding, this rule does not apply to the service of a s.25 notice. As Goff J. acknowledged in *Dodson Bull Carpet Co.* v. *City of London Corporation* [1975] 1 WLR 781, 'There is nothing . . . to authorise a landlord to serve a notice of determination under s.25 as to part only of the premises . . . and indeed quite the reverse, to allow him to do so would cut across and jeopardise the protection afforded by the Act'. The problem was also identified by Oliver L.J. in *Southport Old Links Ltd* v. *Naylor* [1985] 1 EGLR 66 who admitted, 'It may well be (and I think it is) that the Act is defective in not making provisions for this rather unusual situation'.

Accordingly, the landlord's statutory notice must relate to the whole of the property let to the tenant and a notice which relates only to part of the demised premises is simply of no effect. Accordingly, in *Herongrove Ltd* v.

Wates City of London Properties Plc [1998] 24 EG 108, where an office floor and ground floor storage space were demised to one tenant under one lease, the landlord's s.25 notice had to refer to both premises. This can pose particular difficulties for landlords where the reversion has become split. A classic illustration emerges from the *Dodson Bull* case where the head landlord could not serve a valid termination notice in relation to part of the property and was not the competent landlord as regards the remainder. Without the co-operation of both landlords therefore an impasse is reached.

It is possible that the joint reversioners together serve a single s.25 notice (this is best practice) or individually give separate notices operating at the same time. In order for separate notices to take effect however they have to be construed as relating to one single tenancy and not, say, different buildings. Such was illustrated in *M&P Enterprises (London) Ltd* v. *Norfolk Square Hotels Ltd* [1994] 1 EGLR 129 where a single tenancy of five buildings was subject to five notices served by different reversioners. The notices were invalid as they did not make clear that it was a single tenancy that was being determined. A covering letter should spell this out clearly. Nevertheless, this option is not always practicable and ceases to be available where, for example, one landlord does not wish to oppose the grant of a new tenancy or cannot establish a ground of opposition. Hence, when the leases are terminated in accordance with the contract(s), a continuation of the whole property will necessarily arise under s.24.

A limited exception to this general rule occurs where the lease is of two distinct properties and it is clear that the document can be construed as two separate leases. Only in that situation can a s.25 notice refer to one property without relating to the other. For example, in *Moss* v. *Mobil Oil Co. Ltd* [1986] 6 EG 109 two petrol stations were demised in a single document, but it was made expressly clear in the document that there were two tenancies. It is also to be appreciated that two separate tenancies can be converted into a single lease by the agreement of the parties *Latif* v. *Hillside Estates (Swansea) Ltd* [1992] EGCS 75).

The Regulatory Reform (Business Tenancies) (England and Wales) Order 2003, SI 2003/3096 has attempted to clarify the position as regards split reversions and a new s.44(1A) has been added to the 1954 Act. This provision allows, in so far as it affects the whole of the property, landlords collectively both to operate the statutory procedure and to have it operated against them by a tenant. Accordingly, this does nothing in a situation where co-operation between landlords is impractical and they have reached an impasse. As the existing law already catered for the collective service of a termination notice, and it was also thought possible that an effective s.26 request could be served collectively on all landlords of the split reversion, the implementation of this recommendation is likely to achieve little.

4.4   PERSON TO BE SERVED

The landlord's notice must be served on the tenant who is, for these purposes, the person entitled to claim a new lease. The s.25 notice can moreover terminate more than one tenancy. In *Tropis Shipping Co. Ltd* v. *Ibex Properties Corporation Ltd* [1967] EGD 433, three tenancies were terminated by the same s.25 notice. It is however crucial that the notice makes clear that it is to determine each of the tenancies on the date specified therein.

As regards a bankrupt tenant, the notice should be served on the trustee in bankruptcy. Where there are joint tenants, the general rule is that (subject to waiver) the notice must be served on all of them (*Booth Investments Ltd* v. *Reynolds* (1974) NLJ 119). As will be shown, the exception to this rule lies in s.41A and concerns partnership tenants. Subject to certain conditions, this permits the notice to be served only on those partners who are involved in running the business. In relation to trusts, the landlord may experience difficulties when there has been a change of trustees of which the lessor has no knowledge. It might be impossible to guarantee that the tenants are correctly named in the notice. To cater for this situation, it will suffice if the landlord's notice describes the tenant as 'the trustees for the time being' (*London Borough of Hackney* v. *Hackney African Organisation* [1998] EGCS 139).

4.4.1   Effect of sub-letting

As regards a tenant in occupation of the whole premises, few problems are raised. The landlord simply serves the notice on that tenant. More problematic however is where the premises have been sub-let. If the whole of the premises are sub-let and the sub-tenancy is within the scope of the Act, the s.25 notice is to be served directly on the sub-tenant. As the mesne landlord is no longer in occupation of the holding, the protection of the Act does not extend to that head lease. As happened in *Keith Bayley Rogers & Co.* v. *Cubes Ltd* (1975) 31 P & CR 412, if the landlord can prematurely end the head tenant's lease by the exercise of a break clause the landlord will then become the sub-tenant's competent landlord.

Where the premises have been sub-let in part only and the landlord wishes to grant a new lease of the whole premises, the head landlord must serve the s.25 notice on the head lessee. Any new tenancy will be subject to the sub-lease(s). If however the landlord does not wish to grant a renewal of the whole premises, different considerations apply. As made clear in *Rene Claro (Haute Coiffure) Ltd* v. *Halle Concerts Society* [1969] 1 WLR 909, a s.25 notice must be served, first, on the mesne landlord with the result that the server becomes the competent landlord of the sub-tenant(s). The new competent landlord will then serve an additional termination notice directly on each sub-tenant. The renewal process thus fragments in that each termination notice will relate to a different part of the premises. Although the notice must be served first on the mesne landlord, if the notices are served on all the parties on the same day, the presumption is that they are served in the correct order (*Keith Bayley Rogers & Co* v. *Cubes Ltd* (1976) 31 P & CR 412).

4.5 FORMALITIES

4.5.1 Timing

Section 25 requires that the statutory notice be in writing, relate to the whole premises demised and adhere to the form prescribed from time to time by statutory instrument. The notice must also specify a date on which the tenancy is to terminate and that date must fall no more than 12 months and no less than six months after the service of the notice (s.25(2)). It is not necessary that the termination date falls on a rent day (*Westerbury Property & Investment Co Ltd* v. *Carpenter* [1961] 1 All ER 481). If a fixed-term or periodic tenancy is already being continued under s.24, only these time requirements need be satisfied. Accordingly, any date can be specified provided that it falls within the statutory time span.

As regards other tenancies however the date selected cannot be one earlier than that on which the tenancy could be terminated at common law (s.25(3)(*a*)). This means that when the contractual tenancy requires a period of notice longer than six months, the maximum period of 12 months is extended so as to be equal to the duration of the contractual notice plus six months (s.25(3)(*b*)). For example, if the lease requires 10 months' notice to quit, the s.25 notice may be served up to 16 months before the date for termination specified therein.

The general rule means that with regard to a periodic tenancy, the contractual term date will be that on which a notice to quit could have brought the tenancy to an end. In *Commercial Properties* v. *Wood* [1968] 1 QB 15, it was demonstrated that the s.25 notice can terminate a periodic tenancy even though the stated termination date does not fall on the first or last day of a period.

In relation to fixed-term tenancies, the contractual term date will be that on which its original term expires. A statutory notice which specifies the last day of the contractual lease is therefore valid (*Re Crowhurst Park* [1974] 1 WLR 583) whereas one which specifies the day before is not (*Central Estates (Belgravia)* v. *Webster* (1969) 209 EG 1319). Where relevant, and if there is doubt as to the last day of the original lease, several additional days should be added on to the calculation. If the landlord exercises a break clause then, although the contractual term will end, a continuation tenancy will arise under s.24. The landlord is expressly allowed to serve a statutory termination notice timed to follow the break (s.25(3)). If the break clause is irregularly exercised, the s.25 notice which is timed to follow it will be invalid (*Craddock* v. *Fieldman* (1960) 175 EG 1149).

If it is the tenant who exercises the break, the contractual term ends and with it any statutory protection. Accordingly, the tenant cannot then serve a request for a new lease and there is no need for the landlord to serve a termination notice (*Garston* v. *Scottish Widow's Fund & Life Assurance Society* [1998] 3 All ER 596).

Influential factors

The timing of service of a s.25 notice and the selection of the termination date may be driven by a variety of factors:

- the service will put the landlord in the driving seat and, by taking the initiative, allow the landlord to dictate the termination date;
- s.37(2) offers double rate compensation for disturbance payable to a tenant who has been in occupation for 14 years immediately prior to the termination date specified. The landlord may, sensibly, elect for a termination date preceding the lapse of that 14-year period;
- by virtue of s.30(1)(g), renewal can be opposed on the basis of the landlord's desire to occupy, but only if the landlord did not acquire title within the five years preceding the date of termination specified. This may tempt a landlord to postpone the termination date until the five-year requirement is satisfied; and
- as the lessor must be in a position to specify grounds of opposition in the s.25 notice, and must be able to put the opposition into a provable form by the date of the hearing, the landlord may wish to maximise time allowed within which to finalise plans.

4.6 FORM AND CONTENT

Although it is advisable for a *pro forma* document to be used, the Landlord and Tenant Act 1954, Part 2 (Notices) Regulations 2004, SI 2004/1005 permit a limited variation in form by allowing a form 'substantially to the like effect' to be effective for these purposes. This clearly indicates that some departure from the extra-statutory prescription is permissible. While the majority of detail emanates from the delegated legislation, the enabling 1954 Act does itself set out certain matters which must be addressed in the notice. The latter are deemed to be of sufficient importance to merit express mention within the statute and to attract the ultimate sanction imposed by s.25(2), (6)–(8) that, on their omission, the notice 'shall have no effect'. It is to be noted that, in contradistinction to these primary requirements, there is no express sanction attached to non-compliance with the secondary legislation. It is also to be appreciated that the landlord need no longer inquire whether or not the tenant is prepared to give up possession willingly (i.e. s.25(5) has been repealed) and the tenant's counter notice has been abolished.

4.6.1   Stating opposition

Section 25(6) requires the notice to state whether the landlord is opposed to the grant of a new lease. If so, the notice must stipulate the ground(s) of opposition upon which the lessor will rely (s.25(7)). The landlord should think carefully before stipulating any ground as the notice cannot later be amended or withdrawn (*Nursey* v. *P Currie (Dartford) Ltd* [1959] 1 All ER 497). Furthermore, as it may be necessary at a later stage to substantiate the ground stated, a cavalier citation of all or most of the statutory grounds will reduce dramatically the credibility of that landlord's opposition. It is not necessary however that the landlord set out the ground(s) of opposition in full. Instead, it is sufficient that the ground(s) be identified by reference to the appropriate paragraph of s.30(1) or by other expression which indicates the particular ground(s). For example, in *Philipson-Stow* v. *Trevor Square Ltd* (1980) 257 EG 1262 the notice was valid although the landlord had stated the intention to carry out substantial works of 'redecoration' rather than demolition or reconstruction. The overriding issue is that the tenant be given adequate warning of what contention will have to be refuted at the subsequent hearing. Accordingly, in *Sevenarts Ltd* v. *Busvine* [1969] 1 All ER 392 a notice which stated that the landlord sought to occupy, when in reality it was the tenant's company that was to occupy, was upheld. The misstatement was immaterial.

If opposition is stated, but no statutory ground provided, the landlord's notice is invalid. Hence in *Barclays Bank* v. *Ascott* [1961] 1 WLR 717, the consent of the landlord to a new tenancy was made conditional on the finding of a suitable guarantor and this invalidated the notice. The notice did not state on what ground a new tenancy would be opposed if no guarantor was found. On that understanding, the tenant cannot then apply to the court for a new lease.

4.6.2   Stating proposed terms of new lease

Prior to the 2003 Order, and unlike the tenant's s.26 request for a new lease, it had not been necessary for a landlord who did not oppose renewal to set out the proposed terms of the grant. By indicating the terms the landlord will accept, obstacles to agreement will be identified at an early stage. This obligation is now contained in s.25(8) and this provides that such a notice shall not have effect unless it sets out the landlord's proposals as to:

- the property to be comprised in the new lease;
- the rent to be payable under the new lease; and
- the other terms of the new lease.

A 'health warning' is provided in the s.25 notice to the tenant making it clear that there is no obligation to accept the proposed terms and that they are merely suggestions as a basis for negotiation. The warning also invites the tenant to put forward alternative terms.

4.6.3   The 2004 Notices Regulations

The Landlord and Tenant Act 1954, Part 2 (Notices) Regulations 2004 prescribe different forms of s.25 notice to cater for different types of case. For example, Forms 1 and 2 are the standard types of s.25 notice to be employed when the landlord does not oppose renewal and when there is opposition to renewal, respectively. In barest outline, the other, specialist forms are:

- Form 7 where the landlord is opposed to renewal, but the tenant might be entitled to buy the freehold or an extended lease under the Leasehold Reform Act 1967;
- Forms 8, 9, 10, 13 and 14 where a s.57 notice has been served for the change of use or occupation of the property in the public interest;
- Forms 11, 12 and 15 where a s.58 certificate has been issued that the use and occupation should be discontinued or changed in the interests of national security or by reason of the Local Employment Act 1972;
- Forms 16 and 17 where the tenancy is to be ended by the Welsh Development Agency and a s.58 certificate has been issued.

In all cases, the 2004 Regulations prescribe that the s.25 notice is to contain a prominent warning to the tenant that the notice is intended to bring the tenancy to an end and the recommendation that the recipient act quickly and carefully. If in doubt, the tenant is advised to consult a solicitor or surveyor. Appended to the prescribed form are a series of general notes of guidance which explain the basic workings of the 1954 Act and the steps that the tenant should take. In Form 1 the information focuses on negotiation. In Form 2 the emphasis is understandably different and concentrates on the statutory grounds of opposition and compensation for loss of renewal rights. All forms of s.25 notice refer the tenant to the explanatory booklet published by the Office of the Deputy Prime Minister (as was) and entitled *Renewing and Ending Business Leases: A Guide for Tenants and Landlords* (a web page reference is also included at **www.communities.gov.uk**).

4.7   DEFECTS AND OMISSIONS

Although careful drafting of the s.25 notice (and indeed a s.26 request by a tenant) is imperative, it is apparent from case law that the requirements of the Act and the Regulations are not always complied with. Nevertheless, and despite the general rule that if there is a defect or omission the notice will be invalidated, the tenant would be ill-advised to ignore a notice simply in the belief that it is ineffective. This is because the courts have usually adopted a sensible approach to the application of both s.25 and s.26 and have upheld seemingly defective notices on the basis of a liberal construction of either the specific words used or the notice as a whole.

4.7.1   Waiver and estoppel

It is well established that an otherwise invalid notice can be cured by waiver. Following the analysis of Lord Diplock in *Kammins Ballroom Co. Ltd* v. *Zenith Investments (Torquay) Ltd (No.1)* [1971] AC 850, there are two types of waiver:

> the first type of waiver . . . arises in a situation where a person is entitled to alternative rights inconsistent with one another. If he has knowledge of the facts which give rise in law to these alternative rights and acts in a manner which is consistent only with his having chosen to rely on one of them, the law holds him to his choice even though he was unaware that this would be the legal consequence of what he did . . . The second type of waiver which debars a person from raising a particular defence to a claim against him arises when he either agrees with the claimant not to raise that particular defence or conducts himself as to be estopped from raising it.

The consequences of waiver by election (that is, choosing not to rely on the irregularity) are that the tenant loses the right thereafter to object to the validity of the notice and the landlord is prevented also from relying on the defect. For example, in *Bristol Cars Ltd* v. *RKH (Hotels) Ltd* (1979) 38 P & CR 411 the landlord did not realise that the tenant's request was invalid and entered into negotiations for a renewal. Both parties were estopped from denying the validity of the request.

Unlike the second type of waiver, an election is binding even though the other party has suffered no detriment. It is however crucial that the waiving party is aware of the facts which give rise to the right to challenge. In *Tennant* v. *LCC* (1957) 55 LGR 421, the notice was self-evidently not signed by the competent landlord or the landlord's agent (it was clearly marked '*per pro*') and yet the tenant proceeded with a renewal application. In those circumstances, it was held that any defect would be waived. In *Stevens & Cutting Ltd* v. *Anderson* [1990] 11 EG 70, the tenant made a premature application for a new lease, but the landlord failed to raise this in the answer to the tenant's proceedings. Despite lengthy and failed negotiations for a new lease, this first type of waiver had not occurred because the landlord had not been aware of the defect until after the negotiations had broken down. Similarly, in *Morrow* v. *Nadeem* [1987] 1 All ER 237 the incorrect name of the landlord was inserted in the s.25 notice and, consequently, proceedings were commenced against the wrong landlord. The tenant later questioned the validity of the notice and it was held that the defect had not been waived as the tenant had not been aware of the true identity of the competent landlord until after the procedural steps had been taken.

By way of contrast, the tenant in *Keepers & Governors of the Possessions, Revenues and Goods of the Free Grammar School of John Lyon* v. *Mayhew* [1997] 1 EGLR 88 was aware that the landlord had used the wrong form of statutory notice, but proceeded as if the notice was valid and effective. The attempt to challenge validity some two months after the service of the notice failed because a reasonable landlord would have believed that the defect had been waived. Furthermore, this case demonstrates that, where the notice has served the statutory purpose of starting proceedings, and no point of validity has been taken, the notice will not later be the subject of critical examination.

A proprietary estoppel may arise where there has been a representation of fact by one party and the detrimental reliance or change of position by the other. Evidence of each ingredient should normally be presented before the court. There must be a clear and unequivocal assurance (whether by words or spelled out from conduct) which is intended to be relied upon. The statement or conduct must therefore act as an invitation for the other party to take a particular action. As regards a s.25 notice therefore no estoppel can arise in the absence of a representation by the tenant that the defect is not going to be taken up (*Spence* v. *Shell UK Ltd* [1980] 2 EGLR 68). An expression of opinion moreover does not constitute an assurance for these purposes. Although detrimental reliance cannot be presumed, it can be inferred from the circumstances. Usually, it will be expressly proven, for example by showing that the tenant has carried out improvements on the demised premises or incurred other forms of financial expenditure. By way of illustration, in *Keepers & Governors of the Possessions, Revenues and Goods of the Free Grammar School of John Lyon* v. *Mayhew* [1997] 1 EGLR 88 the detriment concerned the incurring of lawyers' and surveyors' fees and the omission to serve a second and valid termination notice. The overriding issue is whether or not it is unconscionable for the representor to resile from the assurance made. If it is, the court can fulfil, either in whole or in part, the representation relied upon. Accordingly, a tenant who accepts a landlord's s.25 notice (which would otherwise be invalid by reason of a defect or omission) as being valid, and persuades the landlord either to take or not to take certain steps under Part II of the 1954 Act, can be estopped from relying upon the defect. In appropriate circumstances, the landlord may also be estopped from relying upon the invalidity of its s.25 notice.

In *Wroe (t/a Telepower)* v. *Exmos Cover Ltd* [2000] 1 EGLR 66, a licensee attempted to estop its landlord from denying it had a tenancy. In the belief that this was the quickest means to regaining possession, the landlord wrote accepting that a s.24 continuation tenancy was in existence and served a s.25 termination notice on Mr Wroe (the licensee). The notice indicated that any renewal application would be opposed on the basis of the owner occupation ground contained in s.30(1)(*g*). As Chadwick L.J. advised, 'A more sensible course, perhaps, would have been to give the s.25 notice without prejudice to the contention that the agreement created a licence and not a tenancy, and to commence proceedings at once to have that issue resolved'. Mr Wroe then made a timely application for a new lease. Thereafter, the matter proceeded on the basis that the office was subject to a tenancy within the provisions of the 1954 Act. Mr Wroe attempted to invoke an estoppel which would prevent the landlord from denying that there was a tenancy. The present facts did not support a tenancy by estoppel because they did not concern a landlord denying that an agreement, which properly construed created a tenancy, was effective to create a tenancy.

The central issue therefore was whether the appellant had relied upon the representation in a manner which caused detriment and made it unfair or inequitable for the respondent to contend that a tenancy had not been created. The tenant's conduct did not justify such protection. Admittedly, the tenant remained in occupation, but this was not in reliance upon the landlord's representation. He would have remained in occupation in any event. Similarly, the subsequent application for a new tenancy could not be viewed as being detrimental to the tenant, 'The appellant applied for a new tenancy because he wanted a new tenancy'. These were necessary steps taken to preserve the appellant's alleged right to a new tenancy. In addition, Chadwick L.J. felt that the landlord's termination notice (while giving the appellant the opportunity to make a renewal application) did not encourage the appellant's application nor did the specification that renewal would be opposed on ground s.30(1)(*g*) (and not on the ground that there was no tenancy) affect the appellant's behaviour. It was apparent that the appellant would not have withdrawn his application had the licence or lease issue been raised in the landlord's answer.

4.7.2 Tenant's response

The appropriate action for a tenant to take, when faced with a potentially defective s.25 notice, is always to apply for a new tenancy. If the landlord purports to withdraw a potentially invalid notice and serves a replacement, the tenant may have to make a new application to the court. The tenant may however expressly reserve the right to challenge the initial notice. This can be achieved by taking the procedural steps 'without prejudice' to any contention as to invalidity (*Rhyl UDC* v. *Rhyl Amusements Ltd* [1959] 1 All ER 257).

This should prevent the tenant being held to have waived the defect. This tactic is not however always sufficient to prevent an estoppel. For example, in *BRB* v. *AJA Smith Transport Ltd* [1981] 2 EGLR 69 the tenant was estopped from denying the validity of the termination notice despite having expressly reserved the right to challenge it. The tenant had simply left it too late in the proceedings to keep both options open. If the first notice is to be challenged, it is also necessary that the tenant makes no representation to the landlord, acts without delay and, where appropriate, adds a plea to the application for a new lease that the notice is invalid and asks for a declaration as a preliminary issue.

4.7.3 Different words, same meanings

Following *Bolton's (House Furnishers) Ltd* v. *Oppenheim* [1959] 3 All ER 90, it is clear that the court will condone, wherever possible, minor deviations in the form and content of a s.25 notice. It remains possible moreover that any shortcomings might be cured by a covering letter containing the omitted information. For example, in *Germax Securities Ltd* v. *Spiegal* (1979) 37 P & CR 204 the wrong date of termination was stated in the notice, but corrected by an appended letter. The notice was held to be valid. The test of validity as expressed by Hodson L.J. in the *Oppenheim* case is simply whether the notice provides the tenant with sufficient information to deal with the landlord's claim. Unless Parliament states that precise and exact language be used, the obligation is merely to indicate the information with sufficient clarity so as to be understood by the tenant. As Hodson L.J. was concerned with the chosen form of expression employed and the ability to ascribe meanings to specific words contained in a document, he did not consider the scenario where the relevant information is entirely omitted. Nevertheless, the inapplicability of the *Oppenheim* test to omissions is sometimes overlooked by the courts and, in consequence, the case is liable to be misused as authority for a more universal proposition.

4.7.4 Construction of the notice

The court is guided by the normal use of grammar and construction and is not entitled to give words a meaning which they do not bear under those rules. Nevertheless, as made clear by Barry J. in *Barclays Bank* v. *Ascott* [1961] 1 WLR 717 the construction can be liberal, 'provided the notice gives the real substance of the information required, then the mere omission of certain details or the failure to embody in the notice the full provisions of the section of the Act referred to will not in fact invalidate the notice'. There the landlord failed to make its opposition clear and to provide any grounds of opposition in the s.25 notice. The notice was therefore manifestly bad as no attempt was made to identify any ground and there was nothing in the wording of the notice which could be construed as imparting the necessary information. If the notice had, on its true construction, stated what was required to be stated then it would have been saved. Nevertheless, as the omitted information was deemed fundamental to the tenant, and because the notice did not satisfy s.25(6), the defect proved fatal.

Barry J.'s approach was subsequently adopted by the Court of Appeal in *Sunrose Ltd* v. *Gould* [1961] 3 All ER 1142 where a notice was upheld even though it failed expressly to specify the year of termination. As the date was readily ascertainable from a formula provided on the back of the notice, there was sufficient specification. Significantly, there was no positive inaccuracy or error on the face of the notice. If there had been, Davies L.J. suspected that the notice would have been incapable of cure. The *Sunrose* case therefore demonstrates that something can be rendered certain by reference to all parts of the document itself and that a notice can be upheld if it does communicate the required information, albeit in a different way than prescribed. In this context moreover it is irrelevant whether the particular requirement is imposed by the 1954 Act or by the secondary legislation. As regards the latter however the 2004 Regulations expressly encourage a liberality of construction and, as previously mentioned, allow a form 'substantially to the like effect' to that prescribed to suffice. In gauging this degree of similarity, Stephenson L.J. in *Sun Alliance & London Assurance Co. Ltd* v. *Hayman* [1975] 1 WLR 177 perceived the role of the judge as being, 'to construct the few relevant words in the regulations and in the . . . notice, and to decide whether in their ordinary significance the . . . words which were in fact used do mean substantially the same as the . . . words which should have been used. If they do not, then the notice . . . is bad . . .'. This case dealt with the use of an out-of-date prescribed form. The methodology of Stephenson L.J. adds little to the general approach to construction. It reiterates that different words from those prescribed will be allowed, provided they communicate substantially the same meanings. This does not however cover the situations where the details are not provided anywhere within the notice or where the information is misstated.

4.7.5 Omissions and mistakes

As regards either an omission to include prescribed information or a positive mistake on the face of the notice, the emphasis upon construction is different. It is no longer a matter of divining a meaning from specific words, but rather it involves the evaluation of the notice as a whole. In this context, there is a distinction between the requirements as imposed by the 1954 Act and those imposed by the 2004 Regulations. As regards the statutory requirements, s.25 unequivocally states that if such information is not provided accurately the notice is invalid. In relation to the Regulations, the phrase 'substantially to the like effect' offers some flexibility, but this of course cannot dilute the statutory provisions. Any purported modification of the statutory provisions by secondary legislation would simply be *ultra vires*. The liberality as promoted in *Barclays Bank* v. *Ascott* [1961] 1 WLR 717 invites the court to determine whether the real substance of the information is communicated to the tenant. The key issues are whether the notice provides the tenant with enough information to proceed and to apply for a renewal and whether it clearly declares the landlord's intentions. In *Tegerdine* v. *Brooks* (1977) 36 P & CR 261, the notice omitted certain marginal notes (as prescribed by the then operative Notices Regulations), but remained valid on the basis that the omitted information was either irrelevant or obvious to the tenant. As the tenant's knowledge would not have been enhanced, the notes were not part of the substance of the notice. As Aldous L.J. explained in *Sabella Ltd* v. *Montgomery* (1999) 77 P & CR 431:

> the decision as to whether the two are substantially to like effect will depend upon the importance of the differences rather than their number or amount ... It follows that a difference can only be disregarded when the information given as to the particular recipient's rights and obligations under the Act is in substance as effective as that set out in the form. Matter that is irrelevant to the recipient's rights and obligations may be omitted as in such a case the notice has given the recipient information substantially to like effect as that in the form.

Not surprisingly, there have been a number of occasions where the courts have felt able to overlook minor deviations in form and content. In *Falcon Pipes Ltd* v. *Stanhope Gate Property (No.1)* (1967) 204 EG 1243, the failure to insert the date that the notice was signed did not prove fatal. Similarly, in *Bond* v. *Graham* (1975) 236 EG 536 a misstatement as to the rateable value of the premises was condoned. Finally, in *Morris* v. *Patel* (1987) 281 EG 419 the use of an outdated prescribed form, which did not contain the same degree of detail as the updated version of the notice, was upheld.

4.7.6 The role of prejudice

Although *Sun Alliance & London Assurance Co. Ltd* v. *Hayman* [1975] 1 WLR 177 concluded that, if the notice is bad, it cannot be saved simply because the particular tenant is not misled, prejudice (or the lack of it) does assume some relevance. Prejudice is important, for example, when assessing the actual degree of similarity between the notice served and that which technically should have been served. As Neill L.J. put it in *Gudka* v. *Patel* (1995) 69 P & CR D20, 'The question is: is the tenant being misled in any way or prejudiced by the omission of the particular words . . .'.

From this perspective 'prejudice' closely links in with the notion of 'materiality' as expressed in *Tegerdine* v. *Brooks* (1978) 36 P & CR 261. In deciding whether the substance of the information is communicated by the notice however the court must ignore the subjective knowledge of the tenant. As

Nourse L.J. emphasised in *Pearson* v. *Alyo* (1990) 60 P & CR 56, 'the validity of a s.25 notice is to be judged, and judged objectively, at the date at which it is given. The question is not whether the inaccuracy actually prejudices the particular person to whom the notice is given, but whether it is capable of prejudicing a reasonable tenant in the position of that person'. Accordingly, if the information is omitted or misstated, the court must decide whether that information is relevant and must be imparted to that tenant. As Nicholls L.J. concluded in *Morrow* v. *Nadeem* [1987] 1 All ER 237, 'a form made out in such a way as not to give the real substance of the information required is not a form substantially to the like effect as the statutory form of notice'. The fact that the consequences may be negligible to the particular tenant is irrelevant. The authorities are consistent in that a material defect is one which prejudices or misleads the hypothetical tenant and that, subject to waiver or estoppel, a notice which embodies such a defect is bad and cannot be validated.

In the *Morrow* case, for example, the notice failed to identify the landlord accurately and, as this would have misled a reasonable tenant, the misstatement could not be overlooked. In contrast, in *M&P Enterprises (London) Ltd* v. *Norfolk Square Hotels Ltd* [1994] 1 EGLR 129 a minor misdescription of the landlord's name did not nullify the effect of a notice. There the landlord was identified as 'Norfolk Square No.2 Ltd' whereas the correct name was 'Norfolk Square Hotels No.2 Ltd'. In *TS Investments Ltd* v. *Langdon* (CA, 13 February 1987) the Court of Appeal held a notice to be invalid because it omitted both a vital warning to the tenant about acting expeditiously and the landlord's name and address as well as not fully describing the premises. An omission of part of the demised premises from the scope of the notice will normally be fatal, but this rule gives way if it is clear to the reasonable tenant that the landlord is intending to terminate the whole of the tenancy. Similarly, in *Pearson* v. *Alyo* (1990) 60 P & CR 56 a notice which provided the name of only one of two joint landlords was void and of no effect. By way of contrast, in *Bridgers & Hamptons Residential* v. *Stanford* (1991) 63 P & CR 18 it was the tenant's name which was misstated (i.e. the notice was addressed not to the tenant, but to a company carrying on the tenant's business). As this would not mislead the hypothetical tenant it did not taint the validity of the notice.

4.7.7 *Sabella* v. *Montgomery*

In *Sabella* v. *Montgomery* (1999) 77 P & CR 431, the tenant was faced with a s.25 notice riddled with omissions from the prescribed form. The notice did not contain an 'act quick' warning, failed to reproduce a number of the marginal notes and omitted to describe all the grounds of opposition upon which the landlord initially sought to rely. It was held that the omission of the 'act quick' notice was fatal because of the vital nature of this warning to the tenant. As Otton L.J. commented, 'He may or may not have or have had legal advice in the past from a solicitor. It is conceivable that he might well not have access to legal advice. In any event, he will be bewildered or overawed by receiving such a notice. If he does not take appropriate and timeous action he may lose his right either to a new tenancy or to compensation'.

As to the omission to provide details of all the grounds of opposition upon which the landlord sought originally to rely, this absence of information was also regarded as being of substance. The fact that the landlord no longer wished to rely upon the omitted ground offered no excuse. As the tenant had not been informed of this change of position, the omitted information remained material to the notice. Although the appellate court did not consider the issue, the logical consequence of this approach is that the failure to refer to compensation for disturbance must also be of invalidating effect. As the tenant was unaware that the landlord no longer sought to rely upon ground (f), equally the tenant could not know that compensation would cease to be available. In relation to the absence of the other notes, the Court of Appeal was unhelpful. It is likely however that the failure to allude to the explanatory booklet should be overlooked where the notice contains an 'act quick' warning and the direction to seek immediate legal advice. The validity of the notice should be adjudged on the direct and internal guidance which it contains and not turn upon the presence or otherwise of a bibliographical reference to an external source. The omissions relating to the negotiation of a new tenancy and the challenging of the validity of the notice served must however be fatal. These notes, respectively, speak of the tenant seeking to negotiate (and not of the landlord's willingness) and alert the tenant to the possibility that the immediate landlord may not be the competent landlord for renewal purposes. Both notes therefore convey potentially important information to the tenant.

4.8 GENERAL RULES OF SERVICE

Section 66(4) of the 1954 Act provides that the rules of service contained in s.23 of the Landlord and Tenant Act 1927 apply to the service of all notices under the 1954 Act. Accordingly, the more extensive service provisions contained in s.196 of the Law of Property Act 1925 do not apply here.

Section 23(1) of the 1927 Act requires that any notice, request, demand or other instrument must be in writing and stipulates that service may occur in one of a number of ways. The purpose of this specification is to ensure that the notice is duly served and to provide actual or deemed proof of service. As Robert Walker L.J. acknowledged in *Blunden* v. *Frogmore Investments Ltd* [2002] 2 EGLR 29, the statutory provisions fulfil two objectives. The first is to allocate risk between the parties where, by some mischance, the notice is not physically received by the addressee. This allocation of risk, of course, favours the serving party. The second objective is to provide a forensic tool which will assist the court in cases of dispute, and 'avoid disputes on issues of fact (especially as to whether a letter went astray in the post or was accidentally lost, destroyed or overlooked after delivery to the premises of the intended recipient) where the true facts are likely to be unknown to the person giving the notice, and difficult for the court to ascertain'.

Although not exhaustive or mandatory, the prescribed modes of service exist therefore to assist the serving party and to simplify matters for the court. Notwithstanding that the specified methods of service are not followed, actual receipt of the notice will always constitute good service. Unspecified methods would include, for example, ordinary post, document exchange and fax. As to the scope for service by fax, e-mail and document exchange, see the supplemental Practice Direction 6 of the Civil Procedure Rules 1998. As regards electronic service, the prior agreement of the other party is necessary and a hard copy should be forwarded at a later date. In *Hastie & Jenkerson* v. *McMahon* [1991] 1 All ER 255 the Court of Appeal accepted that a fax transmission could constitute good service provided that the document received was intact and legible. Service occurs when the transmission is complete. In *Chiswell* v. *Griffon Land & Estates Ltd* [1975] 1 WLR 1181, a counter notice put in the normal post was not received by the landlord's solicitors and it was held that, on a balance of probabilities, it had gone astray. Megaw L.J. drew the following distinction between the authorised methods of service and those not specified in s.23:

> If any of those methods are adopted, they being the primary methods laid down, and in the event of dispute, it is proved that one of those methods has been adopted, then sufficient service is proved. Thus if it is proved, in the event of dispute, that a notice was sent by recorded delivery, it does not matter that that recorded delivery letter may not have been received by the intended recipient. It does not matter, even if it were to be clearly established that it had gone astray in the post . . . But . . . if the person who gives the notice sees fit not to use one of those primary methods, but to send the notice through the post, not registered and not by recorded delivery, that will nevertheless be good notice, if in fact the letter is received by the person to whom the notice has been given. But a person who chooses to use that method instead of one of the primary methods is taking the risk that, if the letter is indeed lost in the post, notice will not have been given.

4.8.1 Can a notice be withdrawn pre-service?

In *Kinch* v. *Bullard* [1998] 4 All ER 650, a notice to sever a joint tenancy, which was delivered by first class post to the joint home of the sender and the recipient, was destroyed by the sender before it was seen by the addressee. The issue before the High Court was whether valid service had occurred and whether this was affected by the sender's change of mind. Neuberger J. stated the general rule as being, 'Once the sender has served the requisite notice, the deed is done and cannot be undone . . . Once the procedure has been set in

95

train, and the relevant notice has been served, it is not open to the giver of the notice to withdraw the notice . . .'. He continued that if it were otherwise:

> The addressee would not be able to rely confidently upon a notice after it had been received, because he might subsequently be faced with the argument that the sender had changed his mind after sending it and before its receipt . . . it is scarcely realistic to think that the legislature intended that the court could be required to enquire into the state of mind of the sender of the notice in order to decide whether the notice was valid.

By way of *obiter* however Neuberger J. outlined two possible qualifications to this general rule. First, that the position would be different if, before the notice was given, the sender had informed the addressee that the notice was withdrawn. His view was that, while it is still in the post and until it is given, the notice can be withdrawn provided that withdrawal is communicated to the addressee before it is served. Secondly, that the sender could not destroy the notice before it is seen by the addressee and later argue that valid service had occurred. The statutory presumption of service could not be relied on by the sender of a notice as an engine of fraud. He explained:

> The very purpose of serving a notice is to convey information, with legal consequences, on the addressee: it cannot be right that the sender of a notice can take positive steps to ensure that the notice does not come to the attention of the addressee, after it has been statutorily deemed to have been served, and then fall back on the Statute to allege that service has nonetheless been effected.

4.8.2 Primary methods of service

Actual delivery

The physical delivery of the notice to the recipient is clearly the most effective and certain means of service. In the case of a local or public authority or statutory or public utility, service can be made on its secretary or other proper officer. Section 23(1) also authorises service on the landlord's duly authorised agent. In *Railtrack Plc* v. *Gojra* [1998] 8 EG 158, for example, where a s.26 request was not addressed to the new landlord, but instead to the former landlord, the latter was on the facts held to be acting as the agent of the successor. There is however no statutory provision for service on the tenant's agent. Nevertheless, the normal rules of agency apply and, hence, the tenant's solicitor or other agent with actual or ostensible authority will be able to accept service.

Service at last known place of abode

Leaving the notice at the party's last known place of abode in England and Wales will suffice for effective service. The term 'leaving' is interpreted as meaning that the document must be deposited in such a place as is reasonable for it to be drawn to the attention of the intended recipient. The notice, as Russell L.J. commented in *Lord Newborough* v. *Jones* [1975] Ch 90, 'must be left there in the proper way, that is to say, in a manner which a reasonable person, minded to bring the document to the attention of the person to whom the notice is addressed, would adopt'. There the notice was slid under the recipient's door, but unfortunately became hidden under the floor covering. It was held to be valid service. Hence, if the premises are shared by a number of firms, and there is only one central letter box, posting through that communal box will suffice (*Henry Smith's Charity Trustees* v. *Kyriakou* [1989] 2 EGLR 110).

The expression 'last known' caters for the situation where one party has moved address and this fact and/or the new address is not known to the other party. It does not mean the address last notified as being the appropriate address for service. In *Kinch* v. *Bullard* [1998] 4 All ER 650, a notice was 'left' at the husband's last place of abode as soon as it was delivered by post regardless that the husband never actually received it. Neuberger J. put forward a simple and clear rule:

> Service of a notice at the last known place of abode . . . of the addressee is good service, and there is no suggestion that it matters how that service is effected, that is, whether it is by the giver of the notice, his agent, courier service, ordinary post, recorded delivery, or registered post or some other method. Provided that it can be established that, irrespective of the identity of the person who delivered the notice to a particular address, it was delivered to that address, then the notice has been validly served at that address, provided that it is the addressee's last known abode or place of business.

Not surprisingly, for the purposes of the business tenancy legislation, the term 'abode' includes place of business as well as home address (*Robertson* v. *Banham & Co* [1997] 1 All ER 79). Accordingly, in *National Westminster Bank* v. *Betchworth Investments* (1975) 234 EG 675 the registered office of a company was regarded as being its place of abode. As regards a local authority, service may occur at an office designated for receiving such notices. In relation to the other bodies, service may be at their principal office.

Registered or recorded mail

Although the use of the ordinary post is not authorised by the 1954 Act, both registered and recorded post are permitted. As a result, the presumption as to service contained in s.7 of the Interpretation Act 1978 has traditionally been thought to have some resonance. This provision sets out the rebuttable presumption that a letter has been delivered in the ordinary course of the post. This presumption is particularly relevant where the notice has to be served within strict time limits because, for example, it leaves it open for the recipient to show that a notice was served too late. The difficulty which has faced the courts on several occasions in recent years is whether s.7 of the 1978 Act tempers the deeming effect of s.23 of the 1927 Act.

Normally, as regards registered and recorded mail there will be documentary proof of service and this will also be determinative of exactly when service has taken place. The existence of the s.7 presumption has enabled the recipient to challenge the timing of service. This could occur, for example, where the delivery is signed for by someone other than the addressee or an agent. The onus of rebutting the presumption however appears to be a heavy burden to shoulder. This was illustrated in *Lex Services Plc* v. *Johns* [1990] 10 EG 67 where a recorded delivery letter was illegibly signed for by someone (identity unknown) and asserted not to have been received by the tenant. Although Mr Johns claimed to be the only person authorised to sign for letters and suggested that the letter had been signed for by someone from another business in the premises, he failed to rebut the statutory presumption that there was a valid service. There was simply no positive evidence that the document had not been received by the recipient. The Court of Appeal added that, even if there was evidence that the document had been received by some other person, it was still necessary to establish that it had not been brought to the addressee's attention. Accordingly, the *Lex Services* case accepted the application of s.7 to the service of renewal documents by recorded delivery. Two subsequent cases have however rejected this conclusion.

In *Egg Stores (Stamford Hill) Ltd* v. *Beanby Estates Ltd* [2004] 3 All ER 184, the landlord sent a s.25 termination notice to the tenant by recorded delivery which was posted on 7 January and physically received by the tenant on 9 January. The date of service was crucial as it determined whether the tenant had made a timely application to court. Neuberger J. noted the effect of s.23 of the 1927 Act and considered any possible interaction with s.7 of the Interpretation Act 1978. As mentioned, the latter states that service by post is deemed, in the absence of contrary intention, to be effected by properly addressing, prepaying and posting a letter and 'unless the contrary is proved, to have been effected at the time at which the letter would be delivered in the ordinary course of post'. The landlord submitted that the effect of s.23 was that, if posted by recorded delivery, the notice is irrevocably deemed to have been received on the date of posting. The tenant argued that there is an implied term under s.23 that the notice is irrevocably deemed to have been served when it would have been received in the ordinary course of post (i.e. the next day, 8 January). In the alternative, the tenant suggested that s.23 had to be read subject to s.7. This would deem the notice to have been served on 8 January unless the contrary was proved. On the present facts the contrary was easily proved so the tenant argued that the notice should be taken as having been served on the date of actual receipt, 9 January. Neuberger J. accepted that, 'if the effect of s.23 is that where a notice is sent through the post by recorded delivery to the addressee at his place of abode it is irrevocably deemed to have been served, then it follows that service is deemed to have been made on the date the notice was put in the post for recorded delivery, and not the date of actual receipt'.

Neuberger J. believed that there were five, possibly overlapping, factors to be taken on board. First, s.23 describes three alternative methods of service: personal service; service at premises; and service through the post by recorded delivery. He explained, 'The first two options clearly envisage service occurring at the moment that is described as effected, i.e. the moment of personal service in one case, and the moment the notice is left at the premises in the other case. Accordingly, logic strongly suggests that, if the act of posting of the notice by recorded delivery effects service, then the moment at which the notice is put in the post is the moment at which service is effected'.

Secondly, if the vital action is posting the notice, actual receipt of the notice is irrelevant, 'It would seem to me to follow that it is the act of posting, rather than the act of receipt, that is vital for the purpose of determining the moment of service'.

Thirdly, if an addressee could say that a notice was received late, this would place the addressee in a better position than one who never received the notice at all, 'the addressee who received a notice very late could rely on the date of late receipt as the date of service, but the addressee who never received the notice could not rely on the fact that he never received the notice, and would be bound to accept that service was effected on posting (or in the ordinary course of post, if the tenant's case is correct)'.

Fourthly, if an addressee was able to contend that a notice sent by recorded delivery, but received much later, was served at the date of actual receipt, 'that would take away much, perhaps most, of the intended effect of s.23 . . . namely, that s.23 deems service to be effective by post'.

Finally, this interpretation was supported by a direct, albeit *obiter*, observation of Wilson J. in *Railtrack Plc* v. *Gojra* [1998] 1 EGLR 63, 'the notice is served – and given – on the date when it is sent by registered post or recorded delivery'.

Neuberger J. cited the Court of Appeal decision in *Lex Services Plc* v. *Johns* [1990] 1 EGLR 92 as authority for the proposition that s.23 should be read subject to s.7. He commented on this case, 'Of all the cases to which I have been referred, it is the most difficult to follow'. He admitted further, 'a little difficulty in understanding the reasoning of the court in *Lex Services* when they came to apply s.7'. Not surprisingly, the tenant attempted to convince the court to follow the *Lex Services* line of approach. It was argued that it would be anomalous and unfair if a tenant was deprived of renewal rights because he was unaware of a notice which had been posted and not yet delivered. Neuberger J. countered that the tenant will usually have nothing to complain about because, if there is no one to accept delivery, notification of the attempted delivery will be left at the premises. He added, 'So far as anomaly is concerned, it seems to me that the purpose of a provision such as s.23 . . . is to introduce an element of certainty and allocation of risk so far as service is concerned. It is important that the parties know where they stand and that the possibility of satellite litigation is kept to a minimum. Any system of service of notices can lead to hardship in particular cases'. Section 23 operates to shift the risk of non-service from the server to the addressee. Hence, Neuberger J. declined to imply any words into s.23 and advised that it is more difficult to imply words into a statute than into a commercial contract. He concluded also that the *Lex Service* case went against the weight of authority and was not to be followed.

On the heels of the *Egg Stores* case, the Court of Appeal in *CA Webber (Transport) Ltd* v. *Network Rail Infrastructure* [2004] 3 All ER 202 again had to consider whether a s.25 notice sent by recorded delivery was deemed to have been served when posted rather than when received by the addressee. Here two notices were served by the landlord on its tenant, terminating the tenancies and stating opposition. The notices were posted on Friday 20 July. By an arrangement with the Post Office, the tenant did not have mail delivered on a Saturday and, accordingly, it received the notices on Monday 23 July. Relying upon service occurring on the Monday, the tenant argued that the notices were invalid because the termination date specified was less than six months hence. Peter Gibson L.J. concluded that, in the light of previous authorities (including the *Egg Stores* case), the consistent approach was that where a notice was served by methods authorised by s.23 of the Landlord and Tenant Act 1927 it mattered not when the notice was received. Service was deemed to have been effected when the notice was entrusted to the Post Office. There was no application of s.7 of the Interpretation Act to notices governed by s.23. He concluded that the decision in *Lex Services Plc* v. *Johns* [1990] 1 EGLR 92 was wrongly decided.

Human rights

In *Egg Stores (Stamford Hill) Ltd* v. *Beanby Estates Ltd* [2004] 3 All ER 184, a novel argument was mooted concerning the Human Rights Act 1998. The argument was that, unless s.23 was construed as subject to s.7, the human rights of an addressee would be infringed. Neuberger J. felt that, on the present facts, no human rights point arose, 'the fact that the tenant was deprived of two days of his two-month period for serving a counter notice, and two days of his four-month period for applying to the court, cannot constitute a significant infringement, or even an infringement, of any of its human rights'. He suggested that the point was more arguable in cases where the notice is returned to the landlord and the very existence of the notice unknown to the tenant. He explained:

> The fact that, in such a case the notice should none the less be deemed to have been served on the tenant on the date it was posted could be said to infringe the tenant's right to property, namely to a new tenancy under the provisions of the 1954 Act, and his right of access to the courts in light of the fact that . . . his application to the court had to be made within four months of receipt or deemed receipt of the notice.

If the human rights argument had prevailed, Neuberger J. admitted that, irrespective of previous decisions, he would have construed s.23 in a way that was subject to s.7. As the argument failed, he did not adopt this construction.

The human rights angle was again followed in *CA Webber (Transport) Ltd* v. *Network Rail Infrastructure* [2004] 3 All ER 202. It was contended that a tenant's renewal rights could be lost when a s.25 notice was sent by recorded delivery and went astray in the post. It followed that s.23 should be construed in a way which catered for a meritorious case. Peter Gibson L.J. took the view that s.23 marked a proportionate and reasonable response by the legislature. The provision is designed to assist the serving party and to establish a fair allocation of the risk of any failure of communication and to avoid disputes of fact (*Blunden* v. *Frogmore Investments Ltd* [2002] 2 EGLR 29). Accordingly, Peter Gibson L.J. concluded that to construe s.23 as excluding the applicability of s.7 of the Interpretation Act, 'does not fall foul of the 1998 Act'. As Longmore L.J. agreed, 'the rules laid down by statute as construed by the courts are in the public interest, and it is impossible to say that the legislature has attached insufficient importance to the tenant's Convention rights'.

4.8.3 Partnerships and joint tenancies

Prior to amendment by the Law of Property Act 1969, a difficulty existed concerning a tenancy held by a partnership in circumstances where not all of the partners were active in the business. Previously, it had been necessary that all of the joint tenants joined in the renewal and termination procedures. In order to remedy this situation, modifications to that rule were introduced by s.41A.

Subject to certain conditions, this provision allows the tenant(s) who carry on the business to act on behalf of any other partner(s). If any of these conditions are not met however it is still necessary for all joint tenants to join together as regards the service and receipt of statutory notices. The conditions are to be found in s.41A(*a*)–(*d*) and, with one exception, refer to the circumstances existing at the end of the contractual term. These conditions are that:

101

- a tenancy is held jointly by two or more persons. This necessarily means that where the tenancy is vested in one partner only, the other partners receive no assistance from s.41A;
- the property comprised in the tenancy is or includes premises occupied for the purposes of a business. If it does not, the tenancy simply falls outside the ambit of the 1954 Act;
- at some time during the subsistence of the current tenancy a business was carried on upon the premises in partnership with all other joint tenants (not just some of them), with or without others, and that the tenancy was held as partnership property. Consequently, if the tenancy is held jointly, but each tenant has always carried out a distinct business, s.41A cannot apply and the landlord's termination notice must be served on all joint tenants; and
- the business is carried on (whether alone or in partnership with other persons) by one or more of the joint tenants and no part is occupied for a business carried on by the other partners.

Where these conditions are met, the tenants carrying on the business at a given time are called 'the business tenants' and it is they who derive benefit from the provision. The remaining partners are termed 'the other joint tenants' (s.41A(2)). The benefit afforded by s.41A is that key notices and applications may be served on or by the business tenants only. It is stated in s.41A(3) that, as regards s.26 requests and s.27 notices, service by the business tenants will be deemed to be service by all the joint tenants, but only when the notice states that it is given by virtue of this provision and sets out the facts showing that it is served by the business tenants. In relation to s.25 notices, s.41A(4) provides that a notice served on the business tenants will automatically be deemed to be service on all the joint tenants. The business tenants may also apply for either a new lease or a termination order under s.24(1), without joining the other joint tenants to the application (s.45A(5)) and, at the court's discretion, the business tenants alone may obtain the new lease or be entitled to compensation in lieu (s.41A(6), (7)).

By virtue of s.41A(6), the new lease may be subject to such conditions (e.g. relating to the provision of guarantors and sureties) as the court thinks equitable, having regard to the omission of the other joint tenants from the grant. It is unclear whether this adds anything to the court's general discretion, under s.35, to include new terms in the renewed lease. It does however highlight that the interests of the other joint tenants should be safeguarded. As s.41A is a facilitating provision, there is, of course, nothing to stop all the joint tenants making the application and receiving the grant.

CHAPTER 5

Tenant's rights: requesting a new tenancy and compensation

Contents

- Introduction
- The section 26 request
- Compensation for loss of renewal rights
- Misrepresentation

5.1 INTRODUCTION

In the same way as the landlord can instigate the Landlord and Tenant Act 1954, Part II machinery by service of a statutory termination notice under s.25, the tenant is able to trigger the renewal machinery by the service on the landlord of a s.26 request for a new lease. As with the landlord's notice, the tenant's request terminates the current lease and activates the jurisdiction of the court to grant a new tenancy. The entitlement to renewal is defeasible only on the grounds specified in s.30(1) and, if the landlord successfully opposes the tenant's claim, compensation in lieu might be available. There is also the possibility that compensation will be payable for any misrepresentation made by the landlord which deleteriously affected the tenant's claim to a new lease. It is with these key entitlements of the tenant that this chapter is concerned.

5.2 THE SECTION 26 REQUEST

5.2.1 Entitlement

Although any protected business tenant who has been served with a s.25 notice is entitled to apply to the court for a new tenancy, not all tenants can make a statutory request for a new tenancy. Indeed, s.26(1) provides that only those tenants holding under a lease originally granted for either a term of years certain (that is a fixed term) exceeding one year or a term of years certain (which can be less than one year (*Re Land & Premises at Liss* [1971] 3 All ER 380)) and thereafter as a yearly tenancy are entitled to make a request. Periodic tenants are excluded because their terms are not 'certain'. A request served by a tenant who does not comply with these basic requirements is invalid and cannot end the tenancy. For example, in *Watkins* v. *Emslie* (1982) 261 EG 1192 the request was invalid as it was served by a periodic tenant. As regards associated companies, care must be taken to ensure that the correct company serves the request. If not, and in a similar vein to the exercise of a break clause, it could be argued that the company is acting as the agent of the tenant (*Dun & Bradstreet Software Services (England) Ltd* v. *Provident Mutual Life Assurance Association* [1998] 2 EGLR 175).

Not surprisingly, it is a criticism levied at s.26 that the availability of the right is unduly restricted. On three occasions however the Law Commission has refused to recommend that the right be extended to periodic tenants. In its 1969 Report, the Commission said, 'We can see no merit in this proposal since a periodic tenancy of its nature continues indefinitely until it is terminated. If the landlord serves a notice under s.25 to terminate the tenancy, a weekly or monthly tenant has the same right as other tenants . . . to apply for a new tenancy'. Some 20 years later, the Commission's Working Paper (1988) reconsidered the matter and arrived at the same conclusion, declaring that to extend the rights to periodic tenants would lead to a proliferation of applications and be of little benefit to such tenants. Finally, in 1992 the fate of this possible reform was sealed in the Report of the Law Commission, 'In the absence of pressing reasons for reform, we consider that this aspect of the legislation is best left as it is. The change could open a door unhelpfully to many applications by short-term tenants, and this seems to be a case in which the balance between landlords and tenants struck by the present provisions is generally accepted and should be maintained'.

On no occasion has the Law Commission expressly considered whether a term *simpliciter* for a year or less than a year should continue to be excluded from the ambit of s.26. As accepted by Goulding J. in *Re Land & Premises at Liss* [1971] 3 All ER 380, the present distinction ensures that a term of exactly one year is excluded whereas a five-month term followed by a yearly tenancy falls within the provisions of s.26(1). It is to be doubted whether, for example, a term of exactly one year followed by a weekly tenancy would suffice. Although it will mean that the tenancy continues for at least one week beyond a year, the periodic tenancy is not certain and will not satisfy the language of s.26(1).

5.2.2 The correct landlord

It is necessary that the request be served on the tenant's competent landlord which is the freeholder or, if sub-tenancies exist, the next landlord above the tenant who has at least 14 months remaining on its lease. The general rule is that, if the request is served on the incorrect landlord, it will be invalid. It is to be appreciated that this conclusion is not disturbed by s.23(2) of the Landlord and Tenant Act 1927 (*Railtrack Plc* v. *Gojra* [1998] 8 EG 158).

Section 23(2) offers some assistance to a tenant where the identity of the reversioner changes without the tenant's knowledge. This provides that, unless and until the tenant is notified that the landlord has ceased to be entitled to rents and profits and provided with the name and address of the new lessor, the tenant is entitled to treat the original landlord as still being the appropriate landlord for the service of notices. The Court of Appeal in *Sector Properties Ltd* v. *Meah* (1974) 229 EG 1097 held that merely providing the name and address of the new landlord's agents will not suffice. The section requires the name and address of the actual landlord.

Section 23(2) of the 1927 Act was considered by the Court of Appeal in *Railtrack Plc* v. *Gojra* [1998] 8 EG 158. There Evans L.J. explained, 'The purpose of s.23(2) ... is to validate a payment made to the original landlord before the required notice is given and has taken effect'. This provision does not require the tenant to wait until the original landlord has ceased to be entitled to the rent before serving a request for a new tenancy. Any contrary conclusion would, as Evans L.J. acknowledged, 'give rise to great difficulties in practice, where the change of landlord occurs at about the same time as the rent becomes due'. It is always to be appreciated however that a landlord can still be in receipt of rents and profits and yet not be the competent landlord for renewal purposes. The statutory fiction can do nothing to assist a tenant who fails to serve a renewal notice on the correct competent landlord. Such is illustrated by *Railtrack Plc* v. *Gojra*, where the tenant sent a request for a new tenancy by ordinary post on 31 March which was received on 6 April. On 1 April however Railtrack Plc had become the statutory assignee of the reversion from the British Railways Board. The request was addressed to the in-house solicitors of the former landlords. The Court of Appeal acknowledged that, because it was not addressed to the correct landlord, normally the consequence would be that the request was invalidated. On the facts, this conclusion was averted because of the operation of Schedule 8 to the Railways Act 1993 which deemed that, from 1 April, Railtrack Plc was substituted as the relevant landlord for the purposes of the renewal proceedings.

5.2.3 Form and content

The s.26 request must be served on the competent landlord by, or on behalf of, the tenant. The request must be in writing and in the form prescribed by the Landlord and Tenant Act 1954, Part 2 (Notices) Regulations 2004, SI 2004/1005 or in a form substantially to like effect. Form 3 is the model to be adopted for these purposes. The Regulations require that the s.26 notice should contain an 'act quick' warning to the recipient which also advises seeking advice from a solicitor or a surveyor and contain a series of notes relating to the grounds of opposition, compensation for disturbance, the steps to be taken and time limits to be satisfied by the parties. Reference should also be made to the explanatory booklet published by the Office of the Deputy Prime Minister and entitled *Renewing and Ending Business Leases: A Guide for Tenants and Landlords* (a web page reference is also included **www.odpm.gov.uk**).

In addition, the 1954 Act itself expressly stipulates that the request must contain certain details and these now fall to be discussed.

Commencement date

The request must state the commencement date for the proposed new tenancy which must be at least six months, and no more than 12 months, after the service of the request (s.26(2)). This mirrors the time limits which regulate the service of the landlord's s.25 notice. On the day before the date specified, s.26(6) provides that the existing tenancy automatically terminates. This is however subject to any interim continuance while the decision of the court as to the grant of a new tenancy is pending (under s.64) and any short extension (under s.36(2)) following the tenant's election not to accept the renewal on the terms decided by the court.

A further limitation is that the commencement date cannot be earlier than that on which the current tenancy can be ended by the effluxion of time (if a fixed term) or a tenant's notice to quit (if a periodic tenancy). The rule, of course, is irrelevant when a continuation tenancy has already arisen. Where the contractual term is in existence however this rule means that a fixed-term tenant cannot serve a request until the last year of the lease. Accordingly, the Act does not allow the tenant to terminate the tenancy early so as to obtain a new lease on more favourable terms. In *Garston v. Scottish Widows Fund & Life Assurance Society* [1998] 3 All ER 596, for example, the tenant sought to exercise an option to break at the end of the tenth year because the premises were over-rented and to obtain a renewal at a lower rent. A s.26 request was served at the same time as the break notice. The Court of Appeal held that the tenant could not exercise a break clause and then serve a request for a new lease. It would otherwise offend the rule that, as regards a fixed-term lease, a request can only be served within 12 months of its contractual term date.

A valid notice to break would moreover operate as a tenant's notice to quit under s.24(2) and should, on that basis alone, disqualify the tenant from engaging the renewal provisions. As Nourse L.J. explained, 'One of the main purposes of Part II of the 1954 Act is to enable business tenants, where there is no good reason for their eviction, to continue in occupation after the expiration of their contractual tenancies. It is not a purpose of the Act to enable a business tenant who has chosen to determine his contractual tenancy to continue in occupation on terms different from those of that tenancy'.

Proposed terms

By virtue of s.26(3), the tenant's request must also include the proposed terms of the new tenancy requested. A failure to do so will render the request void. These proposals must concern:

- the property to be comprised in the new lease (being either the whole or part of the property comprised in the current tenancy). This will normally, but not necessarily, be the tenant's holding, that is, the premises then occupied by the tenant for business purposes. The current holding need not therefore be identical to the premises as originally demised;
- the rent to be payable under the new lease; and
- the other terms of the renewal which, most importantly, include duration.

This requirement may be satisfied by a statement that, other than as to the parcels and the rent, the renewal should be on the same terms as the original lease (*Sidney Bolsom Investment Trust Ltd* v. *E Karmios & Co. (London) Ltd* [1956] 1 QB 529). Although the court's jurisdiction is limited to the order of a 15-year term, the request will not be invalidated by the fact that the tenant proposes a grant of longer duration.

The policy of the 1954 Act is to encourage negotiation and to facilitate agreement between the parties and, it is to be appreciated, the tenant's proposals may not necessarily be reflected in the actual terms of any new lease agreed or ordered. Indeed, the 2004 Notices Regulations make it clear that the tenant's proposals can be discussed and that if the parties cannot agree then either can apply to the court for the terms to be settled.

Similarly, a mistake in this statement of terms will not invalidate the notice. As Denning L.J. explained in *Sidney Bolsom Investment Trust Ltd* v. *E Karmios & Co. (London) Ltd* [1956] 1 QB 529:

> Whatever his inmost state of mind, once a tenant has to all outward appearances made a valid request in the prescribed form setting out his proposals, then he cannot thereafter rely on his own mistake to say that it was a nullity or invalid, no matter how important the mistake was. The validity of the request must be judged by the true interpretation of it, without regard to what happened behind the scenes. It is a formal document with specific legal consequences and it must be treated as such.

Proposals and intentions

The interaction between the right to serve a s.26 request and the right to claim compensation for loss of renewal rights is not always free of difficulty. Such is evident from *Sun Life Assurance Plc* v. *Thales Tracs Ltd* [2002] 1 All ER 64 where the Court of Appeal was invited to consider the role (if any) of the tenant's intentions within this aspect of the legislative framework. The somewhat fundamental issue raised was whether, when serving a s.26 request, the tenant must genuinely intend to take a new lease. If so, a contrary intention to obtain compensation in lieu of renewal would vitiate the legal effect of the request. As Dyson L.J. explained, 'It is common ground that, in a s.26 case, the right to compensation under s.37 depends on a s.26 request which is either valid or which the parties are estopped from contending is invalid. The appeal turns on the meaning of "request" where it appears in s.26 and of "the tenant's proposals" in s.26(3)'.

The respondent, Sun Life Assurance Plc, was the landlord of Thales Tracs Ltd (the tenant formerly known Racal Tracs). The demise expired in December 1998 and the landlord had, from 1996, consistently asserted that it would resist a renewal claim on the basis that the premises were to be redeveloped. During 1997, the tenant decided to relocate to an adjoining site and contracts for its purchase were exchanged. In order to maintain the protection of the 1954 Act however the tenant retained occupation of the demised premises. Completion occurred on 1 April 1998, but prior to that time the tenant had served a s.26 request for a new tenancy. In response, the landlord served a counter notice opposing the grant of a new lease on the ground that it intended to redevelop the premises. The tenant then announced that it would be seeking compensation for the loss of its renewal rights. On 23 April the landlord had a change of heart and offered to renew the tenancy. This tactic does not prevent the tenant claiming compensation, but rather gives the tenant the choice between obtaining a new tenancy and obtaining compensation (*Lloyds Bank Ltd* v. *City of London Corporation* (1982) 262 EG 61). The tenant rejected the landlord's offer, did not apply for a new lease and vacated the premises at the end of the contractual term. The landlord resisted the tenant's claim for compensation on the basis that the s.26 request was invalidated by the fact that, at the time of its service, the tenant did not have any intention of taking a renewal.

The landlord's central argument therefore was that the mental state necessary for a valid request was that the tenant should either want a renewal on reasonable terms or, at least, be undecided as to whether a new lease was wanted. Dyson L.J. could not however accept this interpretation. As a matter of ordinary language the intention of the tenant was irrelevant:

> The words 'request' and 'proposal' are ordinary English words. A request is an act of asking for something. A proposal is something that is put forward for consideration. It may in some circumstances be an offer which, as a matter of law, is

capable of being accepted so as to give rise to a binding contract. But it does not have to be. Both 'request' and 'proposal' are . . . 'performative utterances'. They describe an act. They do something. It is not meaningful whether a request or a proposal say anything about the state of mind of the person who makes the request or puts forward the proposal. The meaning of a request and a proposal is judged objectively. The state of mind of the person who makes the request and the proposal is irrelevant to their meaning. Nor is it meaningful to consider whether they are true.

Dyson L.J. noted that the tenant's intentions are irrelevant when it is the landlord who engages the renewal machinery by the service of a s.25 termination notice. Consequently, he admitted that, 'it is difficult to see why Parliament should have intended that his motives in serving a request for a new tenancy in the first place should be relevant'. Clearly, the availability of compensation should not turn upon which party commences the renewal proceedings. Hence, the terms 'request' and 'proposals' were to be given what Dyson L.J. described as, 'an unqualified objective meaning'. He believed that his approach was consistent with the plain intent of the Act and did not involve absurdity or commercial difficulty. Noting that where the Act requires an intention it does not hesitate to state so expressly, his conclusion was robust:

> there is no justification for reading words into s.26(3) as the judge did. Words should be read into a statute only if there is some necessity to do so . . . The prospect of an inquiry into the tenant's state of mind is not one that the 1954 Act contemplates. The inclusion of proposals in a s.26 request is a statutory formality and does not require the tenant to have any particular intention. It follows that evidence of the tenant's state of mind when he serves his request for a new tenancy is inadmissible because it is legally irrelevant.

Dyson L.J. found it useful to test his hypothesis against several case examples which he felt, 'show that the construction rejected by the judge does not produce results which it can safely be concluded could not have been intended by Parliament'. In the following examples, he felt that the payment of compensation was appropriate and in line with the policy of the Act. They also supported his interpretation of the terms 'request' and 'tenant's proposals'.

- *Case A*: the tenant discovers that the landlord intends to oppose renewal, finds alternative premises and then serves a s.26 request. If the landlord had not intended to oppose a renewal, the tenant would not have taken the alternative site and incurred the associated costs. Dyson L.J. felt that on these facts it would be unfair for the tenant to be denied of compensation and added, 'There is no question of a windfall in favour of the tenant. It might be said that, on the judge's interpretation, case A yields a windfall to the landlord, since it is pure chance that the tenant happens to find the alternative accommodation before he is able to request a new tenancy'.

- *Case B*: the tenant finds alternative accommodation before the end of the contractual term and decides to move. The tenant later discovers that the landlord would oppose the grant of a new tenancy on development grounds. Upon this discovery, the tenant serves a s.26 request. Dyson L.J. admitted that this case may be said to involve some windfall to the tenant.

- *Case C*: and on similar facts to the previous case, the tenant serves the request, but subsequently the alternative accommodation is withdrawn from the market. The tenant then seeks renewal, but unsuccessfully challenges the landlord's opposition. Dyson L.J. felt that, in these circumstances, an entitlement to compensation was not so absurd or surprising so as to indicate that Parliament could not have intended that result.

- *Case D*: the tenant has the intention to take a renewal at the time when the request is served and the landlord serves a counter notice indicating opposition on the basis of an intention to redevelop. The tenant later changes its mind for reasons wholly unconnected with the landlord's response. As Dyson L.J. commented, 'it is anomalous, if not perverse, to allow the tenant compensation if he happens to want a new tenancy when he serves a request, even if he changes his mind immediately afterwards, and yet to refuse compensation if the tenant does not want a new tenancy at the date of his request, although he changes his mind on the following day'.

Waiver and estoppel

Although a failure to comply with the time limits and adhere to the prescribed content *prima facie* renders the request invalid, the landlord should be careful when dealing with what is thought to be a defective request. As discussed in the preceding chapter in the context of the landlord's s.25 notice, waiver and estoppel may have a curative effect in such circumstances. A defect in the tenant's s.26 request can, for example, be expressly or impliedly waived by the landlord's conduct. In *Bristol Cars Ltd* v. *RKH Hotels Ltd* (1979) 251 EG 1279, for example, neither party noticed an error as to the commencement date specified in the s.26 request. The landlord indicated that it would not oppose the grant of a new lease and applied for an interim rent. Subsequently, the defect in the request was discovered and the landlord then served a termination notice. Following *Kammins Ballrooms Co Ltd* v. *Zenith Investments (Torquay) Ltd (No.1)* [1971] AC 850, it was held that a tenant's failure to comply with s.26 could be condoned by the landlord. Both Megaw and Templeman L.JJ. held that, as the landlord had led the tenant to expect that a new lease would not be opposed and the tenant had detrimentally relied on that assurance, the lessor was estopped from denying the validity of the tenant's request. Bridge L.J. however treated the case as one of waiver by election, i.e. by applying for an interim rent and having a full knowledge of the facts, the landlord had affirmed the tenant's request and waived the defect.

Similarly, in *JT Developments Ltd* v. *Quinn* [1991] 2 EGLR 257 statements made in the course of commercial negotiations gave rise to a proprietary estoppel because they created an expectation in the mind of the tenant that a new lease would be granted on the same terms as a specified tenancy of nearby premises. In that case the statements made constituted more than an offer to negotiate, and amounted to an assurance that, irrespective of a formal contract, a renewal would be granted. Estoppel was also raised (albeit unsuccessfully) in *Sidney Bolsom Investment Trust Ltd* v. *E Karmios & Co. (London) Ltd* [1965] 1 QB 529 where Lord Denning M.R. acknowledged that a representation about the legal position can give rise to an estoppel. Nevertheless, he made it clear that a number of hurdles had to be overcome by the claimant:

> But, in order to work an estoppel, the representation must be clear and unequiv-ocal, it must be intended to be acted upon, and it must be acted on. When I say it must be 'intended to be acted on', I would add that a man must be taken to intend what a reasonable person would understand him to intend. In short, the representation must be made in such circumstances as to convey an invitation to act on it. It seems to me that the representation in this case conveyed no such invitation.

5.2.4 Effect of the request

A variety of consequences arise from the service of a valid s.26 request. As mentioned, the request brings to an end the current lease on the day before the date specified as being the commencement date for the new tenancy. The service of a request entitles the landlord to serve a counter notice stating any opposition to renewal itself and/or the terms proposed by the tenant (s.26(6)). The request also enables the tenant to apply to the court within the newly prescribed time limits set out in s.29A(2), (3). If the tenant fails to make an application to the court within this time frame, the current tenancy ends immediately on the expiration of the request (*Smith* v. *Draper* (1990) 60 P & CR 252). Understandably, the tenant then loses the right to a new tenancy and ceases to benefit from the protection of the 1954 Act. This is because the tenant is allowed only to serve one request for a new tenancy and that single request, provided that it is valid (an invalid request is of no effect for these purposes), cannot be abandoned so as to make way for a replacement (*Polyviou* v. *Seeley* [1979] 3 All ER 853). As Edmund Davies L.J. put it in *Stile Hall Properties Ltd* v. *Gooch* [1979] 3 All ER 848:

The suggestion put forward that it is open to the tenant, without the concurrence of the landlord, to withdraw his request for a new tenancy is one which would cut entirely across the statutory scheme. The Act vests radical rights in the tenant of business premises. It also recognises that the landlord also has certain rights and must be protected against exploitation and against harassment.

5.2.5 The pre-emptive strike

It is standard advice to tenants that the use of the s.26 procedure is, in most cases, inadvisable. Despite the facility of an interim rent, the tenant still may gain by prolonging the existing lease, and paying either the old rent or a subsidised interim sum for as long as possible. In this light, and particularly when the landlord shows no sign of serving a s.25 notice, it is rarely advantageous for the tenant to terminate the existing tenancy. Such a step would normally be appropriate only where the tenant either seeks to gain a greater business stability by securing a new lease or wishes to make a pre-emptive strike. This latter tactic assumes relevance only when the tenant suspects that the landlord intends to serve a s.25 notice. The pre-emptive service of a s.26 request will therefore maintain the status quo (and associated rental advantages) for longer than might be desired by the landlord. This is possible because the request takes between six and 12 months to terminate the existing lease and, by choosing the longer period, the tenant may gain half a year. In doing so however the tenant can no longer delay the payment of an interim rent until the later date (s.24B(3)). Once the request is served, s.26(4) prevents the landlord from serving a s.25 notice (and vice versa). Similarly, the tenant cannot serve a s.27 notice or other notice to quit after the service of a s.26 request (and vice versa).

An example of where a tenant could profit from pre-empting the landlord is in the *Sun Life Assurance Plc* v. *Thales Properties Ltd* [2002] 1 All ER 64 scenario. If the tenant does not want a renewal, but does seek compensation in lieu, the tenant may not wish to pay rent until the landlord decides to take the initiative. If the tenant is aware that the landlord will oppose the renewal on a compensation ground, it is an attractive course to serve a s.26 request to expedite matters. The tenant's motives are clearly best not communicated to the landlord until after the service of a s.25 notice or landlord's counter notice. Otherwise the landlord might call the tenant's bluff and not oppose the renewal.

5.2.6 Landlord's counter notice

If the competent landlord seeks to oppose the grant of a new lease, a s.26(6) counter notice must be served on the tenant within two months of receipt of the s.26 request. There is no prescribed form for this counter notice, but it must state the landlord's opposition and the s.30(1) grounds upon which the opposition is based. This is to be expressed in the same way as discussed in Chapter 4 in the context of the landlord's s.25 notice. There is no positive counter notice whereby the landlord can declare the willingness to grant a new lease.

The landlord must respond carefully because once the counter notice is served it is both binding and limiting. The landlord and successors in title remain bound by the grounds set out in the counter notice. Where a new competent landlord emerges, an extant counter notice (unlike a s.25 notice) cannot be withdrawn. If however the predecessor had not served a counter notice, the new landlord can serve one provided that service occurs within the two-month statutory period (*XL Fisheries* v. *Leeds Corporation* [1955] 2 QB 636).

A landlord who does not serve a valid counter notice loses the right to oppose the tenant's application for a new lease. If the landlord has no opposition to the tenant having a renewal, there is no need for the landlord to respond to the tenant's statutory request. It should be understood that where a counter notice is served which contains a ground of opposition which is neither honest nor truthful, as accepted in *Betty's Cafes Ltd* v. *Phillips Furnishing Stores Ltd* [1959] AC 20, the counter notice might be invalidated on the basis of fraudulent misrepresentation. The same principle applies to a fraudulent s.25 notice. Following *Rous* v. *Mitchell* [1991] 1 All ER 676, a similar result may arise in relation to a representation which is made recklessly.

5.3 COMPENSATION FOR LOSS OF RENEWAL RIGHTS

Where the tenant is unable to obtain an order for a new lease, the question of compensation may become the paramount concern. The landlord enjoys no comparable right to claim compensation if the tenant withdraws an application or applies for the revocation of any tenancy ordered. Compensation is payable by the competent landlord under s.37 for what is termed 'disturbance' or, more technically, for loss of the contingent right of renewal. As Ackner L.J. recognised in *Cardshops Ltd* v. *John Lewis Properties Ltd* [1983] QB 161, 'Parliament intended that the tenant should be properly compensated for the disturbance in having to vacate the premises'.

5.3.1 Disturbance

Compensation for disturbance reflects the fact that a tenant's failure to obtain a new lease can prove costly. Apart from a loss of business and goodwill, the tenant will incur expense in locating and moving to alternative premises. This is particularly harsh where the loss of a new lease is not due to any default (e.g. rent arrears and breach of covenant) on the tenant's part. It is this mischief against which the compensation provisions in s.37 are aimed. Before amendment of the 1954 Act by the Law of Property Act 1969, compensation was payable only when the tenant had made an application to the court for a new tenancy and the court was precluded from making the order on grounds: (e) uneconomic sub-letting; (f) demolition and reconstruction; and/or (g) own occupation. The need to make a renewal application was the cause of much criticism. Accordingly, in 1969 the Law Commission recommended that compensation should not be limited to where an application has been made and refused. Instead, it should be available whether or not the tenant bothered to make such an application. As Ward L.J. explained in *Bacchiocchi* v. *Academic Agency Ltd* [1998] 2 All ER 241, 'The disturbance is suffered equally when . . . the tenant withdraws his application for a new tenancy and a tenant in these circumstances is just as much entitled to his compensation'. This recommendation was incorporated within s.37(1).

5.3.2 Availability

For those tenants who fall within the ambit of the 1954 Act, compensation is available under s.37 in two circumstances.

First, when the court is precluded from making an order for a new tenancy or makes a termination order solely on any of the so-called compensation grounds (e), (f) and (g) (s.37(1A), (1B)). These are the mandatory grounds of opposition which do not involve fault on the part of the tenant. If, instead, the court makes a declaration under s.31(2) that either grounds (e) or (f) will be satisfied at a later date, compensation remains payable as the tenant is still denied a renewal. Refusal of renewal or termination on any other ground takes the tenant entirely outside the compensation scheme. Similarly, compensation should not be available where the tenant agrees to take a tenancy of an economically separable part of the previous holding for the purposes of s.31A. The rationale is that the tenant's application has, albeit partially, been successful. On refusing a new tenancy exclusively on one or more of the three specified grounds, the court is, at the behest of the tenant, obliged to certify that fact (s.37(4)). A request for such a certificate is usually made at the end of the renewal hearing, but it can be entertained subsequently. The compensation payable to the tenant will not however form part of the order made by the court when dismissing the tenant's renewal application. As Brightman J. recognised in *Re 14 Grafton Street* [1971] 2 All ER 1, 'It is a debt created by statute, on which the tenant may sue in other proceedings if necessary'.

Secondly, compensation is available when the landlord has served a s.25 notice, or counter notice in response to the tenant's s.26 request, stating only one or more of the grounds of opposition contained in s.30(1)(e)–(g). If other grounds are specified, the tenant must successfully defeat those additional grounds at the hearing stage in order to be entitled to compensation. The general rule therefore is that compensation is available regardless of whether the tenant applies for a new tenancy or withdraws any application made (s.37(1C)). As Slade J. explained at first instance in *Lloyds Bank Ltd* v. *City of London Corporation* (1982) 262 EG 61, the right to compensation is not qualified by any consideration of the tenant's motive:

> Section 37(1), as amended, says nothing whatever about the motives which may prompt a tenant either to omit to apply for a new tenancy or to withdraw his application after it has been made. The motives prompting the tenant to take either of these courses, after he has received a notice under s.25 or s.26(6), relying on one or more of the grounds specified in paragraphs (e), (f) or (g) of s.30, may be many and mixed. I cannot impute an intention to the legislature to withhold compensation from a tenant . . . merely because his motives for omitting to apply to the court, or for withdrawing an application when made, may be of a particular nature.

Special provisions

Where the right to renew is excluded on the grounds of public interest or national security, or a certificate on those grounds prevents renewal beyond a specific date, compensation for disturbance is payable (s.59). If however the Welsh Development Agency is the landlord and a certificate has been issued under ss.60A and 60B by the Secretary of State, compensation is not necessarily available to the tenant. The certification is that the occupation or use of the premises should be changed in order to provide employment in the area. The rule of non-compensation, as set out in s.59(1A), applies where the landlord acquired its interest under ss.7 and 8 of the Welsh Development Agency Act 1975 or the tenant took the lease after the Agency had acquired its interest.

Split reversions

It is an aspect of the catalogue of reforms advocated in 1992 by the Law Commission that, where the ownership of the reversion to a tenancy has been split, the owners of the parts should together be treated as the competent landlord for renewal purposes. In the interests of fairness, the Commission recommended also that compensation payable under s.37 should be apportioned between each part of the property under distinct ownership. This is now to be found in s.37(3B) which provides that the compensation shall be determined separately for each part and be recoverable only from the person who is the competent landlord of that part. Each reversioner's liability would therefore be capped according to the rateable value of, and higher or lower rate applicable to, their respective parts.

5.3.3 Amount of compensation

The tenant is entitled, by virtue of s.37(2), to a flat rate compensation geared to the rateable value of the premises that are occupied by the tenant for business purposes as determined at the time the landlord serves the s.25 notice or counter notice. Compensation is only payable in respect of the tenant's holding (as defined in s.23(3)) which is not necessarily the whole of the premises enveloped within the former tenancy.

The amount payable is the product of an appropriate multiplier (currently one) and either the rateable value of the holding or, in certain circumstances, twice the rateable value (s.37(2)(a), (b)). These rates and the multiplier can be changed by ministerial order (s.37(8)). Such changes have occurred previously so as to reflect significant inflation. The appropriate multiplier to be used is that applicable when the tenant vacates the premises. It is not fixed as at the date of the landlord's notice or counter notice. The tenant moreover has no right to receive compensation until the premises are quit at the end of the tenancy. As Slade J. concluded in *International Military Services Ltd* v. *Capital & Counties Plc* [1982] 1 WLR 575, 'The entitlement arises on the quitting of the holding and not before. In my judgment therefore it is quite plain that the amount of the entitlement must be assessed in accordance with the law as it stands at the date of quitting'. As Walton J. added in *Garrett* v. *Lloyds Bank Ltd* (7 April 1982), 'quitting is the only thing that the tenant is required to do in order to obtain compensation. He is not required to serve any kind of notice or make any kind of application . . .'.

Although the compensation scheme is attractive by reason of its simplicity and certainty, it is to be admitted that the present calculation is purely arbitrary, reflects neither the true loss to the tenant nor the real gain to the landlord and, hence, may produce unfairness.

Rateable values

As regards partly residential premises included within a business tenancy, the abolition of domestic rates has entailed a modification of the compensation scheme. The general rule is that the domestic property is excluded when the rateable value of the premises is calculated, that is, the domestic property does not figure in the calculation of compensation (s.37(5A)). Nevertheless, the tenant can claim reasonable removal expenses for that part, as agreed with the landlord or ordered by the court (s.37(5A)(b), (5B)). Otherwise the rateable value is as shown on the valuation list in force at the date of service of, as appropriate, the landlord's termination notice or counter notice (s.37(5)(a)). If no separate value is given, a proper apportionment or aggregation needs to be made (s.37(5)(b)). Where the rateable value still cannot be ascertained, it is taken to be the value which, apart from any exemption from assessment to rates, would on a proper assessment be the value which would have been entered in the valuation list as the annual value of the holding (s.37(5)(*c*)).

In *Plessey Co. Plc* v. *Eagle Pension Funds* [1990] RVR 29, for example, the central issue was whether the rateable value of the holding was to be ascertained in accordance with s.37(5)(*b*) (as argued by the landlord) or under s.37(5)(*c*) (as argued by the tenant). The difference produced by these calculations was considerable. The landlord was claiming that the rateable value on apportionment was £17; the tenant claimed that the rateable value was £21,097. This discrepancy stemmed from the premises having been damaged by fire and the valuation list consequently being amended to reflect a massively reduced rateable value. Although the premises had been put into a restored state, the rateable value was not upgraded until after the tenant had quit. It was decided that the relevant rateable value was that at the time when the s.25 notice was served (that is, the lower sum). Although a harsh result, the language of s.37(5)(*b*) is clear and unambiguous and the landlord's argument irrefutable.

Procedural rules

Any dispute concerning the determination of the rateable value must be referred to the Commissioners of HM Revenue and Customs for evaluation by an authorised valuation officer (s.37(5)). The valuation officer is not an arbitrator and enjoys much discretion under the present rules. Subject to appeal to the Lands Tribunal, the decision of this officer is final (s.37(5)). Pursuant to s.37(6), rules have been made by the Revenue governing the procedure for such references. Under the Landlord and Tenant (Determination of Rateable Value Procedure) Rules 1954, reference may be made either by one party only or by the parties jointly. The reference moreover must be in the form prescribed in the Rules or in a form substantially to the like effect. Unless all the parties join in the reference, copies of the form must be forwarded immediately to all other parties to the dispute. The valuation officer is also obliged to inform all parties that referral has occurred and to invite them to make written representations, usually within 28 days. The valuation officer can request the parties to furnish such information as reasonably required to assist in the determination. The valuation officer decides the issue in the capacity of an expert, on such evidence as is considered relevant. There is no duty to consider any evidence introduced by the parties, other than their written representations. The valuation officer however has the power to hold a meeting with all the parties before making a determination. Although all must be invited, the meeting can proceed even if a party declines the invitation. On reaching the determination of rateable value, the officer must send notification of the decision to all the parties and to the Revenue Commissioners and this must state the right to appeal to the Lands Tribunal.

5.3.4 Higher rate valuation

As mentioned earlier, in certain cases the rateable value is doubled for the purposes of compensation. The conditions for this higher rate to become payable are twofold. First, by virtue of s.37(3)(*a*) that, during the whole of the 14 years immediately preceding the termination of the current tenancy, the premises (being or comprised in the holding) have been occupied for the purposes of a business carried on by the occupier or for those and other purposes. The relevant termination date here is, by virtue of s.37(7), that specified in the landlord's s.25 notice or the tenant's s.26 request. This may be different from the date the current tenancy ends or the date the tenant quits the premises. The simple logic is that the longer the tenant has spent in the premises the more compensation it should receive. Special provision has been introduced in s.37(3A) to cater for the circumstances where the tenant has occupied only part of the current holding for the 14-year period. This provides that there will be a separate calculation for the part that was occupied for the 14-year period and that which was not. Previously, it was necessary that the whole property have been occupied for this period in order to attract double compensation (*Edicron* v. *William Whitely* [1984] 1 All ER 219).

The second condition is that if during those 14 years there was a change of occupier of the holding, the new occupier must have succeeded to the business of the predecessor (s.37(3)(*b*)). Of crucial relevance here is the continuity of the business and not the identity of the occupier (*Cramas Properties Ltd* v. *Connaught Fur Trimmings Ltd* [1965] 2 All ER 382). Accordingly, this opens the door for the argument that, if the tenant took over the business of the freeholder, the freeholder's period of occupation can, where relevant, count towards the overall 14-year period. Of course, if the 14 years' qualification is not satisfied, the tenant (no matter how short the period of occupation is) will be entitled to compensation at the lower rate.

Traditionally, the requirement of 14 years' business user was strictly applied. The High Court in *Department of Environment* v. *Royal Insurance Plc* (1987) 54 P & CR 26, for example, held that the claim for higher rate compensation was defeated in circumstances where the tenant took a 14-year lease, but entered into physical occupation one day after the term began. In that case, Falconer J. rejected a *de minimis* argument and worked on the premise that the qualification period was not on the facts satisfied because there was not a complete 14-year period. A much different approach was adopted by the Court of Appeal in *Bacchiocchi* v. *Academic Agency Ltd* [1998] 2 All ER 241 where the *Royal Insurance* case was held to be wrongly decided. Simon Brown L.J. acknowledged that the determination of whether business occupation had persisted for the appropriate period should take into account short periods, either at the beginning, mid-term or end of the contractual lease, where the premises stand empty. As Ward L.J. added, 'I find it very difficult to accept Falconer J.'s reasoning that ... there was no intention to occupy the premises on the first day simply because the builders began work on the second day'. Provided that there is no rival claimant to the status of occupier during such periods, fitting out or closing down periods should therefore be included in the calculation. Simon Brown L.J. explained:

> That is to my mind how Part II of the 1954 Act should operate in logic and in justice. It has nothing to do with the *de minimis* principle. Rather it is a recognition that the tenant's business interests will not invariably require permanent physical possession throughout the whole term of the lease and he ought not to have to resort to devices like storage of goods or token visits to satisfy the statutory requirements of continuing occupation. If, of course, the premises are left vacant for a matter of months, the court would be readier to conclude that the thread of continuity has been broken.

5.3.5 Contracting out

The general rule is that the right to compensation can be excluded or modified by an agreement in writing (s.38(3)). This extends also to tenancies terminated in the public interest or due to national security (s.59(2)). Unfortunately, this is catered for in a complex manner. As will become clear, it is ironic that on service of the appropriate notice and on obtaining the appropriate declaration, the parties can contract out a long lease entirely from the Part II proceedings, but their ability to contract out only of the compensation provisions is quite curtailed.

The problems focus on the fact that the general rule gives way where the premises have been occupied for the purposes of the occupier's business (or for those and other purposes) for the whole of five years immediately preceding the date on which the occupier is to quit the holding (s.38(2)(a)). It is clear from *Bacchiocchi* v. *Academic Agency Ltd* that the date the tenant is to quit is that on which the tenant will legally be required to give up possession to the landlord. In that case, due to s.64, the tenant was to quit at the expiry of three months following final disposal of the proceedings. It is not necessarily the date specified in the renewal documentation. In such circumstances, any agreement which purports to exclude or to reduce compensation before its accrual is void. This is regardless of whether such agreement is contained in the lease or in an extraneous document and whether it is entered into before or after the termination of the contractual tenancy. An agreement made after the right to compensation has accrued is however always valid (s.38(2)). It is arguable that the right to compensation accrues when the landlord serves either a s.25 notice or a counter notice which specifies opposition only on the grounds (e), (f) and/or (g). If correct, then the insertion of other grounds of opposition will ensure that the right has not accrued. Indeed, in those circumstances the right will not accrue until the landlord's additional grounds are withdrawn or dismissed by the court.

119

When the identity of the occupier has changed within the five-year period, the agreement is invalidated only if the new occupier was a successor to the business of the previous occupier (s.38(2)(*b*)). Merely being a successor in title to the previous tenant is insufficient to continue the chain of occupation. Nothing in the 1954 Act prevents the parties from entering an agreement which increases the amount of compensation beyond that payable under the statutory calculation. If the lease contains a provision as to compensation payable on termination, the tenant can choose whether to claim under s.37 or the lease. As Ward L.J. commented in *Bacchiocchi* v. *Academic Agency Ltd*:

> Section 38 operates to restrict the freedom of contract which would otherwise allow the parties to agree that no such compensation shall be paid. It operates in favour of the tenant and against the landlord. Its purpose is to ameliorate the tenant's position by imposing the statutory scheme of compensation on the land-lord once the tenant qualifies for relief through five years' occupation for business purposes.

The meaning and timing of occupation

The references in s.38(2)(*a*) to the 'whole of five years' and to 'immediately preceding' indicate, respectively, that continuous occupation is required and must continue up to the date of quitting.

As demonstrated in *London Baggage Company* v. *Railtrack* (11 December 2000) however the calculation of five years for these purposes is not neces-sarily free from difficulty. There the High Court identified five years' contin-uous occupation and yet maintained the validity of the exclusion clause. The reasoning of Pumfrey J. was that occupation *per se* was not the determinative factor. Instead, the legal nature of that occupation was the overriding concern. Here the tenant held over after the expiration of a fixed-term lease, negotiating a renewal. Pumfrey J. concluded that the date of quitting for the purposes of s.37 was the termination date specified in the landlord's notice. The judge felt it significant that the 1954 Act does not extend to tenancies at will. As Pumfrey J. put it, 'So the short question is whether, after the period of the tenancy at will, there was nonetheless a holding which was in fact quitted'. His answer was that the tenancy at will should be ignored. The judge felt that, as regards s.38, Parliament had intended that the five-year period of occupation refers only to occupation under a protected tenancy. He reasoned, 'the reference to "holding" refers to the relevant property comprised in the protected tenancy ... the only period which is to count towards a period for which protection under the Act may be excluded in accordance with section 38(3) is a period of occupation under a tenancy to which the Act applies ...'.

In *Bacchiocchi* v. *Academic Agency Ltd* [1998] 2 All ER 241, the court was faced with a novel point concerning occupation in this context. From 1974 to 1994, the tenant ran a restaurant business in Bath. He held under a 20-year lease and the tenancy fell within the provisions of the 1954 Act. In 1993, the landlords served a s.25 notice on the tenant. The notice stated that they would oppose the tenant's application for renewal on the basis of redevelopment and reconstruction and owner occupation. The tenant applied to the court. The landlords then filed an answer that no longer opposed the application, but did object to the terms proposed by the tenant. The tenant later had a change of heart and decided to retire from business. He withdrew his application on 11 May 1994. By operation of s.64, the tenancy was continued until 11 August 1994 and terminated on that date. The tenant however mistakenly believed that the lease terminated on 29 July and moved out of possession on that date. In the normal course of events, the tenant would be entitled to double rate compensation under s.37. The landlords however contended that no compensation whatsoever was payable because the right had been excluded in the lease. The crucial issue was whether, by moving out 12 days early, the tenant had satisfied the conditions as set out in s.38(2)(a). If so, the contracting-out provision would be invalid. Ward L.J. felt that to give effect to the statutory purpose, 'the question should be approached broadly rather than narrowly'. The case was to turn upon the meaning to be given to the expression 'occupied for the purposes of a business carried on by the occupier'. The appellate court acknowledged that the meaning of occupation in s.38 should bear a meaning allied to that given for the purposes of s.23. On that basis occupation can persist even though the premises are closed (e.g. seasonally). Simon Brown L.J. therefore concluded that it must follow that s.38 can be satisfied where the tenancy comes to an end during such period of closure:

> What is it, therefore, one asks about periods of midterm closure for repairs and the like that in the eyes of the law they do not destroy the continuity of business occupation? That is the critical question and the answer is surely this: each of these events is recognisable as an incident in the ordinary course or conduct of business life. By the same token . . . so also it [occupation] may have to be delayed for the premises to be fitted out in the first place, or may have to end before the term of the lease expires so that the premises may be cleaned up and handed over with vacant possession on the due date.

Accordingly, as the tenant had intended (albeit mistakenly) to quit on the proper date and to remain responsible under the tenancy until that time, it could not be said that occupation for business purposes had prematurely ceased. Instead, the tenant's conduct was viewed as a normal incident of winding down a business at the end of the lease. Ward L.J. added, 'To insist . . . that there be precise coincidence of time between cessation of all activity and the moment when the obligation to quit arises, will produce commercial absurdity. It is an affront to common sense to require a pot and pan to be left on the premises till the clock strikes midnight on the last day. Common sense surely dictates that there be an allowance for reasonable leeway'.

It is not uncommon for compensation to be excluded in a lease for longer than five years. The exclusion is not void *ab initio*, but will be rendered inoperative only when, at the end of the lease, the five years' occupation can be established. Until that time, the agreement will be effective if the lease is prematurely terminated before the qualifying period is satisfied or there is a late change in tenant and the nature of the business carried out on the holding. It is advisable therefore for landlords to include an exclusion in all cases and not merely those leases which are granted for a term less than five years. The tenant should however resist an exclusion clause because it will affect the value of the lease towards the last five or so years of its contractual term. Where relevant, both parties should remain aware of this five-year condition and, hence, the timing of a s.25 notice should be keyed in so as to ensure termination before the five-year period is reached. Conversely, the tenant's s.26 request should attempt to ensure that the five-year mark is passed before the lease can be terminated under the Act. The landlord must also bear in mind the extensions which are possible under the Act and build these into the calculation.

5.4 MISREPRESENTATION

The 1954 Act contains a separate provision for compensation for misrepresentation or concealment. The tenant can obtain compensation under s.37A(1), (2) in two situations.

(1) Where the court has either made a termination order or refused an order for the grant of a new lease. The court has the discretion to order the landlord to compensate the tenant for damage or loss sustained when 'it is subsequently made to appear to the court' that the order was obtained, or the court induced to refuse the grant, by the landlord's misrepresentation or concealment of material facts (s.37A(1)(*a*), (*b*)).

(2) Where the tenant has quit the holding after withdrawing its existing renewal application or without making such an application. The court has the discretion to order the landlord to compensate the tenant for damage or loss sustained as a result of quitting the holding when 'it is made to appear to the court' that the quitting was as a result of misrepresentation or the concealment of material facts (s.37A(2)(*a*), (*b*)).

This remedy is in addition to any common law remedies such as deceit or negligence (*French* v. *Lowen* [1925] EGD 150). The crime of perjury might also be committed by a landlord. The compensation payable under s.37A is not however punitive and the statutory measure of damages is that which is sufficient to compensate the tenant for any loss sustained as a result of the order, refusal or quitting, as appropriate. It is also a discretionary award and not available as of right.

If the tenant is entitled to compensation for disturbance under s.37, that award will be taken into account in the assessment of compensation for misrepresentation or concealment. Loss of expected profits and removal expenses may be included in the calculation under s.37A (*Clark* v. *Kirby-Smith* [1964] Ch 506). Unlike compensation for disturbance, the scope of s.37A is not keyed in to a particular ground of opposition relied on by the competent landlord. It is however most likely to be relevant where the landlord bases opposition on demolition and reconstruction and/or own occupation. This is because, in both instances, the landlord will have to demonstrate the necessary intention and it is to that intention that any misrepresentation will normally strike. The misrepresentation (which can be innocent, negligent or fraudulent) or the concealment (which recognises that the landlord must act in good faith) must cause the court to make the order, induce the rejection of the tenant's application or cause the tenant to quit. Hence, no compensation is available in circumstances where the landlord *bona fide* sets up a ground of opposition and subsequent to the hearing has a change of plans.

Prior to the Regulatory Reform (Business Tenancies) (England and Wales) Order 2003, SI 2003/3096, it was necessary that the tenant had applied for a renewal. This involved the tenant having to go through the motions of a seemingly hopeless application so as to be eligible for compensation. In addition, it was previously the case that the tenant must also establish that the misrepresentation or concealment actually induced the court to reject the tenant's application. Under the old law, no account was taken of any inducement which persuaded the tenant to act in any particular way (see *Deeley* v. *Maison AEL Ltd* (28 July 1989)). Not surprisingly, the requirement of a court application was viewed as unjustifiable and unrealistic in that it ignored totally any misrepresentation that influenced the tenant not to make an application. The introduction of s.37A has remedied these defects, achieved some symmetry between the two compensation schemes and avoided unnecessary applications to the court.

CHAPTER 6

Applications to court

Contents

- Renewal
- Procedural matters
- Pact
- Final disposal
- Following the order
- The effect on reversioners

6.1 RENEWAL

Section 24(1) of the Landlord and Tenant Act 1954 affords to either the tenant or the competent landlord the right to apply to the court for a new lease to be ordered. A number of initial observations can be made about s.24(1), (2):

- the right to make an application is conditional upon the tenancy being within the ambit of the 1954 Act (s.24(1)). This requires that the tenancy must not have been contracted out of the Act and that the tenant remains in occupation for business purposes. Indeed, for the application to be successful, the tenancy must remain within the Act until the proceedings are concluded;
- only one application may be entertained and it must be made subsequent to either the service of a landlord's s.25 notice or the service of a tenant's s.26 request (s.24(2A)). If the landlord has already applied for a termination order under s.29(2), neither can then make a renewal application (s.24(2B)). The other means whereby a tenancy can be terminated under the Act (e.g. tenant's notice to quit, surrender and forfeiture) do not carry with them the right to apply for renewal (s.24(2));
- if the landlord applies for a new lease, the application must be dismissed if the tenant informs the court that it does not want a renewal (s.29(5));

- the application can be entertained only within prescribed, procedural time limits ('the statutory period'). These have been revamped by the Regulatory Reform (Business Tenancies) (England and Wales) Order 2003, SI 2003/3096 and to some extent depend upon whether the renewal machinery is engaged by the landlord or the tenant. If the landlord serves a s.25 notice, either party can apply to the court as soon as the notice is served until the termination date specified in the notice (i.e. between six and 12 months hence). If the tenant serves a s.26 request, either party can make an application following the service of the landlord's counter notice or, if none, the expiry of two months from the date of service. Again, the latest date is the date specified in the request for the termination of the current tenancy (i.e. the date before the stated commencement date for the proposed new lease). These time limits can now be varied by agreement (s.29(B)).

6.1.1   Landlord's motives

The competent landlord might apply for a renewal on behalf of his tenant for a variety of reasons. For example, it might be to ensure that a new lease at a market rent is obtained more quickly than would be the case if matters are left to the tenant's initiative. It may be that the landlord is entitled to an increased interim rent under the new rules of calculation and is looking forward to its receipt. Under the new rules, the arrears are paid only after a new lease has been granted. Nevertheless, it is anticipated that applications for a new lease will remain largely the territory of the tenant whereas land-lords may be more tempted to use the new s.29(2) ability to apply to the court for a termination order.

6.1.2   Termination

Section 29(2) allows the competent landlord to apply to the court to obtain an order for the termination of a tenancy. A number of initial observations can be made about s.29(2):

- the right to make a termination application is dependent upon the tenancy being within the ambit of the 1954 Act (s.29(2));
- the landlord must have served either a s.25 notice stating opposition to the grant of a new tenancy or a s.26(6) counter notice (in response to a tenant's s.26 request) stating opposition (s.29(2)(a), (b));
- neither party must have made a s.24(1) application for a new lease (s.29(3));
- in order to obtain a termination order, the landlord must establish to the satisfaction of the court one of the s.30(1) grounds of opposition. If so, the existing tenancy will terminate in accordance with s.64 and without the grant of a new lease (s.29(4)(a));

125

- if the landlord cannot make out a statutory ground of opposition, the court shall order a new tenancy and the existing tenancy will end immediately before the commencement date of the new lease (s.29(4)(*b*));
- the application must be made within the same time frames ('the statutory period') as an application for renewal (see above) (s.29A(1));
- the landlord may not unilaterally withdraw a termination application (s.29(6)). The consent of the tenant is therefore required.

6.1.3 Extending time limits

The statutory period within which an application must be commenced can, following the 2003 Order, be extended, but in light of s.69(2) only by written agreement. Previously these time limits were inflexible. Section 29B(1) allows scope for extension, but an agreement is valid only if it is made after the service of a s.25 notice or s.26 request and before the end of the statutory period. This, it will be recalled, is the date specified in the renewal documentation (between six and 12 months after service) on which the current tenancy is to expire. An agreement reached outside these time limits will be ineffective.

The parties may from time to time further extend the period for making such an application, but any agreement to do so must be made before the end of the period specified in the existing agreement (s.29B(2)).

If an agreement is made, this does not prevent a party from making an application before the period as specified in the agreement has ended (s.29B(3)).

Where an agreement is, or agreements are, made under s.29B, the landlord's s.25 notice and the tenant's s.26 request are treated as terminating the tenancy at the end of the period specified in the agreement or last of the agreements (s.29B(4)). Any extension must therefore lapse on a stipulated date. It cannot be a general, unspecified extension.

The ability to extend these time limits is intended to give the parties more time to negotiate and to reduce the number of applications made to the court. It is anticipated that this will mark a decline in the number of unopposed renewal applications being made and put to an end to at least one trap for the unwary tenant. Nevertheless, the tenant must still apply before the end of any extended period or lose the right to a new lease. A trap for the unwary therefore remains.

The extension will be geared to whole days and it is sensible to choose, as the last day, a date on which the court office is open. In *Hodgson* v. *Armstrong* [1967] 1 All ER 307, it was held that, when the last day on which an application can be made is one on which the court office is closed (e.g. a Sunday), it is permissible to make the application on the next day the court is open. Matters arising under the Civil Procedure Rules are also subject to this rule (CPR, r.2.8(5)). If the application is made on time, but is defective in some way the court has the power to allow amendment to cure the defect even after the deadline has passed (*Teltscher Bros Ltd* v. *London & India Dock Investments Ltd* [1989] 1 WLR 770). In that case the application was valid even though the landlord was stated to be the 'plaintiff' and not, as was correct, the 'defendant'. The mistake was genuine and did not mislead the landlord.

6.2 PROCEDURAL MATTERS

6.2.1 The court

The application for renewal or termination can be made to either the High Court or the county court. Since 1991, the county court has been given an unlimited jurisdiction to determine applications under the Landlord and Tenant Act 1954 (s.63(2)). Any jurisdictional limitations based upon rateable values were therefore swept away. Accordingly, and although the venue of the High Court remains an option for the tenant, the primary agency dealing with lease renewals is the county court. Indeed, unless there are exceptional circumstances, the claim will be commenced in the county court (CPR, r.56.2(1), PD56.2, para. 2.2).

If the claim is started in the High Court, CPR, r.56.2(2) requires the claimant to file with its claim form a certificate stating the reasons for selecting the Chancery Division. The justifications for starting a claim in the High Court are set out in CPR, PD56.2, para. 2.4 and are where there are complicated issues of fact or there are points of law of general importance. The Practice Direction goes on to state that the value of the property and the amount of any financial claim may be relevant circumstances, but will not alone normally justify the commencement of proceedings in the High Court (CPR, PD56.2, para. 2.5).

The majority of claims therefore will be issued in the county court. The claim must usually be started in the county court for the district in which the land is situated (CPR, r.56.2(1)).

Transfer of proceedings

If the claim is started in the High Court and the Master decides that it should have been commenced in the county court, the claim can be either struck out or transferred to the lower court. The criteria for determining whether a transfer to the county court is appropriate are set out in CPR, Part 30 and PD30. If the proceedings are transferred, they will end up in the Central London County Court or, if requested by the parties, a local county court. The costs of the High Court proceedings and the costs of transfer will normally be disallowed (CPR, PD56.2, para. 2.3).

It is possible that the proceedings are started in the county court, but later transferred to the Chancery Division at the order of the High Court. This is catered for by CPR, r.30.3 which sets out the criteria for a transfer order. The relevant concerns include the value of the claim, issues of convenience and fairness, the availability of a specialist judge, the complexity of the case and the public importance of the claim. There is a right to appeal from a transfer order and a procedure is set out in CPR, PD30.5, paras. 5.1, 5.2.

The county court may also order that the case be transferred to the High Court. This will normally occur when there is some important issue of law that is, or is likely to be, raised.

It is also possible that proceedings may be commenced in the wrong county court. If so, a judge of the county court has several possible responses. The judge may order that the claim be transferred to the county court in which it ought to have been started; the claim continue to be heard in the wrong court; or strike out the claim altogether (CPR, r.30.2(2)). As demonstrated in *Sharma* v. *White* [1986] 1 WLR 757, if the transfer from one county court to another occurs, but arrives at the correct court out of time, it is deemed to have been made within time.

CPR, r.30.2(4) allows transfer within the High Court. Proceedings may be transferred from the Royal Court of Justice to a district registry and vice versa. The criteria for this transfer order are specified in CPR, r.30.3(2)(*a*)–(*h*).

6.2.2 The parties

Where it is the tenant who seeks a new lease, the claimant is the tenant of the holding at the time the originating process is issued. If the tenant assigns the lease after proceedings have been commenced, the assignee will need to be substituted as the new tenant. Where there are joint tenants, the general rule is that all the tenants must join in the application (*Jacobs* v. *Chaudhuri* [1968] 2 QB 470). The court has the discretionary power to order one joint tenant (in the capacity of statutory trustee) to become a party to the proceedings so as to protect trust property (*Harris* v. *Black* (1983) 46 P & CR 366). Even when the tenant is a trustee for the business occupier or where the tenant and the occupier are both members of a group of companies, it is the actual tenant who must be a party to the proceedings. In addition, on obtaining probate, the executor of a deceased tenant can make or continue with, as appropriate, the application to the court (*Re Crowhurst Park* [1974] 1 All ER 991). If there is a misdescription of the tenant, and provided that the landlord is not misled, the application can be amended.

If the landlord initiates proceedings, the tenant becomes the defendant. The above rules apply equally in this situation as they do when the tenant is the claimant.

The appropriate defendant when the tenant seeks a new lease is the competent landlord as defined in s.44 and as assessed at the time the process is issued (CPR, PD56.3, para. 3). If there is a change of competent landlord after the court application is made, the proceedings cease to be properly constituted unless the new landlord is made a party to the application (*Piper* v. *Muggleton* [1956] 2 QB 569). An amendment can occur even after the statutory period in which proceedings could be commenced has passed (*Parsons* v. *George* [2004] 3 All ER 633). The same rules apply when the landlord is seeking renewal or termination and becomes the claimant.

The addition and substitution of new parties is governed by CPR, Part 19 and PD19. Accordingly, if a mortgagee takes possession or a receiver is appointed following the commencement of proceedings, the mortgagee/receiver must be joined (*Meah* v. *Mouskos* [1968] 2 QB 23). Similarly, where a reversionary tenancy is sought by the tenant, the landlord next superior to the competent landlord should be joined (*Birch (A&W)* v. *PB (Sloane) and Cadogan Settled Estates Co.* (1956) 167 EG 283).

Although it is important that the identity of the person intended to be sued is made unequivocal, an error as to the landlord's name or status will not necessarily render the proceedings nugatory. Even if the tenant names the wrong party as landlord, the court may still allow the proceedings to be amended. This is permitted by CPR, r.17.4(3), but only where a mistake was genuine and not one which would cause reasonable doubt as to the identity of the party in question. This, seemingly, reiterates the rule, as established in *Evans Construction Co. Ltd* v. *Charrington & Co. Ltd* [1983] QB 810 that no amendment can be made when the mistake relates to responsibility. In that case the tenant should have commenced proceedings against Bass Holdings, but instead named the landlord's managing agents and associated company (Charrington & Co.) in the application. The amendment was allowed.

Although amendments exist only to correct a simple misnomer, the distinction between name and responsibility is however not always easy to draw. In *Re 55 & 57 Holmes Road, Kentish Town* [1958] 2 WLR 975, for example, it was stressed that a misnomer will occur when the tenant has in mind one party only, but sets down the name incorrectly. It is not however a mere misnomer when the tenant has two entities in mind, correctly names one but wrongly makes that one a party. It is, as Beldam L.J. put it in *Fluoro Engineering Plastics (Linings) Ltd* v. *British Telecommunications Plc* (19 March 1998), 'the distinction between an error in the party and an error in the name of the party'.

6.2.3 The claim procedure

Under the CPR there are two major types of claim procedure: that under Part 7 and that under Part 8. Part 7 claims are intended to deal with the general style of claim while Part 8 caters for claims where the evidence is not likely to be in dispute. With the introduction of two new types of procedure, i.e. the landlord's ability to apply for a termination order or to apply to the court for a renewal, it was necessary to alter CPR, Part 56 accordingly. Part 56 now also draws a distinction between cases where the landlord opposes the tenant's right to a new lease (an 'opposed claim') and those where the landlord does not oppose renewal (an 'unopposed claim'). As regards the former, the Part 7 procedure is to be adopted and a claim form N1 is used. In relation to an unopposed case, the Part 8 procedure is to be followed and claim form N208 is employed. Although the basic structure of these forms remains intact, Part 56 requires more information from the parties to be given in the claim form as well as the acknowledgement of service and any defence served. In both the High Court and the county court, proceedings commence once the claim form is issued by the court.

As regards an unopposed claim, no evidence need be filed unless the court directs otherwise (CPR, PD56.3, para. 14). If a defence is filed, the court will require the landlord to complete a document known as an allocation questionnaire. It is at this stage when the court will usually make directions for the future conduct of the proceedings.

In relation to an opposed claim, evidence (including expert evidence) must be filed as the court directs and the landlord shall be required to file its evidence first (CPR, PD56.3, para. 15). This gives the court a wide discretion as to the management of the claim. Where the landlord asserts the statutory grounds of opposition, this will normally be tried as a preliminary issue (CPR, PD56.3, para. 16).

The claim form must be served on the landlord or tenant by one of the permitted methods of service (CPR, r.6.2). Service can be undertaken either by the court or by the claimant personally. If the claim form is served by the court, the court must notify the claimant when service has occurred, whereas, if service is by the claimant, the claimant must file a certificate of service within seven days of service taking place (CPR, r.6.10). The methods are set out in CPR, r.6.2 and include personal service, first class post, leaving the document at the address for service of the party, document exchange, fax and electronic communication. The Rules also stipulate deemed days of service according to which method is employed (CPR, r.6.7). Service has to occur within two months after the date of issue of the claim form (CPR, r.56.3(b), (4)(b)). The claimant can apply for an extension of time for service under CPR, r.7.6(1).

Once a claim is underway, the claimant can discontinue it by notice and without leave of the court (CPR, r.38.2). The defendant may then apply to have the notice of discontinuance set aside (CPR, r.38.4).

6.2.4   The claim forms

The requirements of a claim form are set out in CPR, PD56. This provides in PD56.3, para. 4 that the claim form must in all cases contain the following details:

- the property to which the claim relates (i.e. the tenant's holding);
- the particulars of the current tenancy (i.e. the date, parties, duration, rent and the date and method of termination);
- every notice or request served under ss.25 and 26 respectively; and
- the expiry date of the statutory period or any agreed extended period.

Tenant's claim for a new lease

If the claimant is the tenant seeking a new lease under s.24, the claim form by virtue of CPR, PD56.3, para. 5 must also contain additional details concerning:

- the nature of the business carried on at the property;
- whether the claimant relies on s.23(1A) (occupation or the carrying on of a business by a company controlled by the tenant or, if the claimant is a company, occupation or the carrying on of a business by a person with a controlling interest in the company tenant), s.41(trusts and occupation by beneficiaries), or s.42 (occupation within a group of companies);
- whether the claimant relies on s.31A (new terms or accepting a tenancy of an economically separable part as a defence to the landlord's opposition under s.30(1)(f));
- whether any part of the property (and, if so, what part) is not occupied for business purposes by the tenant or the tenant's employee;
- the claimant's proposed terms for the new lease; and
- the name and address of anyone known to the claimant who has a leasehold interest in the reversion not exceeding 15 years who is likely to be affected by the grant of a new lease or, if none, the freeholder. The claim form must be served on these named persons.

Landlord's claim for renewal

Where the landlord is claiming a new tenancy on behalf of its tenant, the claim form must contain the following additional details:

- the claimant's proposed terms of the new tenancy;
- whether the claimant wants the parcels of the new lease to be those of the original leases (under s.32(2)) even though parts are no longer occupied by the tenant; and
- the name and address of any other landlord who has a leasehold interest of less than 15 years remaining and who is likely to be affected by the grant of a new tenancy or, if none, the freeholder. The claim form must be served on these named persons.

Landlord's application for termination

Where the claimant is the landlord seeking a termination order under s.29(2), the additional information required concerns:

- the claimant's grounds of opposition;
- full details of those grounds of opposition; and
- the terms of a new tenancy that the claimant proposes if his termination claim fails.

6.2.5 Priority of claims

Where there is more than one application made to the court, either for termination or for a new tenancy, the precedence of claim forms is determined by CPR, PD56.3, para 2. This provides that:

- once an application under s.24(1) has been served on the defendant, no further application under s.24(1) or s.29(2) to the court in respect of the same tenancy may be served by that defendant without permission of the court;
- if more than one s.24 application is served on the same day, the landlord's application will be stayed until the court directs otherwise;
- if an application under s.24 and an application under s.29(2) are served on the same day, the tenant's renewal application will be stayed until further order of the court; and
- if a tenant is served with a s.29(2) application which was issued at a time when an application under s.24(1) had already been made by the tenant, the service of the s.29(2) application will be deemed to be notice under CPR, r.7.7 requiring discontinuance of the s.24 application within 14 days.

6.2.6 Acknowledgement of service

The defendant must file an acknowledgement of service not more than 14 days after the claim form has been served. Not surprisingly, the contents of the acknowledgement differ according to which party is the claimant and whether it is an opposed claim or an unopposed claim. If the defendant fails to respond by filing an acknowledgement of service, the defendant cannot take part in the hearing without the leave of the court (CPR, r.8.4). It is also on the service of the acknowledgement of service that the court will give directions as to the future management of the claim (CPR, r.56.3(3)(c)).

Unopposed claim: tenant as claimant

In this situation, CPR, PD56.3, para. 10 provides that the acknowledgement must be in Form N210 and state with particulars the following:

- whether, if a new lease is granted, the landlord objects to any of the terms proposed by the tenant. If so, the landlord must identify those terms and put forward his own counter proposals;
- whether the landlord's lease has less than 15 years unexpired at the date of termination of the tenant's current lease and, if so, the name and address of any other reversioner;
- the name and address of any person having an interest in the property who is likely to be affected by the grant of a new lease; and
- whether the landlord wishes for the tenant to have a lease of the whole of the property comprised in the tenant's current tenancy under s.32(2) even though this is larger than the tenant's holding.

Unopposed claim: landlord as claimant

The acknowledgement must be in Form N210 and by virtue of CPR, PD56.3, para. 11 must state with particulars the following:

- the nature of the business carried on at the property;
- if the tenant relies on s.23(1A) (occupation or the carrying on of a business by a company controlled by the tenant or, if the claimant is a company, occupation or the carrying on of a business by a person with a controlling interest in the company tenant), s.41(trusts and occupation by beneficiaries), or s.42 (occupation within a group of companies), the basis on which the tenant does so;
- whether any part of the property (and, if so, what part) is not occupied for business purposes by the tenant or the tenant's employee;
- the name and address of anyone known to the tenant who has a leasehold interest in the reversion with less than 15 years remaining who is likely to be affected by the grant of a new lease or, if none, the freeholder; and
- whether the tenant objects to any of the terms proposed by the landlord. If so, the tenant must identify the terms to which he objects and put forward counter proposals.

Opposed claim: tenant as claimant

CPR, PD56.3, para 12 provides that this acknowledgement of service be in Form N9 and the landlord's defence must state with particulars the following:

- the grounds of opposition;
- full details of those grounds of opposition;
- whether the landlord objects to the terms proposed by the tenant. If so, the landlord must identify the terms to which he objects and put forward counter proposals;
- whether the landlord is a tenant under a lease having less than 15 years unexpired at the date of termination of the claimant's current lease and,

if so, the name and address of any person (known to the landlord) of a reversioner who has a lesser interest;

- the name and address of any person having an interest in the property who is likely to be affected by the grant of a new tenancy;
- if the tenant is no longer in occupation of the whole premises as originally demised;
- whether the landlord requires the tenant to take a new tenancy of the whole under s.32(2).

Landlord's claim to termination of tenancy

The acknowledgement of service here is governed by CPR, PD56.3, para. 13 and must be in Form N9. The tenant's defence must state with particulars the following:

- if the tenant relies on s.23(1A) (occupation or the carrying on of a business by a company controlled by the tenant or, if the claimant is a company, occupation or the carrying on of a business by a person with a controlling interest in the company tenant), s.41(trusts and occupation by beneficiaries), or s.42 (occupation within a group of companies), the basis on which the tenant does so;
- whether the tenant relies on s.31A (as a defence to the landlord's claim under s.30(1)(f)) and, if so, the basis on which he does so; and
- the terms of the new tenancy that the tenant would propose if the landlord's claim fails.

6.2.7 Disclosure and expert evidence

Part 31 and PD31 of the CPR set out the rules concerning disclosure and inspection of documents. The court will normally order standard disclosure which requires disclosure of those documents which are to be relied upon or which adversely affect the party's case (CPR, r.31(6)). An application for specific disclosure directed at specified documents or classes of document must be supported by evidence (CPR, r.31.12). The parties are required to make a reasonable search in all the circumstances for such documents and the duty to disclose is ongoing throughout the proceedings (CPR, rr.31.7, 31.11). Each party will serve a disclosure list and a disclosure statement. The latter must describe the extent of the search for the documents and certify that the duty to disclose is understood and has been carried out. The general rule is that a party to whom a document has been disclosed has the right to inspect and copy that document (CPR, rr.31.2, 31.15).

It is usual for experts to be called in to advise on the rent to be payable under a new lease and to decide whether a landlord's redevelopment plans under s.30(1)(g) are feasible. Expert evidence is admissible with the leave of the court (CPR r.35.4(1)). There is some uncertainty however as to the extent to which the court should utilise single joint experts. This practice is encouraged by CPR, r.35.7 which aims to restrict expert evidence only to that reasonably required. In this way, the court can limit the number of experts (CPR, r.35.4(3), (4)). The court has also voiced its view that there should normally be a joint expert (*Peet* v. *Mid-Kent Area Healthcare NHS Trust* [2002] 1 WLR 211). If the parties cannot agree as to a joint expert, the court can appoint one on their behalf (CPR, r.35.7(3)). The court can also offer directions as to the payment of a joint expert (CPR, r.35.8(3)(a)) and, indeed, set a financial limit on the amount that can be paid (CPR, r.35.8(4)).

Despite the encouragement to use one expert who owes his overriding duty to the court and not the party that employs him (CPR, r.35.3), each party is privately entitled to employ its own expert to review the report of the joint expert. The possibility of a joint expert however does serve to focus the minds of the parties on alternative dispute resolution such as the use of the Professional Arbitration on Court Terms scheme (PACT).

6.3   PACT

Although the majority of renewal claims are settled between the parties, some still make it to the court room or are settled on the court steps. Arbitration is well suited for unopposed renewal cases as it concentrates the minds of the parties by meeting with a non-judicial third party. The Law Society and the Royal Institution of Chartered Surveyors (RICS) jointly operate Professional Arbitration on Court Terms (PACT), a scheme which provides an alternative to court room resolution. This offers the parties a means of having disputes over terms, particularly the rent (including interim rent), decided by a surveyor or solicitor acting as an expert or arbitrator.

The PACT procedure involves either party making an application to the court for a new tenancy in the conventional manner. The parties must sort out any argument concerning grounds of opposition and then they may agree that any outstanding matters be referred to a surveyor or solicitor for resolution. The parties decide on the issues to be determined and the order in which those issues are to be addressed. The parties agree as to the capacity of the facilitator, i.e. whether he is to act as an arbitrator or expert. A consent order is drawn up as to the matters agreed and the application to court is suspended. Application is then made to the RICS or Law Society for the appointment of a third party to be made from a panel of trained arbitrators and experts. The third party then proceeds to determine the outstanding issues. Once the decision is reached, either party can apply to the court, under the terms of the consent order, for the grant of a new tenancy.

Once the award is made, the tenant can still exercise the right to decline renewal under s.36(2). The award may also be challenged on appeal on the grounds that there was a serious irregularity or an error of law.

6.3.1   Withdrawal and discontinuance

It might be that, after the tenant's application to the court, the parties reach an agreement as to the grant of a new lease and the terms of that lease. In such a case, there are two options open to the tenant. First, the tenant may proceed with the application and have the agreement embodied in an order of the court. Secondly, the tenant may withdraw the application on the terms agreed. The general rule is that discontinuation is as of right and constitutes the most simple and inexpensive alternative (CPR, r.38.2). The process involves the tenant filing a notice of discontinuance and serving a copy of it on every party. The defendant has the right to apply, within 28 days, to have the notice of discontinuance set aside (CPR, r.38.4). Pre-discontinuation costs will normally be payable by the tenant (CPR, r.38.6). In the context of the Landlord and Tenant Act 1954, withdrawal means that the existing tenancy will come to an end three months after the date of discontinuation and precludes any change of heart. The withdrawal does not however disentitle the tenant to compensation for disturbance or misrepresentation. Similarly, the landlord cannot automatically avoid paying compensation by withdrawing all opposition to the tenant's application. In that situation, the Court of Appeal has acknowledged that the tenant has two options: either to obtain a new tenancy or to discontinue the application and obtain compensation (*Lloyds Bank Ltd* v. *City of London Corporation* [1983] Ch 192).

6.4   FINAL DISPOSAL

As previously mentioned, the date of termination set out in the s.25 notice or s.26 request is not necessarily the date on which (whether the tenant's application is successful or not) the current tenancy will end. Under s.64, where the tenant makes an application to the court for a new tenancy and the termination date specified in the renewal documentation expires within three months of the final disposal of the application, the tenancy automatically continues until the end of that three-month period. The tenant need do nothing and it is the whole tenancy that is continued in this way.

Final disposal occurs when all proceedings (including appeals) have been determined and any time for further appeals has expired. Leave to appeal out of time may however be granted within the three-month period (*Rawashdeh* v. *Lane* [1988] 40 EG 109). Alternatively, final disposal arises when an application has been withdrawn or from the discontinuance of proceedings. In *Austin Reed* v. *Royal Insurance Co. (No. 2)* [1956] 3 All ER 490, for example, the date of final disposal, where the Court of Appeal refused leave to appeal to the House of Lords, was the date on which time to petition the Appeals Committee of the House of Lords expired. The purpose of s.64 was described by Sachs L.J. in *Zenith Investments Ltd* v. *Kammins Ballrooms Ltd* [1971] 1 WLR 1751 as follows:

> The manifest object of s.64 as a whole was to ensure that during the periods, some-times prolonged, whilst litigation between landlord and tenant was pending and neither party knew that a new lease would be granted, there should yet be certainty as between them relating to their interim obligations. It was intended that they should not be beset with the hazy, one is tempted to say crazy, problems that can arise under the law of landlord and tenant between parties who do not know whether the one who is in possession of the property is a trespasser or a tenant – problems which can be of great interest to lawyers but can infuriate laymen . . . it simply intended to produce clarity as between the parties until all real disputes had been finally disposed of.

The Court of Appeal in *Single Horse Properties Ltd* v. *Surrey County Council* [2002] 4 All ER 143 was invited to consider an issue of interpretation relating to the operation of s.64(1)(*c*). This subsection provides for the prolongation of the tenancy in circumstances where, 'apart from this section the effect of the notice or the request would be to terminate the tenancy before the expi-ration of the period of three months beginning with the date on which the application is finally disposed of'. The issue for debate was whether a tenant could, following a renewal application, have a change of heart and, by simply moving out of occupation prior to the contractual term date, avoid a s.64 extension of the tenancy. Arden L.J. offered the following insight, 'In making that determination, s.64(1)(*c*) authorises the making of one assumption, and one assumption only, namely that s.64 has not been enacted. Moreover, since a notice which is ineffective under the 1954 Act is of no effect, s.64(1) cannot apply unless the notice or request took effect under the relevant provision of the 1954 Act'. Accordingly, the central issue was whether (and, if so, when) the landlord's s.25 notice was effective to determine the tenancy. Although on the service of the landlord's notice there existed a tenancy to which the Act applied, Arden L.J. felt that this was not enough. She explained, 's.25(1) does not relate that requirement to the date of service of the notice but rather to the act of termination for which that notice provides'. As a tenancy for a fixed term comes to an end at common law by effluxion of time, the land-lord's s.25 notice cannot terminate the tenancy unless the tenant remains in occupation beyond that time. She acknowledged that the 1954 Act must apply to the tenancy when the notice takes effect:

> A notice under s.25(1) is thus of no effect if the tenancy is not continued by s.24(1). The tenancy is not so continued if it expires on the term date by effluxion of time . . . Whenever the notice is served, there would be nothing for the landlord's termi-nation to 'bite on' . . . [the landlord's] argument amounts to reading into Part II of

the 1954 Act a concept whereby a tenancy is continued beyond its term date if by then the tenant has invoked the jurisdiction of the court by making an application to it. In my judgment, there is no room in s.25 for such a concept.

As the present landlord's s.25 notice was ineffective to terminate the tenancy, it fell outside s.64 and was, thereby, unable to sustain an interim continuation of the tenancy. The tenant was not therefore liable for any rent after the contractual term date.

Although intrinsically reasonable, s.64 is vulnerable to some criticism. First, where the tenant enters a genuine appeal, the period of three months is hardly sufficient within which to locate new premises. If the tenant attempts to find alternative accommodation, it should be borne in mind that the tenant is under a continuing obligation to remain in occupation of the premises throughout all of the proceedings if it wishes to benefit from protection under the 1954 Act (*I&H Caplan Ltd* v. *Caplan (No. 2)* [1963] 2 All ER 930). If the tenant ceases to be in occupation, the protection of the Act is withdrawn and the chance of a renewal is lost. In its 1969 Report, the Law Commission thought it unreasonable to expect a business tenant to wait three months before seeking other premises and unrealistic to suppose that other accommodation will be found in that time. The Commission recommended that the tenant should be required to occupy only up to the time of the court order, any later and intermediate period being of no relevance. This recommendation did not find its way into the Law of Property Act 1969 and has not been championed since.

Secondly, the possibility exists that a tenant can exploit s.64, and so extend the current tenancy for as long as possible, by entering a notice of appeal in circumstances where there is no reasonable prospect of an appeal succeeding, such appeal perhaps destined to be abandoned at the last moment. The motive of the tenant may be merely to gain an extra period of occupation (as in *Photo Centre Ltd* v. *Grantham Court Properties (Mayfair) Ltd* (1964) 191 EG 505) or might be designed to deter the landlord's development plans (*AJA Smith Transport* v. *BRB* (1980) 257 EG 1257). Indeed, in the *Smith* case Brandon L.J. felt that the tenant's use of s.64 was close to an abuse of the judicial process. Nevertheless, the tenant is allowed to manipulate the system and the courts feel obliged to condone unmeritorious appeals. As Glidewell L.J. made clear in *Burgess* v. *Stafford Hotels Ltd* [1990] 3 All ER 222, 'One cannot say that a person who is granted such rights [to appeal] and takes advantage of them is behaving disgracefully or is deserving of moral condemnation. The landlord's remedy . . . is either to apply for an order to strike out . . . or to apply for an order for security of costs, or to make both applications'.

Most cases deal with the scenario where the tenant's quest for a new lease is still technically afoot, albeit perhaps doomed to failure. A different situation arose in *Mark Stone Car Sales Ltd* v. *Howard De Walden Estates Ltd* (1997) 73 P & CR D 43 where the tenant's interest solely concerned compensation without even the possibility of a renewal. The landlord was able to oppose successfully the renewal on the basis of redevelopment, but the appeal concerned whether the landlord had also offered suitable alternative accommodation under s.30(1)(*d*). If so, the tenant would be deprived of compensation. As Brooke L.J. explained:

> Where a landlord has established to the court's satisfaction one or more substantive grounds for opposing the grant of a new tenancy which are not the subject of an appeal it seems quite absurd, if it be correct, that the tenant's current tenancy should automatically continue until three months after the date on which an appeal against a concurrent adverse finding on a s.30(1)(d) issue is finally determined.

Although Brooke L.J. hoped that Parliament would intervene and amend the 1954 Act, he felt that 'imaginative judicial interpretation ... might be employed in order to avoid the obvious injustice which would otherwise befall landlords'. He focused attention on the word 'application' as employed in s.64 and suggested that its final disposal might be construed as meaning 'when a court's unappealed decision put paid to any question of the grant of a new tenancy'. This is a simple and straightforward solution which may readily be employed by those judges who favour the purposive route to statutory interpretation. For those who seek a literal meaning however the impossibility of renewal may be viewed as the disposal of an issue rather than the disposal of the application.

6.5 FOLLOWING THE ORDER

6.5.1 Revocation

Once the tenancy is granted by the court, the tenant is given an opportunity to reconsider. Section 36(2) allows the tenant, within 14 days of the order, to apply to the court for revocation of the grant. In such a case, the court has no option but to accede to the tenant's application. The purpose of this procedure is to ensure that the tenant is not bound to accept a new lease on terms dictated by the court. This is, of course, in contrast to a tenancy which has been agreed with the landlord under s.28 from which the tenant has no right to withdraw. If more than one tenancy has been granted by the court, the tenant has the choice to apply for revocation of any or all of those tenancies.

Following revocation, s.36(2) provides that the current tenancy continues for any such period as the parties agree or, in default, at least until final disposal for the purposes of s.64 or, exceeding that time, for as long as the court deems necessary so as to allow the landlord a reasonable opportunity to re-let or otherwise dispose of the property. If the tenant is appealing against part of the order, it is advisable that the application for revocation is made (within the statutory time frame), but adjourned until the outcome of the appeal is known.

6.5.2 Costs

As to costs of the proceedings, s.38(1) renders void any advance agreement that the tenant pay the costs of the landlord. As is usual, costs remain at the discretion of the court and are likely to follow the event (e.g. if the landlord unsuccessfully opposes the grant of a new lease, costs are likely to be awarded against that landlord). This working presumption can be rebutted however in the light of the parties' conduct, for example, where the successful party had unreasonably refused an offer, raised unjustifiable points or engaged in misconduct or time wasting activities. In *MBI Inc* v. *Riminex Investments SA* [2002] EWHC 2856, the landlord had held out for terms that were deemed by the court to be unreasonable. As a result, it had to pay part of the tenant's costs.

Any 'without prejudice' offers should therefore be subject to the caveat that they can be brought before a judge when dealing with the issue of costs. Revocation does not, of itself, affect any order for costs made, but the court can, if it thinks fit, cancel or vary any such order. If no order for costs had previously been made, s.36(3) allows the court to make an award taking into account the tenant's actions. In *Rom Tyre & Accessories Ltd* v. *Crawford Street Properties Ltd* (1966) 197 EG 565, a tenant who exercised the right to revoke was ordered to pay the landlord's costs, including those connected with the revocation.

6.5.3 Executing the new lease

If there is no revocation and subject to contrary agreement, s.36(1) provides that the competent landlord must execute, and the tenant must accept, the new lease on the terms agreed or determined by the court. If required by the landlord, the tenant is obliged to execute a counterpart or duplicate of the lease. The Act does not stipulate at what date the lease or counterpart must be executed, but this is an understandable omission as the current tenancy will be prolonged under s.64 until after the final disposal of any appeals. Consequently, there is no obligation to comply with the order until the commencement date for the new lease.

The Act is silent as to what redress is available for non-compliance with s.36(1). Nevertheless, it is clear that a refusal would amount to contempt of court and that the court would be able to enforce the order by executing the lease (or counterpart) itself. In this way, the order for a new lease would be regarded as akin to the court ordering specific performance of a contract to grant a lease.

6.6 THE EFFECT ON REVERSIONERS

6.6.1 Binding superior landlords

The court is given the express power to order so-called reversionary leases. Under Sched. 6 to the 1954 Act, the court may grant a new tenancy under the renewal scheme which, whether by agreement or otherwise, extends beyond the date that the immediate landlord's interest comes to an end. This is achieved by creating such reversionary tenancies as may be necessary to secure the grant of the new lease and to ensure that what the Act refers to as the 'inferior tenancy' may be prolonged beyond the term of a superior tenancy. By way of a simple example, X (the head tenant) has three years remaining under a lease not protected by the 1954 Act. X's sub-tenant, Y, obtains a statutory renewal for a full 15-year term. The court must order two leases: one for three years to be granted immediately by the current competent landlord (X); and one for 12 years to be granted when the first lease ends by the next landlord able to grant such a term (Z). These two leases are however deemed to comprise a single 15-year term and no continuation rights emerge at the end of the first tenancy.

Any agreement as to the grant or terms of the new lease made by the competent landlord binds any intervening mesne landlord. A competent landlord cannot however agree for a new tenancy to extend beyond the remainder of its own lease without the consent of all superior landlords. Accordingly, in the above example, X could not agree to grant Y a new lease beyond the remaining three years of its term without the consent of Z.

6.6.2 Provisions as to reversions

By virtue of s.69(1), the protection of the 1954 Act extends to a sub-tenant as to any other tenant. It is therefore possible that under the Act a sub-tenancy can be continued beyond, or a reversionary lease granted to the sub-tenant which subsists beyond, the termination of the head lease. At common law, this would be impossible because the sub-tenancy would fall with the head lease and, in any event, the rules of privity of contract and estate would render the covenants in the sub-tenancy unenforceable by or against the head lessor. In order to overcome these difficulties, s.65 contains a series of facilitating, albeit complex, provisions. In essence, it ensures that when the interest of an intermediate landlord comes to an end, the interest of the next superior landlord shall be deemed to be the reversion. This result is engineered in a variety of ways.

First, and for as long as it subsists, the superior tenancy is preserved and deemed to be an interest in reversion expectant (immediately expectant if no intermediate tenancy exists) upon the termination of the inferior tenancy (s.65(1)). This is so even though the sub-tenancy will continue beyond it. As

141

a result of this fiction, and while the head tenancy and the sub-tenancy exist, both parties to the sub-lease remain able to sue and to be sued on the covenants.

Secondly, when the immediate superior tenancy ends, the sub-tenancy becomes a tenancy held directly under the superior landlord next in the chain (s.65(2)). This landlord has no option other than to accept this, perhaps unwanted, change of status and, of course, will now be bound by the terms of a sub-lease negotiated by others. This simply could not occur at common law.

Thirdly, if a sub-tenancy extends beyond the date on which a lease of the reversion, granted by the landlord, is to commence, the latter takes effect subject to the former, including the sub-tenant's renewal rights (s.65(3)).

Finally, if the statutory renewal is to commence either on the same date or after a landlord's lease of the reversion will take effect, the reversionary lease takes subject to the new tenancy and the new tenant enjoys the right to possession (s.65(4)). Such a reversionary lease is classed an interest expectant on the termination of the renewed tenancy.

CHAPTER 7

Interim rent

Contents

- Introduction
- The applicant
- The application
- Period of payment
- A discretionary award
- Calculation of the interim rent: the old rent rules
- Calculation of the interim rent: the new rent rules

7.1 INTRODUCTION

The facility of an interim rent was created by the Law of Property Act 1969 with the insertion of s.24A into the Landlord and Tenant Act 1954. In general terms, the facility is designed to offer the landlord much needed protection from financial disadvantage during the continuation period between the end of the contractual tenancy and the commencement of a new lease. It is therefore a bridging device which caters for a variation of the former contractual rent until the time when, on renewal, a market rent becomes payable. The interim rent, therefore, constitutes a counterweight to the tenant's right to a continuation tenancy under s.24(1). Accordingly, no interim rent is available when the tenancy is being continued under s.28 in circumstances where renewal has been agreed and is to commence at a future date.

There were two reasons for the introduction of the interim rent. First, experience showed that tenants would engage in delaying tactics so as to keep the continuation tenancy (and, of course, the old rent) alive for as long as possible. Secondly, the United Kingdom had awoken to the effects of an inflationary economy and its effect on rental values. It is to be appreciated that the use of rent review clauses on a wide scale emerged towards the end of the 1960s. The system has long proved deficient and has been the subject of some overhaul by the Regulatory Reform (Business Tenancies) (England and Wales) Order 2003, SI 2003/3096. As will become clear, there remain problems and defects with the revamped interim rent machinery.

7.1.1 Mischief and manipulation

As initially enacted, the 1954 Act provided that, during a s.24 continuation, the original contractual terms (other than those concerning termination) were to be preserved. This ensured that the contractual rent payable to the landlord was frozen until either the continuation tenancy was ended or a new lease came into being. The temptation was offered to the tenant to drag out proceedings so as to engineer a pecuniary advantage over the landlord. The financial incentive could prove considerable. In *Re No. 88, High Road, Kilburn* [1959] 1 All ER 527, for example, the original rent was increased twelve-fold on the order of a new tenancy. The problem was exacerbated for landlords because it was way too easy for the tenant to manipulate the renewal provisions. As Harman J. acknowledged in *Espresso Coffee Machine Co. Ltd* v. *Guardian Assurance Co Ltd* [1958] 1 WLR 900 at 903, a substantial time can elapse 'before every legal artifice is exhausted . . . That may not be a very admirable attitude, but it is one which the law entitled the tenants to take up, and they unblushingly do so'. Although the widely held view was that this produced manifest injustice, the courts felt powerless to assist the landlord. As Wynn-Parry J. admitted in *Re No. 88 High Road, Kilburn* [1959] 1 All ER 527, 'I consider that the result at which I am compelled to arrive is one which is unjust to landlords, but I cannot mitigate that injustice as regards rent'. The court did however seek to mitigate the hardship by ordering a lease of shorter duration than that sought by the tenant.

The most effective course for a tenant to pursue, in order to prolong the life of a continuation tenancy, is to enter an appeal against the decision of the court of first instance. The appeal could relate to the terms of the new lease ordered or the denial of a renewal. By virtue of s.64, a continuation tenancy survives until the end of three months subsequent to the final disposal of the tenant's application. One aim of this provision is to give the tenant a reasonable period within which to find alternative premises, following an unsuccessful application for a new lease on acceptable terms. As final disposal occurs when all proceedings (including any appeal) have been determined and any time for further appeal has expired, the tenant may have much to gain by taking a matter to appeal even when there is no reasonable prospect of that appeal being successful. The appeal might then be abandoned at the last moment and the three-month period of grace will run from the date of that discontinuance. In *Re Sunlight House* (1959) *The Times*, 4 February, the tenant benefited to the tune of £50,000 from manipulating s.64 and delaying the date for final disposal of its application. Although the result may purely be to allow the tenant to prolong the benefit of a low rent, the wording of s.64 is unambiguous and its consequences, seemingly, unavoidable.

An alternative avenue for the tenant to follow, so as to add to the life of the continuation tenancy, is afforded by s.36(2). This enables a tenant who has successfully fought for a new tenancy (possibly one which had in truth never been wanted) to apply to the court within 14 days of its grant for the revocation of that tenancy. Indeed, this occurred in *Re No. 88 High Road, Kilburn* [1959] 1 All ER 527. The tenant is, thereby, given a limited 'cooling off' period within which to decline the renewal. Although the tenant may face an order for costs, as demonstrated in *Rom Tyre & Accessories Ltd* v. *Crawford Street Properties* (1966) 197 EG 565, the court enjoys no power to refuse the application for revocation. Following the order for revocation, s.36(2) ensures that the continuation tenancy subsists for such period as the parties may agree or, in default of agreement, for so long as the court deems reasonable. As it is not a continuation under s.24(1), no interim rent can be applied for during this period of extension. Any existing interim rent will however continue in operation.

Both these statutory provisions enjoy a valid and vital function within the statutory scheme, but it is clear that in 1954 Parliament could not have foreseen the possibility of inflating rents and the scope for tenants to exploit the machinery simply for financial gain. As Wynn-Parry J. admitted in *Re No. 88 High Road, Kilburn* [1959] 1 All ER 527, 'It is not for me to speculate whether the legislature intended as a matter of policy what I hold to have been brought about by these sections or whether there has been some mistake . . . but whether it be a matter of policy or a matter of mistake, I can find no way of giving any other construction to these sections than that which I have given'.

7.1.2 Parliamentary response

There is still little that can be done to prevent tenants utilising the statutory scheme as set out above in order to extend artificially the duration of their continuation tenancies. Instead, reform focused upon how to deter tenants from manipulating the system solely for financial profit. By virtue of the Law of Property Act 1969, and following the recommendation of the Law Commission Report (1969), the 1954 Act was amended. The insertion of s.24A gave the landlord the right to apply for an interim rent during the continuation tenancy. The interim rent was, essentially, the rent which the court decides is reasonable for the tenant to pay while the old tenancy is being continued, in substitution for the historic, contractual rent. This rent was, thereby, intended to be of lesser amount than the market rent which would be awarded on the grant of a new lease. Unfortunately, the system proved to be so complex that even Megarry J. in *English Exporters* v. *Eldonwall* [1973] Ch 415 found the law to be 'difficult and puzzling' and admitted 'to having groped my way to a conclusion ... for reasons which defy any detailed analysis ...'. The system was to prove unsatisfactory on several fronts:

- it was of limited availability;
- it was heavily dependent upon the vagaries of judicial discretion in both its grant and its calculation;
- it was based upon unrealistic comparables;
- it was triggered only following the service of a landlord's s.25 notice or a tenant's s.26 request;
- it was necessary that the landlord make an application for an interim rent to be awarded;
- it was not usually backdated to the end of the contractual lease.

As mentioned above, the 2003 Order has made some key reforms to the interim rent facility. First, is that it has taken some (albeit small) steps to minimise the scope for delay. It was previously the case that the interim rent could be backdated only to the 'termination date' set out in the s.25 notice or s.26 request. It was therefore a simple ploy for the tenant to pre-empt the landlord and serve a s.26 request which stated the latest termination date possible (i.e. 12 months hence). In this way, the earliest date being six months hence, the tenant could steal an extra half-year immune from an interim rent. This tactic has now been rendered redundant as s.24(B)(2), (3) provides that the interim rent is now payable from the earliest date that could have been specified in the notice or request (i.e. six months). This, of course, does nothing to discourage delay by the tenant prior to the service of the renewal documentation.

Secondly, the 2003 Order has now extended to tenants the right to apply for an interim rent. This is contained in s.24(A)(1)(b) and aims to give the impression that tenants and landlords are treated even-handedly for these purposes. It also signals that interim rents can go down as well as up. As the usual trend is towards rising rents, this extension is however destined to achieve little or nothing of practical value for tenants.

Thirdly, the application for an interim rent can be made any time after the service of a s.25 notice or s.26 request. It is not necessary to wait until an application for a new lease or a termination order is made.

Fourthly, different rules as to calculating the interim rent are imposed when, on the service of the s.25 notice or s.26 request, the tenant occupied the whole of the demised premises for the purposes of its business; the landlord has stated in its s.25 notice that it does not oppose renewal or has failed to serve a s.26(6) counter notice stating opposition; and the landlord has now granted (whether by agreement or at the order of the court) a new tenancy of the whole of the property to the tenant. These new rules operate to the advantage of the landlord in that the interim rent is geared more to market values than the old rules which provided a heavy discount in the tenant's favour. The old rules apply by default when the conditions for the new rules are not satisfied (e.g. where the landlord opposes a new lease).

7.2 THE APPLICANT

The interim rent facility was, until the 2003 Order, available only to the 'competent landlord'. This character is defined in s.44 of and Sched. 6 to the 1954 Act. This means that other landlords (e.g. an immediate landlord who does not qualify as 'competent') have no such right. This somewhat awkward distinction between landlords 'competent' and landlords 'immediate' is one drawn throughout Part II of the Act. Although the same body may be both, where sub-leases have been created this is not necessarily the case. As shown in Chapter 2, the 'immediate landlord' is the person who granted the interest to the tenant/sub-tenant, whereas the identity of the 'competent landlord' is more difficult to discern. This is because 'competency' for these purposes is determined on a temporal level.

Section 44(1)(*a*), (*b*) defines the 'competent landlord' as the person who is either a mesne landlord whose lease will not end for at least 14 months or, if none, the freeholder. Even a lessor under a tenancy by estoppel is entitled to apply for an interim rent (*Bell* v. *General Fire and Life Assurance Corporation Ltd* [1998] 17 EG 144). The policy underlying this somewhat arbitrary and inelegant distinction is that the landlord with less than 14 months remaining will not be sufficiently equipped to make long-term decisions about the termination and renewal of sub-tenancies. In that context, the distinction may have the hallmark of common sense, but whether it should extend to the interim rent machinery is questionable. Indeed, the Law Commission in its (1998) Working Paper accepted that, as regards the interim rent, the restrictions upon availability were both anomalous and problematic. It envisaged no insurmountable difficulties in allowing a landlord to make an application regardless of whether or not that landlord satisfied the definition of 'competent', but this view was not to be echoed in the Commission's subsequent Report and has never been pursued since. Indeed, the 2003 Order makes only one alteration to the definition of the competent landlord and this concerns so-called split reversions. Section 44(1A) makes it clear that the reference to the competent landlord shall, where different persons own such different parts of the property, be a reference to all those persons collectively.

As early as 1988, in its Working Paper the Law Commission saw no objections to the statutory right to apply for an interim rent being extended to the tenant. Admittedly, as the usual trend is towards rising rents, this will normally have little practical value, but as the Law Commission acknowledged it would at least 'demonstrate the even-handedness of the law'. The original provisions overlooked entirely the depressive effect of an economic recession on rental values and were firmly rooted in the traditional wisdom that commercial rents would invariably rise. Accordingly, the system was not designed to cater for a downward movement in market values. Although in *Fawke* v. *Viscount Chelsea* [1979] 3 All ER 568 Goff L.J. felt that it would be possible for the court to order a reduced rent where there had been a fall in property prices or, in special cases, a breach by the landlord of repairing covenant, this was to remain an untested jurisdiction. It was also an unsatisfactory state of affairs as, if a decrease was a likely consequence, no right-minded landlord would be prepared to make or, if made, continue with an application.

The only fair and sensible option was to extend to the tenant the right to apply for an interim rent. Section 24A(1) now provides that either the competent landlord or the tenant may make an application to determine an interim rent. The primary restriction is imposed by s.24A(2) and this prevents a party making an application if the other has already made an application and it has not been withdrawn.

7.2.1 The problem with sub-lettings

Under the existing law, potential injustice can still arise because of the artificial distinction between an immediate landlord and a competent landlord. This is pertinent where the premises have been sub-let in whole or part. If the competent landlord and the immediate landlord are not the same individual, there is no incentive for an application for an interim rent to be made against the sub-tenant. The competent landlord will have nothing to gain from initiating the procedure. Only the immediate landlord would benefit and yet that person remains disentitled from commencing proceedings under s.24A. The situation might also arise where the competent landlord applies for an interim rent against the head lessee, but the head lessee is unable to apply for an interim rent against the sub-tenant. On an increase of the head lessee's rent, the sub-tenant would be under no obligation to pay an extra amount. The mesne landlord would be out of pocket to the extent that the increased rent is attributable to the part sub-let. As is clear from *Benedictus* v. *Jalaram Ltd* (1989) 58 P & CR 330, this problem does not occur when the whole of the premises are sub-let. The head lessee would then be outside the ambit of the Act and no interim rent application could be entertained against him.

The stance taken by the law reformers is that, although the sub-letting of business premises is common, in reality very few problems are experienced by intermediate landlords. Hence, to allow any landlord to apply for an interim rent would be to encourage a proliferation of negotiations and court applications and this is viewed as an undesirable consequence.

Some added protection for the intermediate landlord is to be found in s.24D(2)(*b*) which, while dealing only with the calculation of an interim rent under the old rules, requires that the court is to have regard to the rent payable under any sub-tenancy of any part of the property. For reasons which will become clear, this does not have relevance to tenancies which fall within the new interim rent rules.

7.3   THE APPLICATION

Section 24A(1)(*a*), (*b*) makes it necessary that an express application for an interim rent be made and moreover that it be made only subsequent to the service of a landlord's s.25 termination notice or a tenant's s.26 request for a new lease. The earliest date that an application can be made is the date on which such renewal documentation is served. There is no need to wait until a renewal/termination application is made to the court. The latest date on which an application can be entertained is prescribed by s.24A(3) as no more than six months after the termination of the relevant tenancy, that is, the termination of the continuation tenancy. This date will be the date specified in the renewal documentation or, if an application to court is made, the date of final disposal as calculated under s.64. If the parties agree an extension of time limits before a renewal or termination application to court is made under the auspices of s.29B, the relevant termination date will be at the end of the agreed period (s.29B(4)).

Since the Courts and Legal Services Act 1990, the jurisdiction of the county court in these matters is not limited by rateable values. As the county court now shares a concurrent jurisdiction with the High Court, s.63(2) of the 1954 Act accepts the application can be made in either court. Most applications will however be made in the county court. There is, as regards an interim rent application, a unified procedure to be adopted in both the county court and the High Court. As regards both courts, the application may be made by claim form or it may arise in the course of the renewal/termination proceedings. As regards the latter course, the proceedings are regarded as having been commenced at the date of the other party's answer/reply. If it is not possible for both applications to be heard together, it will become necessary for a separate interim rent hearing to occur. This hearing will usually be in private.

In circumstances where the tenant has not applied for a new lease, the landlord must, of course, seek an interim rent by issuing a separate claim form. The claim form has to be served within four months of its issue or six months if service occurs outside the jurisdiction (CPR, r.7.5(2), (3)). The court has the power to extend the time for service under CPR, r.7.6(1)–(4).

Part 56 and PD56 of the CPR deal with landlord and tenant claims. Where proceedings for the grant of a new lease or the termination of an existing tenancy have already been commenced, PD56, paras. 3.14–3.17 require that the claim for an interim rent is to be made in those proceedings. It will be made by the claim form itself (N208), the acknowledgement of service or defence (if any) or by way of an ordinary procedural application

149

under Part 23 of the CPR. The latter is appropriate when the court has ordered a renewal and an interim rent under s.24C (i.e. under the new rules), but subsequently the tenant declines the renewal under s.36(2) or both parties have agreed not to act on the order. Either party can then apply for the fresh determination of an interim rent under the old rules by a Part 23 application to the court where the claim started.

If no proceedings have been commenced, or where such proceedings have already been disposed of, the application for an interim rent is to be made under the alternative, stand-alone procedure in Part 8 of the CPR. The claim form (N208) must then, by virtue of PD56, para. 3.19, include details of:

- the property to which the claim relates;
- the particulars of the relevant tenancy, including the date, duration, parties and the current rent;
- the s.25 notice served by the landlord or the s.26 request served by the tenant where relevant, the date and mode of termination of the relevant tenancy;
- if the landlord has granted a new lease to the tenant, the particulars of the new tenancy. If s.24C(2) applies, but the applicant seeks an interim rent different from the market rent of the new lease, the particulars and matters relied on to justify this exceptional treatment must be provided. This departure from the normal evaluation under the new rules is catered for in s.24C(3).

In practice, a separate claim for an interim rent is undesirable because of the added expense and time involved. Such a step might be appropriate where, for example, the landlord seeks to heighten pressure upon the tenant to quit the premises. As acknowledged by the Court of Appeal in *Homeville Estates Ltd v. Sams* (1976) 243 EG 827, it is usually prejudicial to a tenant if the interim rent is fixed before the terms of the new tenancy. It is however more usual and convenient for the issue of an interim rent to be dealt with at the same time as the tenant's claim for a new lease. Indeed, this is the practice that will be adopted under the new interim rent rules contained in s.24C.

It is interesting to note that, in its 1992 Report, the Law Commission recommended the abolition of the right to make a separate application. Instead, it concluded that the claim for an interim rent should be heard only in the course of proceedings. The underlying rationale was to reduce the number of applications made to the courts. The recommendation was also to be viewed in the light of the additional recommendation that landlords should be able to initiate renewal/termination proceedings under the 1954 Act. Although the latter is now enshrined within s.24(1), the former recommendation never made it to the statute book.

As the application for an interim rent is in the nature of a counter claim, it is unaffected by the discontinuance of the action for a renewal/termination. It is a distinct claim independent of the main proceedings. This was demonstrated by Stephenson L.J. in *Michael Kramer & Co.* v. *Airways Pension Fund Trustees Ltd* (1976) 246 EG 911. Although his reference is to the old law, the sentiment still applies to the new:

> It must be treated separately, and it cannot be discontinued simply by the discontinuance of the . . . proceedings. However described, and whatever its form, the . . . application is in substance an originating application. However labelled, it originates, or starts, or initiates a claim, in some sense countering the tenant's application though affording no defence to it, and has its own distinct and separate life . . .

This explains why it has always been possible for the application to be entertained even after the order for a new lease is made.

If however the proceedings are adjourned, it is up to the applicant to keep the claim alive and to produce appropriate evidence before the court. This was demonstrated in *Arora* v. *Bose* (1998) 76 P & CR D 1 where the landlord's application for an interim rent was adjourned and never formally restored. At the renewal hearing, some four years later, it was held too late for the landlord to resuscitate the application.

It is to be appreciated that the assignment of the reversion does not prevent the new landlord (albeit acquiring title after the application for an interim rent is made) benefiting from, or being detrimentally affected by, those proceedings. The tenancy continues and the rent continues to be payable. If the assignor and assignee cannot agree, say, as to who is to receive the benefit of the order, this is a matter for them to litigate amongst themselves. It does not concern the court's jurisdiction under s.24A. The award of an interim rent is therefore not a money order payable by a party, it is simply an order for the determination of rent payable under the tenancy. As such, the rent concerns particular premises and not a particular person. Lawton L.J. explained in *Bloomfield* v. *Ashwright Ltd* (1983) 47 P & CR 78, 'The ownership of the reversion to the premises may pass from one person to another for various reasons, but when there is such a transfer the tenancy goes on and the rent which is payable in respect of the tenancy continues to be payable. The court is concerned with determining that which is to be paid for the tenancy'.

This means also that if the tenant appeals against the interim rent, the landlord cannot levy distress until the appeal is resolved. It was made clear in *Eren* v. *Tranmac* [1997] 2 EGLR 211 that, as an interim rent is liable to be reduced on appeal, there is no certainty as to what sum could be the subject of distraint.

7.3.1 Case for automatic entitlement

In its 1988 Working Paper, the Law Commission flirted briefly with the idea of abandoning the need to make an express application to the court.

Automatic entitlement to an interim rent was viewed as an alternative, but not favoured. It was however conceded that automatic entitlement would reduce the discretion of the court while circumventing any trap for the ill-advised. Two justifications for maintaining the status quo were offered in the Working Paper. First, automatic entitlement would encourage requests for a rent increase by landlords who would not otherwise bother. Secondly, it would deprive tenants of a positive warning that a rent increase may be on the way. The assumption that such a warning is necessary is not beyond challenge. Indeed, the sentiment was not shared by Nourse L.J. in *French* v. *Commercial Union Life Assurance Plc* [1993] 1 EGLR 113 when he concluded that the shock of an increased rent occurs irrespective of whether the tenant had been forewarned or not. The Court of Appeal was more concerned with the shock to the tenant's pocket than the shock to the tenant's senses. The Law Commission refused the opportunity to examine the argument for change in any greater depth and, in its subsequent Report, declined to investigate the matter further. The case for automatic entitlement may have the hallmark of common sense, but it does not currently enjoy a sponsor.

7.4 PERIOD OF PAYMENT

Prior to the changes brought about by the 2003 Order, the interim rent was payable from either the termination date set out in, as appropriate, the s.25 notice or the s.26 request or, if later, the date that the interim rent proceedings were commenced (that is, when the application for an interim rent is issued by the court). This has now changed and the interim rent is backdated to the 'appropriate date', that is the earliest termination date that could have been specified in the renewal documentation (i.e. six months – s.24B(2), (3)). The interim rent has always been payable until the termination of the continuation tenancy (s.24A(1)).

The commencement date for the interim rent is not normally the day that the original lease ends. In order to achieve this end, it is necessary that the service of the renewal documentation be synchronised with the termination of the contractual lease. Usually, the tenant will enjoy a period of grace, potentially spanning a considerable period of time, free from any rental increase. The service of the renewal documentation, of course, will elicit crucial information as to whether the landlord will oppose a new lease and thereby govern whether the old interim rent rules or the new interim rent rules will operate. The employment of the s.25 notice and s.26 request in such circumstances is therefore understandable. Nevertheless, it is harder to justify why the rent can be backdated only to six months following the service of the renewal documentation. It is surely unrealistic to limit the provisions only to a delay which occurs during the period after such notices have been served. The interim rent provisions, thereby, ignore the period between the end of the contractual term and the initiation of the termination procedures. In view of the fact that the new interim rent rules are designed to encourage a landlord to negotiate a renewal, it is ironic that such negotiations will tend to postpone the date from which the increased rent becomes payable.

7.5 A DISCRETIONARY AWARD

Within the interim rent machinery there exist two distinct means through which the judge must enter what Goulding J. called, 'the realm of pure discretion where it is hardest to condense in words the dialogue of the intracranial jury room . . .'. First, it is at the discretion of the court whether an interim rent should be ordered. Section 24A(1) provides that the landlord or tenant of a tenancy to which this Part of the Act applies may apply to the court to determine a rent 'and the court may order payment of an interim rent'. Secondly, as will become clear, the calculation of an interim rent under the old interim rent rules involves the exercise of much discretion on the part of the judge.

Issues as to whether such discretions are appropriate or necessary components of the system are seldom considered. It was established by Megarry J. in *English Exporters* v. *Eldonwall Ltd* [1973] Ch 415 that there is no obligation on the court to set an interim rent and that s.24A(1) is merely permissive in nature. It has however become the accepted and general rule that the discretion will normally be exercised in favour of the landlord. Indeed, it could be argued that this has now, tacitly, been elevated to a presumption which, unless rebutted by the tenant, will prevail. The circumstances in which any such presumption can be defeated moreover remain vague. As Lawton L.J. admitted in *Bloomfield* v. *Ashwright* (1983) 47 P & CR 78, 'There may be circumstances when it would be unjust to make a tenant pay an interim rent. I find it myself difficult to imagine such circumstances, but no doubt others with a more fertile imagination than I have can do so'. In *English Exporters* v. *Eldonwall Ltd* [1973] 1 Ch 423 Megarry J. was prepared to venture into the realms of speculation, 'Nevertheless, there may be many cases in which proceedings for the fixing of an interim rent might be unreasonable or even oppressive. Thus the gap between the rent being paid and the rent sought by the landlord may be so small; or the proceedings may have marched on apace, so that the period for which any interim rent could operate would be trivial'.

Although the rhetoric of Megarry J. is seductive, the justification for persevering with this brand of judicial discretion is based on a dubious foundation. The assumption that there might be 'many cases' where an interim rent is 'unreasonable' or 'oppressive' is one incapable of substantiation. Certainly, it is arguable that the illustrations provided by Megarry J. do not, in any event, offend 'reasonableness' or constitute 'oppression'. Megarry J. however added two further justifications. First, the tenant has no statutory escape route, akin to s.36(2), from a continuation tenancy. This argument has little force in that s.27 (especially in its newly amended form) offers the tenant an alternative and effective escape route. Secondly, he felt that the discretion was needed in case it was the landlord who delays proceedings under the 1954 Act. This contention is also hollow in that the tenant has never been tied to a continuation tenancy and, following the 2003 Order, the tenant can apply for an interim rent to be determined.

As the primary purpose of s.24A(1) is to protect the financial interests of the parties, particularly those of the landlord, the alleged benefits of retaining judicial discretion here are greatly outweighed by the disadvantage of maintaining a procedural hurdle which if not taken, or taken late, could prove costly. In the context where the court will rarely (if at all) refuse a party's application, the filter can be seen to achieve little and, for practical purposes, to be unnecessary.

7.6 CALCULATION OF THE INTERIM RENT: THE OLD RENT RULES

As explained above, the major reform of the interim rent machinery is to be found in the two alternative systems of rental calculation that now operate. These may for convenience be called the 'old rules' and the 'new rules'. Subject to limited exceptions, the latter set applies where a new tenancy of the whole premises has been granted and the landlord has not opposed renewal (s.24C(1)). In all cases that fall outside the provisions of s.24C, the old rules still apply (s.24D).

Under the old rules the interim rent was payable from the date it was ordered and continued to be payable until final disposal of the proceedings under s.64. As to the quantum of the interim rent under the old rules, the courts have experienced many problems. The difficulties arise from the some-what obscure wording of what is now s.24D and, in particular, its uneasy interaction with s.34. As discussed in Chapter 10, s.34(1) empowers the court to determine a rent on renewal which 'having regard to the terms of the tenancy (other than those relating to rent) the holding might reasonably be expected to be let in the open market by a willing lessor'. It is helpful to outline the ingredients of the statutory formula through which the interim rent is to be assessed:

- account must be taken of the calculus provided within s.34(1), (2) and these provisions applied as if the court is setting a rent under a hypothetical yearly tenancy of the whole property (s.24D(2));
- regard must be had to the rent payable under the existing tenancy (s.24D(2)(a));
- regard must be had to the rent payable under any sub-tenancy of part of the property (s.24D(2)(b)). This is designed primarily to prevent unfair-

ness on an intermediate tenant. Although the Law Commission accepted in its 1992 Report that it is not possible to devise a single rule to cover all cases, 'The matter is, nevertheless, something which should be taken into account';

- the court has to determine a rent which it would be reasonable for the tenant to pay (s.24D(1)). In *Charles Follett Ltd* v. *Cabtell Investments* (1988) 55 P & CR 36, Nourse L.J. concluded that this latter condition imposed what could validly be described as a 'reasonable rent'.

7.6.1 Simple view

The initial occasion on which the court had the opportunity to unravel this curious and complex formula fell to Stamp J. in *Regis Property Co Ltd* v. *Lewis & Peat Ltd* [1970] 1 Ch 695. In a reserved judgment, Stamp J. gave short shrift to arguments that s.24A presented the court with an indefinite and unguided discretion as to what rent was reasonable for the tenant to pay. If it were so, he concluded, 'the rent will in the end be fixed by the length of the judge's foot'. His approach was that the legislature, having set out a formula, could not have 'intended to enable the court to depart from it to an unspecified and arbitrary extent'. Guided by this appealing judicial pragmatism, it was held that the calculation of an interim rent was a single, straightforward operation. The machinery of s.34(1), (2) was to be applied in its normal manner modified only by the concession that the existing rent could be a factor in the assessment. As s.34 was otherwise to be applied to the existing tenancy as if it were a yearly tenancy, the weight given to the existing rent was not such as to provide the tenant with a cushion against a steep rent increase. Stamp J. explained:

> if the existing terms as to rent throw no light on the rent at which the holding might reasonably be expected to be let under a tenancy from year to year, you are no more bound to take the actual rent into account as a relevant element in determining the rent than you would an irrelevant covenant . . . Finding that some of the terms of the existing tenancy and the existing rent do not on the facts of a particular case assist you in determining what the interim rent ought to be, you ignore them.

According to this view, therefore, the existing rent was of evidential value only. Once the valuation exercise under s.34 was complete, the issue was closed and there was to be no modification by reference to 'reasonable' or the existing rent. The attraction of this approach is that it provides greater certainty and is more in accordance with the mischief underlying the existence of the interim rent provisions. Unfortunately, as demonstrated in *English Exporters* v. *Eldonwall Ltd* [1973] Ch 415, it was also the wrong approach to be adopted.

7.6.2 Correct approach

This simplicity of approach did not appeal to the Megarry J. in *English Exporters* v. *Eldonwall Ltd* [1973] Ch 415. Megarry J. did not accept that such an elaborate formula could be reduced to such a convenient and straightforward prescription. In holding that the court had to calculate the market rent of a notional yearly tenancy, identify the existing rent and, aided by the concept of reasonableness, determine the interim rent at some level between those figures, he was critical of the *Regis* approach. Megarry J.'s analysis in the *English Exporters* case was to set the template for future decisions. The following points can be distilled from this influential judgment.

First, the conclusion drawn in *Regis* that what is now s.24D was not concerned with rent under a new tenancy, but with a rent to be paid under an existing tenancy was viewed as wrong, giving 'scant weight' to the wording of that section. The interpretation favoured by Megarry J. was that, once the market rent of the hypothetical annual tenancy had been assessed under s.34, regard must, in all cases, be had to the existing rent under the continuation tenancy. This regard is a separate and independent requirement. It does not however mean that the market rent and the existing rent are to be given equal weight, rather it is a process 'of applying one factor, namely, the market rent, and, where appropriate, suitably tempering it by reference to the existing rent'. The idea that s.24D and s.34 could be applied, within one operation, to the existing tenancy was rejected. The statutory provisions spoke of two different tenancies and two different calculations.

Secondly, the requirement that the interim rent be one which is reasonable for the tenant to pay, did not give the court a roving commission to consider every relevant fact. It merely provided 'for the rent that it would be reasonable for the tenant to pay to be worked out in a particular way, namely, by taking the market rent and then having regard to the existing rent; and that is all'. As apparent from *Harwood* v. *Borough of Reigate & Banstead* (1982) 43 P & CR 336, the court must take into account all relevant circumstances in a broad and commonsense fashion, giving such weight as it thinks fit to the various factors, in order to reach a right and fair conclusion. It is to be appreciated that, despite the original recommendation of the Law Commission in its 1969 Report, the Act does not allude to a 'fair rent' and, accordingly, the court is precluded from considering the interests of the landlord. As Lawton L.J. commented in *Bloomfield* v. *Ashwright* (1983) 47 P & CR 78, 'whether or not a particular landlord is rich or poor, flush with money or nearly impoverished is irrelevant'. Instead, the wording focuses solely upon the tenant who has to pay the rent. In this way, Megarry J. argued that the restrictive formula now contained in s.24D undermined the 'length of the judge's foot' criticism. In the light of subsequent cases, this assertion appears little more than ill-founded optimism. Megarry J.'s interpretation clearly views the old rent as a depressive factor and does not cater for the situation where the market rent is valued at less than the old contractual rent. In the circumstances that the old rent merely provides a cushion for the tenant, the landlord would not be able to rely on the higher figure in order to produce an interim rent above the market value.

Thirdly, the elaboration of the language used by Parliament must be for some purpose. If a market value was to be fixed (which is, essentially, what occurred in *Regis*), then the complex formula within s.24D would stand redundant. Megarry J. could not accept that the legislature would go to such elaborate lengths for nothing when it could more simply have allowed the permanent rent under a new tenancy to be backdated or the interim rent to be calculated purely on the basis of s.34.

Finally, the conclusion that the award of an interim rent is at the discretion of the court emphasises that s.24D is not designed to provide a rigid valuation according to market values. As Megarry J. explained, 'If this were not so, the discretion would have to be exercised on the footing that the court must either refuse to fix an interim rent at all, and so leave the existing rent to continue, or else an interim rent at full market value, with no intermediate rent possible. To me s.24A does not read as if it were intended to provide for all or nothing'. Accordingly, Parliament was seen as offering a cushion for the tenant with the extent of that temperance being decided on the facts of each case. This view does however appear to gloss over the additional subsidy afforded by the valuation being of a hypothetical tenancy and not the existing lease.

7.6.3 Practical consequences

The divergence of statutory interpretation does not, necessarily, ensure a different outcome to the case according to which construction is followed. The alternative views are, indeed, capable of producing disparate results, but the likelihood of that occurring in practice may not be as great as might be feared. It should not be overlooked that *Regis* recognised that the existing rent was an evidential factor to be taken on board where relevant. The *English Exporters* case, while recognising that the contractual rent must always be looked at, did not set down any rule other than that, where appropriate, the existing rent can temper the market valuation under s.34. In many cases, the 'evidential factor' will govern the discretion of the court and produce either a cushion for the tenant or no discount on this basis. The two routes, therefore, lead towards a similar destination. As Goff L.J. explained in *Fawke* v. *Viscount Chelsea* [1979] 3 All ER 568:

> In the result, therefore, both agreed, though for different reasons, that the court and the expert witnesses appearing before it should have regard to the existing rent if it has evidentiary value, but the difference between them lies in Stamp J.'s view that, apart from that, it is irrelevant and the matter ends with the valuation,

whereas in Megarry J.'s view it then has in any event to be considered in order to determine whether it is reasonable to adopt the valuation without modification.

The danger, of course, lies primarily with the flexibility of discretion and the potential for its erratic exercise. The *English Exporters* case clearly opened the door wide for the unguided and uncertain use of discretion in this area. The operation of s.24D is, therefore, purely dependent on the sense and perceptions of the individual judge. As Nourse L.J. concluded in *Charles Follett Ltd v. Cabtell Investments* (1988) 55 P & CR 36, 'that I think is the inescapable result of Parliament having given no guidance as to the consequences which are to flow from the mandatory regard to the old rent'. The potential consequences of a maverick decision moreover are exacerbated by the reluctance of the appellate courts to interfere with the findings at first instance. As the calculation of the interim rent is primarily a question of fact, an appeal will succeed only if there is an error of law. For example, in *Romulus Materials Ltd v. W T Lamb Properties Ltd* (18 February 1999) the judge engaged in contradictory reasoning and failed to take regard of comparables.

7.6.4 Fiction of a yearly tenancy

The modifications to the normal s.34 valuation procedure operate to the advantage of the tenant and produce an interim rent discounted below the true market rent for the property. A reduction may occur because the calculation is based upon the fictional premise that what is being valued is a yearly tenancy. It is due to the continuation tenancy being a creature of indeterminate duration that Parliament elected for the yardstick, admittedly arbitrary, of an annual lease of the holding. This is thought necessary because a market rent can have little meaning unless it can be applied to a tenancy of a calculable period. There is however no automatic entitlement to a discount under this head and a case must be made out by the tenant. Nevertheless, by employing the gauge of a yearly tenancy a deduction will occur in the normal course of events. This is because the tenant under the hypothetical lease will enjoy less security of tenure, and fewer safeguards against increasing rent levels and inflation, than a tenant under a term of years certain. The assessment of this rent reduction can prove varied and considerable, for example:

- 33 per cent in *Regis Property Co Ltd v. Lewis & Peat* [1970] 1 Ch 695;
- 10 per cent in *Lawson v. Hartley-Brown* (1996) 71 P & CR 242;
- 12.5 per cent in *Department of Environment v. Allied Freehold Property Ltd* [1992] 45 EG 156;
- 15 per cent in *Ratners (Jewellers) Ltd v. Lemnoll* (1980) 255 EG 987;
- 20 per cent in *Halberstam v. Tandalco Corp. NV* [1985] 1 EGLR 90.

7.6.5 Factors to be taken into account

Both parties have the right to be heard and to introduce expert evidence. The judge is not however bound to accept the evidence of an expert. Nevertheless, in *Conway* v. *Arthur* [1988] 2 EGLR 113, the judge clearly erred in setting the interim rent at £4,234 where the landlord introduced no evidence and the tenant had argued for an interim rent of only £2,500. If no valuations are agreed, the court will look at comparable properties when assessing the interim rent. Before reliance can be placed on such evidence, the court will need to know how those comparables were arrived at, how the figures were calculated and the reasoning behind them. In *Romulus Materials Ltd* v. *W T Lamb Properties Ltd* (18 February 1999), for example, the court discounted down for shortcomings that the comparables demonstrated. The Court of Appeal also criticised the judge at first instance for plucking figures from the air.

Where there is nothing comparable, the rents of neighbouring properties might be used as a guide. In all cases, the comparable rents to be used are those current at the time the interim rent period commences, which may be years before the application is heard. Consequently, if it appears that rents are to rise sharply in the foreseeable future, the landlord may be tempted to wait and make an application later than otherwise advisable in order to take advantage of inflated comparables. In *French* v. *Commercial Union Life Assurance Plc* [1993] 1 EGLR 113, Nourse L.J. accepted that the effects of an economic recession must be built into the calculation and that this could produce a reduced interim rent. As emphasised in *Rogers* v. *Bulleid Leeks & Co.* (4 November 1992), the recession must be shown to impact on the particular premises. In the *French* case therefore the fact that a large supermarket was moving out of a shopping centre and the impending refurbishment of the building operated to depress market values, which fell to be reflected in the interim rent.

In addition, the condition of the premises, and any obligation of either party as to repairs, may be taken into account when it will, for example, involve expense during the continuation period. Although the reference in s.24D is to a hypothetical letting, the court cannot simply shut its eyes to known facts existing at the commencement of the interim period. Accordingly, the court should have regard to the actual condition and state of the premises at the commencement date of the interim rent. In *Fawke* v. *Viscount Chelsea* [1979] 3 All ER 568, the premises were infested with dry rot arising from many years of neglect by the landlord. In addition to the discount for disrepair, the interim rent was also to reflect the inconvenience to the tenant and limited use of the premises while the repair work was to be carried out. Goff L.J. made it clear that this leaves unaffected the tenant's right to sue for breach of covenant, except of course that credit for the reduction of interim rent must be given from any damages awarded. Facts which come into being afterwards cannot however form part of the calculation.

If appropriate, the court can order a differential rent (that is, one varying with the state of repair of the property) but, seemingly, only where the disrepair is of a very serious nature. As Brandon L.J. admitted *in Fawke* v. *Viscount Chelsea* [1979] 3 All ER 568, 'I should not however wish to encourage the view that this is a power which the court should exercise at all frequently'. In theory at least, it is possible that a nil interim rent could be set if the state of repair of the premises was such that they would be worthless to a lessee for a certain period.

7.6.6 Potential disadvantages

There are however two potential disadvantages for the tenant arising from the objective yardstick of s.24D(2). First, as the hypothetical lease is from year to year, if the tenant seeks a shorter term on renewal the interim market valuation will necessarily be higher than that of the new lease. This occurred in *Woodbridge* v. *Westminster Press Ltd* (1987) 284 EG 60 where the tenant was seeking a nine-month renewal.

Secondly, the valuation is of a hypothetical tenancy of the whole premises. It may be that any new lease sought by a tenant could comprise less property than under the original lease because, for example, the tenant has sub-let or is willing to accept a tenancy of an economically separable part of the holding under s.31A(1)(*b*). Accordingly, it might be considered unfair for the tenant to pay an interim rent for the whole premises. This argument however is one lacking in force. It should not be viewed as the responsibility of the landlord to subsidise the tenant for the latter's inability to secure either an adequate financial return from any sub-letting or a new lease of the whole property. Few would argue that, as it is the original lease which is being continued, it is improper for the landlord to receive an interim rent of the entire premises which comprised the subject matter of that grant.

Although for rental purposes the calculation is on the basis of a yearly tenancy, it is common for a continuation tenancy to span a number of years. For example, in *French* v. *Commercial Union Life Assurance Plc* [1993] 1 EGLR 113 the continuation tenancy spanned more than six years. As there can only be one award of an interim rent, the landlord's predicament is compounded by the likelihood that, in such cases, the rent set will become unrealistically low by the end of the continuation tenancy. Nevertheless, this does not justify the court setting initially an interim rent which is above the market value as assessed at the time of the hearing nor can the court achieve this end with hindsight where the matter of the interim rent is disposed of at the same time as the application for a new lease. Such is illustrated by *Conway* v. *Arthur* [1988] 2 EGLR 113 where proceedings were delayed for three years and, eventually, the interim rent was fixed at a level some 330 per cent above the contractual rent. This assessment was reduced on appeal because, for part of the three years, the rent ordered exceeded the market rent of a yearly tenancy.

7.6.7 Effect of the existing rent

The need to have regard to the existing rent may, as shown, have a further depressive effect. As Nourse L.J. concluded in *Charles Follett Ltd* v. *Cabtell Investments Ltd* (1988) 55 P & CR 36, this cushion exists to protect the tenant from the shock of an inflated rent taking effect in full directly the lease has determined. Accordingly, the market rent of the hypothetical tenancy will, where appropriate, be suitably tempered with reference to the former contractual rent. It was however made clear in *English Exporters* v. *Eldonwall Ltd* [1973] Ch 415 that there is no obligation on the court to make such an adjustment and that it is necessary for the tenant to establish a case for reduction. The decision lies solely at the discretion of the court and is not an issue for expert evidence.

Once the case has been made out however the weight given to it and its translation into financial terms can vary dramatically. As Paul Baker Q.C. acknowledged in *Woodbridge* v. *Westminster Press* (1987) 284 EG 60, 'One does have regard to it, but with the weight from zero to perhaps predominant in a continuous line'. Admittedly, each case turns on its own facts, but the variations indicated below do little to erase the imprint of the 'judge's foot' from the proceedings. This is particularly so in the light of judicial admissions that mathematical precision is not necessary and the adoption of a broad brush approach. The scope for variation is readily apparent from case law:

- 0 per cent was allowed in *Halberstam* v. *Tandalco Corporation NV* [1985] 1 EGLR 90 because there had been a three-year delay, since the application for a new lease, before the landlord applied for an interim rent;
- 0 per cent was allowed in *Department of the Environment* v. *Allied Freehold Property Trust Ltd* [1992] 45 EG 156. The tenant had already had the considerable benefit of a low rent in inflationary times and the shock element was unreal. There was seen to be no reason to perpetuate what inflation and the passage of time had turned into an injustice for the landlord;
- 6.66 per cent discount was made in *English Exporters* v. *Eldonwall Ltd* [1973] 1 Ch 423 in circumstances where the tenant had entered into the lease three years before the Law of Property Act 1969 and had held the expectation that the lease would continue for some time at a low rent;
- 10.63 per cent discount was given in *Ratners (Jewellers) Ltd* v. *Lemnoll* (1980) 255 EG 987;
- 50 per cent was allowed in *Charles Follett Ltd* v. *Cabtell Investments Ltd* (1988) 55 P & CR 36. Although this case is to be regarded as exceptional,

the computation was justified on the basis of a dramatic increase in market rental value.

7.6.8 Last day rent reviews

It is hardly surprising that under these old rules landlords traditionally negotiate and agree (from a position of weakened bargaining strength) a figure for an interim rent without taking part in this uncertain and financially risky courtroom lottery. As regards interim rents settled by agreement, a practice of deducting an amount in the region of 10 per cent from the agreed market value is discernible. Indeed, landlords might be better served if they sidestep the interim rent machinery totally. This may be done by the insertion in the original lease of an 'upwards only' rent review which would be geared to take effect prior to the termination of the original fixed term (e.g. the day before). Owing to the provision against contracting out of the 1954 Act, contained in s.38, a review clause designed to operate during the continuation itself would be void as repugnant to the nature of a continuation tenancy. As demonstrated in *Willison* v. *Cheverell Estates* [1996] 1 EGLR 116, the review clause has relevance only to a fixed term while it exists and therefore cannot apply during the continuation tenancy.

A 'last day' review would be based on the assumption that the tenant will remain in occupation under the aegis of s.24 and is likely to produce a figure higher than any interim rent as fixed by the court. Interest on rent falling due may also be dealt with by the review clause. There would also be no need for the service of a s.25 notice or s.26 request to activate the rent increase and that increase would be based upon contemporary valuations and run from the date of the review. In short, this produces a much more advantageous position for the landlord. It should be appreciated that, if the continuation period spans a number of years, the landlord may later apply for an interim rent.

7.7 CALCULATION OF THE INTERIM RENT: THE NEW RENT RULES

Although the Law Commission in 1992 acknowledged that there was major discontent amongst landlords, unfortunately it could find no consensus as how best to proceed. Hence, it attempted to provide a fair compromise between landlord and tenant in promoting a revised scheme under which, 'the interim rent should be raised in those cases in which there is no sustainable case for a discount from the full market figure, but in other cases the rent should be assessed in accordance with the present formula'. This novel proposal was drawn from the deliberations of its previous Working Paper. As regards those tenants whose renewals are not in doubt, a system of 'new rent rules' was advocated as a replacement for the current interim rent. For this class of tenancy, no special interim rent would be necessary and, instead, the tenant would be under a 'continuous' obligation to pay a market rent. The notion was that the rent would be equal to the rent to be payable at the commencement of the renewed term. As the Working Paper explained, 'Effectively, therefore, that new rent would date back to the date given, in the landlord's notice or the tenant's request, for ending the current lease'. This was also designed to speed up the renewal process as neither party will now have as much to gain by delaying proceedings and, indeed, landlords may have a financial incentive to acquiesce in the tenant obtaining a renewal.

The general features of the revamped scheme as contained in s.24C are that:

- it avoids the need for reference to a hypothetical yearly tenancy;
- it sidesteps the requirement that regard be had to the existing rent;
- when renewal is guaranteed there would no longer be any cushion for the tenant;
- whether or not an interim rent is to be awarded remains within the discretion of the court;
- as the procedure remains tied to the service of renewal documentation, the new rent may not necessarily operate from the expiry of the contractual term;
- the backdated interim rent is payable only after the new lease has been ordered or agreed. It would seem that there is no scope for interest to be claimed during the intervening period.

7.7.1 Conditions and qualifications

On the satisfaction of three conditions, the calculation of the interim rent is intended to be a straightforward exercise. Under the new rules, s.24C(2) states the general rule that, 'the rent payable under and at the commencement of the new tenancy shall also be the interim rent'. This general rule that the new rent will be the interim rent gives way in delimited and, at times, complex circumstances.

The conditions which need to be satisfied before the new rent rules can apply are identified in s.24C(1)(a), (b). These provide, first, that the tenant was in occupation of the whole of the property demised for business purposes at the time the s.25 notice or s.26 request was served. Hence, the new rent must be calculated by reference to the premises which the tenant is entitled to enjoy under the current tenancy. It is possible that, after the service of the renewal documentation and the termination of the contractual lease, the tenant will sub-let. If so, and in order for the new interim rent rules to apply, the sub-letting must normally be terminated and the tenant back in occupation before the hearing date. It is to be appreciated that here the timing of occupation by the tenant is crucial.

Secondly, that the landlord either stated in its s.25 notice that it did not oppose the grant of a new lease to the tenant or did not serve a s.26(6) counter notice opposing the new tenancy. It is to be remembered that the landlord cannot have a change of heart after this time. Of course, if the landlord opposes the renewal from the outset and subsequently withdraws its opposition, the new rent rules are inapplicable.

Thirdly, that whether by agreement or by order of the court the landlord grants a new tenancy of the whole of the property comprised in the former lease. The new rules are conditional upon a new lease actually being granted to the tenant. This caters for the possibility that, despite a sub-letting that occurs after the renewal documentation is served and remains extant, if the landlord agrees to a new lease of the entire premises the new rules will still apply. The same would arise where the court ordered a new tenancy of the whole premises following the landlord's insistence under s.32(2). It is not occupation that is vital here, but instead the emphasis is upon the parcels of the new lease.

An exception to the general rule is where either party demonstrates that the interim rent calculated under s.24C(2) differs substantially from the 'relevant rent' (s.24C(3)(a)). The expression 'relevant rent' is the market rent that would be determined under s.34 to be payable under the new tenancy if the new tenancy has started on the 'appropriate date'. The appropriate date is defined in s.24B as the date from which the interim rent is payable (i.e. six months after the service of the s.25 notice or s.26 request). This exception is based on the possibility that the market rental valuation at the appropriate date will be greater or lesser than the valuation carried out at the end of the renewal hearing. Take, for example, a landlord who serves a s.25 notice on 1 December 2002. Any interim rent will be payable from 1 June 2003 (six months after service, i.e. the 'appropriate date'). The new lease is ordered by the court in June 2006. On the assumption that rental values have increased substantially in the intervening three years, the tenant will be prejudiced if the current rental values are used in order to gauge the interim rent which is backdated to 1 June 2003. Of course, in the less likely event that rental values plummeted recently, it would be unfair on the landlord to be adjudged solely by contemporary valuations. The party claiming this special treatment must show that the difference is substantial (which raises issues of fact and degree) and this must be demonstrated on a balance of probabilities.

If the s.24C(3)(a) qualification is made out the interim rent is based upon the historic market values prevailing at the 'appropriate date' (in the above example, 1 June 2003). The possibility of a differential rent is not catered for here. Hence, it is highly likely that, even under the new rules, the tenant will benefit from a financial cushion during the continuation tenancy.

A further exception to the general rule occurs when one party shows to the satisfaction of the court that the terms of the new tenancy differ from the terms of the old tenancy with the effect that the s.34 valuation of the old tenancy is substantially different from the s.34 valuation of the new lease (s.24C(3)(*b*)). For example, if the new lease is of a longer duration than its predecessor, the new lease will carry a substantially higher rental valuation. It would be unfair if the tenant had to pay this higher valuation by virtue of an interim rent, payable from six months after the service of renewal documentation (i.e. the 'appropriate date'), during the continuation of a less valuable tenancy. Of course, this can work also to the benefit of a landlord where, for example, the new lease has a much stricter user covenant. This will operate to depress the market value and, if this reduced valuation was the one backdated to the appropriate day, it would prejudice the landlord's interests.

If the s.24C(3)(*b*) qualification is made out (whether alone or in conjunction with s.24C(3)(*a*)), the interim rent will be one which the court considers it reasonable for the tenant to pay while the tenancy was continued (s.24C(6)). This, at least partially, has echoes of the 'old rules' in that s.24C(7)(*a*), (*b*) requires that, for these purposes, the court must have regard to the rent payable under the terms of the old tenancy and to the rent payable under any sub-tenancy of part of the property. There is, of course, no reference to the hypothetical yearly tenancy as the duration of the continuation tenancy will now be known.

Change of rules

Section 24D(3)(*a*), (*b*) contemplates the situation where an interim rent has been ordered under the new s.24C rules, but subsequent events require a recalculation under the old s.24D rules. This can occur in two situations:

- where the tenant subsequently revokes the new tenancy within the 14-day window of opportunity offered by s.36(2); or
- where the tenancy is ordered, but both parties agree not to act on it (i.e. the tenancy is not to be taken at all or is to be granted on different terms than those ordered by the court).

In both these scenarios, either party can apply to the court under the CPR, Part 23 procedure without the need for a stand-alone application under s.24A. The court shall then determine a revised interim rent under s.24D. The court here has no discretion as to whether or not to make an award because it exercised that discretion prior to the rule changing events.

CHAPTER 8

Discretionary grounds of opposition

Contents

- Introduction
- General observations
- Ground (A): disrepair
- Ground (B): persistent rent arrears
- Ground (C): other breaches
- Ground (E): uneconomic sub-letting

8.1   INTRODUCTION

Section 29(1) of the Landlord and Tenant Act 1954 enshrines the primary right of the business tenant, which is to apply for and obtain the grant of a new lease following on from the determination of the current tenancy. The jurisdiction of the court is limited by the requirement that the tenant must have adhered to any prescribed time limits and procedures. Accordingly, the right to renew can be sacrificed through slowness and inaction. In order for the court to grant a renewal, it is necessary that the tenancy is within the ambit of the Act and remains so until the proceedings are concluded. The tenancy must therefore still be in existence and the premises demised must be occupied for the purposes of a business carried on by the tenant. As it is necessary that the tenant holds under a subsisting tenancy, where the landlord forfeits the contractual or continuation tenancy, for example, there will be nothing remaining with which the renewal machinery can engage. The tenant then simply falls outside the statutory provisions.

If the tenancy remains within the protection of the Act, the tenant may make a renewal application or the landlord may take pre-emptive action by making an application for a termination order under s.29(2). The landlord can, however, successfully oppose the tenant's application or obtain a termination order only on strictly delimited grounds. Refusal of a new lease may be based on one of the seven statutory grounds set out in s.30(1)(*a*)–(*g*). The statutory grounds divide into two categories: those grounds that are discretionary (grounds (a), (b), (c) and (e)) and those that are mandatory (grounds (d), (f) and (g)). The statutory grounds are:

- failure to repair (ground (a));
- persistent rent arrears (ground (b));
- other breaches of obligation or prejudicial acts connected with the use and management of the holding (ground (c));
- suitable alternative accommodation (ground (d));
- uneconomic sub-letting (ground (e));
- demolition and reconstruction (ground (f)); and
- owner occupation (ground (g)).

8.2 GENERAL OBSERVATIONS

8.2.1 Identifying the statutory grounds

Each of the statutory grounds is distinct and proof of any allows the landlord to overcome the tenant's entitlement to a new lease. The grounds may be relied upon exclusively, cumulatively or in the alternative. It is necessary, however, that the statutory grounds upon which the landlord intends to rely are stated in the s.25 notice or s.26(6) counter notice served in response to the tenant's request for a new tenancy. This requirement does not, however, apply to the common law ground of illegality which is considered below. The statutory grounds in their full form are set out on the reverse of each of the *pro forma* versions of the s.25 notice or s.26(6) counter notice. On the front of both forms moreover the landlord is required to indicate such ground(s) as are relevant to the opposition and to do so with sufficient clarity so that the tenant can appreciate the basis of the landlord's objection. In *Sevenarts Ltd v. Busvine* [1969] 1 All ER 392, for example, the trustee landlord stated ground (g), but wrongly claimed to want occupation for its own business. Although occupation was, in reality, sought for occupation by the beneficiary, the notice remained valid because it did not mislead the tenant and the misstatement was of no practical importance.

8.2.2 Election and evidence

The landlord must decide upon its tactics prior to the service of the s.25 notice or counter notice. The landlord's election of grounds must moreover be taken with care. Although once stated a ground can subsequently be abandoned, grounds cannot otherwise be amended or added to. As the landlord's ability to defeat the tenant's claim is limited to the grounds set out in the renewal documentation, not surprisingly, this election will also bind any successor in title of the landlord. If the landlord omits to specify any grounds of opposition or states only grounds that cannot be established, its opposition must fail and the tenant will be granted a new lease. This occurred in *Nursey* v. *P Currie (Dartford) Ltd* [1959] 1 All ER 497 where the landlord failed to establish the stated ground (i.e. that the premises were wanted for owner occupation) and was unable to rely upon the intended demolition and reconstruction of the premises because the latter ground had not been disclosed in its s.25 notice.

As regards the fault-based grounds ((a)–(c)) the landlord may still be able to adduce evidence of an unexpressed ground, but only in so far as it throws light upon a stated ground. This occurred in *Hutchinson* v. *Lambeth* [1984] 1 EGLR 75 where the landlord introduced evidence concerning a nuisance (which is covered by ground (c), but that ground had not been stated). This was regarded as relevant in establishing whether the tenant should be denied a renewal under the pleaded grounds (a)–(b). The landlord could adduce evidence of all collateral matters relating to the occupancy of the premises. Similarly, in *Eichner* v. *Midland Bank Executor and Trustee Co. Ltd* [1970] 2 All ER 597 the judge was allowed to take into account matters not specified in the landlord's notice of opposition. Lord Denning M.R. held that, in relation to grounds (a)–(c), the judge was entitled to consider a wide range of factors, including the tenant's conduct and the history between the parties. He observed, 'It was, I think, open to him to look at all the circumstances in connection with that breach; also I may add, to look at the conduct of the tenant as a whole in regard to his obligations under the tenancy. The judge was not limited to the various grounds stated in the notice'. Although ground (b) was not relied upon by the landlord, the court felt that the tenant's past rental defaults clearly demonstrated the unhappy relationship between the parties.

The reliance upon a ground of opposition must be *bona fide*. If not, as suggested by the House of Lords, in *Betty's Cafes Ltd* v. *Phillips Furnishing Stores Ltd* [1959] AC 20, the landlord's notice (or counter notice) would be invalidated. In that case Denning L.J. admitted that, 'It would be deplorable if a landlord could be allowed to get an advantage by misrepresenting his state of mind or any other fact . . . I should have thought it clear that the notice would be bad – voidable – liable to be set aside for fraudulent misrepresentation . . . If it was avoided, the original tenancy would continue'.

Of course, if it is too late to avoid the notice, the tenant will be able to obtain damages at common law for fraud or under s.37A(1) for possession obtained by misrepresentation. The court, however, is given no power to re-open proceedings and s.37A(1) implicitly operates on the basis that the notice or counter notice was effective despite the *mala fides* of the landlord.

8.2.3 Compensation grounds

The ground(s) of possession relied on by the landlord will also dictate whether the tenant is entitled to flat rate compensation for disturbance under s.37. Section 37(1A) limits the tenant's entitlement to cases where the landlord's opposition was based exclusively upon one or more of grounds (e)–(f). The reasoning that unfolds is that: the tenant in default does not deserve compensation; the tenant deprived of possession in furtherance of the landlord's management interests should be recompensed; and the tenant offered suitable alternative accommodation has no need of compensation. Clearly, in the hope of defeating the tenant's entitlement to compensation, the landlord might be well advised, if relevant, to rely also upon a ground drawn from the categories (a)–(d).

8.2.4 When must the ground be established?

In *Betty's Cafes* v. *Phillips Furnishing Stores* [1959] AC 20, the House of Lords considered when the landlord must be able to prove the statutory grounds of opposition. It was made clear that this will differ depending on which ground the landlord relies on. Although the appeal concerned ground (f) (redevelopment), wide-ranging *obiter* provided guidance relating to the other grounds. Three points may safely be distilled from the case. First, notwithstanding the fact that grounds (e)–(g) involve a future element relating to the landlord's intentions and use of the property, the time for proving intention is at the date of the hearing and not at the date the notice or counter notice is served. Viscount Simonds explained, 'All is still in the future, and except for purposes of challenging his [the landlord's] *bona fides* . . . nothing that has happened in the past has any relevance'.

Secondly, as regards grounds (a)–(c), there must be a breach by the tenant at the date of the landlord's notice or counter notice and that default must be proven at the hearing. As Lord Keith noted, 'I cannot understand a landlord, who wishes to terminate a tenancy, being thought to state a ground of opposition to a possible application for a new tenancy that did not exist at the time of his notice'.

Thirdly, in connection with ground (d), the landlord must express a willingness to provide or secure suitable alternative accommodation in the notice or counter notice and persist in this willingness throughout the proceedings. These basic propositions will be considered again as each ground is analysed during this and the following chapter.

8.2.5 The role of discretion

Grounds (a)–(c) invoke the court's discretion by adding the requirement that the tenant 'ought not to be granted a new tenancy'. Ground (e) also employs this discretion, but the emphasis there, as will become clear, is upon the land-lord's needs and not the tenant's default. The general discretion exists, as Ormerod L.J. put it in *Lyons* v. *Central Commercial Properties Ltd* [1958] 1 WLR 869, 'to enable the judge to refuse to grant a new lease to a tenant who has shown himself to be unsatisfactory in the performance of his obligation under the contract of tenancy'. In the same case, Morris L.J. acknowledged, 'It is to be noted that the discretion is one whereby a tenant may be deprived of that which under the Act he was in a position to receive. The discretion does not operate to give something, but to take something away'.

The exercise of discretion must be tailored to the facts of a particular case and the reported cases provide mere illustrations of how, in appropriate circumstances, the discretion should be exercised. Accordingly, as Millett L.J. observed in *Jaggard* v. *Sawyer* [1995] 1 WLR 269, 'The most that any of them can demonstrate is that in similar circumstances it would not be wrong to exercise the discretion in the same way. But it does not follow that it would be wrong to exercise it differently'.

8.2.6 Illegality

No renewal can be granted in circumstances where the tenant intends to use the property for an illegal purpose. In circumstances where the illegality is directly concerned with the use of the land, and is implicit in the proposed new tenancy, the court cannot enforce the new lease. As the court will neither countenance nor facilitate the illegal user of the land, the lease is void and its terms unenforceable. The user has to be illegal and moreover it has to be a current activity. Accordingly, in *Beard* v. *Williams* (1986) 278 EG 1087 the common law did not avail the landlord because the actual user of the land was not illegal. The 'illegality' (arguably a trespass only) consisted of parking a decrepit van on or near the adjacent highway. It was therefore relevant only in so far as it was 'connected with the tenancy or management of the holding' under s.30(1)(c) below. Similarly, if the unlawful user was in the past, the court will not deny the tenant a renewal on the basis of illegality. Nevertheless, it also would be a consideration under ground (c).

The common law ground of illegality was successfully raised in *Udechuku* v. *Lambeth LBC* (1982) 262 EG 1308 where a lease granted by a landlord, who was aware that a demolition order had become operative in relation to the premises, was void and any rent irrecoverable. The grant amounted to a criminal offence. This approach is illustrated further in *Turner & Bell* v. *Searles (Stanford-le-Hope) Ltd* (1977) 33 P & CR 208 where, contrary to a planning enforcement notice, the tenant continued to operate its coaching business from the demised premises. Although no prosecution had been brought, this conduct constituted a criminal offence. The tenant then applied for a new lease so as to carry on the same business, but the application was unsuccessful. As Bridge L.J. explained:

quite independently of the express provisions of the statute, this is a case where the court would be bound to refuse the relief claimed on the simple ground that if the court were to order a new tenancy in the circumstances indicated it would be ordering the parties to enter into an illegal contract which the court could not enforce because the illegal purpose of the tenant was clearly known to both parties. That would be an absurdity.

The attractions of relying on the common law, in circumstances where the premises are actually being used for an illegal purpose, are that, in contradistinction to s.30(1)(c), the landlord does not have to specify this reliance in any of the renewal documentation and the court does not enjoy any discretion. Instead, it is the duty of the court, whether or not the point is taken by the parties, to raise on its own motion any issue of illegality.

8.3   GROUND (A): DISREPAIR

Section 30(1)(a) offers the court the discretion to refuse renewal if, due to the failure to observe repairing and maintenance obligations under the existing lease, the tenant ought not, in view of the state of repair of the holding, to be granted a renewal. This ground therefore has relevance only where there is some repair obligation (express or implied) imposed upon the tenant that has been breached. This will normally be evidenced by the competent landlord serving a schedule of dilapidations on the tenant.

Obviously, the breach of repair or maintenance must exist at the date when the landlord serves the notice or counter notice. This timing element should not cause the landlord any difficulties because, as Viscount Simonds commented in *Betty's Cafes Ltd* v. *Phillips Furnishing Stores Ltd* [1959] AC 20, 'It is not to be supposed that a landlord will base his opposition under ground (a) . . . if in fact the state of repair at that date gives him nothing to complain of. He will state that he will rely on ground (a) if and only if at the date of the notice it gives him solid support'. If the disrepair is remedied during the intervening period before the date of the hearing, the landlord can still rely upon ground (a). The court must take into consideration the state of repair or disrepair, not only at the date of the notice, but also at the date of the hearing. The present state of the premises may well influence the exercise of discretion as to whether to grant the landlord possession. Hence, it might prove beneficial for the tenant to carry out any repair work before the hearing date.

8.3.1 Meaning of repair

The 1954 Act offers some guidance to the meaning of the word 'repair' and it is to be widely defined as including 'maintenance, decoration and restoration' (s.69(1)). As the term 'premises' is not limited to buildings, a failure to maintain, for example, landlord's fixtures, fencing or garden area should fall within ground (a). Section 30(1)(*a*), however, focuses only upon disrepair to the tenant's 'holding' which may be less in extent than the premises originally demised. Accordingly, where the tenant is in occupation of the entire premises for business purposes, disrepair to any part will enable the landlord to oppose the tenant's application. Different considerations apply, however, when the tenant has ceased to occupy part of the premises as originally leased. The parts that are not occupied for the purposes of a business cease to be part of the tenant's holding by virtue of s.23(1). Hence, if the tenant has granted a sub-tenancy, the landlord cannot rely upon the disrepair to the sub-tenant's premises when opposing the mesne tenant's application for a new lease. Similarly, if the tenant has discontinued business use of part of the premises, renewal rights in relation to that part are lost and, correspondingly, the landlord cannot rely on the disrepair of that part under ground (a). The disrepair of premises no longer comprising the tenant's holding can, however, be a relevant consideration under s.30(1)(*c*) below.

8.3.2 Discretion

As should now be clear, ground (a) is a discretionary ground for possession. This means that it is insufficient for the landlord merely to show a breach of repairing covenant existing at the date of the notice. The court must also be satisfied that the breach is of such a serious nature as to justify the tenant losing the right to a new lease. As Ormerod L.J. acknowledged in *Lyons* v. *Central Commercial Properties Ltd* [1958] 1 WLR 869, the disrepair must be 'substantial'. It follows that where there is disrepair, but the landlord intends to demolish the premises, the court is unlikely to decline renewal on the basis of ground (a). The breach would there be seen to have no deleterious effect on the landlord and the performance of the tenant's obligation would stand redundant. In such circumstances therefore the landlord would be wise to place primary reliance upon ground (f).

In deciding whether the tenant 'ought not' to be granted a new tenancy, the court must examine the factual matrix and look to all the circumstances. This will normally include factors such as the extent of the tenant's liability, the physical state of the premises, the conduct of the tenant, the relationship of the parties, the reasons for the breach, and the consequences of the tenant's failure. For example, in the *Lyons* case, the fact that the tenant had a small business and faced the loss of livelihood was regarded as a persuasive factor. It is on the basis of such wide-reaching evidence that the court must then decide how to exercise its discretion. In doing so, the court will adopt a broad brush approach in order to determine whether it would be unfair to the landlord, having regard to the tenant's past behaviour, if the tenant obtained a new lease. In the *Lyons* case, it was made clear that it is only the relationship between the landlord and the present tenant which must be adjudged. The willingness of, say, a proposed assignee to perform the covenants is irrelevant.

The tenant's willingness at the hearing to remedy the breach is not necessarily decisive. In the *Lyons* case, for example, there was a serious breach of repair obligation which the tenant had left unremedied for one year. Although the tenant offered an undertaking to carry out the necessary works, the court declined to award a new lease. The tenant was viewed as unworthy of relief. A new lease should not be granted to a bad tenant unless there exist exculpatory circumstances which can forgive the past misdoing. In contrast, however, the tenant in *Nihad* v. *Chain* [1956] EGD 234 was given the benefit of the doubt on the basis that he was prepared to consent to the new lease containing both a covenant to put the property into immediate repair and a forfeiture clause. The provisions offered sufficient protection to the landlord against future defaults occurring. These two cases therefore demonstrate that existing breaches may be overlooked, but only when the court is satisfied as to the future performance of the repair obligations.

In *Hazel* v. *Akhtar* [2002] 07 EG 124, the landlords claimed that the property had been allowed to fall into a poor condition. They had initially prepared a schedule of dilapidations, which the tenant attended to. Subsequently, the landlords had a further schedule prepared which required further work. The estimated cost of these additional works was disputed before the trial judge. The landlords claimed that they would cost £25,000 whereas the tenant claimed that they could be undertaken at a cost of £5,000–£7,000. The judge felt that the tenant had substantially underestimated the actual costs of the repairs and, on the limited evidence before him, concluded that the tenant could not afford a market rent coupled with the costs of carrying out the repairs. The judge upheld the landlords' opposition under ground (a). In the Court of Appeal, however, Sir Anthony Evans considered that the judge had been unduly sceptical about the tenant's ability to finance the corrective works. Additional evidence put before the appellate court suggested that the tenant would be able to carry out the works provided that costs were at or near the lower estimate put forward by his surveyor. In addition, one item of disrepair concerned the presence of dry rot which, it was now suggested, stemmed from water leakage from a neighbouring property owned by the landlords. This matter had not been investigated at the trial. It was also clear that, during the 12 months leading up to the trial, the tenant had carried out a considerable amount of repair work on the property. There was simply nothing to suggest that, if a new lease was granted there would be a future breach of repairing obligation. In these circumstances, the decision not to grant a new tenancy had been unduly severe.

8.4 GROUND (B): PERSISTENT RENT ARREARS

Section 30(1)(*b*) concerns where the tenant ought not to be given a new tenancy because of persistent delay in the payment of rent which has become due. The term 'rent' was defined by Lord Diplock in *United Scientific Holdings Ltd* v. *Burnley BC* [1978] AC 904 as, 'a payment which a tenant is bound by his contract to pay to the landlord for the use of his land'. The lease will normally contain a rental covenant in which the sum payable is expressed. It is, however, possible that the lease will describe other types of payment as 'rent', for example, service charges and insurance premiums. This entitles the landlord to exercise the remedy of distress to defaults in such payments and to proceed in forfeiture. Ground (b) will therefore extend to any non-payment of sums which are described in the lease as 'rent'.

The reference to 'persistent' necessitates either that there has been a delay on more than one occasion or that at least one instalment of arrears has been outstanding for some time. The non-payment was 'persistent' in *Maison Kaye Fashions Ltd* v. *Horton's Estate Ltd* (1967) 202 EG 23 where for over three years every monthly payment of rent was paid after the due date, mostly one to two months late. Accordingly, the issue is one of fact and degree. As Stocker L.J. admitted in *Gill* v. *Moore* (CA, 3 August 1989), 'The word "persistent" must import some consideration of past events, although these events should be considered at the time of the hearing, and if there were then no arrears at that time then that would be a factor to be taken into account by the judge in the exercise of his discretion'. The landlord should therefore support the opposition with a schedule of rental payments which can be served either before or at the time of the hearing. This is not a requirement, but it does save time and avoids going through each item orally. It assists both parties and the court.

The size and duration of the arrears need not be substantial and the arrears need not cover the whole duration of the lease. All that is necessary is that some arrears have been sustained over a period of time. The landlord is therefore required to demonstrate a history of bad payment. A classic example is to be found in *Gill* v. *Moore* where the tenant had been persistently late in paying rent throughout a long period, had given the landlord dishonoured cheques and had been subject to the landlord's distraint on two occasions. The court was of the opinion that, in this type of case, it would be very unfair to the landlord if a new tenancy was granted. Indeed, Fox L.J. admitted that, 'This is really an overwhelming case, and it would be perverse of me to grant a new tenancy in the light of this admitted record'. An appalling record of late payment emerged also in *Hutchinson* v. *Lambeth* [1984] 1 EGLR 75 where no rent was paid for the first four years of the lease and in *Rawashdeh* v. *Lane* [1988] 2 EGLR 109 where payments were regularly months overdue.

8.4.1 Tenant's response

In order to persuade the court to grant a renewal, the tenant has two potential counter-strategies. First, to show that there was good reason why the rent fell into arrears. In *Electricity Supply Nominees Ltd* v. *Truman* (CA, 14 December 1994), it was made clear that the effects of a recession do not offer the tenant a good reason for these purposes. The Court of Appeal warned of tenants who resist payments of rent and then seek a pretext to justify having done so. A lack of financial organisation or oversight will not provide any justification. Hence, the court was unsympathetic to the tenant in *Gill* v. *Moore* who claimed that the late payment and bounced cheques arose from uncleared items in her bank account and the fact that she had overstretched her business interests.

Some mitigation might be found, however, in circumstances where the rent has been withheld because of a breach of the landlord's covenant and the tenant is pursuing a genuine counter claim against the landlord. If the counter claim succeeds, the tenant has a defence to any action for rent arrears. In *Televantos* v. *McCullock* [1991] 1 EGLR 123, the tenant had a well-founded counter claim for a sum in excess of the rent withheld. Nicholls L.J. commented, 'when one takes that into account, I have the greatest difficulty in seeing how it could be regarded as reasonable in the circumstances of this case to say that an order for possession should be made'. Even if the counter claim fails, the fact that the rent was withheld for this reason will be a factor in favour of the tenant. It is a factor which relates to discretion. It is, however, necessary for the tenant to be equipped to make immediate payment or, at least, to make some provision for the discharge of outstanding arrears. As Waite J. admitted in *London Borough of Haringey* v. *Stewart* (1991) 23 HLR 557:

> In ordinary circumstances it will not be reasonable to make a possession order if the tenant has made arrangements in the event of failure of his counterclaim to clear the arrears by an anticipatory payment into court (to give one example), or by setting aside funds which can be devoted for that purpose (to give another), or, at the very least, to put forward proposals for an early discharge of the arrears.

This does not invariably offer a guarantee for the tenant because, as Waite J. added:

> In exceptional circumstances, however, as for example where the tenant has already a very poor record for persistent late payment of rent, the ordinary benevolent course will not be followed, and the making of an order would be regarded as reasonable upon the ground that the tenant has disqualified himself from the court's sympathy by the persistency of his past defaults.

The second type of response that a tenant may make is to offer a rent deposit and/or a surety for the new lease. This additional protection for the landlord might persuade the court to overlook previous defaults and to favour the tenant's application. As Birkett L.J. commented in the Court of Appeal in *Betty's Cafes Ltd* v. *Phillips Furnishing Stores Ltd* [1957] 1 All ER 1, 'if the tenant has some very good reasons to explain delays and very good grounds for assuring the court that the like situation would never arise again, it seems difficult to say that the court should not listen to evidence to show how completely the situation had changed at the date of the hearing, from what it was at the date of the notice'.

8.4.2 Landlord's forbearance

In *Hazel* v. *Akhtar* [2002] 07 EG 124, the landlords opposed a new lease partly on the ground of the tenant's persistent rent arrears. The tenant accepted in evidence that he had never paid the rent on the due date and, accordingly, that on each occasion he was in arrears. A schedule of rental payments showed that the duration of the arrears was invariably short, payment usually being only a few days later. The tenant pleaded that his business did not have cash flow problems and that he had not consciously profiteered by earning interest on the overdue rent. The trial judge was not favourably impressed by the lack of any expression of apology or regret by the tenant. He concluded that this was a bad case and that no landlord should be expected to put up with such behaviour from a tenant.

Although it appeared to be a hopeless case, the Court of Appeal held that the landlords could not rely upon s.30(1)(*b*). The judge had fallen into error because he had failed to take into account that, for the first 14 years of the tenancy, the landlords' predecessor in title had not complained about late payments. The judge had also ignored the fact that, by accepting conditional payments by cheque, the previous landlord had assented to the practice of 'slightly' late payments on those occasions. Accordingly, and akin to estoppel, the record of late payments should not have been held against the tenant as it was. Ironically, the longevity of the practice of making late payments here supported the tenant's case rather than, as is usual, providing evidence of a 'persistent' disregard for the purposes of ground (b). Sir Anthony Evans explained, 'This did not amount, of course, to a variation of the terms of the lease, but it did mean that the landlords were, in legal and equitable terms, estopped from insisting that the appellant should revert to strict compliance with the lease unless they gave reasonable notice to that effect'. The landlord's forbearance of rental breaches had therefore acted as an encouragement to make late payment. The defendants as assignees of the reversion were subject to the same restraints concerning both the method (cheque) and date ('slightly late') of payment adopted by the tenant. The landlords were, thereby, estopped from relying on ground (b) until they gave clear notice that strict compliance was required.

Consequently, the only breaches that could assume relevance for the purposes of ground (b) were those occurring after such a change of heart was communicated to the tenant. Admittedly, the giving of the s.25 notice would offer an antidote to forbearance, but this came too late in the day to help the landlords' claim for possession. It will be remembered that the lessor must be able to establish persistent delay at the time the termination notice is served, and, of course, this is precisely what the current landlords were estopped from showing.

8.4.3 Exercise of discretion

Whether or not a renewal is declined turns upon the perceptions of the judge and the evidence put before the court. As Lord Greene put it in *Cumming* v. *Danson* [1942] 2 All ER 653, the judge must act in a 'broad commonsense way as a man of the world, and come to his conclusion giving such weight as he thinks right to the various factors in the situation. Some factors may have little or no weight, others may be decisive, but it is quite wrong for him to exclude from his consideration matters which he ought to take into account'. The court may, in exercising this discretion, have regard to such matters as the frequency of delay, the reasons for the delay, the measures taken by the landlord to secure payment and any safeguards that the landlord has against future arrears. The inconvenience and expense to the landlord incurred in having had to chase a tenant for rent is also a material factor for the court to take on board. The court can moreover take account of the tenant's cavalier attitude towards the payment of other creditors as indicating that it is unsatisfactory to foist a further term on the landlord. In *Bede Securities (Property Management) Ltd* v. *Margolis* (CA, 7 March 1985), for example, the court took account of the bankruptcy of one of the tenants and the judgment debts that were outstanding against the other tenant.

As the court has to rely on past conduct in order to predict future behaviour, the poorer the tenant's record the more likely that the landlord's opposition will succeed. As Millett L.J. commented in *Secretary of State for Transport* v. *Jenkins* (CA, 30 October 1997), 'a landlord is not to be saddled with a poor tenant who habitually pays rent late and is therefore unlikely if any new tenancy is granted, to be punctual in his payments'. It should be recalled, that unlike relief against forfeiture, the payment of arrears pending proceedings does not necessarily protect the tenant. This is particularly so in the context that a substantial rent increase is likely to occur on renewal and this will cast even further doubt upon the tenant's ability and willingness to pay. In *Gill* v. *Moore* (CA, 3 August 1989), Fox L.J. considered the tenant's new-found punctuality following the service of the landlord's s.25 notice and commented, 'The resistance to the tenant's claim and the onset of proceedings may have caused her to beware. It does not alter the fact that the persistent delay previously occurred and it is highly conjectural whether, if a new tenancy were granted, she would not revert back to her old practices'.

The wide discretion given to the court means that one case is no sure guide to another. Although it is up to the landlord to establish the ground, there is an obligation on the tenant to explain away the past failures and to satisfy the court that there will be no recurrence. Accordingly, each case turns upon its own facts. Unless the judge errs at law, the decisions of these fact-finding tribunals will not be disturbed by the higher courts. In *Hurstfell Ltd* v. *Leicester Square Property Co.* [1988] 2 EGLR 105, for example, a renewal was ordered even though the tenant had been in arrears for 11 consecutive rent instalments and had given the landlord dishonoured cheques. In that case the judge was satisfied that there would be no future repetition, notwithstanding that the viability of the tenant's business was questionable. As Nicholls L.J. concluded, 'at the end the matter comes down to this. Here was a question of fact on which the judge . . . saw the witnesses, heard their evidence, heard the submissions and reached a conclusion for which there was supporting evidence. In those circumstances it seems to me that there is no justification for this court interfering with the judge's conclusion of fact'. He did, however, express the view that he, on the evidence, 'would not have been wholly surprised if the judge had reached a different conclusion on the crucial question'.

In *Rawashdeh* v. *Lane* [1988] 2 EGLR 109, a renewal was denied to the tenant, who had been late in rent payments regularly during the course of the lease, because the delays were regarded as sufficiently serious to justify the rejection of the application. This was so even though the tenant was prepared to pay a quarter's rent in advance and to agree to payment by a monthly standing order. Similarly, in *Hopcutt* v. *Carver* [1969] 209 EG 1069 the tenant had occupied for 20 years, but the evidence showed that, during the last two years, he had regularly been in arrears with rent. At one stage the tenant went five months without making any payment. The judge carefully prepared a table relating to past payments which showed that, while proceedings were pending, the tenant had become more punctual. The renewal was, however, refused and the appellate court felt that it was significant that the tenant had made no offer for the rent to be payable in advance and offered no security to the landlord. There was simply no certainty that the rent would be paid if the renewal was granted. These cases demonstrate that the onus is on the tenant to persuade the court that there will be no future arrears and that this will normally require the offer of effective safeguards for the landlord.

8.5   GROUND (C): OTHER BREACHES

Section 30(1)(*c*) enables the landlord to oppose the renewal application on the basis that the tenant ought not to be granted a new lease in the light of other substantial breaches of the obligations under the lease or for any other reason connected with the use or management of the holding. In opposing the new lease on the basis of ground (c), the landlord should take care to specify all allegations made and to support them with evidence. A vague, general statement of the tenant's conduct will not be sufficient. The wording of ground (c) makes it apparent that this ground deals with two distinct sets of circumstances.

8.5.1 The first set

Any substantial breach of leasehold covenant (except one caught by grounds (a) and (b)) can be relied upon by the landlord. Accordingly, the landlord can invoke a breach of a user covenant (as in *Jones* v. *Jenkins* (1985) 277 EG 644) or a covenant prohibiting the tenant from causing a nuisance or annoyance (as in *Norton* v. *Charles Deane Productions Ltd* (1969) 214 EG 559). It would also include a breach of repairing obligation which fell outside ground (a) because it referred to premises which were not comprised in the tenant's holding. Similarly, the first set would embrace rent arrears which were not persistent and non-payments of sums not designated as rent in the lease.

For the landlord to be successful in this opposition, however, the breach must be more than trivial and its consequences must be serious. For example, if the tenant seeks the renewal of shop premises from which he has unlawfully sold cigarettes in breach of covenant, this would not be viewed as substantial. A breach of a covenant against alienation, however, will be regarded as sufficiently substantial to allow the landlord's opposition under ground (c) to succeed. The determination lies at the court's discretion and, in its exercise, the court will take into account the nature of the breach, whether it can be remedied, any proposals made by the tenant for remedy, and whether the landlord has either acquiesced in or waived the breach. In deciding whether the breach is substantial, the court will look at the whole of the tenant's conduct during the tenancy and is therefore not restricted to issues set out in the landlord's notice or counter notice. The tenant's expected future conduct should also be of relevance. There must, however, be cogent evidence introduced by the landlord proving the breach. In *Jones* v. *Jenkins* (1986) 277 EG 644, the landlord alleged that three rooms in a basement flat had been converted into a laundry in breach of user covenant. Although the county court upheld the landlord's opposition, the decision could not stand as no evidence of this breach had been introduced. Despite the fact that another breach (relating to the use of a flat as a massage parlour) was established, the lower court's exercise of discretion was tainted and a retrial was ordered.

8.5.2   The second set

Ground (c) is widened considerably by the allusion to 'any other reason' relevant to the use and management of the holding. It is to be appreciated that, if the reason impacts solely upon land which has been sub-let by the tenant, it will no longer concern the tenant's holding and will fall outside the ambit of this second set. In contrast, the conduct of the tenant on land not comprised in the demise may be relevant to the extent that it reflects on the tenant's ability to manage the holding properly. Accordingly, in *Beard* v. *Williams* (1986) 278 EG 1087 the unlawful parking of a van (in which the tenant lived) 100 yards from the demised premises meant that the van could be moved on which would jeopardise the tenant's dog breeding business and, thereby, potentially prejudice the landlord. These precarious living arrangements were clearly connected to the tenant's use and management of the holding.

The court can, seemingly, look to both past and future use and there is no requirement of substantiality here. The underlying consideration is whether the landlord will be prejudiced by the tenant's conduct. In *Turner & Bell* v. *Searles (Stanford-le-Hope) Ltd* (1977) 33 P & CR 208, Roskill L.J. adopted a liberal stance and suggested that any factor which could be said to be relevant to use or management might legitimately be taken on board. Clearly, this includes matters which are beyond the tenant's legal obligations to the landlord, but it is not certain how far this extension reaches. It covers, for example, a breach of either criminal law or planning law by the tenant. It might cater for the situation where, following a change in the neighbourhood, it is no longer desirable that the tenant's business be continued on the premises. It could be invoked moreover when the tenant has run the business in such a fashion that, although in compliance with the terms of the lease, it is undesirable that the business continues to operate as before. Indeed, the Court of Appeal in *Cheryl Investments Ltd* v. *Saldanha* [1979] 1 All ER 5 acknowledged that even a lawful change of user might give the landlord the ability to oppose renewal.

Albeit usually present, fault on the part of the tenant is not, however, a necessary ingredient under this second set. Nevertheless, the absence of fault would be a material consideration for the court to take on board in exercising its discretion. Similarly, the ready availability of alternative accommodation for the tenant is a factor which may influence the court to deny renewal.

8.6   GROUND (E): UNECONOMIC SUB-LETTING

Section 30(1)(*e*) is relevant where the current tenant is a sub-lessee of part only of the premises which previously had been let by the competent landlord under a superior tenancy of the whole. It is a discretionary ground which can only be relied upon when the competent landlord can demonstrate the reasonable expectation that the aggregate of the rents, reasonably obtainable on separate lettings of the sub-tenant's holding and the remainder of the premises, would be substantially less than if the property was let as a whole. In addition, it must be shown that, on the termination of the current tenancy, the landlord requires possession of the holding for the purpose of letting or otherwise disposing of the whole premises. Consequently, ground (e) enables the competent landlord to recover possession in order to effect a more lucrative re-letting or sale. This ground is seldom used in practice owing to its difficulties and limited application. Indeed, Viscount Simonds in the House of Lords in *Betty's Cafes Ltd* v. *Phillips Furnishing Stores Ltd* [1959] AC 20 described ground (e) as not being '. . . wholly intelligible'.

8.6.1 Checklist

For ground (e) to have relevance it is necessary that a number of features be present:

- it must be the sub-tenant who applies for a new lease and the sub-tenancy must be of part only of the premises (not the whole);
- the intermediate landlord's interest must be due to end within 14 months, following the notice or counter notice, as otherwise the head landlord would not be the sub-tenant's competent landlord for the purposes of the 1954 Act, Part II renewal scheme. This is crucial as the ground cannot be used by a landlord against an immediate tenant;
- the time for determining whether a sub-tenancy is in existence is the date of the tenant's application. Previous relationships are to be ignored. Accordingly, if a merger of the interests of the competent landlord and the mesne landlord occurs before this date, the competent landlord will be unable to rely upon ground (e). The opposition should not, however, be affected if, after the date of the tenant's application, the mesne landlord's tenancy ends, for example by expiry of time or surrender. If it were otherwise, the outcome would turn upon how quickly it was possible to obtain a hearing date;
- the head landlord must demonstrate at the hearing that substantially more rent (presumably calculated at a net value) would be received if the premises were let as whole, rather than subject to separate lettings. This difference in rental values may be difficult to prove and will necessarily hinge upon detailed, comparative valuation evidence of the premises as let on different tenancies and as let in their entirety on a hypothetical single lease. The court will then make a comparison between these competing valuations and decide whether the former is substantially less than the latter. The court cannot consider the effect on other property outside the underlease. This limited calculation, therefore, overlooks the possibility

that the sub-letting may diminish the value of the landlord's reversion from an investment viewpoint. Nevertheless, if there is no substantial diminution of rental income then ground (e) is unavailable. Such was demonstrated in *Greaves Organisation Ltd* v. *Stanhope Gate Property Co. Ltd* (1973) 228 EG 725 where a diminution could be proved, but it was not shown to be substantial;

- the landlord must demonstrate at the hearing a genuine intention and ability to dispose of the property as a whole when possession of the tenant's holding is recovered. This means that the competent landlord must be able to convince the court that vacant possession of the remainder of the building can be obtained. In the context of the limited sphere of ground (e), the remainder will be occupied by the mesne landlord and, where relevant, any other sub-tenants. If, for example, the mesne landlord's tenancy is protected by the 1954 Act, then ground (e) will, except where the mesne landlord's co-operation is obtained, be redundant;
- the court must be persuaded to exercise its discretion and decide whether the sub-tenant 'ought not to be granted a new tenancy'. In doing so, the court will take into account all the circumstances of the case and, particularly, whether the superior landlord had originally consented to the sub-letting. Adopting a broad brush approach, the court will balance the respective hardships to the competent landlord and to the sub-tenant. The landlord's case is presumably strengthened by the fact that, if the renewal is denied under ground (e), compensation for disturbance is available to the sub-tenant for disturbance under s.37.

CHAPTER 9

Mandatory grounds of opposition

Contents

- Introduction
- Ground (D): suitable alternative accommodation
- Ground (F): redevelopment
- Ground (G): owner occupation

9.1 INTRODUCTION

Having considered the common law objection to a new lease on the basis of illegality and the discretionary grounds set out in s.30(1)(*a*), (*b*), (*c*) and (*e*), it is now necessary to consider the mandatory grounds. Grounds (d), (f) and (g) are mandatory grounds because, if the landlord can establish one or more of these grounds, the court enjoys no discretion and must deny to the tenant a new lease. As demonstrated in the previous chapter, grounds (f) (redevelopment) and (g) (owner occupation) carry with them the possibility that the tenant may be awarded flat rate compensation for loss of renewal rights. As ground (d) is posited upon there being suitable alternative accommodation available to the tenant, the Landlord and Tenant Act 1954 adopts the stance that there is no loss for which compensation is payable.

9.2 GROUND (D): SUITABLE ALTERNATIVE ACCOMMODATION

Section 30(1)(*d*) provides that the tenant's application can be successfully opposed if the landlord has offered, and is willing to provide or to secure, suitable alternative accommodation on reasonable terms. The court enjoys no discretion here and, if the landlord can establish certain facts, must refuse the tenant's application. Ground (d) is, however, attractive only where the landlord is both able and prepared to offer the tenant other premises from which to conduct business. Owing to the restrictions upon what is suitable, many

183

landlords will not be in a position to satisfy the necessary requirements and, even if they can, the temptation may exist (although compensation for disturbance will then become payable) to rely instead upon one of the other non-discretionary grounds.

There is, however, much that remains unclear about the operation of ground (d) for, as Judge Aron Owen acknowledged in *Chaplin (M) Ltd* v. *Regent Capital Holdings Ltd* [1994] 1 EGLR 249, 'The Act has now been in operation for nearly three decades, but it appears that the implications of this paragraph have never had to be fully and directly considered'. Little assistance, moreover, is to be drawn from the cases decided in relation to residential tenancies. As emphasised by the House of Lords in *Singh* v. *Malayan Theatres* [1953] AC 632, this is because of the different considerations which apply to residential property and the different wording of the respective statutory codes. As Lord Porter explained, 'principles applicable to the retention by tenants of places which are required as a home have very little bearing on the position of a tenant who requires a place in which to conduct his business'.

9.2.1 An offer

A suitable alternative must have been offered by the landlord to the tenant and this offer must be firm, *bona fide* and capable of immediate acceptance. This requires that the landlord must be able to comply with the offer. As to the timing of the offer, in *Chaplin (M) Ltd* v. *Regent Capital Holdings Ltd* [1994] 1 EGLR 249 the county court held that it was unnecessary for the offer to be made prior to the service of the landlord's s.25 notice or counter notice. To tie the landlord's hands prematurely would mark a disadvantage to the landlord without achieving any corresponding benefit to the tenant. Indeed, it would be impractical always to expect the landlord to make an offer within the period of two months following the service of the tenant's s.26 request for a new tenancy.

While being preferable that the landlord makes the offer either before or at the time of the notice/counter notice, it will suffice if ground (d) is merely indicated at that stage and details provided later. This is consistent with a central tenet of ground (d) which is that matters that need to be established must be established at the date of the hearing. It is also sensible that, as will be shown, the landlord can revise an offer both before and during the court proceedings.

9.2.2 Suitability

The landlord must be willing to provide or to secure the accommodation and this willingness must continue throughout the hearing. It is also at the hearing that questions of suitability are to be answered. There the judge will normally see plans and photographs of both the existing and the alternative premises and consider the reports of surveyors. The judge might even feel obliged to inspect the respective premises personally.

As regards suitability, it is not necessary that the accommodation is identical or even similar to the present premises. Indeed, the alternative accommodation may consist of part only of the premises currently leased to the tenant. In gauging suitability, the court is expressly directed by s.30(1)(d) to consider a variety of issues: the preservation of goodwill (where relevant); the nature of the tenant's business as permitted by the lease; the location of the existing holding; and the extent of the holding and facilities presently afforded. Accordingly, the alternative might (but not necessarily) be regarded as unsuitable where the tenant can show that existing goodwill will be detrimentally affected as a result of the business being moved. Of course, the loss of goodwill will be easier to show as regards a retailing business than, say, a wholesale or manufacturing enterprise. Similarly, if the premises are less spacious than the current holding, it might be argued that they are ill-suited to the tenant's needs. Although the landlord carries the primary burden to show that the current business can be adequately carried out in the alternative premises, the tenant should be ready to produce evidence so as to demonstrate some deleterious impact upon that business. In *Chaplin (M) Ltd* v. *Regent Capital Holdings Ltd* [1994] 1 EGLR 249, for example, accommodation offered on the second floor of a building was held to be a suitable alternative to the existing ground floor premises because the change would not affect the tenant's business as a wholesale jeweller. It is a working rule that the premises cannot, however, be regarded as suitable when their occupation would cause change to the conduct of the tenant's business and require it to be carried out in a different or diminished fashion.

9.2.3 Reasonable terms

The alternative accommodation must be available on terms which, having regard to the terms of the 'current tenancy' and all other relevant circumstances, are deemed to be reasonable. Somewhat surprisingly, in *Chaplin (M) Ltd* v. *Regent Capital Holdings Ltd* [1994] 1 EGLR 249 the county court accepted the concession that, '... "terms of the current tenancy" in this context refer not to the old terms under which the tenant holds his existing tenancy, but to such terms as the parties agree or the court would determine in a grant of the tenant's application for a new tenancy of his holding'. This interpretation is, simply put, unsustainable as it totally disregards the clear and obvious meaning of Parliamentary expression. Nevertheless, the reference to 'all other relevant circumstances' does invite some comparison between the terms of the tenancy which would be granted on renewal and those of the proposed alternative.

The expense to be incurred in moving premises is not usually a factor which will affect reasonableness or suitability. It is, instead, an inevitable risk which all tenants face at the expiry of their contractual terms. If, however, the landlord's payment of such costs is a term of the offer then the adequacy of the sum prescribed might be relevant in deciding whether the offer is on reasonable terms. The accommodation must moreover be available on those reasonable terms throughout the hearing. Although the landlord will normally take care to specify all the terms of the offer, it is permissible for the landlord to invite the court to determine terms as a preliminary issue. Hence, in *Chaplin (M) Ltd* v. *Regent Capital Holdings Ltd*, the judge considered as a preliminary issue what would constitute a reasonable rental figure for the alternative premises.

9.2.4 Revising the offer

A novel argument faced the Court of Appeal in *Mark Stone Car Sales Ltd* v. *Howard De Walden Estates Ltd* (1997) 73 P & CR D 43 and this concerned the evidence upon which issues of suitability fall be adjudged. The tenant argued that the court was limited solely to considering the terms of the original offer and could not have regard to the terms of an improved offer made by the landlord during the trial. The 1954 Act provides no direct assistance on this matter of timing and there is no definite answer to be drawn from case law. Unfortunately, the appellate court found it unnecessary to provide a definite answer and this important issue still remains in some doubt. It is, however, strongly arguable that the 1954 Act allows the offer of alternative accommodation to be revised while the hearing is continuing. There are several reasons for reaching this conclusion.

First, the general policy of the 1954 Act is to encourage negotiation and to promote agreement between the parties. The court is intended to be a venue of last resort. It would therefore be curious if the landlord's pre-trial offer was regarded as immutable and the landlord denied the opportunity to overcome the tenant's objections which, in all likelihood, would then remain undisclosed until the commencement of the trial. A landlord would be placed in the awkward position of having to couch an offer in such terms as would overcome any future pitfalls which might emerge at the trial stage. As Judge Aron Owen admitted in *Chaplin (M) Ltd* v. *Regent Capital Holdings Ltd* [1994] 1 EGLR 249, 'It would be an impossible, or almost impossible feat for a landlord to make an offer which is "spot on" from inception and will remain so throughout the lengthy period that is going to elapse'. As this would frustrate rather than facilitate negotiation, this approach would seriously undermine the flexible spirit and intendment of the statutory scheme.

Secondly, there is nothing within the wording of s.30(1)(*d*) which supports such a restrictive approach. Indeed, the emphasis upon reasonableness and suitability as measured at the time of the hearing, seemingly, reinforces the notion that the landlord can refine the offer once the trial is under way. Certainly, the Act envisages that the tenant's circumstances may change between the landlord's initial offer and the conclusion of the trial and allows challenge on this basis at the hearing. It should surely follow that the landlord is able to amend an offer at an equivalently late stage so as to reflect the tenant's change of circumstances. It would then be for the tenant to apply for an adjournment so as to consider the landlord's revised offer.

Thirdly, the county court in *Chaplin (M) Ltd* v. *Regent Capital Holdings Ltd* has already established the practice that an offer of alternative accommodation can be revised after the service of the landlord's s.25 notice or counter notice. Although the scope of that judgment was limited to pre-trial amendments, it would seem illogical to prevent further revision merely because the trial has commenced. This is not a radical proposition as ground (f) (demolition and/or reconstruction) clearly allows the landlord's case to be put in a provable form once the trial is underway. Some support can also be distilled from s.31(2) which provides that, where the landlord fails to establish the alternative accommodation at the hearing, but the court believes that it could be established within a specified period (not exceeding one year from the termination date specified in the renewal documentation), if at the end of that period the landlord again fails to satisfy the court, it is only then that a new lease can be granted. This surely undermines any argument that the landlord's hands are tied from the commencement of the hearing. It would be most peculiar for the landlord to be denied the opportunity to revise the offer during the hearing and yet be allowed to prove the ground of opposition during the subsequent months.

Finally, it should be borne in mind that the statutory scheme is designed to protect the tenant's business and not the tenant *per se*. The central issue for the court to decide is whether the alternative premises are suitable for that business and considerations such as the tenant's reluctance to relocate or desire to obtain compensation are simply irrelevant. Meanwhile the tenant is safeguarded in that the landlord's opposition will succeed only if the alternative accommodation is both suitable and reasonable. If it is, then the business will not be prejudiced and can be carried out from the new premises. Continued negotiations about the suitability of the proposed accommodation are therefore of even-handed benefit. While the landlord can strengthen the case for rejection of the tenant's application, the tenant's business will benefit by having more reasonable and suitable premises from which it can operate in future. In the context of a provision which attempts to achieve a compromise between the commercial interests of the parties, it would be most peculiar for the tenant to be able to reject the landlord's enhanced offer and yet rely on the inadequacy of the original.

9.2.5 Keeping the offer open

The landlord's offer of, and willingness to provide/secure, suitable accommodation must be maintained throughout the hearing. There is, however, no requirement that the offer be kept open for acceptance after that time, for example, while the tenant's appeal is pending. Similarly, the tenant is not compelled to accept the landlord's offer. If the offer is withdrawn post-hearing therefore the tenant may be placed in an unenviable situation. There is no provision for the court to order that the landlord keep the offer on the table for a reasonable period. Subject to s.37A compensation being payable for any misrepresentation by the landlord, the tenant will be unable to accept the offer, must quit the premises and will be unable to claim compensation for disturbance. There can be no argument that a binding contract exists at this stage because, regardless of any oral offer and acceptance, the formal requirements of the Law of Property (Miscellaneous) Provisions Act 1989 remain unsatisfied. If an appeal is outstanding, the tenant's only remaining hope is that it is successful because, if the determination is that the accommodation is not suitable, the tenant will be entitled to a renewal or, if the landlord has established additional compensation grounds of opposition, compensation for loss of renewal rights.

9.3 GROUND (F): REDEVELOPMENT

By virtue of s.30(1)(*f*), the tenant's application will be dismissed if the competent landlord can show that, on the termination of the existing lease, it is its *bona fide* intention that the premises (or a substantial part of them) comprised in the holding are either to be demolished or reconstructed; or that substantial works of construction are to be carried out on the holding. A number of introductory points may be made:

- work carried out on property other than the tenant's holding is to be disregarded for these purposes. It does not matter how substantial the works are on other parts of the premises; it is only works on the tenant's holding which count;
- as regards demolition and reconstruction, this ground is only available where there is some building already on the holding. As Robert Walker L.J. observed in *Coppen* v. *Bruce-Smith* (1998) 76 P & CR D 7, 'premises in s.30(1)(*f*) cannot mean bare land with no building on it';
- in relation to construction, however, bare land would suffice provided that there is the intention either to erect some building on it or to convert it for a different use such as, for example, a roadway or runway. In *Cook* v. *Mott* (1961) 178 EG 637, preparatory works for a caravan site sufficed for these purposes;

- subject to two qualifications contained in s.31A below, the landlord must also show that the development could not occur without first gaining possession of the tenant's holding.

Where the landlord takes the initiative by serving a s.25 notice, a strategy should be planned in advance. This may be more difficult, however, when it is the tenant who initiates the renewal proceedings by the service of a s.26 request. An unprepared landlord may then have to respond with some haste to ensure that the intention to develop is put into a provable form. Nevertheless, the landlord does not have to prove the full extent of what is claimed in the notice or counter notice. In *Biles* v. *Caesar* [1957] 1 All ER 151, the renewal documentation claimed that the landlord intended to reconstruct the whole of the premises, whereas the real intention was to reconstruct a substantial part. The landlord was still able to recover possession. As Lord Denning M.R. explained, 'It is a settled rule of pleading that if a pleader alleges more than is necessary, he is entitled to rely on any lesser facts covered by the allegation which are sufficient for the purpose he has in hand . . . The greater allegation includes the less'.

For these purposes it is the genuineness of the landlord's intention that is crucial and the burden rests with the tenant to show that the landlord's professed intentions are fictitious. The motives underlying the landlord's intention are moreover irrelevant. In *Fisher* v. *Taylor's Furnishing Stores Ltd* [1956] 2 All ER 78, the Court of Appeal emphasised that the use to which the premises are ultimately put is of no concern. Hence, the landlord may wish to dispose of the redeveloped premises or may not have come to any decision as to their future use. At the outset, however, it should be appreciated that ground (f) is unavailable in circumstances where the landlord intends to gain possession, sell the site to a developer and then leave the premises. It must be the competent landlord who intends to develop. In contrast, there is no problem where the landlord intends to lease or sell after the development is completed.

9.3.1 Firm and settled intention

The competent landlord must have an unequivocal and fully formed intention to demolish, reconstruct or carry out works of construction. This requires the landlord to have both a genuine desire to carry out the works and a reasonable chance of putting those plans into effect. As Lord Denning M.R. stated in *Reohorn* v. *Barry Corp* [1956] 2 All ER 742, 'Intention connotes an ability to carry it into effect. A man cannot properly be said to intend to do a work of reconstruction when he has not got the means to carry it out. He may hope to do so; he will not have the intention to do so'. A vague or general assertion of intention will not therefore suffice. The classic exposition of what constitutes an intention emerges from the speech of Lord Asquith in *Cunliffe* v. *Goodman* [1950] 2 KB 237:

> Not merely is the term 'intention' unsatisfied if the person professing it has too many hurdles to overcome, or too little control of events; it is equally inappropriate if at the material date that person is in effect not deciding to proceed but feeling his way and reserving his decision until he shall be in a possession of financial data sufficient to enable him to determine whether the payment will be commercially worthwhile ... In the case of neither scheme did she [the landlord] form a settled intention to proceed. Neither project moved out of the zone of contemplation – out of the sphere of the tentative, the provisional and the exploratory – into the valley of decision.

In order to move into this 'valley of decision', the landlord must have a definite attitude to redevelopment, formed plans and overcome any serious obstacles. There is, however, no requirement that the landlord has taken all necessary steps towards the achievement of the development and the proposal need not be examined by the court in detail. It is also possible for the landlord to promote alternative plans and maintain both up to and throughout the hearing. All that is necessary is a genuine and realistic intention to implement one of those schemes. *Yoga for Health Foundation* v. *Guest & Utilini* [2002] EWHC 2658 (Ch) shows that the court is much less concerned with the specific details of the project than with the genuineness and practicality of the landlord's intention. Accordingly, the burden of proof rests heavily with the tenant to demonstrate that the landlord's professed intentions are fictitious, vague or unrealistic. It is during the course of such a challenge that matters of detail, such as an absence of planning permission or sufficient funding, might assume importance. These issues are, however, limited only to the determination of whether or not there is a reasonable prospect of the ground (f) development works occurring.

It is sufficient that there is a reasonable prospect of bringing about that which is intended and, hence, there must not be so many obstructions which undermine that prospect. In this context, a reasonable prospect was described by Saville L.J. in *Cadogan* v. *McCarthy & Stone Developments Ltd* [1996] EGCS 94 as, 'a real chance, a prospect that is strong enough to be acted on by a reasonable landlord minded to go ahead with plans . . . as opposed to a prospect that should be treated as merely fanciful or as one that should sensibly be ignored by a reasonable landlord'.

As will be shown, intention is primarily evidenced by the ability, both financial and legal, of the landlord to put the plans into operation. In *Yoga for Health Foundation* v. *Guest & Utilini*, for example, a number of factors assumed relevance. The landlord was a property developer who had acquired the land on the sole basis that it would be developed. It had a proven track record of completed development projects and adequate funds to undertake this particular project. The scope for development had moreover been reflected in a higher price paid for the site. This heightened cost (some £130,000) offered the strongest indication that the works would go ahead. This was reinforced by the fact that, if the development did not take place, it would spell financial ruin for the landlord.

The fact that the landlord proposes a technical breach of planning conditions does not, however, prevent the landlord from establishing the requisite intention. In addition, entrusting the work to another (e.g. an agent or a contractor) does not disqualify the landlord from relying upon ground (f), provided that some form of control is retained over the works. In the absence of control, the landlord will be regarded as merely intending to dispose of the property with vacant possession. It is evident that the current provisions do not adequately cater for the contemporary trend towards redevelopment on a grand scale when the development process is so long and complex that the landlord is unable to satisfy the intended requirement when the first leases of properties forming part of the site expire. It is suggested that, in such cases, the landlord should argue for a short term on renewal and the insertion of a development break clause.

9.3.2 Evidencing intention

As mentioned above, the landlord must show an ability to undertake the works and demonstrate the reasonable prospect of them being carried out. This is a question of fact and degree and there are a number of ways in which the landlord can establish the firm and settled intention to redevelop.

Sworn testimony

The court may accept the uncorroborated sworn testimony of the landlord, but to rely on this course alone is somewhat unsafe. The court must be careful as the landlord may assert the intention at the hearing, but may have a change of heart once in possession. In such cases, short of awarding compensation for misrepresentation, there is nothing that the court can do.

An undertaking

An undertaking to the court may add evidential weight to the landlord's opposition. In *London Hilton Jewellers Ltd* v. *Hilton International Hotels Ltd* [1990] 20 EG 69, the landlord's undertaking tipped the scales in favour of rejecting the application for a new lease. The undertaking does however have to be both specific and realistic as a vague or implausible undertaking is of little evidential worth. Furthermore, as illustrated in *Coppen* v. *Bruce-Smith* (1998) 76 P & CR D 7, the terms of any undertaking given should be carefully scrutinised by the landlord. In that case the undertaking included the demolition of recreational facilities which meant that planning permission would remain unavailable. If the undertaking had not made reference to these works, the landlord would have succeeded on the basis of the demolition of the buildings situated on the property. Although there are no hard-and-fast rules, it is not surprising that the court will normally look for some outward sign that the landlord is serious in intent.

Planning permission

The landlord will usually have obtained planning permission or, at the least, should be able to demonstrate a reasonable prospect that planning permission will be granted if the landlord is awarded possession. For these purposes, as made clear by Saville L.J. in *Cadogan* v. *McCarthy & Stone Developments* [1996] EGCS 94, 'A reasonable prospect does not entail that it is more likely than not that [planning] permission will be obtained'. As Mance L.J. put it in *Dogan* v. *Semali Investments Ltd* [2005] 50 EG 92, '"Reasonable prospect" is a low threshold, not to be equated with probability'. Instead, the landlord must show that there is a real and not a merely fanciful chance of permission being forthcoming. A similar approach applies also to any listed building consent which the landlord requires.

The issue is determined therefore according to whether a reasonable man would expect permission to be granted. As demonstrated in *Coppen* v. *Bruce-Smith* (1998) 76 P & CR D 7, where there is no reasonable prospect of obtaining planning permission it cannot be said that the landlord has the requisite intention. In that case, as the landlord had previously been refused permission because the proposed construction would entail a loss of recreational facilities, it was apparent that planning permission would again be refused on the same grounds, even though the landlord now sought to turn the tennis courts into a derelict 'brown field' site. If there is uncertainty as to whether such permission is necessary the court normally should not try to resolve the issue. It was moreover established in *Gatwick Parking Services Ltd* v. *Sargent* [2000] 25 EG 141 that an appellate court can take into account the grant of planning permission, even though it had not been obtained at the date of the original hearing.

Financial viability

The landlord should also be able to demonstrate the availability of adequate finance. The tenant should therefore require the landlord (under CPR, Part 31) to produce for inspection any disclosed documents which purport to support this intention, ability and preparations to carry out the works. This approach is equally applicable to ground (g) below.

This demonstration of financial ability can adopt a number of forms and the court is entitled to look at any relevant documentation, even if such documents remain undisclosed before the hearing. For example, in *DAF Motoring*

Centre (Gosport) Ltd v. *Hatfield & Wheeler* (1982) 263 EG 976 a letter from a bank manager promising finance was held to suffice for these purposes. Similarly, in *Adams* v. *Glibbery (JR) & Sons Ltd* (CA, 22 January 1991) a faxed message from the landlord's bank proved decisive. The court is not, however, concerned with the precise source of the funds and, instead, simply concentrates upon whether the funds available are sufficient to implement the proposed development. Accordingly, where the landlord has cash flow problems and is dependent upon the support of a bank, it will be expected that some evidence of the bank's willingness to provide continued (and increased) finance will be brought before the court.

If the landlord does not have the necessary financial resources, it will generally follow that the intention to redevelop is incomplete. It is, however, open to the landlord to arrange for the work to be carried out by another. This occurred in *Gilmour Caterers Ltd* v. *St. Bartholomew's Hospital Governors* [1956] 1 All ER 314 where the landlord established its intention by entering into an agreement for a building lease under which the lessees were to do the rebuilding. This flexibility therefore leaves it open to the landlord to have a change of tactics prior to the hearing. For example, in *Spook Erection Ltd* v. *British Railways Board* [1988] 21 EG 73 the landlord had initially intended to develop through the sale of the site with vacant possession. This would have taken the landlord outside ground (f), but a successful change of strategy occurred when the landlord then decided to grant a long building lease to a developer who would undertake the work.

Although for these purposes it is not necessary that binding contracts have been entered into between reversioner and developer, in *Edwards* v. *Thompson* (1990) 60 P & CR 222 the landlord was deemed unable to carry out the works because, at the time of the hearing, he had not selected an independent developer and had not reached any agreement as to the cost of the redevelopment. There was, simply, no guarantee that the whole development would go ahead if the landlord obtained possession. The landlord is also expected to incur expenditure on developing plans prior to obtaining possession. This does not, however, pose a great risk for the landlord. In *Peter Goddard & Sons Ltd* v. *Hounslow London BC* [1992] 1 EGLR 281, for example, the fact that the landlord had spent £70,000 by way of preparatory expenditure indicated strongly that the works would go ahead. Similarly, in *BP International Ltd* v. *Newcastle International Airport Ltd* [2005] 1 P & CR D G 18 the construction of a new fuel farm by the landlord at the airport was a strong indicator that the landlord intended to carry out the works on the tenants' old fuel farms. The steps taken by the landlord in carrying out works and seeking tenders for future works demonstrated that the intention expressed by the landlord was a genuine intention.

Corporate intentions

As regards a company, it is necessary to evidence a corporate intention to redevelop. The mere evidence of a company representative, whether secretary or director, should not of itself suffice. This is because the mere appointment of such officers does not give them adequate powers to form a company intention. Usually therefore a corporate intention will be evident from a formal board resolution, but even then it should be coupled with an additional resolution authorising a specified director or manager to give evidence of the company's intention, if required. In *BP International Ltd* v. *Newcastle International Airport Ltd* (18 January 2005), the directors of the landlord company approved the expenditure of £4.5 million in respect of the construction of a new fuel farm. This gave great weight to the landlord's case. Alternatively, a director could be given express or implied authority to take the necessary decisions and, in this case, the director's intention would constitute the corporate intention. It may moreover be possible to overcome the absence of a formal resolution where the intention of a number of directors is such that it is to be regarded as the company intention. Much turns upon the officers' positions within the company, the nature of the matter under consideration and other relevant circumstances. If, however, the directors do not possess adequate powers either to pass a resolution or to formulate the company's intention, a resolution in a general meeting will be necessary.

9.3.3 Timing of intention

Although the landlord's intention must be established at the hearing, it can be put into a provable form after the hearing has begun. In order to promote convenience and to keep costs at a minimum, however, it is normally desirable that the determination of intention be dealt with as a preliminary matter before any other issue in the proceedings. The attraction of a two-stage trial is that if the landlord succeeds on ground (f) there is no need for the parties to collate valuation evidence as to the new rent. One hearing might be appropriate when the terms of the new lease sought by the tenant are not in much dispute.

The intention need not be supported by evidence at the date of service of the landlord's notice or counter notice and there is no need for the landlord, at that time, to disclose precise intentions. It is sufficient for the landlord merely to indicate that ground (f) will be relied upon. This means that the landlord is able to advance the development plans in the intervening period between the service of the renewal documentation and the hearing. It is also permissible for the landlord to express alternative schemes of proposed development both up to and throughout the hearing. All that is necessary is the intention to carry out one of them. In addition, last minute changes to the proposals do not automatically damage the credibility of the landlord's claim. Neither does it matter if the identity of the competent landlord changes between the service of the landlord's renewal documentation and the date of the hearing. If this occurs, it is the new competent landlord's intention which is relevant and this will be unaffected by the seriousness or otherwise of the intention of the former landlord. As Denning M.R. said in *Marks v. British Waterways Board* [1963] 1 WLR 1008, 'If the subsequent landlord can prove that at the date of the hearing he has the requisite intention, the new lease must be refused'.

9.3.4 Timing of works

While it is at the time of the hearing that the competent landlord must establish the existence of a firm and settled intention, that intention is necessarily one that cannot be put into effect until the termination of the existing lease. Accordingly, the landlord must also demonstrate the intention to start work on, or within a reasonable time after, the date vacant possession will be obtained. An intention to commence work within three months of termination, for example, was held to be sufficient in *Livestock Underwriting Agency v. Corbett & Newton* (1955) 165 EG 469. The tenant's cause moreover will not be advanced by deferring the termination date (e.g. lodging an appeal against the refusal of a new lease) and then arguing that the landlord is less able to effect the development. In addition, the tenant is not entitled to argue that the landlord should use a contractor as a way of speeding up the development process. It should also be recalled that, once possession is gained, the landlord is free to have a change of mind and the tenant (except if there has been misrepresentation) is left with no remedy. Such occurred in *Bentley & Skinner (Bond St. Jewellers) Ltd* v. *Searchmap Ltd* [2003] EWHC 1621 (Ch). This possibility explains why it is necessary for the landlord to have a fixed and settled intention to redevelop.

Section 31(2)

If there is no intention to start the works within a reasonable time, but the landlord can show that they will be commenced within one year of the termination date stated in the s.25 notice or s.26 request, the court must by virtue of s.31(2) (which applies also to grounds (d) and (e)) dismiss the tenant's application and declare when the landlord will be able to satisfy the court. This provision leaves unaltered the date when the intention must be established and focuses instead upon when it is to be implemented.

Following the declaration, the tenant has 14 days to make an *ex parte* application in chambers (High Court) or to the district judge (county court) requiring the court to substitute the date specified in the declaration for the original termination date. This 14-day period cannot be extended. If the tenant fails to respond promptly to the declaration, the tenancy will end on the date specified in the renewal documentation or, if later, on final disposal of the tenant's application. On the tenant taking the positive step envisaged by s.31(2), the existing tenancy continues beyond the original termination date until the later date specified in the declaration. It is to be stressed that the tenant has the choice of whether or not to accept this extension.

9.3.5 Premises

In *Pumperninks of Piccadilly Ltd* v. *Land Securities Plc* [2002] Ch 332, the Court of Appeal had to consider the degree to which these statutory provisions applied to a so-called eggshell tenancy. This is a tenancy that does not include any structural, load-bearing element and where the demise is merely of the internal skin of a building, that is, an enclosed space without structural parts. The landlord intended to carry out major works to the building and proposals were of such a far-reaching nature that they undoubtedly amounted to works of both demolition and reconstruction. The tenant countered that its holding did not consist of premises that could be demolished or reconstructed. In other words, the works were not to be carried out on 'premises' comprised within its 'holding'. The tenant's reasoning was that the need for 'premises' operated to limit ground (f) to redevelopment only of those parts of the holding which performed some structural function. If correct, ground (f) could not be invoked in relation to the present demise of an airspace within a thin enclosing skin. Any works done to the eggshell would therefore amount merely to works of redecoration and fall outside ground (f).

Chadwick L.J. thought that the meanings of 'demolish' and 'reconstruct' for the purposes of ground (f) hinged, in all cases, upon three questions. First, what are the physical features of the property comprised in the tenancy? Secondly, what amongst those features is capable of being demolished and reconstructed? Thirdly, can what is to be done to those features properly be described as demolition or reconstruction of those features or a substantial part of them? He added, 'It is, I think, wrong to start from the premise that physical features that are not load-bearing are incapable of being demolished and reconstructed'. The structure was the fabric which enclosed the demise and the physical boundaries of that demise (whether walls, ceilings, floors or only their surfaces) were held to constitute premises within the meaning of ground (f). Hence, the holding consisted of premises which were to be the subject of the landlord's redevelopment plans. The appellate court could find nothing in the authorities to support the tenant's contention that 'premises' had to be confined to those parts which performed a structural function. As Charles J. concluded, 'in my judgment the ordinary meaning of the words demolish and reconstruct is wide enough to apply to an eggshell'.

This approach was shared also by Lawrence Collins J. in *Ivorygrove Ltd* v. *Global Grange Ltd* [2004] 4 All ER 144 when he concluded, 'There is plainly nothing in the wording of s.30(1)(*f*) which requires the demolition or construction of structural or load-bearing features as a condition of its applicability'. It followed that whether the relevant parts of the premises are load bearing is simply one factor to be taken on board and does not operate as any precondition. In that case proposed works were undoubtedly extensive in nature, but only 10 per cent of the scheme was to impact directly upon the load-bearing elements of the building.

9.3.6 The works

Ground (f) details what it is that the landlord must intend. The landlord is required to intend to demolish or reconstruct the premises comprising the holding (or a substantial part of the premises); or to carry out substantial construction work on the holding. Whether or not the proposed works fit within one of these categories is an issue of fact and degree. In *Bewlay (Tobacconists) Ltd* v. *British Bata Shoe Co. Ltd* [1958] 3 All ER 652, Evershed M.R. demonstrated that the court must, 'look at the totality of what is proposed to be done and, as a matter of fact and commonsense, to ask . . . whether these proposals . . . satisfy the language of ground (f)'. There the removal of a wall and its replacement by screens amounted to works of reconstruction. It was also made clear that the landlord's opposition is not limited to works appropriate to turn to modern use an old or out-of-date building.

Demolition

Where the landlord intends to demolish all the buildings on the holding, this is clearly within the scope of ground (f). Similarly, if the intention is not to destroy all the buildings, but to demolish a substantial part of the premises, the landlord will also be able to rely upon this ground of opposition. In *Wessex Reserve Forces and Cadets Association* v. *White* [2005] EWCA Civ 1744, the tenant occupied the land for Air Training Corps activities and it was not in doubt that these activities constituted a business for the purposes of the 1954 Act. The landlord (Mr White) opposed the grant of a new tenancy on the basis of s.30(1)(*f*) (i.e. redevelopment). More specifically, the landlord claimed that he wanted to demolish the premises (or a substantial part of them) and could not reasonably do so without obtaining possession of the tenant's holding. The unusual feature of this case was that, apart from a small shed, every other structure (i.e. several large huts, sheds and a Portakabin) on the site had been introduced by the tenant. The tenant moreover was under an obligation to remove all buildings at the end of the lease. The Court of Appeal concluded that the landlord could not make out a case

RENEWAL OF BUSINESS TENANCIES

to demolish premises when, as here, there would be no buildings remaining at the end of the lease. Chadwick L.J. was pragmatic, 'The buildings will not be available for demolition; because they would not be there'.

Although 'substantial' connotes something that is 'big', 'solid' and 'considerable', in *Housleys* v. *Bloomer-Holt Ltd* [1966] 2 All ER 966 the demolition of a brick wall and a wooden garage (covering one-third of a timber yard) and replacement with concrete hardstanding for lorries, was held to be sufficient for the purposes of ground (f). As Sellers L.J. said:

> The fact is that what was to be demolished was all that there was to demolish on the site, the garage and the wall, and all that seems to be demolishing the whole of the premises so far as any structure was to be demolished. It seems to me that fulfils the requirements sufficiently. I am not concerned at the moment to consider what would be the position if the structure to be demolished had been some very small dog-kennel or very small hut on a very large area.

While the latter examples might still amount to demolition, it is probable that the landlord would not succeed under ground (f) because the need for possession to carry out the works could not be made out. In *Coppen* v. *Bruce-Smith* (1998) 76 P & CR D 7 therefore the demolition of a clubhouse and garage alone would have satisfied ground (f). If it had been left at that, planning permission would not have been necessary and the landlord's ground of opposition most certainly made out. Unfortunately for the landlord, however, the additional intention to demolish the tennis courts both required and prevented the grant of planning permission and defeated the claim to possession.

Reconstruction

It has been held that the term 'reconstruct' is akin to a building exercise following a measure of demolition and entails more than mere works of improvement and repair or mere changes of identity. It is analogous with the term 'rebuild'. As Lawrence Collins J. explained in *Ivorygrove Ltd* v. *Global Grange Ltd* [2004] 4 All ER 144, '"Reconstruction" connotes a physical reconstruction of the premises, and means a substantial interference with the structure of the premises and then a rebuilding of such part of the premises as has been demolished by reason of the interference with the structure'. Accordingly, in *Cook* v. *Mott* (1961) 178 EG 637 the term 'reconstruction' was viewed as involving the demolition of an existing fixed structure in whole or part as opposed to 'construction' which connotes works of an original or additional nature. The terms 'demolition' and 'reconstruction' here fall to be construed conjunctively. The court will therefore assess the degree of the proposed demolition and building work against the background of the premises as they currently exist. Work which is not constructional, but is subsidiary to work that is, can be taken into account in this overall evaluation of substantiality. As Lawrence Collins J. commented in *Ivorygrove Ltd* v.

Global Grange Ltd, 'Work associated with demolition and reconstruction, such as works of preparation ancillary to such works, or re-plastering and rewiring, or the laying of cables and drains, may be considered when looking at the totality of the work to determine whether the work is construction or is substantial or is on a substantial part of the premises'. Hence, in *Romulus Trading Co. Ltd* v. *Henry Smiths Charity Trustees (No.1)* [1990] 32 EG 41 the plastering of a new load-bearing wall was regarded as part of the reconstruction of the wall itself. Other examples of reconstruction include:

- the proposed change from a small shop with two storage areas into part of a large amusement arcade was held to be reconstruction (*Joel* v. *Swaddle* [1957] 3 All ER 325);
- the physical removal of most of an office suite and its replacement by a different floor level, new suspended ceilings, new partition walls and the removal of a brick wall constituted reconstruction in *City Offices (Regent St) Ltd* v. *Europa Acceptance Group Plc* [1990] 5 EG 71.

In *Cadle (Percy E) & Co Ltd* v. *Jacmarch Properties Ltd* [1957] 1 All ER 148 however the turning of three floors, in separate occupation, into a self-contained unit was not regarded as falling within ground (f). The actual construction work to be done was very little indeed. Similarly, the installation of a new shop front was held not to be reconstruction in *Atkinson* v. *Bettison* (1985) 273 EG 1217. Also, the landscaping of a field, removal of material and infilling was not classified as work of reconstruction in *Botterill* v. *Bedfordshire CC* [1985] 1 EGLR 82. In that case the council was merely intending to alter the shape of the land and to give a slightly new composition to the field. It was not open to the council to contend that it was constructing a domed field with some trees situated on it.

Construction

Ground (f) deals also with new construction, whether on the whole holding or on part of it (e.g. an extension to an existing building). Construction, therefore, connotes either new building or adding to what is already there. The construction work, however, needs to be substantial which again raises issues of fact and degree. The laying of a sufficient area of concrete and the resurfacing with hardstanding was regarded as construction for these purposes in *Housleys* v. *Bloomer-Holt Ltd* [1966] 2 All ER 966. Similarly, in *Cook* v. *Mott* (1961) 178 EG 637 the making of a road and the laying of pipes, cables and drains so that the land could be used as a caravan site was sufficient. The work must, however, amount to more than refurbishment or improvement. In *Barth* v. *Pritchard* [1990] 20 EG 65, for example, electrical re-wiring, provision of new toilet facilities and installation of a new central heating system were, in relation to the holding, deemed neither to be works of construction nor to be substantial. The works proposed there could more properly be classified as refurbishment or improvements. In contrast, the extension of a factory by the building of a second storey on top of one section and erection of a wall between that section and the tenant's holding were designated as being works of construction in *Fernandez* v. *Walding* [1968] 2 WLR 583.

9.3.7   Need for possession

The landlord has to show that the works of demolition, reconstruction or construction cannot be reasonably carried out without obtaining possession of the tenant's holding. Possession in this context means both physical and legal possession and the landlord is required to establish that the work could not be undertaken without bringing the tenancy to an end. Accordingly, in *Bewlay (Tobacconists) Ltd* v. *Bata Shoe Co Ltd* [1958] 3 All ER 652, Sellers L.J. felt that the installation of a new shop front did not require possession of the holding as the business could continue as usual. Similarly, in *Heath* v. *Drown* [1973] AC 498 it was concluded that, where there is an express right to enter and to carry out works reserved in the lease, the landlord cannot successfully oppose the tenant's application for a new lease under ground (f). This is because legal possession is not then dependent upon the termination of the tenancy. Instead, the legal right to undertake the works was granted by the lease itself and this reasoning applies even though the tenant will have to close his business for a temporary period. This general rule will give way, however, where the work when completed would deprive the tenant of facilities necessary to carry on trade and amount to a derogation from the landlord's grant. In *Leathwoods Ltd* v. *Total Oil (GB) Ltd* (1986) 51 P & CR 20, the landlord, having a right to carry out alterations, improvements and additions, proposed a scheme of works which would have prevented the tenant continuing the business of selling and repairing cars. To carry out such works lawfully, the landlord will still need to acquire legal possession as well as physical possession.

9.3.8   Section 31A: calling the landlord's bluff

Even though the landlord can show the necessary intention, where there is no existing term in the lease which gives a right to enter, the tenant can still obtain a renewal where possession of the entire holding is not required in order to carry out the redevelopment. This brings into relevance the somewhat complicated s.31A(1)(*a*)–(*b*) which, by way of an escape route for the tenant, provides that the landlord is unable to demonstrate the need for possession in two circumstances. These are, first, where the tenant agrees to the inclusion of new terms which would reasonably allow the landlord to undertake the works without obtaining possession and without substantial interference with the tenant's business. Secondly, when the tenant is willing to accept an economically separable part of the holding which will allow the landlord to carry out the intended works.

As this provision is relevant only when the landlord can establish the necessary intention to carry out works within the scope of ground (f), it does not concern a landlord who is unable to show such intention. Section 31A is designed to benefit the tenant and does not offer assistance to the landlord who wants to repossess. The relationship between ground (f) and s.31A was considered in *Romulus Trading Company Ltd* v. *Henry Smith's Charity Trustees (No. 2)* [1991] 11 EG 112. The Court of Appeal felt it proper for the tenant to put forward conditional arguments. Accordingly, and in the alternative, the tenant can: dispute the genuineness of the landlord's intention; contend that the work does not fall within ground (f); propose that the work can be carried out by the means of access and facilities contemplated by s.31A(1)(*a*); and suggest that the work can be done if there was a grant of part only of the premises under s.31A(1)(*b*). This avoids the need for any election on the tenant's part.

New terms: section 31A(1)(a)

The tenant may prevent the landlord recovering possession under ground (f) when it agrees to the inclusion within the new lease of new terms. These terms must facilitate the landlord's access and ability to carry out the work and allow the landlord to execute the work without retaking possession or disrupting to a substantial extent and for a substantial time the tenant's use of the holding. This provision is therefore relevant only where the existing lease does not contain a term allowing the landlord to carry out the work. The tenant will not be able to utilise s.31A(1)(*a*) if the landlord's works will be made unreasonably more protracted or expensive. This provision is also unavailable where the landlord intends to demolish the entire premises. The aim of the provision is to reduce the ability of the landlord to recover possession, except where major demolition or reconstruction is proposed.

The assessment of interference is one of fact and degree. It is the effect on the tenant's present use which is relevant and not the effect on the tenant's business. Accordingly, the fact that the tenant's goodwill will not be affected by the tenant temporarily moving out of possession is irrelevant. The key issue is whether the work can go ahead with only minor and temporary inconvenience to the tenant's use of the holding or whether it will involve a total disruption of that use. The onus rests on the tenant to show that the proposed term will allow the landlord to undertake the work and the court's determination will be based on a detailed description of the works intended. In fairness to the landlord, the court may require the tenant to particularise the case put under s.31A(1)(*a*).

In *Cerex Jewels Ltd* v. *Peachey Property Corporation* (1986) 52 P & CR 127, for example, the closure of the tenant's business for two weeks was regarded as a minor interference, whereas in *Blackburn* v. *Hussain* [1988] 22 EG 78 a closure for 12 weeks was sufficiently disruptive to prevent the operation of s.31A. In *Pumperninks of Piccadilly Ltd* v. *Land Securities Plc* [2002] Ch 332, it was accepted that new terms relating to access and other facilities would allow the landlord to carry out the intended works within a period of approximately three weeks. Nevertheless, if granted a new lease the tenant would, in order to resume its business, need to return the premises to their previous state and condition. Charles J. observed that the calculation should include also the time it would take to reinstate the premises. These cases illustrate the basic proposition that the longer the interruption the less likely it is that the court will protect the tenant. The tenant is unable to waive the interference with the use of the holding because the section does not confer on the tenant the ability to disregard any disruption. The landlord is under no duty to minimise the interference.

The underlying rationale of s.31A(1) is that the landlord's plans can still be reasonably carried out and that they can coexist with the grant of a new lease. On the facts of *Pumperninks of Piccadilly Ltd* this patently was not the case. First, the landlord's works would be entirely frustrated if the tenant obtained a new lease. This undermined any argument as to reasonableness of effecting the works. As much of the landlord's works would have to be undone by the tenant in order to occupy, the landlord could not reasonably do what it intended to do if the tenant obtained a renewal.

Secondly, there was no possibility of coexistence because the proposed redevelopment would destroy the nature of the holding and prevent the tenant's occupation of it. On completion of the works, the eggshell and rights enjoyed with it would no longer exist and, hence, would be incapable of occupation by the tenant. Chadwick L.J. believed that these results rendered the statutory defence inoperative, 'It follows, as it seems to me, that if the proposed works were carried out with access and facilities given pursuant to the terms of a new tenancy, the property comprised in the new tenancy would thereafter be unusable by the tenant for the purposes of its business'. Section 31A could not operate in circumstances where, as a consequence of the work, the holding would become unusable indefinitely for the purpose of the tenant's business.

New letting of part: section 31A(1)(b)

This operates when the tenant is willing to accept a tenancy of an economically separable part of the holding. This offers the tenant a partial shield in that the new lease will be granted, but only of that economically separable part of the existing holding. The meaning of 'an economically separable part' is provided by s.31A(2) which states that a part is economically separable when, after the completion of the intended work, the aggregate of the rents which would be reasonably obtainable on separate lettings of that part and the remainder of the premises is not less than the rent which is reasonably obtainable on a letting of those premises as a whole. Accordingly, whether the separation of the part is economic depends purely upon valuation evidence of the landlord's alternative rental incomes. It has nothing to do with the tenant's business.

For the tenant to rely upon this provision, it is necessary that a further condition be satisfied. This additional requirement is expressed in the alternative: first, that the tenant is willing to grant access and facilities (under s.31A(1)(a)) in respect of the economically separable part and the proposed works can be carried out without substantially affecting the tenant's business. Secondly, that the landlord can reasonably carry out the proposed works (without being granted access and facilities over the separable part) on the excluded part which, of course, will no longer form part of the tenant's holding. The burden of proof lies on the tenant and it is necessary that the tenant's willingness be established at the date of the hearing. It should be borne in mind, however, that the tenant cannot insist that there be an alteration to the landlord's plans so as to minimise the impact of the redevelopment. As Charles J. admitted in *Pumperninks of Piccadilly Ltd* v. *Land Securities Plc* [2002] Ch 332, 'for the purposes of s.31A the court is to look at the work the Landlord intends to do and not some other work which might be said to achieve the same object, or additional work that the Landlord might have carried out'. It is the *bona fide* intentions of the landlord which prevail and the court cannot consider whether the landlord's proposals are reasonable or modify those plans. This was illustrated in *Decca Navigator Co Ltd* v. *GLC* [1974] 1 All ER 1178 where the tenant argued that the landlord did not need all of the holding for the purposes of building a fire station and that a 15-foot strip should be retained for the tenant's car parking purposes. The contention was that the landlord could construct a perfectly adequate fire station in a different way. The tenant's argument was roundly rejected.

9.4   GROUND (G): OWNER OCCUPATION

Under s.30(1)(g) the tenant's application for a new tenancy can be opposed if the competent landlord intends to occupy the entirety of the tenant's holding for use (either in whole or part) as a residence or for a business carried on therein by the landlord or a company controlled by the landlord. As will be shown, this is qualified by the so-called five-year rule imposed by s.30(2). To succeed under this ground there are a number of factors which must be established: there must be a sufficiency of intention; the intention must be to occupy; and occupation must be for business or residential purposes.

9.4.1 Intention

The requirement as to the landlord's settled and genuine intention to occupy is subject to a similar standard of proof (and similar judicial gloss) as considered above in connection with ground (f). It contains therefore both subjective and objective elements. Consequently, the landlord must be able to demonstrate both a *bona fide* intention to occupy for business/residential purposes and the reasonable prospect of bringing about this occupation. A noticeable difference between grounds (f) and (g) however is that it is not normally appropriate to test the reasonable practicability of the landlord's intention under ground (g) by reference to the presence or absence of detailed financial and structural plans, consents and planning permission. In *Dolgellau Golf Club* v. *Hett* (1998) 76 P & CR 526, for example, the landlord succeeded even though he produced little to demonstrate the detail and practicality of his intentions. As Balcombe L.J. explained in *Palisade Investments Ltd* v. *Collin Estates Ltd* [1992] 2 EGLR 94, 'the Act was intended to be construed sensibly, so as to hold a fair balance between landlord and tenant. It is not . . . to be construed so as to create a series of artificial hoops through which the landlord must jump before he must satisfy the necessary intention'. Nevertheless, where there is a proposed change of use, the likelihood of being granted planning permission will become a relevant factor.

It is also important to appreciate that the ground (g) is concerned only with the reality of the landlord's intention of setting up a business and not the probability of achieving its start or its ultimate success. In *Cox* v. *Binfield* [1989] 1 EGLR 97, the evidence was that the landlord would have difficulties in financing the necessary equipment and that the economic advantages of the venture were doubtful. Nevertheless, the opposition succeeded even though the future plans for the holding were ill thought out and might fail. As O'Connor L.J. observed, 'Objectively, the judge must be able to say that this intention is one which is being capable of being carried out in the reasonable future in the circumstances which will prevail when possession is achieved by the landlord'. Similarly, in *Dolgellau Golf Club* v. *Hett*, the landlord's plans were incomplete and the proposed business was likely to fail in the longer term. Nevertheless, the landlord's opposition prevailed because the proposal was at least capable of succeeding. This was so even though the landlord's business proposals were modified in the intervening period between the service of the renewal documentation and the hearing. In that case the landlord's counter notice stated that the landlord sought to operate an 18-hole golf course, but because of financial constraints successfully claimed possession to run a nine-hole course. Auld L.J. took an overview:

> It is not an incident of the statutory formula, nor of the present judicial gloss on it, that a landlord, in seeking to satisfy the court of the reality of his intention, should be subjected to minute examination of his finances with a view to determining the financial viability and durability of the business he intends to establish.

The Court is not there to police a landlord's entitlement to recover possession of his own property by examining the financial wisdom of his genuinely held plans for it.

Subjective and objective intentions

The court will evaluate the efficacy of the landlord's intention from both a subjective and an objective standpoint. This duality of approach demands that the landlord must not only demonstrate a *bona fide* intention, but must also show that there exists a realistic prospect of that intention being brought into effect. Hence, a subjective desire is insufficient unless there is also evidence of the objective ability to occupy. In *Zarvos* v. *Pradhan* [2003] 26 EG 180, the Court of Appeal was invited to test the professed intentions of the landlord and to determine whether they were sufficiently genuine and realistic for the purposes of s.30(1)(*g*). In the course of this appraisal, Ward L.J. provided an astute examination of the fusion of subjective and objective factors which govern whether or not the landlord has a sufficiency of intention. He considered which intention was to be considered first and concluded that there existed nothing in principle or practice which demanded any type of sequential treatment. Ward L.J. added, 'Ultimately there is a single question for the judge to decide, namely the question posed by s.30(1)(*g*) itself: does the landlord on the termination of the current tenancy intend to occupy the holding for the purposes of a business to be carried on by him therein?' This means:

- if there is no genuine intention to run the business then, as Ward L.J. explained, 'The landlord falls at the first fence. One need not investigate the reality or the fantasy of his business plan'. In such a case, the judge should make it plain that he does not believe the landlord and, wherever possible, should explain why;
- if there is a lack of reasonable prospects, there is no need to consider the landlord's *bona fides*. As Ward L.J. put it, 'If he hangs his judgment on the second limb he does not have to disbelieve the landlord when he sets out his stall. Indeed, the second limb is there precisely to cater for the case where the landlord does genuinely believe in what he says he intends to do';
- only when the finding is that the landlord has real prospects of setting up the business does the issue of genuineness assume vitality.

Proving the subjective intention

In *Europark (Midlands) Ltd* v. *Town Centre Securities* (1985) 274 EG 289, the landlord's intention to occupy was demonstrated by the minutes of a board meeting, an affidavit of a director, and obtaining quotations for equipment to

205

be used by the landlord on regaining possession. In *Page* v. *Sole* (CA, 24 January 1991), a minute of a partnership meeting and the evidence of one partner was sufficient for the court to make the factual finding of intention. Similarly, in *Skeet* v. *Powell-Sneddon* [1988] 40 EG 116 the evidence of the landlord that she wanted to go into the hotel business with her husband and to give employment to her daughter sufficed, even though no partnership agreement had been entered and no application had been made for a liquor licence. Although some doubt has been expressed concerning the appropriateness of an undertaking to occupy because of the inability at law to enforce such an undertaking, it is common for such an undertaking to support the landlord's claim. While an undertaking alone is not conclusive, at the least it evidences intention and can only assist the landlord's case.

Proving the objective intention

The landlord will usually experience no difficulties in showing the financial resources to start a business. The finances of the competent landlord might, however, be questioned in circumstances where the premises need expensive refurbishment before they can be occupied. In this instance, a detailed examination of the financial viability of the landlord's proposals might be appropriate and become a key factor in determining whether the intention is genuine and realistic. The landlord may also have difficulties where occupation is sought for business purposes which are prohibited under a head lease. In such a situation, the competent landlord should secure the relaxation of the user covenant before the hearing date. Problems can arise where the premises need expensive refurbishment before they can be occupied and the finances of the landlord are insufficient to undertake the work; or where the landlord will need planning permission, but has no reasonable prospect of obtaining such authority.

In *Zarvos* v. *Pradhan* [2003] 26 EG 180, the landlord opposed the tenant's renewal on the basis that he wished to take over occupation of the demised restaurant. Some £40,000 would have to be borrowed to get the business up and running. Mr Zarvos was somewhat economical with the truth and refused to disclose fully his financial situation. The trial judge also viewed the economic projections for the proposed business as overly optimistic and believed that a prudent bank manager would be sceptical about the business plan. Although subsequent to the trial Mr Zarvos did obtain the necessary finance, this new evidence was not admitted by the appellate court. Ward L.J. believed that this evidence could have been obtained with reasonable diligence for use at the hearing and that to allow its subsequent introduction would compromise the interests of justice, 'This may be harsh on the landlord but it would be more harsh on the tenants to give the landlord a chance to put his house in order and subject them to a retrial'.

The decision in *Zarvos* serves also as a practical reminder that, although the landlord is not expected to produce much in the way of evidence, he is expected to provide enough to persuade the trial judge that ground (g) is made out. It follows that where the landlord is economical with the evidence, proves to be unduly reticent to disclose documents and is evasive in the witness box, the risk is run that the tenant will be granted a new lease. The moral which emerges is that, in practice, the landlord will only have one chance to promote its opposition. By failing to seize his opportunity, Mr Zarvos was undoubtedly the author of his own downfall.

In *Gatwick Parking Services Ltd* v. *Sargent* [2000] 25 EG 141, the tenant operated the business of a car park from the demised premises. The tenant had the benefit of planning permission subject to a personal occupancy condition. The landlord intended to occupy the premises for the purposes of a similar business. The onus lies on the landlord to show the prospect of success (but he is not expected to do so on a balance of probabilities) and the court must undertake a practical appraisal of the evidence before it. In the light of the previous planning history, the county court concluded that the landlord had no chance of lifting the personal occupancy condition and, hence, could not establish the necessary intention. Running contrary to the county court's prediction, planning permission was later granted to the landlord.

Laws L.J. admitted that the central question was whether there was a realistic prospect that planning permission would be granted if the landlord was awarded possession. As Laws L.J. put it, 'the hurdle to be surmounted by the appellant . . . is by no means a high one . . . He has to show that there is a real, not merely a fanciful, chance'. He concluded that the judge should have acceded to the landlord's case on the strength of the evidence presented at the hearing. The judge had too lightly set aside the view of the planning officials that conditions should not act to protect local businesses against market competition. There was simply no planning reason why the business should be operated by one firm and not another. At the very least, the trial judge should have thought that there was a real prospect that planning permission would eventually be granted. The fact that permission was subsequently granted was admissible evidence which served to demonstrate this prospect.

9.4.2 Occupation

It is necessary that the evidence shows that the competent landlord will actually occupy the holding. The landlord, however, need not seek to occupy the holding personally as it is well established that there are a number of other ways in which occupation can arise. The landlord can occupy, for example, through an agent, a manager, a partnership, a beneficiary under a trust s.41(2)), and a company which is a member of a group of companies which includes the landlord company (s.42(3)). Section 30(1A) now provides that where the landlord has a controlling interest in a company, the reference to the landlord in ground (g) is to be construed as a reference to the landlord or the company. Similarly, s.30(1B) makes it clear that, where the landlord is a company, a person who has a controlling interest in that company can be in occupation for the purposes of ground (g).

A 'controlling interest' in a company is defined in s.144 of the Companies Act 1989 as arising when either the landlord is a member of it and able (without the consent of any other person) to appoint or remove at least a majority of its directors or the landlord holds (disregarding shares held in a fiduciary capacity or as a nominee) more than one-half of its equity share capital. In *Ambrose* v. *Kaye* [2002] 15 EG 134, the Court of Appeal heard an appeal by the tenant who claimed that, during an adjournment of proceedings, Mr Kaye acquired an increased shareholding to ensure that he had the requisite controlling interest. The point which then arose was whether this transfer came too late to be taken into account for the purposes of ground (g). Chadwick L.J. acknowledged that the judge had the discretionary powers to adjourn and to admit new evidence (CPR, r.3.1(2)). If the judge erred in principle when exercising these powers, the court must treat the judge's exercise of discretion as flawed and must set it aside. The overriding objective however was to deal with cases justly (CPR, r.1.1) and, in order to ensure this, the courts are encouraged to take active management of cases (CPR, r.1.4(2)). Chadwick L.J. took the view that a tenant who deliberately declined to raise a point and who at the trial argued that it was too late for the landlord to meet it by a transfer of shares was not deprived of an advantage by the judge granting an adjournment, 'I would be sorry if that were the position under the Civil Procedure Rules. If it were, the courts could, I think, be criticised for treating civil litigation as though it were indeed a game of skill and chance. The courts could be criticised for losing sight of the overriding objective, which is to deal with cases justly'. The judge had properly exercised his discretion. Indeed, if it had been exercised differently, the case would not have been dealt with justly. Chadwick L.J. emphasised that landlord and tenant cases were not to be treated differently from other types of dispute. He concluded, 'the tenant wished to take a point of law . . . in opposition to the landlord's attempt to establish ground (g). If the tenant wished to take that point then, in my view, he was required to identify it, if possible in advance of the hearing, so that the court could deal with the manner in an appropriate way; if necessary, by directing a preliminary hearing to address that point of law'.

Occupation need not be immediate and the court may be prepared to accept the landlord's undertaking to occupy at a later date. Nevertheless, in *Method Development Ltd* v. *Jones* [1971] 1 All ER 1027 it was made clear that occupation must be intended to be within a reasonable time following the date of termination. This gives rise to an issue of fact and, in approaching the matter, the court must adopt a sensible and business-like attitude. In

London Hilton Jewellers Ltd v. *Hilton International Hotels Ltd* [1990] 20 EG 69, it was admitted that, for these purposes, a month or so would not be unreasonable.

There is also no mention within ground (g) as to how long the landlord must intend to occupy the holding. The rule which has emerged however is that it will not be sufficient for the landlord to show the intention to occupy for a temporary period before selling the property. Hence, the landlord cannot rely upon ground (g) when the occupation is merely to redecorate. In other circumstances, an intended occupation of a number of months may suffice, but as mentioned above, only when there is intended to be no outright sale of the premises to a cash purchaser. In *Willis* v. *Association of Universities of the British Commonwealth (No.1)* [1964] 2 All ER 39, Salmon L.J. stated, by way of analogy, that a landlord who has not long to live, and who seeks possession under ground (g), could not be said by the tenant to intend to pass the property to the heirs. He also considered the situation where, following a restructuring exercise, the landlord company was to be dissolved. If dissolution occurred before the hearing, the new landlord would stand in the shoes of the old. In relation to a dissolution planned to occur after the hearing, he felt that the landlord could still rely on ground (g): 'the law does not make the rights of the parties depend on the fortuitous circumstance whether the transfer is executed sooner than later'.

Occupation of the holding

It should be appreciated that the landlord must intend to occupy the whole of the tenant's holding and not merely part of it, no matter how substantial that part may be. In contrast with s.31A(1)(*b*) which relates to part development, this may be regarded as an unduly onerous and unreasonable requirement. Ground (g) does not however require that each and every part of the holding be physically used for the landlord's business or residential purposes.

In the context of ground (g), the term 'holding' has been subject to judicial scrutiny. In *Nursey* v. *P Currie (Dartford) Ltd* [1959] 1 All ER 497, the Court of Appeal concluded that the landlord could not successfully oppose the tenant's renewal under ground (g) where it was the intention to demolish the buildings on the current holding (a petrol station) and to build replacements. The reasoning was that the landlord could then no longer occupy the holding as it was. As Wynn-Parry J. commented, 'it is not permissible to take into account the wider scheme which the landlords had in mind, and merely to treat the land comprised in the holding as land which, in one way or another, will be used for the purpose of the wider undertaking'. Willmer L.J. added, 'in applying s.30(1)(*g*) one must look at the particular holding comprised in the particular tenancy which is before the court in the particular case'. This decision however appears to confuse the meaning of the terms 'holding' and 'premises' and appears to be confined to the situation when there is to be the demolition and replacement of existing buildings. Accordingly, if the holding consists of a vacant site (such as a car park), the landlord can rely on ground (g) even though the intention is to build upon the site once in occupation. In *Cam Gears Ltd* v. *Cunningham* [1981] 2 All ER 560, the holding consisted of a vacant site with hardstanding for the parking of cars. The landlord sought to take possession and to erect a building which would cover about one-third of the site. The claim under ground (g) was successful. Owing to this lingering uncertainty promoted by the *Nursey* case, if the landlord intends to redevelop before taking up occupation it is advisable to rely on both grounds (f) and (g). Provided that the necessary intentions are established, it is practicable for both to be relied on together.

A further point of interest arises in the context of the amalgamation of the premises. In *JW Thornton Ltd* v. *Blacks Leisure Group* (1987) 53 P & CR 223, it was held that a landlord who wished to demolish two partition walls (between the landlord's present premises and those of the tenant) and to occupy the enlarged holding remained within ground (g). The Court of Appeal distinguished the *Nursey* case on the ground that here the demolition and reconstruction work was not substantial.

9.4.3   Business or residential purposes

The occupation needs to be wholly or partially for the landlord's business or residence and a mixed user is permissible. As regards residential use, it should be of no consequence that the landlord has other residences provided that the intention to occupy the tenant's holding is made out. Although the landlord must occupy the whole of the holding, it is not necessary that the entirety is used for business or residential purposes. The term 'business' is widely interpreted for these purposes. It has, for example, been held to include the running of a community centre, managed in conjunction with a local church. It extends to storage purposes ancillary to the business and advantageous for the development of the business in the future. In *Jones* v. *Jenkins* (1986) 277 EG 644, it was accepted that, where the landlord is in the business of letting accommodation and intends to let the property to others while providing services and management, this may also constitute occupation for business purposes. Following *Graysim Holdings Ltd* v. *P & O Property Holdings Ltd* [1995] 4 All ER 831 however this approach can no longer be sustained because, as Lord Nicholls emphasised, the sub-lessor would neither occupy the property nor be said to be carrying on a business from the premises.

A further potential problem arises for the landlord where, on the grant of the original tenancy, the existing goodwill of the business was assigned to the tenant and the landlord now seeks to resume that same business. It was held in *Daleo* v. *Iretti* (1972) 224 EG 61 that, as this use could be restrained by the tenant, the landlord could not rely on ground (g). In all other circumstances however the continuation by the landlord of the tenant's business is acceptable.

9.4.4 The five-year rule

It is a curious, but general rule of the 1954 Act, that a change in the personality of the landlord during the course of the opposition to a new tenancy does not alter the landlord's position. An exception to this rule concerns the right of the landlord to oppose the tenant's application or to seek a termination order under ground (g). The right is subject to an important qualification contained in s.30(2) which is commonly called 'the five-year rule'. This rule precludes reliance upon ground (g) where the landlord's interest was purchased or, if leasehold, created within the five years preceding the termination of the tenancy and the holding has throughout that time been subject to a business tenancy within the protection of the 1954 Act. Although the general tendency is now to treat occupation by a company or a person with a controlling interest in the company as amounting to the same thing (s.30(1A), (1B)), one difference emerges in the context of the five-year rule. This exception operates when a company is the landlord, but the occupation intended under ground (g) is that of a person with a controlling interest. If that person acquired the controlling interest within five years ending with the termination date of the current tenancy, the intended occupation by that person does not allow the landlord to utilise ground (g).

The aim of this complex restriction is simply to prevent a speculator buying over the head of a sitting tenant and then, as soon as possible, claiming possession on the ground of owner occupation. This explains why the rule has no relevance if the current landlord was the grantor of the tenancy. In *VCS Car Park Management Ltd* v. *Regional Railways North East Ltd* [2000] 1 All ER 403, the landlord had started out as a freeholder and then became a leaseholder. The change of status did not hurt the landlord's opposition under ground (g). Sir Richard Scott explained, 'The mischief at which the Act is aimed is not offended by allowing such a person to object to the grant of a new tenancy under ground (g) ... we should allow an interest held first as a freehold and then under a lease or successive leases to qualify'.

The rule means that a landlord who acquired the reversion in the last five years will be unable to use ground (g) unless there was no business tenancy in existence at any given time within that period (e.g. there had been a cessation of occupation or business user). It is to be appreciated that the five-year rule does not apply to ground (f) and that reliance on the latter may be an attractive possibility for a new landlord. Although the operation of s.30(2) may thwart the landlord's opposition under ground (g), it might still be to the landlord's advantage to rely upon the ground. If the landlord can satisfy the other aspects of this ground, the court might be persuaded to order a new lease of shorter duration than it would otherwise have granted.

Conversely, in the scenario where the landlord is waiting until the five-year period expires before serving a s.25 notice, the tenant might be able to defeat this tactic by the peremptory service of a s.26 request.

Key points

A series of further observations need to be made about the intricacies of the five-year rule contained in s.30(2):

- the landlord's interest may be in either the freehold or the leasehold estate. The rule applies, for example, if the landlord has been granted a reversionary lease;
- the five-year rule does not apply where the landlord is a company and the interest has been acquired by another company landlord within the same group of companies. The expression 'group of companies' is defined in s.42(1);
- for the purpose of determining when the landlord acquired a leasehold interest, a succession of tenancies is to be treated as a single tenancy. Seemingly, it does not matter that the capacity in which the landlord held the interest has changed during the five-year period as what counts is the interest which originally arose;
- the term 'purchased' is to be given its ordinary meaning (that is, buying for money) and does not include a surrender by operation of law or acquisition in consideration of a covenant. The date of purchase is deemed to be the time that contracts are exchanged. If there is doubt as to whether a purchase has occurred, the court will look at the whole transaction, including any preceding contract;
- the term 'created' refers to the creation of the competent landlord's interest. This can give rise to difficulties where the landlord's interest is subject to a trust and it is a beneficiary who seeks to be treated as the landlord and to rely upon s.30(1)(g). In this situation, the landlord's interest will be treated as created when the trust was declared and not the date when the beneficiary landlord actually acquires the interest. This does not apply however where it is a trustee landlord who seeks possession;
- where the landlord's interest is leasehold, and a contract preceded the acquisition of that interest, the date of creation is the date of the contract. Otherwise, the general rule is that the relevant date is that when the lease is executed;
- the termination date of the current lease is the date specified in the landlord's s.25 notice or the tenant's s.26 request. As it is from this point that the five years are counted back, it appears that the landlord could serve a

s.25 notice, then sell the reversion leaving it open for the new landlord to rely on ground (g);
- when issuing a notice or request, the date selected for termination should take into account the five-year rule. Hence, the landlord might insert a date more distant in time and the tenant might be wise to choose an earlier date.

CHAPTER 10

New lease

Contents

10.1 INTRODUCTION

The most significant aspect of Part II of the Landlord and Tenant Act 1954 is that which deals with the grant of the new lease and, in particular, the precise form that it will adopt. It is, of course, on renewal that the tenant's abstract statutory entitlements finally become translated into reality. The 1954 Act proceeds on two fronts. First, its primary purpose is to stimulate agreement between the parties as to the grant and its terms. Secondly, by way of a default mechanism the court is afforded the jurisdiction to order a new lease, essentially on such terms as it deems appropriate.

Although this chapter is concerned primarily with the ability of the court to divine the terms of a new lease, the role of agreement and its effect on the judicial process will be considered at the outset. It is also to be appreciated that, although the 1954 Act focuses on the jurisdiction of the court, the use of alternative dispute resolution is nowadays encouraged in all litigation. As regards lease renewals, it is possible for the parties to settle disputes out of court with the assistance of a non-judicial mediator. This is particularly suitable to cases where the renewal is unopposed. It offers a speedier, cheaper and more flexible method of resolving disputes over terms.

It is also possible for the parties to elect for Professional Arbitration on Court Terms (PACT) which is a scheme operated jointly by the Law Society and the Royal Institution of Chartered Surveyors. This would bypass a court hearing and instead allow for, say, the determination of the rent by a surveyor acting as an arbitrator/expert. Disputes as to other terms could be decided by an experienced conveyancer sitting as arbitrator/expert.

10.2 AGREEMENT

Part II of the 1954 Act is designed to facilitate agreement between the parties without recourse to the courts. The statutory rights afforded to the tenant are therefore intended to ensure that the parties negotiate on a more equal footing. While this undoubtedly strengthens the position of the tenant at the negotiation table, the onus remains on it to strike the best bargain available. The parties' freedom to contract on whatever terms they see fit is thenceforth reinstated. As Judge Brandt admitted in *Ganton House Investments* v. *Crossman Investments* [1995] 1 EGLR 239, 'We are dealing with business people who are perfectly entitled to drive as hard a bargain as they can'.

While negotiations between the parties are ongoing, it is crucial that the tenant complies with any time limits and procedural requirements imposed by the Act. If the tenant fails to do so, and a binding agreement is not reached, all rights to a new lease may be sacrificed.

10.2.1 Complete agreement

The Act expressly allows the competent landlord (as ascertained at the date of the agreement) and the tenant to agree to a total package, that is, both the grant and the terms of the grant. Such an agreement would otherwise be void under s.38 because it would preclude the tenant 'from making an application of request' and/or would provide 'for the termination or the surrender of the tenancy'.

On reaching a complete agreement, s.28 ousts the jurisdiction of the court and automatically sustains the existing lease (whether or not it is a contractual or a continuation tenancy) until the agreed date for the commencement of the new tenancy. It is to be appreciated that this negotiated commencement date can be earlier than the current tenancy could otherwise have been determined at common law. Following agreement, the existing tenancy is taken outside the ambit of Part II of the 1954 Act. The agreement ensures therefore that the parties lose the *locus standi* to commence proceedings and that any ongoing application is invalidated. In relation to the existing tenancy, the statutory protection cannot be revived and this is so even if the contract is rescinded or for some reason not carried through. Unless there is contracting out of the statutory scheme however the Part II provisions will apply to the new agreed lease.

Formalities

In order to satisfy s.28, the agreement must constitute a valid and enforceable contract. It must not be marked 'subject to contract'. If the agreed tenancy is not a periodic tenancy and the duration of the proposed lease exceeds three years, it would seem that the formalities of s.2 of the Law of Property (Miscellaneous Provisions) Act 1989 must be complied with. This requires that a contract for a lease be in writing, signed by both the tenant and the competent landlord and contain all the express terms agreed. Although the 1989 Act has no application to periodic tenancies and leases for three years or less, even with such tenancies it appears necessary that the agreement be in writing (1954 Act, s.69(2)) and its terms expressed therein (1954 Act, s.28).

Although it is a much safer practice to ensure that the formalities are observed, there is some lifeline offered for those who do not. In *Lambert* v. *Keymood Ltd* [1997] 43 EG 131, Laws J. mooted the possibility that the s.28 agreement falls entirely outside the ambit of the 1989 Act:

> I do not think it necessarily requires the execution of a document exhaustively containing all the terms agreed, such that no parol evidence could be introduced to explain the full intentions of the parties. The writing must, in my judgment, demonstrate that the parties have come to terms upon a new contract for the tenancy of the property ... if it is only signed by the party against whom it is raised in later proceedings ... that will be sufficient.

If this interpretation is correct, it drives the proverbial coach and horses through the prescription contained in the 1989 Act. It is however strongly arguable that this departure from the general formalities is unjustified.

Subject matter of the agreement

It is a requirement of s.28 that the property relating to this future agreed lease includes, at the very least, the tenant's holding as at the date of the agreement. It is perfectly permissible however for the parcels to include additional land. Accordingly, an agreement relating to property which is less than the current holding cannot comply with s.28 and, instead, will be viewed as an agreement to surrender at a future date and void under s.38(1). The court's jurisdiction would, thereby, remain unaffected and any ongoing application unaffected.

One way of bypassing this restriction is to agree to the grant of an immediate tenancy. Such an agreement falls outside s.28 (as it is not a 'future tenancy of the holding') and will operate as a valid surrender by operation of law. From the ashes of the former tenancy, the new lease would emerge which, on this occasion, may concern property less in extent than the former holding. Unless contracting out occurs however the new lease will fall within the protection of the 1954 Act.

Enforcing the agreement

Although subsequent to a valid s.28 agreement the tenant loses statutory protection, neither party can unilaterally withdraw from the transaction. The normal contractual remedies are available and, hence, the agreement may be specifically enforced and the landlord compelled to execute the lease. If the agreement does not reflect the common intention of the parties however the court has the discretion to rectify the contract. For example, rectification was appropriate in *Coles* v. *William Hill Organisation Ltd* [1998] EGCS 40 where the landlord submitted a draft lease mistakenly including a break clause in favour of the tenant. As the tenant's solicitor was aware of the mistake, the High Court concluded that it would be unconscionable to deny the landlord the remedy of rectification. The contract was rewritten to reflect the true agreement reached between the parties.

As with any land contract however it is imperative that the agreement is capable of binding third party purchasers. To ensure this happens, the tenant should, if the title is unregistered, enter a Civ land charge under the auspices of the Land Charges Act 1972. In relation to registered land, under the Land Registration Act 2002 the agreement may be passively protected as an over-riding interest (by virtue of the tenant's actual occupation) or, alternatively, may be actively protected by the entry of a notice on the Land Register. The danger which exists in both systems is that an unprotected contract will fail to bind a purchaser of the landlord's reversion. This would produce the unfortunate situation that the agreement would exclude the jurisdiction of the court while, at the same time, being unenforceable against the new reversioner.

10.2.2 Terms only agreement

It is to be appreciated that the parties may agree the terms, whether in whole or in part, of a prospective tenancy without the landlord conceding the tenant's right to a new lease. In such a case, if the landlord's opposition is unsuccessful, the agreed terms will then be embodied in the order for a new tenancy with the court filling in any gaps that remain. To be effective for these purposes, the 1954 Act requires the agreement to be in writing and to be intended by the parties to be binding. The agreement must therefore be unconditional and final. It is thought that this contract falls beyond the reach of the Law of Property (Miscellaneous Provisions) Act 1989. First, it is arguable that the agreement is for the purposes of an application to court and not for the grant of a lease. Secondly, as its terms are divorced from the grant itself, the agreement should not constitute a land contract. If this general approach is correct, it will be possible for a formal offer to be made, for example in correspondence or in the pleadings of the application which, on acceptance, becomes binding.

217

It is not permissible for the parties to agree privately to the grant of a new lease without reaching consensus as to its terms. Any attempt to do so will be void for uncertainty and offend the all terms rule set out in s.2 of the Law of Property (Miscellaneous Provisions) Act 1989. Absent a claim in proprietary estoppel, such informal assurances are of no weight. The lifeline for the tenant exists when the landlord has indicated that there will be no opposition to a new lease in its s.25 notice or counter notice. This election will be binding on the landlord.

10.2.3 In the absence of agreement

The parties are not obliged to negotiate. If agreement is not achieved, and where the landlord does not successfully oppose the tenant's application for a renewal, the court must order a new lease under s.29. The difficulty which then faces the court concerns, of course, the terms that will form the basis of the new lease. The court has, perhaps surprisingly, been offered only sketchy guidance by Parliament as how to carry out this important judicial function. This guidance is to be found in ss.32–35 of the 1954 Act and is grouped around four headings: property, duration, rent and other terms. Beyond this, the judges are left to their own discretion and will look for direction from previously decided cases and generally accepted norms applicable in the context of dealings with commercial property. It is now necessary to look at the groupings and, in the light of the admittedly limited statutory prescription, to examine how the court goes about its task.

10.3 PROPERTY: SECTION 32

As to the parcels of the new lease, absent agreement between the parties the court is empowered by s.32 to grant a new lease only of the holding as it determines and designates. The meaning of 'holding' is provided in s.23(3) as those parts demised that are occupied by the tenant (or the tenant's employee) for the purposes of the business carried out on the premises, but excluding those parts not so occupied. Subject to limited exceptions contained in s.32(2) and s.32(1A) (below), the court can order no more and no less. As Winn L.J. commented in *Fernandez* v. *Walding* [1968] 2 WLR 583, 'it is abundantly plain that "holding" cannot mean the same as "part of the holding", nor can part of the "holding" mean the same as "holding"'.

10.3.1 Timing

Section 32(1) states that the tenant's 'holding' is to be ascertained as at the date of the court order for renewal. In *I&H Caplan Ltd* v. *Caplan (No.2)* [1963] 2 All ER 930, the House of Lords made it clear that the crucial time is not the commencement of the hearing or the date of any ancillary or preliminary order. Lord Reid explained:

> The policy of the Act appears to be that not only the extent of the holding but also the rent, duration and other terms of the new tenancy should be determined as nearly as may be at the time when the tenancy is granted, and this seems right because circumstances may alter and the tenancy ought not to be granted in light of obsolete conditions. It is quite true that s.32 cannot be applied with literal accuracy because there may have to be some interval between the hearing of the evidence and the making of the order, but circumstances are unlikely to change in so short a time.

He did however accept that, if a considerable time elapses and there has been a material change of circumstances, the court would be prepared to hear new evidence.

10.3.2 Occupation

Section 32 requires that the tenant or the tenant's employee be in 'occupation' of something for business purposes in order for that to constitute the holding. The term 'tenant' is, by virtue of s.23(1A), (1B), to be construed as including a company in which the tenant has a controlling interest or, where the tenant is a company, a person with a controlling interest in the company. This means that, if sub-letting has occurred, it is the sub-tenant who benefits from the renewal rights in relation to the property that it occupies. If the tenant sub-lets only part of the property, the tenant's holding is defined according to the parts remaining within its occupation. Hence, it might be advisable for the head tenant to terminate any sub-lease and move back into occupation before the court order is made. Such retaking of possession may occur even after the tenant's application for a new lease is made. It is the fact of occupation, and not the motive underlying it, that is crucial.

10.3.3 Limited exceptions

The general rule, which allows only the tenant's holding to be the subject matter of the renewal, gives way in two situations. First, when the landlord opposes the lease under s.30(1)(f) (redevelopment) and the tenant is willing to accept a new tenancy of an economically separable part of the holding so that the landlord can carry out work on the remainder. This escape route for the tenant is offered by s.31A(1)(b). In such an instance, s.32(1A) limits the parcels of the new lease to the part that the tenant is willing to accept. As s.31A provides a fall-back position for the tenant, there is no obligation on the tenant to choose an option until the final determination of the landlord's ground of opposition. If the tenant does not wish to obtain a lease of part as opposed to the whole of the holding, the application can then be withdrawn.

Secondly, where other premises are included in the original lease in addition to the tenant's current holding, s.32(2) enables the landlord to insist that the parcels of the new tenancy include the whole of the property as originally demised. The court has no discretion here and must accede to the landlord's wishes. The object of this facility is to protect the landlord against any fragmentation of dealings by reason of sub-interests in the property. It does not however give the landlord the opportunity to select which sub-let parts are to be excluded or included in the new lease.

10.3.4 Tenant's ancillary rights

The general rule, as set out in s.32(3), is that ancillary rights (e.g. relating to access, drainage and light) which are enjoyed at the date of the hearing by the tenant under the current lease will be included in the new tenancy. This rule of thumb however gives way in the face of a contrary agreement between the parties or a contrary determination by the court. The judicial discretion to exclude ancillary rights is likely to be exercised so as to exclude or modify rights granted at the beginning of the current lease which are no longer necessary or appropriate.

Ancillary rights may be included in the new lease whether they were granted in the original lease or acquired by the tenant subsequently. Section 32(3) however applies only to property rights and does not extend to mere personal rights. Distinct contractual arrangements or mere *de facto* use will not alone be regarded as sufficient for these purposes and the court cannot hijack s.32 as a means of enlarging the holding beyond that contained in the original grant. As will become clear, the creation of new rights falls within the territory of s.35 (below). In *Orlik G (Meat Products)* v. *Hastings & Thanet Building Society* (1974) 29 P & CR 126, for example, a bare licence to park two vehicles on the landlord's land, which was not a term of the original lease, did not pass as part of the tenant's holding. Any rights granted after the lease should therefore be contained in a deed which is expressed to be supplemental to the lease.

10.3.5 Landlord's rights

As regards any rights originally reserved for the landlord, s.32 is silent. It is therefore apparent that nothing in s.32 allows the court to reduce, add to or modify such provisions contained in the old lease. This limitation could cause problems for a landlord who seeks to refurbish a building in which the tenant has a lease of a part. Section 32 does not facilitate the landlord being given new rights over the tenant's holding. As it is unlikely that the rights would be given by virtue of s.35 (below), the refurbishment scheme might be thwarted. Accordingly, there is some force in the argument that the court should be given the power to extend the landlord's rights beyond that currently available.

10.4 DURATION: SECTION 33

Section 33 (as amended) enables the court to order a term up to a maximum of 15 years, as considered reasonable in all the circumstances. This means that, if deemed appropriate, the court could order a periodic tenancy. The imposition of the statutory maximum is designed to offer adequate security of tenure, without unduly prejudicing the landlord's position, and yet is to be sufficiently flexible to cater for the tenant who does not wish to be bound too far into the future. It does not matter that the original lease was for a term in excess of 15 years. An agreed duration can however be incorporated into the court order, even though it exceeds the statutory maximum. In *Janes (Gowns) Ltd* v. *Harlow Development Corporation* [1979] 253 EG 799, for example, the parties agreed a term of 20 years.

The recent increase of the ceiling from 14 years to 15 years was designed to match modern rent review clauses (usually at five-yearly intervals) and to generate more accurate comparables. In practice, 14-year leases were uncommon and rents negotiated for new lettings were usually based on 5-, 15-, 25- and 35-year terms. At the end of the renewal, of course, the provisions of Part II of the 1954 Act can still apply and the tenant may be entitled to another term.

Subject to the 15-year maximum, s.33 offers the court a wide discretion, limited only by the concept of reasonableness. No guidance is to be found in the 1954 Act as to how this discretion is to be exercised. No directions are given as to what duration is appropriate and, in determining what is reasonable, the Act provides no hint as to what factors are relevant and the weight to be given to them. Although no one case is a sure guide to another, a series of influential factors can however be deduced from the authorities. As will now become clear, these influences are varied and, at times, conflicting.

10.4.1 Duration of the original lease

The term of the original grant offers to the court a useful and convenient starting point. It has become clear that the court will be reluctant to grant a lease for a term longer than the current lease. The Court of Appeal in *Betty's Cafes Ltd* v. *Phillips Furnishing Stores Ltd* [1957] 1 All ER 1 reduced a 14-year term as ordered by the lower court to a five-year lease on this basis. While it is common for the new lease to be of the same duration as its predecessor, the judge is not obliged to order a new lease of identical duration. It is likely that, if the original lease contained a break clause, the new lease will contain a similar provision. This tendency to reproduce the terms of the

221

original lease might make the task easier, but it is unlikely to reflect market forces, reasonableness or the circumstances of the case (which are likely to have changed over the intervening years).

10.4.2 Duration of the continuation tenancy

The longevity of the continuation tenancy might exert influence over the length of lease ordered on renewal. Unfortunately, its precise influence is unpredictable. As in *London & Provincial Millinery Stores* v. *Barclays Bank Ltd* [1962] 2 All ER 163, if the tenant has been holding over for a long time, it could be successfully argued that the new lease should be longer than the original. As in *CBS (UK) Ltd* v. *London Scottish Properties Ltd* [1985] 2 EGLR 125 however the same trait might offer a justification for a shorter lease. In *Upsons Ltd* v. *E Robins* [1956] 1 QB 131, the fact that the tenant had already benefited from a one-year extension to his lease was a relevant and reductive factor for the judge to take into account. To instil further confusion, in *Becker* v. *Hill Street Properties* [1990] 38 EG 107, Dillon L.J. felt that the length of the continuation was of no effect at all.

10.4.3 Comparative hardship and needs

An inequality of bargaining power between the parties is a relevant factor for the court to consider. As Morris L.J. explained in *Upsons Ltd* v. *E Robins Ltd* [1956] 1 QB 131, 'A consideration of "all the circumstances" of a case, if it is careful and complete ... may inevitably involve considering how the "circumstances" tell on the fortunes of those concerned'. This means that, if the tenant seeking renewal is a one-shop company, the potential hardship to, and the need of, that tenant might persuade the court to grant a lease longer than that desired by the landlord. Such was recognised in *CBS (UK) Ltd* v. *London Scottish Properties Ltd* [1985] 2 EGLR 125. If however the tenant is a company with numerous retail outlets, but the landlord owns only one shop, it is likely that the tenant will be granted only a short-term lease. This was demonstrated in *Upsons* case where the tenant operated some 250 retail outlets, but the landlord (apart from the demised premises) owned only one shop. The landlord moreover was facing potential eviction from his current premises. This cumulative hardship tipped the scales in favour of a one-year renewal instead of the seven-year term sought by the tenant.

Hardship may also become relevant when, for example, the tenant seeks a short-term lease which would damage the value of the landlord's reversion. Such a situation was faced in *Charles Follett Ltd* v. *Cabtell Investments Co. Ltd* (1988) 55 P & CR 36 where the court granted a lease of longer duration than the tenant sought. This is not however a hard-and-fast rule. In *CBS (UK) Ltd* v. *London Scottish Properties Ltd* [1985] 2 EGLR 125, the High Court was aware that the value of the reversion would be substantially reduced if a short lease was ordered. Nevertheless, it granted the tenant a one-year lease even though the landlord sought a 14-year term. The court admitted that the outcome would have been different had the landlord intended to sell the reversion. The one-year term allowed the tenant sufficient time to relocate its business. The landlord would also be better placed to re-let the premises during the one-year term than the tenant would be to assign a 14-year lease.

By way of an aside, Micklem J. suggested that, as the policy of the 1954 Act was primarily to protect the tenant, it could not justify more protection than the tenant needed. This does not sit well with other (and higher) author-ities (e.g. *Charles Follett Ltd* v. *Cabtell Investments Co Ltd* (1988) 55 P & CR 36) and is, at best, a dubious assertion. Not surprisingly, in *Rumbelows* v. *Tameside Metropolitan BC* [1994] 13 EG 102 the tenant's practice of taking only short-term renewals was a factor to be disregarded by the court. Similarly, in *Re Sunlight House* [1959] 173 EG 311 the tenant was granted a longer lease than was wished for because of the landlord's difficulty in re-letting in the short term.

10.4.4 Landlord's plans for the property

The lessor's intentions are, undoubtedly, a relevant factor to be taken on board. By way of example, the landlord intends to redevelop or to occupy the premises. If it cannot establish this intention at the date of the renewal hearing, the court must grant a new lease. Nevertheless, the duration of that new tenancy might be significantly affected by those intentions. In *Millet (Peter) & Sons Ltd* v. *Salisbury Handbags Ltd* [1987] 2 EGLR 104, the tenant sought a 12-year lease, but as the landlord genuinely intended to occupy the property at a future date the court granted a three-year term subject to a break clause exercisable on six months' notice. Similarly, in *Upsons Ltd* v. *E Robins Ltd* [1956] 1 QB 131 the landlord's opposition on the basis of its inten-tion to occupy floundered because it had acquired the property two months before the end of the statutory five-year disqualification period. This influ-enced the court to grant a short-term lease. Perhaps the position was best summarised by Denning L.J. in *Wig Creations* v. *Colour Film Services* (1969) 20 P & CR 870:

> Section 33 is in very wide terms. It empowers the court to do what is 'reasonable in all the circumstances'. Suppose a landlord bought five years ago, plus one day. He could resist a new tenancy altogether on the ground that he wanted the place for his own business. Suppose he buys it five years ago less one day. Should he be kept out of the place for several years simply by the two-day difference? I think not. The policy of the Act is to give a landlord (who has purchased more than five years ago) an absolute right to get possession for his own business; leaving it to the court to do what is reasonable if he has purchased less than five years. In doing

what is reasonable, the five-year period is a factor which is permissible for the judge to take into account. The weight is for him.

It is to be appreciated that, for the landlord's future plans to have a reductive effect on the duration of the new lease, the landlord must have a firm and settled intention to develop (or to occupy, as appropriate) and that intention must be genuine. This was clearly signalled in *Adams (E & B) Ltd* v. *Chesterfield Properties* (1961) 178 EG 561 where the landlord's evidence was so unconvincing that the court ordered a 10-year lease instead of the two-year term contended for by the lessor.

Once the landlord has demonstrated its future intentions to the satisfaction of the court, two alternative responses are possible. First, the court might order a short letting so as to allow the tenant to find alternative premises. In *London & Provincial Millinery Stores* v. *Barclays Bank Ltd* [1962] 2 All ER 163, the landlord wanted to redevelop dilapidated premises and on appeal the nine-year lease ordered in the lower court was reduced to a one-year term. In somewhat similar circumstances, a short fixed-term lease, determinable by either party on six months' notice, was deemed appropriate in *Reohorn* v. *Barry Corporation* [1956] 2 All ER 742.

Secondly, a longer lease may be granted, but subject to a break clause allowing for early termination. In *Adams* v. *Green* (1978) 247 EG 49, for example, the county court originally ordered a seven-year term without a break clause. This was increased on appeal to a 14-year lease including an option to break for rebuilding, exercisable on two years' notice. The power to insert the break clause is afforded by s.35 (below). Of course, the rent to be paid under the renewed lease would be reduced accordingly. It is possible moreover that a mutual break clause will be included. The award of a longer lease, subject to a right to break, appears appropriate when the development is not immediately in prospect, but is reasonably likely. In *NCP Ltd* v. *Paternoster Consortium Ltd* [1990] 15 EG 53, the court felt able to insert a break clause to allow comprehensive redevelopment which was a real possibility within the next 10 years, even though the plans were not finalised. The prevailing ethos is that the landlord should not be deterred from works of redevelopment by being saddled with a long lease without provision for an early determination. The issue is returned to in the context of s.35 below.

10.4.5 Relationship between the parties

The past and present behaviour of the parties may assume relevance in the calculation of the duration of the new lease. If, for example, the court believes that one party has acted unreasonably during the original tenancy, the term of the renewal may be influenced by that behaviour. A poor tenant could, thereby, be punished by being given a new lease of a lesser duration than would otherwise have been granted. As Ackner L.J. explained in *Orenstein* v. *Donn* (5 May 1983):

> The relationship between landlord and tenant is important. It is a business relationship, and if the conflict between the parties is such that it is not a relationship which should continue longer than is really necessary, there is, in my judgment, no reason why a judge in that situation should not grant a somewhat shorter term rather than the longer term in the hope that the parties, if they cannot maintain a harmonious relationship, can sever that relationship, the tenant going somewhere else, thereby enabling both parties to achieve the advantage of a peaceful and quiet existence which *ex hypothesi* their continued relationship would not make possible.

Conversely, it is possible that a good working relationship between the parties could be put forward as a justification for a longer lease than might otherwise be ordered.

10.4.6 Other potential influences

Although the more common influences have required somewhat more detailed consideration, other factors that have influenced the courts include:

- market forces. In *Ganton House Investments* v. *Crossman Investments* [1995] 1 EGLR 239, it was held that the court had to take into account the state of the market as a material circumstance. The court added that it was desirable in the letting market to achieve stability and that this aim was served by the granting of long renewals. Such factors do not however always carry weight. In *CBS (UK) Ltd* v. *London Scottish Properties Ltd* [1985] 2 EGLR 125, the tenant's desire to relocate its business was the main factor in the decision to grant a one-year term instead of the 14-year lease sought by the landlord. A market forces argument was rejected;
- the age and state of the repair of the premises. For example, if the disrepair is due to the tenant's breach of covenant this might warrant a shorter term than that wished for by the tenant. If the premises are tired and in need of refurbishment, again this might suggest a shorter lease so that the landlord can upgrade the property;
- the age and nature of the tenant's business. The preservation of the tenant's goodwill might influence the court to order a long lease. Such was accepted by the Court of Appeal in *Upsons Ltd* v. *E Robins Ltd* [1956] 1 QB 131 when it concluded that the fact that the tenant had been in business since 1927 was a relevant consideration;
- the interests of good estate management. If, for example, a tenant of a public house is running the business in an inefficient and unprofitable manner then this could be a reductive factor to be taken on board when the new lease is ordered; and

- where the court has ordered a renewal following the landlord having unsuccessfully relied on a discretionary ground of opposition. If the court has doubts as to the future ability of the tenant, say, to pay rent or keep the property in repair, this might be reflected in a shorter lease than the tenant was seeking.

10.4.7 Commencement date of new lease

Section 33 provides that the new tenancy commences when the current one terminates under the provisions of the Act. Owing to the possibility of appeal from the court order, and with it an interim continuance under s.64, the commencement date will however be uncertain. As Dunn L.J. admitted in *Turone* v. *Howard de Walden Estates* (1983) 267 EG 440, 'The difficulty is that it is impossible to say with precision at the time when the judge of first instance makes the order granting a new tenancy when that new tenancy will commence; and if one does not know when it will commence and nothing is said, it is equally impossible to ascertain when it will expire'.

This gives rise to potential difficulties where it is necessary to synchronise the termination date with other leases forming part of the same premises. Accordingly, it is standard practice for the order to state that the lease will begin from the date of final disposal of the application (whenever that may be) and to specify the end date of the new tenancy. This is particularly important in relation to short-term leases. Although the court may not know exactly when the lease will begin, it will be sure of when it will end. The parties can however agree a different commencement date and that will then be incorporated into the order. Such an agreed date might, for example, be the day immediately following the expiry of the original contractual term.

10.5 RENT: SECTION 34

As with the other terms of the new lease, the rent under the new tenancy may be the subject of agreement between the parties. The appropriate rental value of the holding is, not surprisingly, often the major contention between the parties. In default of agreement, s.34 allows the court to set the new rent. This section prescribes parameters beyond which the court's jurisdiction cannot transgress. It provides that the new rent to be ordered is that at which, having regard to the terms of the new lease, the holding might reasonably be expected to be let in the open market by a willing lessor. A number of disregards are also specified. Although this provision invokes an interplay between reality and hypothesis which is apt to cause some difficulty, the ambition is not to immunise the tenant from market forces. The emphasis is therefore upon what rent the landlord could command for the premises and not what the tenant is able and willing to pay. As Denning L.J. commented in *McLaughlin*

v. *Walsall Arcade Ltd* [1956] 167 EG 356, 'on a new lease the tenant has to pay the fair market value of the premises . . . the only advantage which the tenant gets . . . is security of tenure provided that he is ready to pay the fair market price'. Once the market rent has been determined therefore the court cannot order either a lower or higher rent.

Before examining the key concepts that pervade the s.34 prescription, it is to be noted that the issue of rent is the final matter to be concluded after all other terms are settled. Hence, if on appeal a variation of any other term occurs, this must be reflected in a reconsideration of the rent. Although the appropriate time for calculation is at the date of the order, if appropriate the court should factor in any foreseeable changes that might occur between that date and the time that the new lease will take effect. The calculation of rent may therefore have a prospective element.

10.5.1 An open market

There is no statutory definition of the term 'open market', but the courts have provided guidance as to its meaning. In *Baptist* v. *Masters of the Bench and Trustees of the Honourable Society of Gray's Inn* [1993] 2 EGLR 136, the court had to consider the open market value of the tenancy of chambers in Gray's Inn. The court emphasised that 'open market' is not a technical term and is an ordinary and commonly used expression. In the context of s.34, an open market should include various features:

- there must be a sufficient number of lessors and lessees to constitute a market and to create the opportunity of comparing rents (that is, an opportunity for the forces of supply and demand to operate). This does not however exclude a monopoly situation because, although there may be only one landlord, the market is generated by the number of potential tenants;
- there must be a willing lessor and lessee in this market. The screening of tenants or a restricted user does not vitiate the concept of an open market;
- there has to be a reasonable period in which the parties can negotiate at arm's length, taking into account the state of the market at such time. Accordingly, if there is a downturn in the market, this must be taken on board; and
- the property must be freely exposed to the market and account is not to be taken of any higher rent that might be paid by a potential lessee with a special interest. The market does not cease to be an 'open market' because the persons occupying the premises in the market belong to a particular profession or engage in a particular trade. As Judge Aron Owen concluded, 'In such an open market the landlord will seek to obtain the best rent for the premises on the terms offered and the tenant will seek to agree the lowest rent which he can persuade the landlord to accept'.

It is possible that, where the premises are of a type not normally associated with market rack rents (e.g. licensed premises and units in shopping centres), the court could order a turnover rent to be determined by a prescribed formula. As regards turnover rents, the tenant should always ensure that rental formula closely reflects the actual profit. Although a turnover rent may not necessarily be a 'true' market rent as it reflects the profits of an individual business, it will be deemed to be the open market rent. The device of linking rents to something such as the Retail Price Index is not always to the advantage of the landlord as the base figure of the index may be altered, producing a decrease in rent. In addition, rents can rise more rapidly than the index selected.

10.5.2 Willing lessor

The allusion within s.34(1) to a 'willing lessor' is accepted as referring to a hypothetical landlord and not to the actual landlord. It should be appreciated that the section, unlike many rent review clauses, does not expressly assume a 'willing lessee'. Nevertheless, the fact that the renewal procedure is sustained by the tenant must involve the tacit assumption that the tenant is 'willing'. In addition, the allusion to an 'open market rent' appears to contemplate a 'willing tenant' as otherwise it might be said that no market would exist. The objective standard imposed by s.34 reinforces the notion that the rent to be ordered is that which the landlord could command for the premises on the open market and not what the tenant is able and willing to pay.

In *Northern Electric Plc* v. *Addison* [1997] 39 EG 175, the Court of Appeal felt that the application of the statutory formula in the calculation of the rental value of an electricity substation was a straightforward exercise. The task of the court was merely to determine the rent for the new tenancy subject to a restrictive and specialist user clause. This case demonstrated also that any 'ransom' element, whereby in order to relocate the tenant would have to incur great cost (e.g. the payment of a premium for a lease not subject to such a restrictive user provision) was to be ignored and could not justify a higher rent. As the Court of Appeal concluded, to base a rent on a ransom value presupposes a lessor 'unwilling' to let premises for the restricted use contemplated by the lease. Presumably, the same line of reasoning would prevent a ransom value creeping in to private rent reviews where the hypothetical negotiation is expressed to be between willing lessor and willing lessee.

10.5.3 Land-locked close properties

This type of property gives rise to difficulties concerning the concept of an 'open market' and the effects of employing by implication the objective yardstick of a willing lessee. In *Murphy & Sons Ltd* v. *Railtrack Plc* [2002] 31 EG 99, Railtrack Plc owned the freehold reversion to a tenancy granted in favour of Murphy & Sons Ltd. The subject matter of the demise was an irregular shaped piece of land which had previously been used as a goods yard. The tenant had bought the freehold of adjacent land from Railtrack Plc with the curious result that the landlord could no longer grant a right of way allowing access to the demised property. Owing to the landlord's lack of legal ability, the demised property fell to be viewed as land-locked. The question before the Court of Appeal was whether, for the purposes of s.34(1), the court should depart from reality and value the premises on the hypothesis that there was no restriction of access. The landlord's reasoning was that, if the premises were to be valued as land-locked, there would be neither a 'willing lessee' nor an 'open market'. As no other bidder would be 'willing' to take on such a lease, it followed that the only interest would emanate from the sitting tenant. Accordingly, the limited access to the property should be disregarded.

The Court of Appeal rejected the landlord's appeal and emphasised that the purpose of s.34 is to generate an open market rent of a real lease with real terms. It is, thereby, divorced from the sophistry and artifice which characterises the modern rent review clause. Accordingly, it is the intention of Parliament that is paramount and not the intentions of the parties. The entitlement of the parties under s.34 should therefore turn upon the facts of the case. The grounds for rejecting the landlord's argument are entirely convincing.

First, while s.34 tacitly assumes that the tenant is 'willing' it did not follow that this hypothetical lessee would be sufficiently 'willing' to pay an additional rent for fictitious access rights. Secondly, an 'open market' may exist even though there is only one potential bidder for the premises. As Peter Gibson L.J. put it, 'An open market is one from which no-one is excluded and if there is a purchaser interested there can be a sale in the open market'. Thirdly, the landlord's arguments ran contrary to the tenor of ss.32 and 35 which deal, respectively, with the property to be the subject matter of the new lease and the introduction of new terms. Although any ancillary rights which are enjoyed by the tenant under the current tenancy will normally be included within the renewal, s.32 cannot operate to resurrect historic rights or impose rights that could not be granted by the landlord. Put simply, the s.34 valuation focuses exclusively upon the actual terms of an actual lease. Fourthly, if Parliament had intended for there to be an additional disregard within s.34 it would have said so. Peter Gibson L.J. concluded:

> When Parliament has specified what should be taken into account and what should be disregarded, it is a bold submission that it is permissible, nevertheless, for the court to imply a further disregard . . . it seems to me impossible for the court to depart from the reality of the situation as a matter of statutory interpretation in

order to imply into the tenancy some right which it does not confer. It would be very surprising if Parliament intended that a tenant should be required to pay rent for a right which he already has by reason of his ownership of land adjoining the demised premises.

10.5.4   Premises in disrepair

The state of repair of the premises is also a relevant factor. If the premises are in disrepair, owing to a breach of covenant by one of the parties, the issue is whether the premises should be valued as they stand or, alternatively, on the assumption that the covenants have been performed. Although the Act makes no reference to this issue, and the courts have not always spoken with one voice, the answer seemingly lies according to which party is in breach. If the tenant is in default, the assumption is that the covenants have been performed. Where the landlord is in breach, the court will conclude that the proper market rent is less than it would have been had the repair covenants been observed. Although it is not possible with a private rent review clause, in *Fawke* v. *Viscount Chelsea* [1980] 2 QB 441 it was accepted that the court can, in exceptional circumstances, order a differential rent until the landlord's obligations are fulfilled. The general policy running through the disrepair cases is that the tenant is not allowed to set up breaches of the tenant's repair covenant in order to depress the market rent and that the landlord cannot profit from its failure to observe repairing obligations.

10.5.5   Abolition of original tenant liability

Since the enactment of the Landlord and Tenant (Covenants) Act 1995, s.34(4) has been added to the 1954 Act, Part II scheme. This expressly requires the court to take into consideration any effect on rent of the 1995 covenants legislation. As the 1995 Act abolishes original tenant liability following assignment of the lease, it is likely that this will be used by landlords as a justification for a higher rent on renewal. Presumably, if a qualified covenant against assignment is imposed on renewal (thereby, paving the way to the negotiation of an authorised guarantee agreement) the market rent might be depressed accordingly.

10.5.6   Valuation process

The 1954 Act offers no guidance as to how the open market rent is to be deduced. It has therefore been left to the court to devise methods through which a rental figure can be obtained. The process involves questions of fact and invariably hinges on expert valuation evidence, often adduced on a square-foot basis and supported by comparables. An important feature of valuation evidence is therefore the rent reserved on recent lettings of comparable properties in the area, taking into account the terms of the new lease. For example, if a user restriction in the new lease is more onerous than that in the comparable lease, the rent payable should be suitably depressed. The court can also look at offers in relation to comparables even though the transaction did not go through. Although this forensic exercise might be viewed as overly imprecise and heavily impressionistic, it should not be forgotten that, as Mummery J. observed in *British Airways Plc* v. *Heathrow Airport* [1992] 1 EGLR 141, 'The parties have invoked the decision of a judicial tribunal and not an oracular pronouncement by an expert'.

Expert evidence

At the case management stage, an order will be made either for the appointment of a joint, impartial expert or for the appointment of experts to represent each side. There is a discernible movement towards the appointment of a single joint expert. Nevertheless, if the court appoints a single expert, both sides may still employ their own experts so that the joint report can be challenged in court. If the court allows separate experts for each party, they will be subject to pre-trial written questions. The experts must disclose the substance of all material instructions given to them and will be expected to reach agreement where possible and to identify any remaining issues of dispute between them.

Although in theory the expert's duty is to assist the court and to provide an objective, unbiased opinion, in practice the landlord's expert will tend to support the best rent for the premises on the terms offered, whereas the tenant's expert will usually argue for the lowest rent which can be achieved. The court must take such evidence into account and should take care not to trespass on the territory of the expert valuer. Traditionally, the judge has been left to make a value judgment and choose between rival and equally authoritative views. The judge is therefore entitled to rely on the evidence of one party only. In undertaking this task, the court will often deal with the calculation with a broad sword and not by the application of exact mathematics. Nevertheless, some judges might prefer a more detailed analysis. In *Simonite* v. *Sheffield City Council* [1992] 1 EGLR 105, for example, Harman J. felt able to disregard and modify the evidence of 'honest, experienced and skilled' valuers on the basis that, 'Since both are human neither is infallible'. The judge went on, with an air of infallibility, to calculate a rent which was so precise as to include pence as well as pounds. The understandable tendency is for the court to test the evidence of the experts (which might be dramatically divergent) and to settle on a figure which will, in all likelihood, fall somewhere between the rival valuations.

Evidence of comparables

The utilisation of evidence of comparables was explained by Forbes J. in *GREA Real Property Investment Ltd* v. *Williams* [1979] 1 EGLR 121 where he stated:

> It is a fundamental aspect of valuation that it proceeds by analogy. The valuer isolates those characteristics of the object to be valued which in his view affects the value and then seeks another object of known or ascertainable value possessing some or all of those characteristics with which he may compare the holding he is valuing. Where no directly comparable object exists the valuer must make allowances of one kind or another, interpolating or extrapolating from his given data. The less closely analogous the object chosen for comparison the greater the allowances which have to be made and the greater the opportunity for error.

Although the parties will normally come to trial having exchanged lists of comparable properties, it is for the court to decide in which area the comparables should be located. In *Baptist* v. *Masters of the Bench and Trustees of the Honourable Society of Gray's Inn* [1993] 2 EGLR 136, for example, the court looked only at comparables within Gray's Inn itself. The cachet of having offices within this area thereby drove the rent upwards. In *Ganton House Investments* v. *Crossman Investments* [1995] 1 EGLR 239 however the court looked beyond the existing location of a betting shop and drew comparables from the surrounding area. In general, the precise location of the premises does not matter if the value of the business is unaffected by it. If comparables exist within the selected area, the matter is relatively straightforward and, unless one of the parties can show that special circumstances apply, the up-to-date rental figures for such properties will guide the court. The ideal comparable rarely exists and, in this light, the judge may have to make some modifications to reflect, for example, differences in view, parking facilities, access, ventilation and layout between the two premises.

In *Hood Sailmakers Ltd* v. *Berthon Boat Company Ltd* (17 August 2000) there was only one comparator, a more recent tenancy of a smaller part of the marina site. This tenancy carried with it the right to park 10 vehicles on the marina car park. The tenant argued that these car parking spaces had a separate commercial value that should be deducted from the rent of the comparable before computing its square-foot value. This approach would operate to depress the yearly rent payable by more than £6,000. The landlord countered that this approach was wrong in principle and that the availability of parking space had only a limited impact on the rent a hypothetical tenant would be prepared to pay. In addition, the landlord contended that the needs of individual tenants varied so greatly that car parking should not be isolated as a separate element in the payments they were making. In the county court, the landlord's arguments prevailed. Hale L.J. admitted that there had been a stark conflict in expert views and that the county court judge had been entitled to choose between them. She accepted also that there would be a major difficulty in isolating a car parking element in the overall rent when it had not been subject to separate bargaining or pricing.

Unfortunately, comparables are sometimes difficult to adduce and too frequently properties are introduced in evidence that are not at all truly comparable to the property in question. For example, in *Newey & Eyre* v. *J Curtis & Son Ltd* (1984) 271 EG 891, a 'down market' comparable had been applied to 'up market' premises. It follows that if there is nothing comparable, or no modifications which can be made to make an adduced comparable truly comparable, the court must look elsewhere for assistance.

Alternative guides

A variety of alternative options may be available to the court and each can produce a markedly different outcome. For example:

- in *NCP* v. *Colebrook Estates* (1983) 266 EG 810, the court looked to the general rent increases in the area for inspiration;
- in *Re 52, Osnaburgh Street* [1956] CLY 1947, the landlord's proof that he had a firm offer from a prospective tenant was accepted as good evidence of the open market rent. This case marks a departure from reliance upon expert valuation because the landlord's evidence was preferred to the (standard) square-foot basis of assessment. This is a potentially dangerous precedent as it may encourage the landlord to canvass offers without obligation on the part of those who make them. Those offers may be far from representative of the true value;
- in *Harewood Hotels Ltd* v. *Harris* [1958] 1 All ER 104, evidence of the profitability of the tenant's business was relevant. The court indicated that a similar approach could be applied to other businesses with special features such as theatres, petrol stations and racecourses. Traditionally however the general rule has been that the tenant's trading accounts are inadmissible in evidence and that rental comparables will normally suffice. The rationale for their exclusion is that, as 'haggling' parties in the real world cannot see trading accounts, they should be denied to the hypothetical landlord under s.34;
- in *Aldwych Club Ltd* v. *Copthall Property Co Ltd* (1963) 185 EG 219, the fact that the club premises could be employed for a more profitable purpose (that is, as offices) justified a higher rent valuation. Provided that the alternative use is not prohibited under the terms of the original lease or the proposed new tenancy, the more valuable use can be taken into account. Not surprisingly, the court will not relax a user covenant on renewal merely to justify a higher valuation;
- in *Davies* v. *Brighton Corporation* [1956] CLY 4963, the rateable value of the holding was used to calculate the rent under a yearly tenancy. The

rateable value is however a poor guide to rental levels. This is because the terms of a tenancy will rarely be comparable to the underlying basis of the property's rating.

10.5.7 Mandatory disregards

Section 34(1)(*a*)–(*d*) contains a series of disregards that are not to enter into the calculation of the new rent. Note that the disregards of goodwill (*b*) and improvements (*c*) are traditionally not thought to extend to increases in rental value emanating from a sub-tenant. Nevertheless, following *Oscroft* v. *Benabo* [1967] 2 All ER 548, it could be argued that the court should disregard a sub-tenant's goodwill and improvements. The statutory disregards are:

(a) the effect on rent attributable to *occupation by the tenant* (or a predecessor in title) of the holding. The premises will therefore be valued on the assumption of vacant possession. This prevents the tenant from benefiting from any sitting tenant discount and avoids the landlord claiming any accretion to the rent attributable to such occupation. The 1954 Act does not allow the landlord to argue that a sitting tenant should be prepared to outbid the rest of the market. As discussed above, the disrepair of the premises, due to the tenant's breach of covenant, will also be disregarded;

(b) any *goodwill* attaching to the premises by reason of the business carried on by the tenant (or by a predecessor in both title and business) is to be discounted. The policy is that, if the goodwill belongs to the tenant, additional rent should not be levied because of it. The court must therefore calculate whether there is any difference in the value of the holding with and without goodwill. If such a difference exists, it must be disregarded. The burden of proof lies with the tenant who must show, on a balance of probabilities, that the goodwill has enhanced the letting value of the holding. Whether or not a person is a predecessor in business is an issue of fact and is determined by such matters as whether, for example, the new tenant continues to trade under the same name, had the goodwill assigned and purchased the predecessor's stock-in-trade;

(c) the court must disregard any increase in value attributable to *relevant improvements* carried out by a tenant or a predecessor in title, other than in pursuance of an obligation to the immediate landlord. This is considered in more detail below;

(d) in the case of a holding comprising *licensed premises*, any addition to its value attributable to that licence, where the benefit of the licence belongs to the tenant, must be discounted. This was designed with public houses in mind, but the disregard also extends to licensed betting shops. Section 34(2A) clarifies that, for these purposes, the term 'tenant' shall be construed as including a company in which the tenant has a controlling interest or, where the tenant is a company, a person with a controlling interest in the company.

Disregard of tenant's improvements

The term 'improvement' is not defined in the 1954 Act and most certainly does not cover every alteration made by the tenant. It is however necessary to evaluate the work from the tenant's perspective. In addition, so-called 'tenant's fixtures', which by their nature are removable, do not fall within the understanding of an improvement nor do they form part of the demise. An improvement would therefore embrace such matters as the installation of central heating, external storage spaces, suspended ceilings and double glazing. The apparent purpose of this disregard is to protect a tenant against having to pay a higher rent by reason of such personal expenditure.

In order to defeat this disregard, it is traditionally understood that a positive, legal obligation (whether general or specific) to have carried out the works of improvement is required. The disregard is dependent on the work being carried out by a tenant and does not apply to improvements carried out pre-term or during a licence occupancy. As made clear in *Hambros Bank* v. *Superdrug Stores Ltd* [1985] 1 EGLR 99, the person making the improvement must be the tenant at the time the work is carried out.

The Law of Property Act 1969 expanded the class of tenant's improvements that fall to be disregarded under s.34(1)(c). This amendment ensured that it was no longer necessary for the improvement to be carried out during the current tenancy. If it was not, the improvement still falls to be disregarded if it satisfies certain further conditions now set out in s.34(2). These somewhat elaborate conditions are:

- that the tenant can prove that the improvement was completed not more than 21 years before the application for a new tenancy was made. This ceiling recognises that, in relation to previous tenancies, with the passage of time it becomes impractical to assess what effect the improvement has had on the letting value under the current lease. Accordingly, in these circumstances the improvement is, beyond 21 years, presumed to have no enhancing effect and the building and costs are deemed to have been written off. This ceiling also serves as an encouragement for tenants to retain documentary evidence to show what improvements were carried out, when and by whom;
- that the holding, or any part of it, has at all times since the improvement was completed been comprised in tenancies which fell within the provisions of the 1954 Act. There is no requirement that the same business has been carried out since the improvement. This condition means that a tenancy existing prior to the 1954 Act will be caught if it would,

otherwise, have fallen within the scope of the 1954 Act. Similarly, the condition will not be defeated by showing that, at some stage, a tenancy had been contracted out of the Act. It is unclear what consequences would arise if it could be proved that, for some time in the 21-year period, a tenancy had ceased to fall within the protection of the Act (e.g. the tenant had for some reason ceased to occupy for business purposes);

- that at the termination of each of those tenancies, the tenant did not quit. If the tenant did quit, compensation for improvements might be claimed under Part I of the Landlord and Tenant Act 1927. This condition under-scores the fact that the tenant can disregard only improvements made by himself or by an assignor.

10.5.8 Insertion of a rent review clause

Since the Law of Property Act 1969, and as a concession to inflationary times, the court is expressly enabled to include a rent review clause in the order for a new tenancy. This power is contained in s.34(3). It is generally thought that the court had this power anyway, but at least s.34 removes any doubt. The prospect of a rent review clause may help to reduce the landlord's opposition to a new tenancy of a reasonably long duration. The court is not however obliged to include a rent review clause but such insertion has, for longer leases, become standard practice. Indeed, there is some force in the suggestion that all renewals should automatically contain review clauses. As the tenant is expected to pay a market rent, there can be no justification for maintaining the discretion as to whether to include in the lease such a standard, market mechanism. In the interests of fairness, the tendency is to order review clauses which permit the rent to move upwards or downwards. This is so even though the open market tendency is towards upwards-only reviews. The frequency of any review will be geared to any relevant terms of the current tenancy or, if none, prevailing market trends (currently, five-year reviews). The review clause will generally require the involvement of an arbitrator/expert if the parties fail to agree on a new rent.

The court may decline to insert a review clause where it is deemed uneconomic and wasteful. On admittedly unusual facts, in *Northern Electric Plc v. Addison* [1997] 39 EG 175 the court refused to include a review clause in relation to a tenancy of an electricity substation for a period of 14 years at a rent of £40 per annum. The cost of surveyors and negotiations involved in any review would clearly outweigh any benefit that the landlord could achieve.

It is unclear what influence a review clause in the current tenancy will have on the court. Although, s.34(3) does not oblige the judge to have regard to the original tenancy, the current terms will be highly persuasive and it will usually follow that a similar review clause will be maintained in the new lease. In such a case however the court should take the opportunity to update the review clause in the light of recent developments in the drafting of such provisions. It appears moreover that s.34(3) requires the rent review clause to be considered after the market rent has been calculated. If this is correct, it might produce a benefit for the landlord in that the market rent might be higher if the review clause has not been included in the calculation. It is however apparent that a potentially downward review clause will not generate a discounted rent for the tenant.

10.6 OTHER TERMS

In the absence of agreement, s.35 places the onus on the court to determine the remaining terms of the new tenancy. In undertaking this task, the court is obliged to 'have regard to the terms of the current tenancy and to all relevant circumstances'. Beyond this, the judiciary has been left to devise its own rules, presumptions and principles on a case-by-case basis. The judicial task must involve taking account of current market trends and changes to the premises that have occurred (e.g. the need for immediate or future repairs) since the original lease was granted. This general requirement is elastic in the sense that it compels something between a reproduction of the existing terms and an unfettered right to substitute others. This elasticity is more pronounced when the previous lease was created orally. Subject to two exceptions, the 1954 Act offers no explanation and no indication of what was intended to be covered by the section. The first exception relates to split reversions and the second concerns the operation of the Landlord and Tenant (Covenants) Act 1995.

10.6.1 Split reversions

In amended form, s.35(1) deals expressly with the, admittedly rare, situation of when a split reversion exists. Understandably, if the reversion is divided between two separate landlords, potential headaches lie ahead for the tenant seeking renewal. For the purposes of this chapter, the pertinent issue is whether the tenant should be granted a single tenancy with the same landlords as before or be granted two separate tenancies, each with a different landlord. The amendment to s.35 is that when the court considers the issue of rent under s.34 it can, when the reversion has been severed, apportion the rent payable. Hence, if the market value of one part is greater than the other, this can be reflected in the rents payable to the respective landlords. Section 35 supports the view that the court should order a single tenancy of the entire holding.

10.6.2 Effect of the Landlord and Tenant (Covenants) Act 1995

Section 35(2) has been introduced by the Landlord and Tenant (Covenants) Act 1995 and this expressly makes the abolition of original tenant liability a relevant consideration for the court to take on board. Unfortunately, the 1954 Act offers no explanation and no indication of how this provision is to affect the terms of the renewal. Nevertheless, as Neuberger J. put it in *Wallis Fashion Group Ltd* v. *CGU Life Assurance Ltd* [2000] 27 EG 145, 'the 1995 Act requires radical surgery effectively to be done to an alienation covenant when translating it into a new tenancy . . .'. Such surgery might, for example, involve the grafting on of a qualified alienation covenant so as to protect the landlord from possible breaches by a future assignee and/or (as argued for in the *Wallis* case) a requirement that the outgoing tenant guarantees an assignee's performance of the covenants.

The issue that vexed Neuberger J. was whether an alienation covenant in the renewed lease should give the landlord the automatic right to require an authorised guarantee agreement (AGA) on assignment. In the alternative, it was argued that such a guarantee should be required only 'where reasonable'. It was accepted that, if this lease was privately negotiated in the open market, the covenant regulating assignment would almost certainly include a condition that the outgoing tenant provided such a guarantee. Neuberger J. focused on the wording of s.16(3)(*b*) of the 1995 Act which states that a landlord's requirement for an AGA is valid and enforceable only if it is a requirement which is 'lawfully imposed'. Where an assignment requires the landlord's consent and the alienation covenant is silent on the specific issue of whether or not he can demand an AGA, then the landlord can refuse consent if it is reasonable to do so. Neuberger J. concluded, 'In those circumstances it seems to me that it follows he can only impose a condition on the grant of his consent if that condition is reasonable. If it is reasonable to demand an AGA as a condition of his consent, then that demand is lawfully imposed. If it is unreasonable to make such a demand, then it is not lawfully imposed'. He took the view that, if Parliament had intended that, on every assignment the landlord could insist upon an authorised guarantee agreement being taken, it would have made this clear. As the judge acknowledged, it would not then have been necessary to require the guarantee to be 'lawfully imposed'. Hence, there is no automatic right to call for an AGA to be inserted into a new lease when the original lease was either created before the 1995 Act or, if subsequently granted, when it was negotiated without such a provision. This should cause no undue hardship to the landlord for as Neuberger J. noted, 'the standard of unreasonableness is not ungenerous to the landlord. In order to show that the landlord's requirement for an AGA was unreasonable the tenant would have to show that no reasonable landlord could, in the circumstances, require it'.

10.6.3 Exercise of discretion

The requirement that the court have regard to all relevant circumstances offers to the court a very liberal discretion. Nevertheless, the court will operate on the presumption that the current terms (except as to duration and rent) will pervade the new lease. For example, in *Aldwych Club Ltd* v. *Copthall Property Co Ltd* (1963) 185 EG 219 the fact that rent had been payable in arrears under the original lease resulted, despite the landlord's objections, in a similar term being inserted into the new lease. This cautious approach does not necessarily mean that a term will be automatically reproduced in the new lease. Instead, it requires that the party arguing for change will have to convince the court that the alteration is fair and reasonable. The overarching concern of the court is to draw a reasonable balance between the interests of the landlord (including any superior landlord) and the interests of the tenant. As Lord Wilberforce put it in *O'May* v. *City of London Real Property* [1982] 1 All ER 660, '[a] party seeking to introduce new, or substituted, or modified terms [has] to justify the change, with reasons appearing sufficient to the court . . . if such reasons are shown, then the court . . . may consider giving effect to them: there is certainly no intention shown to freeze . . . or to "petrify" the terms of the lease'. Lord Wilberforce refused to allow the landlord, in relation to a short lease, to impose a fluctuating service charge in return for a fixed-rent reduction. As a consequence, the landlords lost an estimated £2 million accretion to the freehold value. Lord Wilberforce was forced to acknowledge that s.35 may place the tenant on statutory renewal in a stronger position than a new tenant negotiating in the open market.

In *Hood Sailmakers Ltd* v. *Berthon Boat Company Ltd* (17 August 2000), the dispute concerned the type of break clause which should be inserted into the new lease. The original 25-year lease had provided the landlord with the ability to break, for the purposes of development, on the giving of six months' written notice. In such circumstances, and by way of compensation, the tenant was entitled to a lease of nearby premises for the unexpired period of the term. In addition, the tenant was to be indemnified against the costs of moving and re-erecting a building. On renewal, the landlord sought to retain the right to break, but without any compensating provision. The tenant resisted this change and argued that to implement it would be analogous to imposing a break clause for the first time. Hale L.J. admitted that the context in which this clause originally emerged was an important consideration. The tenant's need for protection, while still in existence, had been substantially diminished in that they had now had the benefit from their investment in the building for the last 25 years. The probable consequences to the landlord of having to comply with the compensating provision had also altered greatly. The relocation which once could have been achieved easily by recourse to readily available land could not be achieved at all some two decades down the line. Hale L.J. felt that a clean break clause would still offer the usual degree of protection afforded to business tenants, that is, security of tenure or compensation in lieu.

The court will be reluctant to impose new terms that serve merely to improve the position of one party, particularly when the change would be detrimental to the other. In *Cardshops Ltd* v. *Davies* [1971] 2 All ER 721, the landlord failed in an attempt to change a qualified covenant against assignment into an absolute covenant because the proposal was harsh and would imperil the tenant's goodwill. This protective tendency may prevail even if current market practices would suggest a different outcome.

In *Charles Clements (London) Ltd* v. *Rank City Wall Ltd* (1978) 246 EG 739, the court rejected an attempt by the landlord to relax a user covenant with the purpose of increasing the rental value of the premises. As Goulding J. commented, 'If the parties are to be at liberty to insist on changes in the terms of the existing tenancy simply because they consider them beneficial to themselves, a field would be opened which I think the court would find it bewildering to traverse'. Similarly, in *Aldwych Club Ltd* v. *Copthall Property Co* (1963) 185 EG 219 the tenant failed to tighten a user covenant so as to reduce the rental value. In that case Pennycuick J. accepted that it would be contrary to both the policy of the Act and 'reasonable justice' to allow the tenant to depress the rent in this way. He added however that had it been the landlord who sought the restriction then, provided it was fair, the court would here have favoured the change.

The emphasis upon fairness was reiterated in *Gold* v. *Brighton Corporation* [1956] 3 All ER 442 where the Court of Appeal refused to tighten a user covenant at the request of the landlord so as to prevent the premises being used as a second-hand clothes shop. To do so would have prevented the tenant carrying out her existing business and, as Parker L.J. concluded, 'in the ordinary case . . . it is difficult to think of any considerations which would justify changing restriction on user in such a way as to alter or limit the nature of the business which the tenant has lawfully carried out on those premises and which it is clearly the object of the Act to preserve'. The burden of persuading the court to change the terms lay with the landlord and there was no evidence to show that the continuance of this type of business would depress property values in the area or damage the reversion in any way.

10.6.4 Break clauses

In the context of the duration of the new lease, the authorities demonstrate that the genuine intention of the landlord to redevelop at a future time will offer a compelling reason for the inclusion of a break clause. The tenant will, of course, be adequately compensated by a corresponding rental reduction. The break clause will be introduced under the auspices of s.35. As illustrated in *Davy's of London (Wine Merchants) Ltd* v. *City of London Corporation* [2004] EWHC 2224, the difficulty lies in casting the terms of the break clause and, in particular, when it is to become exercisable and following what period of notice. While it is settled law that the lease should not deprive the landlord from using the premises for the purposes of development, the tenant should not be prejudiced unduly by the landlord's professed and, as yet unproven, future intentions. The tenant must still be afforded a reasonable degree of security of tenure. Lewison J. acknowledged, 'This necessarily presupposes that the landlord may have to wait for some time (though not so long as to prevent redevelopment) before being able to regain possession'. The judge believed that, while redevelopment should not be prevented, it was perfectly permissible for those plans to be delayed. He explained, 'There is no indication in the formulation of the legal test that the landlord's desire to redevelop necessarily trumps the tenant's desire for security of tenure'. Hence, it is standard practice for the break clause to be made operative only on the expiry of an initial fixed period. Lewison J. determined that the break clause should be exercisable upon the lapse of 42 months (and not five years as ordered by the court) and with an 11-month notice period. In *Amika Motors Ltd* v. *Colebrook Holdings Ltd* (1981) 259 EG 243, a five-year term was ordered with the break exercisable at the end of the third year. Similarly, in *Edwards (JH) & Sons Ltd* v. *Central London Commercial Estates Ltd* (1984) 271 EG 697 the court ordered a seven-year lease with the break exercisable after the fifth year. In the *Adams* v. *Green* (1978) 247 EG 49 however the court felt it appropriate to offer the tenant stability by imposing the requirement of two years' notice before the break could become operable. This ploy was designed simply to give the tenant at least two years' security of tenure.

In taking this overview, the court is allowed to look at all the evidence admitted and this is so even if that arises in a post-trial context. Once fresh evidence is admitted, it must be taken on board. Indeed, it would be ludicrous for such evidence to be validly introduced and then ignored. In *Davy's of London (Wine Merchants) Ltd* v. *City of London Corporation* [2004] EWHC 2224, Lewison J. explained, 'Unlike the position in most civil cases, the judge in an application for a new tenancy is not deciding what happened in the past, but what terms should govern the future. This, perhaps, explains why the court is more ready to admit evidence of post-trial events in such cases. The point is all the stronger in a case in which, as here, the dispute turns on an evaluation of future events'.

10.6.5 Limitations

The authorities demonstrate that the court should not exercise its discretion so as to create a new saleable asset for the tenant. Accordingly, in *Kirkwood* v. *Johnson* (1979) 38 P & CR 392 the tenant was denied its claim to a fresh option to purchase to be inserted into the new lease. Ormrod L.J. suggested that if the option to purchase in the original lease had not lapsed it could have been transmitted under s.32 as it appertained to the tenant's holding.

Nevertheless, it could not fall within the jurisdiction conferred by s.35. Similarly, the court should not employ s.35 as a means of enlarging the tenant's holding or conferring rights over the landlord's land not previously enjoyed. Hence, in *Orlik G (Meat Products)* v. *Hastings & Thanet Building Society* (1974) 29 P & CR 126, the tenant's claim, that an existing licence to park two vehicles on the landlord's land should be converted into a term of the new lease, was doomed. Similarly, in *Murphy & Sons Ltd* v. *Railtrack Plc* [2002] 31 EG 99 the Court of Appeal felt that it was an untenable assertion that rights that were incapable of grant could somehow be included in the new lease by virtue s.35. The holding cannot be enlarged to include an easement which was neither enjoyed at the termination of the contractual lease nor capable of existing at all.

The court does not enjoy the jurisdiction to deprive the tenant of statutory protection. It would not be possible therefore for the court to impose a term in the lease under which the parties are to contract out of the 1954 Act. Accordingly, in *Cairnplace* v. *CBL (Property Investment) Co. Ltd* [1984] 1 All ER 316 the court felt that it could not include a term as to the payment of the landlord's costs and, thereby, deprive the tenant of the protection afforded by s.1 of the Costs of Leases Act 1958. Such a term can only be included by express written agreement between the parties. This theme was pursued also by Neuberger J. in *Wallis Fashion Group Ltd* v. *CGU Life Assurance Ltd* [2000] 27 EG 145 where the landlord was seeking the revision of a pre-existing term so as to sidestep the statutory protection otherwise afforded to the tenant under the Landlord and Tenant (Covenants) Act 1995. Neuberger J. acknowledged that, where Parliament has relieved tenants of a specific obligation, the court could not use its s.35 discretion to deprive a tenant of that protection. He believed that the exercise of his discretion should not run contrary to the apparent intention of the legislature.

Outside these parameters, and as a rule of thumb, the court may insert any provision that can become contractually binding on the new lease being executed. The introduction or modification of user and alienation covenants however feature most frequently in the case law. Although the court does not have the ability to bind third parties, it can impose a term which will depend upon third parties for efficacy and co-operation (e.g. a term that the tenant provide a guarantor or insure the premises). Such occurred in *Cairnplace* v. *CBL (Property Investment) Co. Ltd* [1984] 1 All ER 316 where two guarantors were required in the context of a new company which took the assignment of a lease towards the end of its term.

10.6.6   Justifying change

It is clear that the party seeking the change of terms (however minor) must produce evidence in support. It is usually the landlord who seeks the revision and the tenant who resists it. As mentioned earlier, the need to permit subsequent redevelopment of the property is a sufficient justification for the insertion of a break clause. A change might also be justified so as, first, to bring the lease into line with current practice or to revamp old and unsuitable terms. This should be more than a mere revision of the language of the lease and should reflect changes in, for example, the law, building techniques and management practices. The House of Lords in *O'May* v. *City of London Real Property Co. Ltd* [1983] 2 AC 726 was of the view that new terms will not be introduced to reflect market practices if to do so would prove unfair to the tenant. The alteration may be designed to overcome the previously demonstrated unreasonableness of one of the parties. In *Re 5 Panton Street, Haymarket* (1959) 175 EG 49, the landlord had for some time been troublesome over the tenant making minor alterations to the premises. On renewal, the court revised a term in order to prohibit only 'structural alterations' without the lessor's consent. The change might be geared to ensure that there is no future default in rental payments. As mentioned, and owing to the Landlord and Tenant (Covenants) Act 1995, it is likely that any alienation covenant imported into the new lease will be qualified. This will enable the landlord to insist that the tenant enter into an authorised guarantee agreement, when the lease is next assigned, to ensure the performance of the covenants by the assignee. Lord Wilberforce in *O'May* v. *City of London Real Property Co Ltd* [1983] 2 AC 726 promoted a four-stage test which must be satisfied before allowing a variation:

- a valid reason must be shown for the variation;
- the other party must be adequately compensated for the effect that the new term will have on rent;
- the tenant's business must not be impaired; and
- it must be fair and reasonable to make the change.

APPENDIX A

Landlord and Tenant Act 1954, Part II (as amended at 1 June 2006)

PART II SECURITY OF TENURE FOR BUSINESS, PROFESSIONAL AND OTHER TENANTS

TENANCIES TO WHICH PART II APPLIES

23 Tenancies to which Part II applies

(1)   Subject to the provisions of this Act, this Part of this Act applies to any tenancy where the property comprised in the tenancy is or includes premises which are occupied by the tenant and are so occupied for the purposes of a business carried on by him or for those and other purposes.

(1A)   Occupation or the carrying on of a business –

      (a) by a company in which the tenant has a controlling interest; or

      (b) where the tenant is a company, by a person with a controlling interest in the company,

      shall be treated for the purposes of this section as equivalent to occupation or, as the case may be, the carrying on of a business by the tenant.

(1B)   Accordingly references (however expressed) in this Part of this Act to the business of, or to use, occupation or enjoyment by, the tenant shall be construed as including references to the business of, or to use, occupation or enjoyment by, a company falling within subsection (1A)(a) above or a person falling within subsection (1A)(b) above.

(2)   In this Part of this Act the expression 'business' includes a trade, profession or employment and includes any activity carried on by a body of persons, whether corporate or unincorporate.

(3)   In the following provisions of this Part of this Act the expression 'the holding', in relation to a tenancy to which this Part of this Act applies, means the property comprised in the tenancy, there being excluded any part thereof which is occupied neither by the tenant nor by a person employed by the tenant and so employed for the purposes of a business by reason of which the tenancy is one to which this Part of this Act applies.

(4)   Where the tenant is carrying on a business, in all or any part of the property comprised in a tenancy, in breach of a prohibition (however expressed) of use for business purposes which subsists under the terms of the tenancy and extends to the whole of that property, this Part of this Act shall not apply to the tenancy unless the immediate landlord or his predecessor in title has consented to the breach or the immediate landlord has acquiesced therein.

      In this subsection the reference to a prohibition of use for business purposes does not include a prohibition of use for the purposes of a specified business, or of use for purposes of any but a specified business, but save as aforesaid includes a prohibition of use for the purposes of some one or more only of the classes of business specified in the definition of that expression in subsection (2) of this section.

CONTINUATION AND RENEWAL OF TENANCIES

24 Continuation of tenancies to which Part II applies and grant of new tenancies

(1)   A tenancy to which this Part of this Act applies shall not come to an end unless terminated in accordance with the provisions of this Part of this Act; and, subject to the following provisions of this Act either the tenant or the landlord under such a tenancy may apply to the court for an order for the grant of a new tenancy –

    (a) if the landlord has given notice under section 25 of this Act to terminate the tenancy, or

    (b) if the tenant has made a request for a new tenancy in accordance with section 26 of this Act.

(2)   The last foregoing subsection shall not prevent the coming to an end of a tenancy by notice to quit given by the tenant, by surrender or forfeiture, or by the forfeiture of a superior tenancy unless –

    (a) in the case of a notice to quit, the notice was given before the tenant had been in occupation in right of the tenancy for one month;

    (b) [*Repealed*]

(2A) Neither the tenant nor the landlord may make an application under subsection (1) above if the other has made such an application and the application has been served.

(2B) Neither the tenant nor the landlord may make such an application if the landlord has made an application under section 29(2) of this Act and the application has been served.

(2C) The landlord may not withdraw an application under subsection (1) above unless the tenant consents to its withdrawal.

(3)   Notwithstanding anything in subsection (1) of this section –

    (a) where a tenancy to which this Part of this Act applies ceases to be such a tenancy, it shall not come to an end by reason only of the cesser, but if it was granted for a term of years certain and has been continued by subsection (1) of this section then (without prejudice to the termination thereof in accordance with any terms of the tenancy) it may be terminated by not less than three nor more than six months' notice in writing given by the landlord to the tenant;

    (b) where, at a time when a tenancy is not one to which this Part of this Act applies, the landlord gives notice to quit, the operation of the notice shall not be affected by reason that the tenancy becomes one to which this Part of this Act applies after the giving of the notice.

24A Applications for determination of interim rent while tenancy continues

(1)   Subject to subsection (2) below, if –

    (a) the landlord of a tenancy to which this Part of this Act applies has given notice under section 25 of this Act to terminate the tenancy; or

(b) the tenant of such a tenancy has made a request for a new tenancy in accordance with section 26 of this Act,

either of them may make an application to the court to determine a rent (an 'interim rent') which the tenant is to pay while the tenancy ('the relevant tenancy') continues by virtue of section 24 of this Act and the court may order payment of an interim rent in accordance with section 24C or 24D of this Act.

(2) Neither the tenant nor the landlord may make an application under sub-section (1) above if the other has made such an application and has not withdrawn it.

(3) No application shall be entertained under subsection (1) above if it is made more than six months after the termination of the relevant tenancy.

24B Date from which interim rent is payable

(1) The interim rent determined on an application under section 24A(1) of this Act shall be payable from the appropriate date.

(2) If an application under section 24A(1) of this Act is made in a case where the landlord has given a notice under section 25 of this Act, the appropriate date is the earliest date of termination that could have been specified in the land-lord's notice.

(3) If an application under section 24A(1) of this Act is made in a case where the tenant has made a request for a new tenancy under section 26 of this Act, the appropriate date is the earliest date that could have been specified in the tenant's request as the date from which the new tenancy is to begin.

24C Amount of interim rent where new tenancy of whole premises granted and landlord not opposed

(1) This section applies where –

(a) the landlord gave a notice under section 25 of this Act at a time when the tenant was in occupation of the whole of the property comprised in the relevant tenancy for purposes such as are mentioned in section 23(1) of this Act and stated in the notice that he was not opposed to the grant of a new tenancy; or

(b) the tenant made a request for a new tenancy under section 26 of this Act at a time when he was in occupation of the whole of that property for such purposes and the landlord did not give notice under subsection (6) of that section,

and the landlord grants a new tenancy of the whole of the property comprised in the relevant tenancy to the tenant (whether as a result of an order for the grant of a new tenancy or otherwise).

(2) Subject to the following provisions of this section, the rent payable under and at the commencement of the new tenancy shall also be the interim rent.

(3) Subsection (2) above does not apply where –

(a) the landlord or the tenant shows to the satisfaction of the court that the interim rent under that subsection differs substantially from the relevant rent; or

(b) the landlord or the tenant shows to the satisfaction of the court that the terms of the new tenancy differ from the terms of the relevant tenancy to such an extent that the interim rent under that subsection is substantially different from the rent which (in default of such agreement) the court would have determined under section 34 of this Act to be payable under a tenancy which commenced on the same day as the new tenancy and whose other terms were the same as the relevant tenancy.

(4) In this section 'the relevant rent' means the rent which (in default of agreement between the landlord and the tenant) the court would have determined under section 34 of this Act to be payable under the new tenancy if the new tenancy had commenced on the appropriate date (within the meaning of section 24B of this Act).

(5) The interim rent in a case where subsection (2) above does not apply by virtue only of subsection (3)(a) above is the relevant rent.

(6) The interim rent in a case where subsection (2) above does not apply by virtue only of subsection (3)(b) above, or by virtue of subsection (3)(a) and (b) above, is the rent which it is reasonable for the tenant to pay while the relevant tenancy continues by virtue of section 24 of this Act.

(7) In determining the interim rent under subsection (6) above the court shall have regard –

(a) to the rent payable under the terms of the relevant tenancy; and
(b) to the rent payable under any sub-tenancy of part of the property comprised in the relevant tenancy,

but otherwise subsections (1) and (2) of section 34 of this Act shall apply to the determination as they would apply to the determination of a rent under that section if a new tenancy of the whole of the property comprised in the relevant tenancy were granted to the tenant by order of the court and the duration of that new tenancy were the same as the duration of the new tenancy which is actually granted to the tenant.

(8) In this section and section 24D of this Act 'the relevant tenancy' has the same meaning as in section 24A of this Act.

24D Amount of interim rent in any other case

(1) The interim rent in a case where section 24C of this Act does not apply is the rent which it is reasonable for the tenant to pay while the relevant tenancy continues by virtue of section 24 of this Act.

(2) In determining the interim rent under subsection (1) above the court shall have regard –

(a) to the rent payable under the terms of the relevant tenancy; and
(b) to the rent payable under any sub-tenancy of part of the property comprised in the relevant tenancy, but otherwise subsections (1) and (2) of section 34 of this Act shall apply to the determination as they would apply to the determination of a rent under that section if a new tenancy from year to year of the whole of the property comprised in the relevant tenancy were granted to the tenant by order of the court.

(3) If the court –

(a) has made an order for the grant of a new tenancy and has ordered payment of interim rent in accordance with section 24C of this Act, but

(b) either –

    (i)   it subsequently revokes under section 36(2) of this Act the order for the grant of a new tenancy; or

    (ii) the landlord and tenant agree not to act on the order,

the court on the application of the landlord or the tenant shall determine a new interim rent in accordance with subsections (1) and (2) above without a further application under section 24A(1) of this Act.

25   Termination of tenancy by the landlord

(1)   The landlord may terminate a tenancy to which this Part of this Act applies by a notice given to the tenant in the prescribed form specifying the date at which the tenancy is to come to an end (hereinafter referred to as 'the date of termination'):

      Provided that this subsection has effect subject to the provisions of section 29B(4) of this Act and the provisions of Part IV of this Act as to the interim continuation of tenancies pending the disposal of applications to the court.

(2)   Subject to the provisions of the next following subsection, a notice under this section shall not have effect unless it is given not more than twelve nor less than six months before the date of termination specified therein.

(3)   In the case of a tenancy which apart from this Act could have been brought to an end by notice to quit given by the landlord –

(a)   the date of termination specified in a notice under this section shall not be earlier than the earliest date on which apart from this Part of this Act the tenancy could have been brought to an end by notice to quit given by the landlord on the date of the giving of the notice under this section; and

(b)   where apart from this Part of this Act more than six months' notice to quit would have been required to bring the tenancy to an end, the last foregoing subsection shall have effect with the substitution for twelve months of a period six months longer than the length of notice to quit which would have been required as aforesaid.

(4)   In the case of any other tenancy, a notice under this section shall not specify a date of termination earlier than the date on which apart from this Part of this Act the tenancy would have come to an end by effluxion of time.

(5)   [*Repealed*]

(6)   A notice under this section shall not have effect unless it states whether the landlord is opposed to the grant of a new tenancy to the tenant.

(7)   A notice under this section which states that the landlord is opposed to the grant of a new tenancy to the tenant shall not have effect unless it also specifies one or more of the grounds specified in section 30(1) of this Act as the ground or grounds for his opposition.

(8)   A notice under this section which states that the landlord is not opposed to the grant of a new tenancy to the tenant shall not have effect unless it sets out the landlord's proposals as to –

(a)   the property to be comprised in the new tenancy (being either the whole or part of the property comprised in the current tenancy);

(b)   the rent to be payable under the new tenancy; and

(c)   the other terms of the new tenancy.

26 Tenant's request for a new tenancy

(1) A tenant's request for a new tenancy may be made where the current tenancy is a tenancy granted for a term of years certain exceeding one year, whether or not continued by section 24 of this Act, or granted for a term of years certain and thereafter from year to year.

(2) A tenant's request for a new tenancy shall be for a tenancy beginning with such date, not more than twelve nor less than six months after the making of the request, as may be specified therein;

Provided that the said date shall not be earlier than the date on which apart from this Act the current tenancy would come to an end by effluxion of time or could be brought to an end by notice to quit given by the tenant.

(3) A tenant's request for a new tenancy shall not have effect unless it is made by notice in the prescribed form given to the landlord and sets out the tenant's proposals as to the property to be comprised in the new tenancy (being either the whole or part of the property comprised in the current tenancy), as to the rent to be payable under the new tenancy and as to the other terms of the new tenancy.

(4) A tenant's request for a new tenancy shall not be made if the landlord has already given notice under the last foregoing section to terminate the current tenancy, or if the tenant has already given notice to quit or notice under the next following section; and no such notice shall be given by the landlord or the tenant after the making by the tenant of a request for a new tenancy.

(5) Where the tenant makes a request for a new tenancy in accordance with the foregoing provisions of this section, the current tenancy shall, subject to the provisions of sections 29B(4) and 36(2) of this Act and the provisions of Part IV of this Act as to the interim continuation of tenancies, terminate immediately before the date specified in the request for the beginning of the new tenancy.

(6) Within two months of the making of a tenant's request for a new tenancy the landlord may give notice to the tenant that he will oppose an application to the court for the grant of a new tenancy, and any such notice shall state on which of the grounds mentioned in section 30 of this Act the landlord will oppose the application.

27 Termination by tenant of tenancy for fixed term

(1) Where the tenant under a tenancy to which this Part of this Act applies, being a tenancy granted for a term of years certain, gives to the immediate landlord, not later than three months before the date on which apart from this Act the tenancy would come to an end by effluxion of time, a notice in writing that the tenant does not desire the tenancy to be continued, section 24 of this Act shall not have effect in relation to the tenancy, unless the notice is given before the tenant has been in occupation in right of the tenancy for one month.

(1A) Section 24 of this Act shall not have effect in relation to a tenancy for a term of years certain where the tenant is not in occupation of the property comprised in the tenancy at the time when, apart from this Act, the tenancy would come to an end by effluxion of time.

(2) A tenancy granted for a term of years certain which is continuing by virtue of section 24 of this Act shall not come to an end by reason only of the tenant ceasing to occupy the property comprised in the tenancy but may be brought to an end on any day by not less than three months' notice in writing given by the tenant to the immediate landlord, whether the notice is given after the date

on which apart from this Act the tenancy would have come to an end or before that date, but not before the tenant has been in occupation in right of the tenancy for one month.

(3) Where a tenancy is terminated under subsection (2) above, any rent payable in respect of a period which begins before, and ends after, the tenancy is terminated shall be apportioned, and any rent paid by the tenant in excess of the amount apportioned to the period before termination shall be recoverable by him.

28 Renewal of tenancies by agreement

Where the landlord and tenant agree for the grant to the tenant of a future tenancy of the holding, or of the holding with other land, on terms and from a date specified in the agreement, the current tenancy shall continue until that date but no longer, and shall not be a tenancy to which this Part of this Act applies.

APPLICATIONS TO COURT

29 Order by court for grant of new tenancy or termination of current tenancy

(1) Subject to the provisions of this Act, on an application under section 24(1) of this Act, the court shall make an order for the grant of a new tenancy and accordingly for the termination of the current tenancy immediately before the commencement of the new tenancy.

(2) Subject to the following provisions of this Act, a landlord may apply to the court for an order for the termination of a tenancy to which this Part of this Act applies without the grant of a new tenancy –

(a) if he has given notice under section 25 of this Act that he is opposed to the grant of a new tenancy to the tenant; or

(b) if the tenant has made a request for a new tenancy in accordance with section 26 of this Act and the landlord has given notice under subsection (6) of that section.

(3) The landlord may not make an application under subsection (2) above if either the tenant or the landlord has made an application under section 24(1) of this Act.

(4) Subject to the provisions of this Act, where the landlord makes an application under subsection (2) above –

(a) if he establishes, to the satisfaction of the court, any of the grounds on which he is entitled to make the application in accordance with section 30 of this Act, the court shall make an order for the termination of the current tenancy in accordance with section 64 of this Act without the grant of a new tenancy; and

(b) if not, it shall make an order for the grant of a new tenancy and accordingly for the termination of the current tenancy immediately before the commencement of the new tenancy.

(5) The court shall dismiss an application by the landlord under section 24(1) of this Act if the tenant informs the court that he does not want a new tenancy.

(6) The landlord may not withdraw an application under subsection (2) above unless the tenant consents to its withdrawal.

29A Time limits for applications to court

(1)   Subject to section 29B of this Act, the court shall not entertain an application –

    (a) by the tenant or the landlord under section 24(1) of this Act; or
    (b) by the landlord under section 29(2) of this Act,

if it is made after the end of the statutory period.

(2)   In this section and section 29B of this Act 'the statutory period' means a period ending –

    (a) where the landlord gave a notice under section 25 of this Act, on the date specified in his notice; and
    (b) where the tenant made a request for a new tenancy under section 26 of this Act, immediately before the date specified in his request.

(3)   Where the tenant has made a request for a new tenancy under section 26 of this Act, the court shall not entertain an application under section 24(1) of this Act which is made before the end of the period of two months beginning with the date of the making of the request, unless the application is made after the landlord has given a notice under section 26(6) of this Act.

29B Agreements extending time limits

(1)   After the landlord has given a notice under section 25 of this Act, or the tenant has made a request under section 26 of this Act, but before the end of the statutory period, the landlord and tenant may agree that an application such as is mentioned in section 29A(1) of this Act may be made before the end of a period specified in the agreement which will expire after the end of the statutory period.

(2)   The landlord and tenant may from time to time by agreement further extend the period for making such an application, but any such agreement must be made before the end of the period specified in the current agreement.

(3)   Where an agreement is made under this section, the court may entertain an application such as is mentioned in section 29A(1) of this Act if it is made before the end of the period specified in the agreement.

(4)   Where an agreement is made under this section, or two or more agreements are made under this section, the landlord's notice under section 25 of this Act or tenant's request under section 26 of this Act shall be treated as terminating the tenancy at the end of the period specified in the agreement or, as the case may be, at the end of the period specified in the last of those agreements.

30 Opposition by landlord to application for new tenancy

(1)   The grounds on which a landlord may oppose an application under section 24(1) of this Act, or make an application under section 29(2) of this Act, are such of the following grounds as may be stated in the landlord's notice under section 25 of this Act or, as the case may be, under subsection (6) of section 26 thereof, that is to say:

    (a) where under the current tenancy the tenant has any obligations as respects the repair and maintenance of the holding, that the tenant ought not to be granted a new tenancy in view of the state of repair of the holding, being a state resulting from the tenant's failure to comply with the said obligations;

   (b) that the tenant ought not to be granted a new tenancy in view of his persistent delay in paying rent which has become due;

   (c) that the tenant ought not to be granted a new tenancy in view of other substantial breaches by him of his obligations under the current tenancy, or for any other reason connected with the tenant's use or management of the holding;

   (d) that the landlord has offered and is willing to provide or secure the provision of alternative accommodation for the tenant, that the terms on which the alternative accommodation is available are reasonable having regard to the terms of the current tenancy and to all other relevant circumstances, and that the accommodation and the time at which it will be available are suitable for the tenant's requirements (including the requirement to preserve goodwill) having regard to the nature and class of his business and to the situation and extent of, and facilities afforded by, the holding;

   (e) where the current tenancy was created by the sub-letting of part only of the property comprised in a superior tenancy and the landlord is the owner of an interest in reversion expectant on the termination of that superior tenancy, that the aggregate of the rents reasonably obtainable on separate lettings of the holding and the remainder of that property would be substantially less than the rent reasonably obtainable on a letting of that property as a whole, that on the termination of the current tenancy the landlord requires possession of the holding for the purpose of letting or otherwise disposing of the said property as a whole, and that in view thereof the tenant ought not to be granted a new tenancy;

   (f) that on the termination of the current tenancy the landlord intends to demolish or reconstruct the premises comprised in the holding or a substantial part of those premises or to carry out substantial work of construction on the holding or part thereof and that he could not reasonably do so without obtaining possession of the holding;

   (g) subject as hereinafter provided, that on the termination of the current tenancy the landlord intends to occupy the holding for the purposes, or partly for the purposes, of a business to be carried on by him therein, or as his residence.

(1A) Where the landlord has a controlling interest in a company, the reference in subsection (1)(g) above to the landlord shall be construed as a reference to the landlord or that company.

(1B) Subject to subsection (2A) below, where the landlord is a company and a person has a controlling interest in the company, the reference in subsection (1)(g) above to the landlord shall be construed as a reference to the landlord or that person.

(2) The landlord shall not be entitled to oppose an application under section 24(1) of this Act, or make an application under section 29(2) of this Act, on the ground specified in paragraph (g) of the last foregoing subsection if the interest of the landlord, or an interest which has merged in that interest and but for the merger would be the interest of the landlord, was purchased or created after the beginning of the period of five years which ends with the termination of the current tenancy, and at all times since the purchase or creation thereof the holding has been comprised in a tenancy or successive tenancies of the description specified in subsection (1) of section 23 of this Act.

(2A) Subsection (1B) above shall not apply if the controlling interest was acquired after the beginning of the period of five years which ends with the termination of the current tenancy, and at all times since the acquisition of the controlling interest the holding has been comprised in a tenancy or successive tenancies of the description specified in section 23(1) of this Act.

(3)   [*Repealed*]

31   Dismissal of application for new tenancy where landlord successfully opposes

(1)   If the landlord opposes an application under subsection (1) of section 24 of this Act on grounds on which he is entitled to oppose it in accordance with the last foregoing section and establishes any of those grounds to the satisfaction of the court, the court shall not make an order for the grant of a new tenancy.

(2)   Where the landlord opposes an application under section 24(1) of this Act, or makes an application under section 29(2) of this Act, on one or more of the grounds specified in section 30(1)(d) to (f) of this Act but establishes none of those grounds, and none of the other grounds specified in section 30(1) of this Act, to the satisfaction of the court, then if the court would have been satisfied on any of the grounds specified in section 30(1)(d) to (f) of this Act if the date of termination specified in the landlord's notice or, as the case may be, the date specified in the tenant's request for a new tenancy as the date from which the new tenancy is to begin, had been such later date as the court may determine, being a date not more than one year later than the date so specified, –

(a)   the court shall make a declaration to that effect, stating of which of the said grounds the court would have been satisfied as aforesaid and specifying the date determined by the court as aforesaid, but shall not make an order for the grant of a new tenancy;

(b)   if, within fourteen days after the making of the declaration, the tenant so requires the court shall make an order substituting the said date for the date specified in the said landlord's notice or tenant's request, and thereupon that notice or request shall have effect accordingly.

31A   Grant of new tenancy in some cases where section 30(1)(f) applies

(1)   Where the landlord opposes an application under section 24(1) of this Act on the ground specified in paragraph (f) of section 30(1) of this Act, or makes an application under section 29(2) of this Act on that ground, the court shall not hold that the landlord could not reasonably carry out the demolition, reconstruction or work of construction intended without obtaining possession of the holding if –

(a)   the tenant agrees to the inclusion in the terms of the new tenancy of terms giving the landlord access and other facilities for carrying out the work intended and, given that access and those facilities, the landlord could reasonably carry out the work without obtaining possession of the holding and without interfering to a substantial extent or for a substantial time with the use of the holding for the purposes of the business carried on by the tenant; or

(b)   the tenant is willing to accept a tenancy of an economically separable part of the holding and either paragraph (a) of this section is satisfied with respect to that part or possession of the remainder of the holding would be reasonably sufficient to enable the landlord to carry out the intended work.

253

(2) For the purposes of subsection (1)(b) of this section a part of a holding shall be deemed to be an economically separate part if, and only if, the aggregate of the rents which, after the completion of the intended work, would be reasonably obtainable on separate lettings of that part and the remainder of the premises affected by or resulting from the work would not be substantially less than the rent which would then be reasonably obtainable on a letting of those premises as a whole.

32   Property to be comprised in new tenancy

(1) Subject to the following provisions of this section, an order under section 29 of this Act for the grant of a new tenancy shall be an order for the grant of a new tenancy of the holding; and in the absence of agreement between the landlord and the tenant as to the property which constitutes the holding the court shall in the order designate that property by reference to the circumstances existing at the date of the order.

(1A) Where the court, by virtue of paragraph (b) of section 31A(1) of this Act, makes an order under section 29 of this Act for the grant of a new tenancy in a case where the tenant is willing to accept a tenancy of part of the holding, the order shall be an order for the grant of a new tenancy of that part only.

(2) The foregoing provisions of this section shall not apply in a case where the property comprised in the current tenancy includes other property besides the holding and the landlord requires any new tenancy ordered to be granted under section 29 of this Act to be a tenancy of the whole of the property comprised in the current tenancy; but in any such case –

   (a) any order under the said section 29 for the grant of a new tenancy shall be an order for the grant of a new tenancy of the whole of the property comprised in the current tenancy, and

   (b) references in the following provisions of this Part of this Act to the holding shall be construed as references to the whole of that property.

(3) Where the current tenancy includes rights enjoyed by the tenant in connection with the holding, those rights shall be included in a tenancy ordered to be granted under section 29 of this Act, except as otherwise agreed between the landlord and the tenant or, in default of such agreement, determined by the court.

33   Duration of new tenancy

Where on an application under this Part of this Act the court makes an order for the grant of a new tenancy, the new tenancy shall be such tenancy as may be agreed between the landlord and the tenant, or, in default of such an agreement, shall be such a tenancy as may be determined by the court to be reasonable in all the circumstances, being, if it is a tenancy for a term of years certain, a tenancy for a term not exceeding fifteen years, and shall begin on the coming to an end of the current tenancy.

34   Rent under new tenancy

(1) The rent payable under a tenancy granted by order of the court under this Part of this Act shall be such as may be agreed between the landlord and the tenant or as, in default of such agreement, may be determined by the court to be that at which, having regard to the terms of the tenancy (other than those relating

to rent), the holding might reasonably be expected to be let in the open market by a willing lessor, there being disregarded –

    (a)   any effect on rent of the fact that the tenant has or his predecessors in title have been in occupation of the holding,

    (b)   any goodwill attached to the holding by reason of the carrying on thereat of the business of the tenant (whether by him or by a predecessor of his in that business),

    (c)   any effect on rent of an improvement to which this paragraph applies,

    (d)   in the case of a holding comprising licensed premises, any addition to its value attributable to the licence, if it appears to the court that having regard to the terms of the current tenancy and any other relevant circumstances the benefit of the licence belongs to the tenant.

(2)   Paragraph (c) of the foregoing subsection applies to any improvement carried out by a person who at the time it was carried out was the tenant, but only if it was carried out otherwise than in pursuance of an obligation to his immediate landlord, and either it was carried out during the current tenancy or the following conditions are satisfied, that is to say –

    (a)   that it was completed not more than twenty-one years before the application to the court was made; and

    (b)   that the holding or any part of it affected by the improvement has at all times since the completion of the improvement been comprised in tenancies of the description specified in section 23(1) of this Act; and

    (c)   that at the termination of each of those tenancies the tenant did not quit.

(2A)   If this Part of this Act applies by virtue of section 23(1A) of this Act, the reference in subsection (1)(d) above to the tenant shall be construed as including –

    (a)   a company in which the tenant has a controlling interest, or

    (b)   where the tenant is a company, a person with a controlling interest in the company.

(3)   Where the rent is determined by the court the court may, if it thinks fit, further determine that the terms of the tenancy shall include such provision for varying the rent as may be specified in the determination.

(4)   It is hereby declared that the matters which are to be taken into account by the court in determining the rent include any effect on rent of the operation of the provisions of the Landlord and Tenant (Covenants) Act 1995.

35   Other terms of new tenancy

(1)   The terms of a tenancy granted by order of the court under this Part of this Act (other than terms as to the duration thereof and as to the rent payable thereunder), including, where different persons own interests which fulfil the conditions specified in section 44(1) of this Act in different parts of it, terms as to the apportionment of the rent, shall be such as may be agreed between the landlord and the tenant or as, in default of such agreement, may be determined by the court; and in determining those terms the court shall have regard to the terms of the current tenancy and to all relevant circumstances.

(2)   In subsection (1) of this section the reference to all relevant circumstances includes (without prejudice to the generality of that reference) a reference to the operation of the provisions of the Landlord and Tenant (Covenants) Act 1995.

36 Carrying out of order for new tenancy

(1) Where under this Part of this Act the court makes an order for the grant of a new tenancy, then, unless the order is revoked under the next following sub-section or the landlord and the tenant agree not to act upon the order, the landlord shall be bound to execute or make in favour of the tenant, and the tenant shall be bound to accept, a lease or agreement for a tenancy of the holding embodying the terms agreed between the landlord and the tenant or determined by the court in accordance with the foregoing provisions of this Part of this Act; and where the landlord executes or makes such a lease or agreement the tenant shall be bound, if so required by the landlord, to execute a counterpart or duplicate thereof.

(2) If the tenant, within fourteen days after the making of an order under this Part of this Act for the grant of a new tenancy, applies to the court for the revocation of the order the court shall revoke the order; and where the order is so revoked, then, if it is so agreed between the landlord and the tenant or determined by the court, the current tenancy shall continue, beyond the date at which it would have come to an end apart from this subsection, for such period as may be so agreed or determined to be necessary to afford to the landlord a reasonable opportunity for reletting or otherwise disposing of the premises which would have been comprised in the new tenancy; and while the current tenancy continues by virtue of this subsection it shall not be a tenancy to which this Part of this Act applies.

(3) Where an order is revoked under the last foregoing subsection any provision thereof as to payment of costs shall not cease to have effect by reason only of the revocation; but the court may, if it thinks fit, revoke or vary any such provision or, where no costs have been awarded in the proceedings for the revoked order, award such costs.

(4) A lease executed or agreement made under this section, in a case where the interest of the lessor is subject to a mortgage, shall be deemed to be one authorised by section 99 of the Law of Property Act 1925 (which confers certain powers of leasing on mortgagors in possession), and subsection (13) of that section (which allows those powers to be restricted or excluded by agreement) shall not have effect in relation to such a lease or agreement.

37 Compensation where order for new tenancy precluded on certain grounds

(1) Subject to the provisions of this Act, in a case specified in subsection (1A), (1B) or (1C) below (a 'compensation case') the tenant shall be entitled on quitting the holding to recover from the landlord by way of compensation an amount determined in accordance with this section.

(1A) The first compensation case is where on the making of an application by the tenant under section 24(1) of this Act the court is precluded (whether by subsection (1) or subsection (2) of section 31 of this Act) from making an order for the grant of a new tenancy by reason of any of the grounds specified in paragraphs (e), (f) and (g) of section 30(1) of this Act (the 'compensation grounds') and not of any grounds specified in any other paragraph of section 30(1).

(1B) The second compensation case is where on the making of an application under section 29(2) of this Act the court is precluded (whether by section 29(4)(a) or section 31(2) of this Act) from making an order for the grant of a new tenancy by reason of any of the compensation grounds and not of any other grounds specified in section 30(1) of this Act.

(1C)   The third compensation case is where –

    (a)   the landlord's notice under section 25 of this Act or, as the case may be, under section 26(6) of this Act, states his opposition to the grant of a new tenancy on any of the compensation grounds and not on any other grounds specified in section 30(1) of this Act; and

    (b)   either –

        (i)   no application is made by the tenant under section 24(1) of this Act or by the landlord under section 29(2) of this Act; or

        (ii)   such an application is made but is subsequently withdrawn.

(2)   Subject to the following provisions of this section, compensation under this section shall be as follows, that is to say –

    (a)   where the conditions specified in the next following subsection are satisfied in relation to the whole of the holding it shall be the product of the appropriate multiplier and twice the rateable value of the holding,

    (b)   in any other case it shall be the product of the appropriate multiplier and the rateable value of the holding.

(3)   The said conditions are –

    (a)   that, during the whole of the fourteen years immediately preceding the termination of the current tenancy, premises being or comprised in the holding have been occupied for the purposes of a business carried on by the occupier or for those and other purposes;

    (b)   that, if during those fourteen years there was a change in the occupier of the premises, the person who was the occupier immediately after the change was the successor to the business carried on by the person who was the occupier immediately before the change.

(3A)   If the conditions specified in subsection (3) above are satisfied in relation to part of the holding but not in relation to the other part, the amount of compensation shall be the aggregate of sums calculated separately as compensation in respect of each part, and accordingly, for the purpose of calculating compensation in respect of a part any reference in this section to the holding shall be construed as a reference to that part.

(3B)   Where section 44(1A) of this Act applies, the compensation shall be determined separately for each part and compensation determined for any part shall be recoverable only from the person who is the owner of an interest in that part which fulfils the conditions specified in section 44(1) of this Act.

(4)   Where the court is precluded from making an order for the grant of a new tenancy under this Part of this Act in a compensation case, the court shall on the application of the tenant certify that fact.

(5)   For the purposes of subsection (2) of this section the rateable value of the holding shall be determined as follows –

    (a)   where in the valuation list in force at the date on which the landlord's notice under section 25 or, as the case may be, subsection (6) of section 26 of this Act is given a value is then shown as the annual value (as hereinafter defined) of the holding, the rateable value of the holding shall be taken to be that value;

(b) where no such value is so shown with respect to the holding but such a value or such values is or are so shown with respect to premises comprised in or comprising the holding or part of it, the rateable value of the holding shall be taken to be such value as is found by a proper apportionment or aggregation of the value or values so shown;

(c) where the rateable value of the holding cannot be ascertained in accordance with the foregoing paragraphs of this subsection, it shall be taken to be the value which, apart from any exemption from assessment to rates, would on a proper assessment be the value to be entered in the said valuation list as the annual value of the holding;

and any dispute arising, whether in proceedings before the court or otherwise, as to the determination for those purposes of the rateable value of the holding shall be referred to the Commissioners of Inland Revenue for decision by the valuation officer.

An appeal shall lie to the Lands Tribunal from any decision of a valuation officer under this subsection, but subject thereto any such decision shall be final.

(5A) If part of the holding is domestic property, as defined in section 66 of the Local Government Finance Act 1988 –

(a) the domestic property shall be disregarded in determining the rateable value of the holding under subsection (5) of this section; and

(b) if, on the date specified in subsection (5)(a) of this section, the tenant occupied the whole or any part of the domestic property, the amount of compensation to which he is entitled under subsection (1) of this section shall be increased by the addition of a sum equal to his reasonable expenses in removing from the domestic property.

(5B) Any question as to the amount of the sum referred to in paragraph (b) of subsection (5A) of this section shall be determined by agreement between the landlord and the tenant or, in default of agreement, by the court.

(5C) If the whole of the holding is domestic property, as defined in section 66 of the Local Government Finance Act 1988, for the purposes of subsection (2) of this section the rateable value of the holding shall be taken to be an amount equal to the rent at which it is estimated the holding might reasonably be expected to let from year to year if the tenant undertook to pay all usual tenant's rates and taxes and to bear the cost of the repairs and insurance and the other expenses (if any) necessary to maintain the holding in a state to command that rent.

(5D) The following provisions shall have effect as regards a determination of an amount mentioned in subsection (5C) of this section –

(a) the date by reference to which such a determination is to be made is the date on which the landlord's notice under section 25 or, as the case may be, subsection (6) of section 26 of this Act is given;

(b) any dispute arising, whether in proceedings before the court or otherwise, as to such a determination shall be referred to the Commissioners of Inland Revenue for decision by a valuation officer;

(c) an appeal shall lie to the Lands Tribunal from such a decision, but subject to that, such a decision shall be final.

(5E) Any deduction made under paragraph 2A of Schedule 6 to the Local Government Finance Act 1988 (deduction from valuation of hereditaments used for breeding horses etc.) shall be disregarded, to the extent that it relates to the holding, in determining the rateable value of the holding under subsection (5) of this section.

(6)   The Commissioners of Inland Revenue may by statutory instrument make rules prescribing the procedure in connection with references under this section.

(7)   In this section –

the reference to the termination of the current tenancy is a reference to the date of termination specified in the landlord's notice under section 25 of this Act or, as the case may be, the date specified in the tenant's request for a new tenancy as the date from which the new tenancy is to begin;

the expression 'annual value' means rateable value except that where the rateable value differs from the net annual value the said expression means net annual value;

the expression 'valuation officer' means any officer of the Commissioners of Inland Revenue for the time being authorised by a certificate of the Commissioners to act in relation to a valuation list.

(8)   In subsection (2) of this section 'the appropriate multiplier' means such multiplier as the Secretary of State may by order made by statutory instrument prescribe and different multipliers may be so prescribed in relation to different cases.

(9)   A statutory instrument containing an order under subsection (8) of this section shall be subject to annulment in pursuance of a resolution of either House of Parliament.

37A   Compensation for possession obtained by misrepresentation

(1)   Where the court –

(a) makes an order for the termination of the current tenancy but does not make an order for the grant of a new tenancy, or

(b) refuses an order for the grant of a new tenancy,

and it is subsequently made to appear to the court that the order was obtained, or the court was induced to refuse the grant, by misrepresentation or the concealment of material facts, the court may order the landlord to pay to the tenant such sum as appears sufficient as compensation for damage or loss sustained by the tenant as the result of the order or refusal.

(2)   Where –

(a) the tenant has quit the holding –

(i)   after making but withdrawing an application under section 24(1) of this Act; or

(ii) without making such an application; and

(b) it is made to appear to the court that he did so by reason of misrepresentation or the concealment of material facts, the court may order the landlord to pay to the tenant such sum as appears sufficient as compensation for damage or loss sustained by the tenant as the result of quitting the holding.

38   Restriction on agreements excluding provisions of Part II

(1)   Any agreement relating to a tenancy to which this Part of this Act applies (whether contained in the instrument creating the tenancy or not) shall be void (except as provided by section 38A of this Act) in so far as it purports to

preclude the tenant from making an application or request under this Part of this Act or provides for the termination or the surrender of the tenancy in the event of his making such an application or request or for the imposition of any penalty or disability on the tenant in that event.

(2) Where –

(a) during the whole of the five years immediately preceding the date on which the tenant under a tenancy to which this Part of this Act applies is to quit the holding, premises being or comprised in the holding have been occupied for the purposes of a business carried on by the occupier or for those and other purposes, and

(b) if during those five years there was a change in the occupier of the premises, the person who was the occupier immediately after the change was the successor to the business carried on by the person who was the occupier immediately before the change,

any agreement (whether contained in the instrument creating the tenancy or not and whether made before or after the termination of that tenancy) which purports to exclude or reduce compensation under section 37 of this Act shall to that extent be void, so however that this subsection shall not affect any agreement as to the amount of any such compensation which is made after the right to compensation has accrued.

(3) In a case not falling within the last foregoing subsection the right to compensation conferred by section 37 of this Act may be excluded or modified by agreement.

(4) [Repealed]

38A Agreements to exclude provisions of Part II

(1) The persons who will be the landlord and the tenant in relation to a tenancy to be granted for a term of years certain which will be a tenancy to which this Part of this Act applies may agree that the provisions of sections 24 to 28 of this Act shall be excluded in relation to that tenancy.

(2) The persons who are the landlord and the tenant in relation to a tenancy to which this Part of this Act applies may agree that the tenancy shall be surrendered on such date or in such circumstances as may be specified in the agreement and on such terms (if any) as may be so specified.

(3) An agreement under subsection (1) above shall be void unless –

(a) the landlord has served on the tenant a notice in the form, or substantially in the form, set out in Schedule 1 to the Regulatory Reform (Business Tenancies) (England and Wales) Order 2003 ('the 2003 Order'); and

(b) the requirements specified in Schedule 2 to that Order are met.

(4) An agreement under subsection (2) above shall be void unless –

(a) the landlord has served on the tenant a notice in the form, or substantially in the form, set out in Schedule 3 to the 2003 Order; and

(b) the requirements specified in Schedule 4 to that Order are met.

GENERAL AND SUPPLEMENTARY PROVISIONS

39   Saving for compulsory acquisitions

(1)   [*Repealed*]

(2)   If the amount of the compensation which would have been payable under section 37 of this Act if the tenancy had come to an end in circumstances giving rise to compensation under that section and the date at which the acquiring authority obtained possession had been the termination of the current tenancy exceeds the amount of the compensation payable under section 121 of the Lands Clauses Consolidation Act 1845 or section 20 of the Compulsory Purchase Act 1965 in the case of a tenancy to which this Part of this Act applies, that compensation shall be increased by the amount of the excess.

(3)   Nothing in section 24 of this Act shall affect the operation of the said section 121.

40   Duty of tenants and landlords of business premises to give information to each other

(1)   Where a person who is an owner of an interest in reversion expectant (whether immediately or not) on a tenancy of any business premises has served on the tenant a notice in the prescribed form requiring him to do so, it shall be the duty of the tenant to give the appropriate person in writing the information specified in subsection (2) below.

(2)   That information is –

(a)   whether the tenant occupies the premises or any part of them wholly or partly for the purposes of a business carried on by him;

(b)   whether his tenancy has effect subject to any sub-tenancy on which his tenancy is immediately expectant and, if so –

(i)   what premises are comprised in the sub-tenancy;

(ii)   for what term it has effect (or, if it is terminable by notice, by what notice it can be terminated);

(iii)   what is the rent payable under it;

(iv)   who is the sub-tenant;

(v)   (to the best of his knowledge and belief) whether the sub-tenant is in occupation of the premises or of part of the premises comprised in the sub-tenancy and, if not, what is the sub-tenant's address;

(vi)   whether an agreement is in force excluding in relation to the sub-tenancy the provisions of sections 24 to 28 of this Act; and

(vii)   whether a notice has been given under section 25 or 26(6) of this Act, or a request has been made under section 26 of this Act, in relation to the sub-tenancy and, if so, details of the notice or request; and

(c)   (to the best of his knowledge and belief) the name and address of any other person who owns an interest in reversion in any part of the premises.

(3)   Where the tenant of any business premises who is a tenant under such a tenancy as is mentioned in section 26(1) of this Act has served on a reversioner or a reversioner's mortgagee in possession a notice in the prescribed form requiring him to do so, it shall be the duty of the person on whom the notice is served to give the appropriate person in writing the information specified in subsection (4) below.

261

(4)   That information is –

    (a) whether he is the owner of the fee simple in respect of the premises or any part of them or the mortgagee in possession of such an owner,

    (b) if he is not, then (to the best of his knowledge and belief) –

        (i)   the name and address of the person who is his or, as the case may be, his mortgagor's immediate landlord in respect of those premises or of the part in respect of which he or his mortgagor is not the owner in fee simple;

        (ii) for what term his or his mortgagor's tenancy has effect and what is the earliest date (if any) at which that tenancy is terminable by notice to quit given by the landlord; and

        (iii) whether a notice has been given under section 25 or 26(6) of this Act, or a request has been made under section 26 of this Act, in relation to the tenancy and, if so, details of the notice or request;

    (c) (to the best of his knowledge and belief) the name and address of any other person who owns an interest in reversion in any part of the premises; and

    (d) if he is a reversioner, whether there is a mortgagee in possession of his interest in the premises and, if so, (to the best of his knowledge and belief) what is the name and address of the mortgagee.

(5)   A duty imposed on a person by this section is a duty –

    (a) to give the information concerned within the period of one month beginning with the date of service of the notice; and

    (b) if within the period of six months beginning with the date of service of the notice that person becomes aware that any information which has been given in pursuance of the notice is not, or is no longer, correct, to give the appropriate person correct information within the period of one month beginning with the date on which he becomes aware.

(6)   This section shall not apply to a notice served by or on the tenant more than two years before the date on which apart from this Act his tenancy would come to an end by effluxion of time or could be brought to an end by notice to quit given by the landlord.

(7)   Except as provided by section 40A of this Act, the appropriate person for the purposes of this section and section 40A(1) of this Act is the person who served the notice under subsection (1) or (3) above.

(8)   In this section –

'business premises' means premises used wholly or partly for the purposes of a business;

'mortgagee in possession' includes a receiver appointed by the mortgagee or by the court who is in receipt of the rents and profits, and 'his mortgagor' shall be construed accordingly;

'reversioner' means any person having an interest in the premises, being an interest in reversion expectant (whether immediately or not) on the tenancy;

'reversioner's mortgagee in possession' means any person being a mortgagee in possession in respect of such an interest; and

'sub-tenant' includes a person retaining possession of any premises by virtue of the Rent (Agriculture) Act 1976 or the Rent Act 1977 after the coming to an end of a sub-tenancy, and 'sub-tenancy' includes a right so to retain possession.

40A   Duties in transfer cases

(1)   If a person on whom a notice under section 40(1) or (3) of this Act has been served has transferred his interest in the premises or any part of them to some other person and gives the appropriate person notice in writing –

(a)   of the transfer of his interest; and
(b)   of the name and address of the person to whom he transferred it,

on giving the notice he ceases in relation to the premises or (as the case may be) to that part to be under any duty imposed by section 40 of this Act.

(2)   If –

(a)   the person who served the notice under section 40(1) or (3) of this Act ('the transferor') has transferred his interest in the premises to some other person ('the transferee'); and
(b)   the transferor or the transferee has given the person required to give the information notice in writing –

(i)   of the transfer; and
(ii)   of the transferee's name and address,

the appropriate person for the purposes of section 40 of this Act and subsection (1) above is the transferee.

(3)   If –

(a)   a transfer such as is mentioned in paragraph (a) of subsection (2) above has taken place; but
(b)   neither the transferor nor the transferee has given a notice such as is mentioned in paragraph (b) of that subsection,

any duty imposed by section 40 of this Act may be performed by giving the information either to the transferor or to the transferee.

40B   Proceedings for breach of duties to give information

A claim that a person has broken any duty imposed by section 40 of this Act may be made the subject of civil proceedings for breach of statutory duty; and in any such proceedings a court may order that person to comply with that duty and may make an award of damages.

41   Trusts

(1)   Where a tenancy is held on trust, occupation by all or any of the beneficiaries under the trust, and the carrying on of a business by all or any of the benefici-aries, shall be treated for the purposes of section 23 of this Act as equivalent to occupation or the carrying on of a business by the tenant; and in relation to a tenancy to which this Part of this Act applies by virtue of the foregoing provi-sions of this subsection –

(a)   references (however expressed) in this Part of this Act and in the Ninth Schedule to this Act to the business of, or to carrying on of business, use, occupation or enjoyment by, the tenant shall be construed as including references to the business of, or to carrying on of business, use, occupation or enjoyment by, the beneficiaries or beneficiary;

(b) the reference in paragraph (d) of subsection (1) of section 34 of this Act to the tenant shall be construed as including the beneficiaries or beneficiary; and

(c) a change in the persons of the trustees shall not be treated as a change in the person of the tenant.

(2) Where the landlord's interest is held on trust the references in paragraph (g) of subsection (1) of section 30 of this Act to the landlord shall be construed as including references to the beneficiaries under the trust or any of them; but, except in the case of a trust arising under a will or on the intestacy of any person, the reference in subsection (2) of that section to the creation of the interest therein mentioned shall be construed as including the creation of the trust.

41A Partnerships

(1) The following provisions of this section shall apply where –

(a) a tenancy is held jointly by two or more persons (in this section referred to as the joint tenants); and

(b) the property comprised in the tenancy is or includes premises occupied for the purposes of a business; and

(c) the business (or some other business) was at some time during the existence of the tenancy carried on in partnership by all the persons who were then the joint tenants or by those and other persons and the joint tenants' interest in the premises was then partnership property; and

(d) the business is carried on (whether alone or in partnership with other persons) by one or some only of the joint tenants and no part of the property comprised in the tenancy is occupied, in right of the tenancy, for the purposes of a business carried on (whether alone or in partnership with other persons) by the other or others.

(2) In the following provisions of this section those of the joint tenants who for the time being carry on the business are referred to as the business tenants and the others as the other joint tenants.

(3) Any notice given by the business tenants which, had it been given by all the joint tenants, would have been –

(a) a tenant's request for a new tenancy made in accordance with section 26 of this Act; or

(b) a notice under subsection (1) or subsection (2) of section 27 of this Act;

shall be treated as such if it states that it is given by virtue of this section and sets out the facts by virtue of which the persons giving it are the business tenants; and references in those sections and in section 24A of this Act to the tenant shall be construed accordingly.

(4) A notice given by the landlord to the business tenants which, had it been given to all the joint tenants, would have been a notice under section 25 of this Act shall be treated as such a notice, and references in that section to the tenant shall be construed accordingly.

(5) An application under section 24(1) of this Act for a new tenancy may, instead of being made by all the joint tenants, be made by the business tenants alone; and where it is so made –

(a) this Part of this Act shall have effect, in relation to it, as if the references therein to the tenant included references to the business tenants alone; and

(b) the business tenants shall be liable, to the exclusion of the other joint tenants, for the payment of rent and the discharge of any other obligation under the current tenancy for any rental period beginning after the date specified in the landlord's notice under section 25 of this Act or, as the case may be, beginning on or after the date specified in their request for a new tenancy.

(6) Where the court makes an order under section 29 of this Act for the grant of a new tenancy it may order the grant to be made to the business tenants or to them jointly with the persons carrying on the business in partnership with them, and may order the grant to be made subject to the satisfaction, within a time specified by the order, of such conditions as to guarantors, sureties or otherwise as appear to the court equitable, having regard to the omission of the other joint tenants from the persons who will be the tenants under the new tenancy.

(7) The business tenants shall be entitled to recover any amount payable by way of compensation under section 37 or section 59 of this Act.

42 Groups of companies

(1) For the purposes of this section two bodies corporate shall be taken to be members of a group if and only if one is a subsidiary of the other or both are subsidiaries of the third body corporate or the same person has a controlling interest in both.

(2) Where a tenancy is held by a member of a group, occupation by another member of the group, and the carrying on of a business by another member of the group, shall be treated for the purposes of section 23 of this Act as equivalent to occupation or the carrying on of a business by the member of the group holding the tenancy; and in relation to a tenancy to which this Part of this Act applies by virtue of the foregoing provisions of this subsection –

(a) references (however expressed) in this Part of this Act and in the Ninth Schedule to this Act to the business of or to use occupation or enjoyment by the tenant shall be construed as including references to the business of or to use occupation or enjoyment by the said other member;

(b) the reference in paragraph (d) of subsection (1) of section 34 of this Act to the tenant shall be construed as including the said other member; and

(c) an assignment of the tenancy from one member of the group to another shall not be treated as a change in the person of the tenant.

(3) Where the landlord's interest is held by a member of a group –

(a) the reference in paragraph (g) of subsection (1) of section 30 of this Act to intended occupation by the landlord for the purposes of a business to be carried on by him shall be construed as including intended occupation by any member of the group for the purposes of a business to be carried on by that member; and

(b) the reference in subsection (2) of that section to the purchase or creation of any interest shall be construed as a reference to a purchase from or creation by a person other than a member of the group.

43 Tenancies excluded from Part II

(1)   This Part of this Act does not apply –

    (a) to a tenancy of an agricultural holding which is a tenancy in relation to which the Agricultural Holdings Act 1986 applies or a tenancy which would be a tenancy of an agricultural holding in relation to which that Act applied if subsection (3) of section 2 of that Act did not have effect or, in a case where approval was given under subsection (1) of that section, if that approval had not been given;

    (aa) to a farm business tenancy;

    (b) to a tenancy created by a mining lease; or

    (c) [Repealed]

    (d) [Repealed]

(2)   This Part of this Act does not apply to a tenancy granted by reason that the tenant was the holder of an office, appointment or employment from the grantor thereof and continuing only so long as the tenant holds the office, appointment or employment, or terminable by the grantor on the tenant's ceasing to hold it, or coming to an end at a time fixed by reference to the time at which the tenant ceases to hold it:

    Provided that this subsection shall not have effect in relation to a tenancy granted after the commencement of this Act unless the tenancy was granted by an instrument in writing which expressed the purpose for which the tenancy was granted.

(3)   This Part of this Act does not apply to a tenancy granted for a term certain not exceeding six months unless –

    (a) the tenancy contains provision for renewing the term or for extending it beyond six months from its beginning; or

    (b) the tenant has been in occupation for a period which, together with any period during which any predecessor in the carrying on of the business carried on by the tenant was in occupation, exceeds twelve months.

43A Jurisdiction of county court to make declaration

Where the rateable value of the holding is such that the jurisdiction conferred on the court by any other provision of this Part of this Act is, by virtue of section 63 of this Act, exercisable by the county court, the county court shall have jurisdiction (but without prejudice to the jurisdiction of the High Court) to make any declaration as to any matter arising under this Part of this Act, whether or not any other relief is sought in the proceedings.

44 Meaning of 'the landlord' in Part II, and provisions as to mesne landlords, etc.

(1)   Subject to subsections (1A) and (2) below, in this Part of this Act the expression 'the landlord' in relation to a tenancy (in this section referred to as 'the relevant tenancy'), means the person (whether or not he is the immediate landlord) who is the owner of that interest in the property comprised in the relevant tenancy which for the time being fulfils the following conditions, that is to say –

    (a) that it is an interest in reversion expectant (whether immediately or not) on the termination of the relevant tenancy, and

(b) that it is either the fee simple or a tenancy which will not come to an end within fourteen months by effluxion of time and, if it is such a tenancy, that no notice has been given by virtue of which it will come to an end within fourteen months or any further time by which it may be continued under section 36(2) or section 64 of this Act,

and is not itself in reversion expectant (whether immediately or not) on an interest which fulfils those conditions.

(1A) The reference in subsection (1) above to a person who is the owner of an interest such as is mentioned in that subsection is to be construed, where different persons own such interests in different parts of the property, as a reference to all those persons collectively.

(2) References in this Part of this Act to a notice to quit given by the landlord are references to a notice to quit given by the immediate landlord.

(3) The provisions of the Sixth Schedule to this Act shall have effect for the application of this Part of this Act to cases where the immediate landlord of the tenant is not the owner of the fee simple in respect of the holding.

45 *[Repealed]*

46 Interpretation of Part II

(1) In this Part of this Act: –

'business' has the meaning assigned to it by subsection (2) of section 23 of this Act;
'date of termination' has the meaning assigned to it by subsection (1) of section 25 of this Act;
subject to the provisions of section 32 of this Act, 'the holding' has the meaning assigned to it by subsection (3) of section 23 of this Act;
'interim rent' has the meaning given by section 24A(1) of this Act;
'mining lease' has the same meaning as in the Landlord and Tenant Act 1927.

(2) For the purposes of this Part of this Act, a person has a controlling interest in a company if, had he been a company, the other company would have been its subsidiary; and in this Part –

'company' has the meaning given by section 735 of the Companies Act 1985; and
'subsidiary' has the meaning given by section 736 of that Act.

Landlord and Tenant Act 1927, s.23

23 Service of notices

(1) Any notice, request, demand or other instrument under this Act shall be in writing and may be served on the person on whom it is to be served either personally, or by leaving it for him at his last known place of abode in England or Wales, or by sending it through the post in a registered letter addressed to him there, or, in the case of a local or public authority or a statutory or a public utility company, to the secretary or other proper officer at the principal office of such authority or company, and in the case of a notice to a landlord, the person on whom it is to be served shall include any agent of the landlord duly authorised in that behalf.

(2) Unless or until a tenant of a holding shall have received notice that the person theretofore entitled to the rents and profits of the holding (hereinafter referred to as 'the original landlord') has ceased to be so entitled, and also notice of the name and address of the person who has become entitled to such rents and profits, any claim, notice, request, demand, or other instrument, which the tenant shall serve upon or deliver to the original landlord shall be deemed to have been served upon or delivered to the landlord of such holding.

CPR, PD56: Landlord and tenant claims and miscellaneous provisions about land

SECTION I – LANDLORD AND TENANT CLAIMS

1.1   In this section of this practice direction –

(1) 'the 1927 Act' means the Landlord and Tenant Act 1927;
(2) 'the 1954 Act' means the Landlord and Tenant Act 1954;
(3) 'the 1985 Act' means the Landlord and Tenant Act 1985; and
(4) 'the 1987 Act' means the Landlord and Tenant Act 1987.

56.2 – STARTING THE CLAIM

2.1   Subject to paragraph 2.1A, the claimant in a landlord and tenant claim must use the Part 8 procedure as modified by Part 56 and this practice direction.

2.1A   Where the landlord and tenant claim is a claim for –

(1) a new tenancy under section 24 of the 1954 Act in circumstances where the grant of a new tenancy is opposed; or
(2) the termination of a tenancy under section 29(2) of the 1954 Act,

the claimant must use the Part 7 procedure as modified by Part 56 and this practice direction.

2.2   Except where the county court does not have jurisdiction, landlord and tenant claims should normally be brought in the county court. Only exceptional circumstances justify starting a claim in the High Court.

2.3   If a claimant starts a claim in the High Court and the court decides that it should have been started in the county court, the court will normally either strike the claim out or transfer it to the county court on its own initiative. This is likely to result in delay and the court will normally disallow the costs of starting the claim in the High Court and of any transfer.

2.4   Circumstances which may, in an appropriate case, justify starting a claim in the High Court are if –

(1) there are complicated disputes of fact; or
(2) there are points of law of general importance.

2.5   The value of the property and the amount of any financial claim may be relevant circumstances, but these factors alone will not normally justify starting the claim in the High Court.

2.6   A landlord and tenant claim started in the High Court must be brought in the Chancery Division.

CLAIMS FOR A NEW TENANCY UNDER SECTION 24 AND TERMINATION OF A TERNANCY UNDER SECTION 29(2) OF THE 1954 ACT

3.1   This paragraph applies to a claim for a new tenancy under section 24 and termination of a tenancy under section 29(2) of the 1954 Act where rule 56.3 applies and in this paragraph –

    (1)   'an unopposed claim' means a claim for a new tenancy under section 24 of the 1954 Act in circumstances where the grant of a new tenancy is not opposed;

    (2)   'an opposed claim' means a claim for –

      (a)   a new tenancy under section 24 of the 1954 Act in circumstances where the grant of a new tenancy is opposed; or

      (b)   the termination of a tenancy under section 29(2) of the 1954 Act; and

    (3)   'grounds of opposition' means –

      (a)   the grounds specified in section 30(1) of the 1954 Act on which a landlord may oppose an application for a new tenancy under section 24(1) of the 1954 Act or make an application under section 29(2) of the 1954 Act; or

      (b)   any other basis on which the landlord asserts that a new tenancy ought not to be granted.

Precedence of claim forms where there is more than one application to the court under section 24(1) or section 29(2) of the 1954 Act

3.2   Where more than one application to the court under section 24(1) or section 29(2) of the 1954 Act is made, the following provisions shall apply –

    (1)   once an application to the court under section 24(1) of the 1954 Act has been served on a defendant, no further application to the court in respect of the same tenancy whether under section 24(1) or section 29(2) of the 1954 Act may be served by that defendant without the permission of the court;

    (2)   if more than one application to the court under section 24(1) of the 1954 Act in respect of the same tenancy is served on the same day, any landlord's application shall stand stayed until further order of the court;

    (3)   if applications to the court under both section 24(1) and section 29(2) of the 1954 Act in respect of the same tenancy are served on the same day, any tenant's application shall stand stayed until further order of the court; and

    (4)   if a defendant is served with an application under section 29(2) of the 1954 Act ('the section 29(2) application') which was issued at a time when an application to the court had already been made by that defendant in respect of the same tenancy under section 24(1) of the 1954 Act ('the section 24(1) application'), the service of the section 29(2) application shall be deemed to be a notice under rule 7.7 requiring service or discontinuance of the section 24(1) application within a period of 14 days after the service of the section 29(2) application.

Defendant where the claimant is the tenant making a claim for a new tenancy under section 24 of the 1954 Act

3.3   Where a claim for a new tenancy under section 24 of the 1954 Act is made by a tenant, the person who, in relation to the claimant's current tenancy, is the landlord as defined in section 44 of the 1954 Act must be a defendant.

Contents of the claim form in all cases

3.4   The claim form must contain details of –

(1) the property to which the claim relates;

(2) the particulars of the current tenancy (including date, parties and duration), the current rent (if not the original rent) and the date and method of termination;

(3) every notice or request given or made under sections 25 or 26 of the 1954 Act; and

(4) the expiry date of –

(a) the statutory period under section 29A(2) of the 1954 Act; or

(b) any agreed extended period made under section 29B(1) or 29B(2) of the 1954 Act.

Claim form where the claimant is the tenant making a claim for a new tenancy under section 24 of the 1954 Act

3.5   Where the claimant is the tenant making a claim for a new tenancy under section 24 of the 1954 Act, in addition to the details specified in paragraph 3.4, the claim form must contain details of –

(1) the nature of the business carried on at the property;

(2) whether the claimant relies on section 23(1A), 41 or 42 of the 1954 Act and, if so, the basis on which he does so;

(3) whether the claimant relies on section 31A of the 1954 Act and, if so, the basis on which he does so;

(4) whether any, and if so what part, of the property comprised in the tenancy is occupied neither by the claimant nor by a person employed by the claimant for the purpose of the claimant's business;

(5) the claimant's proposed terms of the new tenancy; and

(6) the name and address of –

(a) anyone known to the claimant who has an interest in the reversion in the property (whether immediate or in not more than 15 years) on the termination of the claimant's current tenancy and who is likely to be affected by the grant of a new tenancy; or

(b) if the claimant does not know of anyone specified by sub-paragraph (6)(a), anyone who has a freehold interest in the property.

3.6   The claim form must be served on the persons referred to in paragraph 3.5(6)(a) or (b) as appropriate.

Claim form where the claimant is the landlord making a claim for a new tenancy under section 24 of the 1954 Act

3.7   Where the claimant is the landlord making a claim for a new tenancy under section 24 of the 1954 Act, in addition to the details specified in paragraph 3.4, the claim form must contain details of –

(1) the claimant's proposed terms of the new tenancy;
(2) whether the claimant is aware that the defendant's tenancy is one to which section 32(2) of the 1954 Act applies and, if so, whether the claimant requires that any new tenancy shall be a tenancy of the whole of the property comprised in the defendant's current tenancy or just of the holding as defined by section 23(3) of the 1954 Act; and
(3) the name and address of –
    (a) anyone known to the claimant who has an interest in the reversion in the property (whether immediate or in not more than 15 years) on the termination of the claimant's current tenancy and who is likely to be affected by the grant of a new tenancy; or
    (b) if the claimant does not know of anyone specified by sub-paragraph (3)(a), anyone who has a freehold interest in the property.

3.8 The claim form must be served on the persons referred to in paragraph 3.7(3)(a) or (b) as appropriate.

Claim form where the claimant is the landlord making an application for the termination of a tenancy under section 29(2) of the 1954 Act

3.9 Where the claimant is the landlord making an application for the termination of a tenancy under section 29(2) of the 1954 Act, in addition to the details specified in paragraph 3.4, the claim form must contain –

(1) the claimant's grounds of opposition;
(2) full details of those grounds of opposition; and
(3) the terms of a new tenancy that the claimant proposes in the event that his claim fails.

Acknowledgment of service where the claim is an unopposed claim and where the claimant is the tenant

3.10 Where the claim is an unopposed claim and the claimant is the tenant, the acknowledgment of service is to be in form N210 and must state with particulars –

(1) whether, if a new tenancy is granted, the defendant objects to any of the terms proposed by the claimant and if so –
    (a) the terms to which he objects; and
    (a) the terms that he proposes in so far as they differ from those proposed by the claimant;
(2) whether the defendant is a tenant under a lease having less than 15 years unexpired at the date of the termination of the claimant's current tenancy and, if so, the name and address of any person who, to the knowledge of the defendant, has an interest in the reversion in the property expectant (whether immediate or in not more than 15 years from that date) on the termination of the defendant's tenancy;
(3) the name and address of any person having an interest in the property who is likely to be affected by the grant of a new tenancy; and
(4) if the claimant's current tenancy is one to which section 32(2) of the 1954 Act applies, whether the defendant requires that any new tenancy shall be a tenancy of the whole of the property comprised in the claimant's current tenancy.

Acknowledgment of service where the claim is an unopposed claim and the claimant is the landlord

3.11 Where the claim is an unopposed claim and the claimant is the landlord, the acknowledgment of service is to be in form N210 and must state with particulars –

(1) the nature of the business carried on at the property;

(2) if the defendant relies on section 23(1A), 41 or 42 of the 1954 Act, the basis on which he does so;

(3) whether any, and if so what part, of the property comprised in the tenancy is occupied neither by the defendant nor by a person employed by the defendant for the purpose of the defendant's business;

(4) the name and address of –

    (a) anyone known to the defendant who has an interest in the reversion in the property (whether immediate or in not more than 15 years) on the termination of the defendant's current tenancy and who is likely to be affected by the grant of a new tenancy; or

    (b) if the defendant does not know of anyone specified by sub-paragraph (4)(a), anyone who has a freehold interest in the property; and

(5) whether, if a new tenancy is granted, the defendant objects to any of the terms proposed by the claimant and, if so –

    (a) the terms to which he objects; and

    (b) the terms that he proposes in so far as they differ from those proposed by the claimant.

Acknowledgment of service and defence where the claim is an opposed claim and where the claimant is the tenant

3.12 Where the claim is an opposed claim and the claimant is the tenant –

(1) the acknowledgment of service is to be in form N9; and

(2) in his defence the defendant must state with particulars –

    (a) the defendant's grounds of opposition;

    (b) full details of those grounds of opposition;

    (c) whether, if a new tenancy is granted, the defendant objects to any of the terms proposed by the claimant and if so –

        (i) the terms to which he objects; and

        (ii) the terms that he proposes in so far as they differ from those proposed by the claimant;

    (d) whether the defendant is a tenant under a lease having less than 15 years unexpired at the date of the termination of the claimant's current tenancy and, if so, the name and address of any person who, to the knowledge of the defendant, has an interest in the reversion in the property expectant (whether immediately or in not more than 15 years from that date) on the termination of the defendant's tenancy;

    (e) the name and address of any person having an interest in the property who is likely to be affected by the grant of a new tenancy; and

    (f) if the claimant's current tenancy is one to which section 32(2) of the 1954 Act applies, whether the defendant requires that any new tenancy shall be a tenancy of the whole of the property comprised in the claimant's current tenancy.

Acknowledgment of service and defence where the claimant is the landlord making an application for the termination of a tenancy under section 29(2) of the 1954 Act

3.13   Where the claim is an opposed claim and the claimant is the landlord –

    (1)   the acknowledgment of service is to be in form N9; and

    (2)   in his defence the defendant must state with particulars –

        (a)   whether the defendant relies on section 23(1A), 41 or 42 of the 1954 Act and, if so, the basis on which he does so;

        (b)   whether the defendant relies on section 31A of the 1954 Act and, if so, the basis on which he does so; and

        (c)   the terms of the new tenancy that the defendant would propose in the event that the claimant's claim to terminate the current tenancy fails.

Evidence in an unopposed claim

3.14   Where the claim is an unopposed claim, no evidence need be filed unless and until the court directs it to be filed.

Evidence in an opposed claim

3.15   Where the claim is an opposed claim, evidence (including expert evidence) must be filed by the parties as the court directs and the landlord shall be required to file his evidence first.

Grounds of opposition to be tried as a preliminary issue

3.16   Unless in the circumstances of the case it is unreasonable to do so, any grounds of opposition shall be tried as a preliminary issue.

Applications for interim rent under section 24A to 24D of the 1954 Act

3.17   Where proceedings have already been commenced for the grant of a new tenancy or the termination of an existing tenancy, the claim for interim rent under section 24A of the 1954 Act shall be made in those proceedings by –

    (1)   the claim form;

    (2)   the acknowledgment of service or defence; or

    (3)   an application on notice under Part 23.

3.18   Any application under section 24D(3) of the 1954 Act shall be made by an application on notice under Part 23 in the original proceedings.

3.19   Where no other proceedings have been commenced for the grant of a new tenancy or termination of an existing tenancy or where such proceedings have been disposed of, an application for interim rent under section 24A of the 1954 Act shall be made under the procedure in Part 8 and the claim form shall include details of –

    (1)   the property to which the claim relates;

    (2)   the particulars of the relevant tenancy (including date, parties and duration) and the current rent (if not the original rent);

    (3)   every notice or request given or made under sections 25 or 26 of the 1954 Act;

    (4)   if the relevant tenancy has terminated, the date and mode of termination; and

(5) if the relevant tenancy has been terminated and the landlord has granted a new tenancy of the property to the tenant –

    (a) particulars of the new tenancy (including date, parties and duration) and the rent; and

    (b) in a case where section 24C(2) of the 1954 Act applies but the claimant seeks a different rent under section 24C(3) of that Act, particulars and matters on which the claimant relies as satisfying section 24C(3).

OTHER CLAIMS UNDER PART II OF THE 1954 ACT

4.1 The mesne landlord to whose consent a claim for the determination of any question arising under paragraph 4(3) of Schedule 6 to the 1954 Act shall be made a defendant to the claim.

4.2 If any dispute as to the rateable value of any holding has been referred under section 37(5) of the 1954 Act to the Commissioners for HM Revenue and Customs for decision by a valuation officer, any document purporting to be a statement of the valuation officer of his decision is admissible as evidence of the matters contained in it.

CLAIM FOR COMPENSATION FOR IMPROVEMENTS UNDER PART I OF THE 1927 ACT

5.1 This paragraph applies to a claim under Part I of the 1927 Act.

The claim form

5.2 The claim form must include details of:

    (1) the nature of the claim or the matter to be determined;

    (2) the property to which the claim relates;

    (3) the nature of the business carried on at the property;

    (4) particulars of the lease or agreement for the tenancy including:

        (a) the names and addresses of the parties to the lease or agreement;

        (b) its duration;

        (c) the rent payable;

        (d) details of any assignment or other devolution of the lease or agreement;

    (5) the date and mode of termination of the tenancy;

    (6) if the claimant has left the property, the date on which he did so;

    (7) particulars of the improvement or proposed improvement to which the claim relates; and

    (8) if the claim is for payment of compensation, the amount claimed.

5.3 The court will fix a date for a hearing when it issues the claim form.

Defendant

5.4 The claimant's immediate landlord must be a defendant to the claim.

5.5 The defendant must immediately serve a copy of the claim form and any document served with it and of his acknowledgment of service on his immediate landlord. If the person so served is not the freeholder, he must serve a copy of these documents on his landlord and so on from landlord to landlord.

Evidence

5.6   Evidence need not be filed – with the claim form or acknowledgment of service.

Certification under section 3 of the 1927 Act

5.7   If the court intends to certify under section 3 of the 1927 Act that an improvement is a proper improvement or has been duly executed, it shall do so by way of an order.

Compensation under section 1 or 8 of the 1927 Act

5.8   A claim under section 1(1) or 8(1) of the 1927 Act must be in writing, signed by the claimant, his solicitor or agent and include details of –

    (1) the name and address of the claimant and of the landlord against whom the claim is made;
    (2) the property to which the claim relates;
    (3) the nature of the business carried on at the property;
    (4) a concise statement of the nature of the claim;
    (5) particulars of the improvement, including the date when it was completed and costs; and
    (6) the amount claimed.

5.9   A mesne landlord must immediately serve a copy of the claim on his immediate superior landlord. If the person so served is not the freeholder, he must serve a copy of the document on his landlord and so on from landlord to landlord.
(Paragraphs 5.8 and 5.9 provide the procedure for making claims under section 1(1) and 8(1) of the 1927 Act – these 'claims' do not, at this stage, relate to proceedings before the court)

TRANSFER TO LEASEHOLD VALUATION TRIBUNAL UNDER 1985 ACT

6.1   If a question is ordered to be transferred to a leasehold valuation tribunal for determination under section 31C of the 1985 Act the court will:

    (1) send notice of the transfer to all parties to the claim; and
    (2) send to the leasehold valuation tribunal:
        (a) copies certified by the district judge of all entries in the records of the court relating to the question;
        (b) the order of transfer; and
        (c) all documents filed in the claim relating to the question.
(Paragraph 6.1 no longer applies to proceedings in England but continues to apply to proceedings in Wales)

CLAIM TO ENFORCE OBLIGATION UNDER PART I OF THE 1987 ACT

7.1   A copy of the notice served under section 19(2)(a) of the 1987 Act must accompany the claim form seeking an order under section 19(1) of that Act.

CLAIM FOR ACQUISITION ORDER UNDER SECTION 28 OF THE 1987 ACT

8.1   This paragraph applies to a claim for an acquisition order under section 28 of the 1987 Act.

Claim form

8.2   The claim form must:

(1)   identify the property to which the claim relates and give details to show that section 25 of the 1987 Act applies;

(2)   give details of the claimants to show that they constitute the requisite majority of qualifying tenants;

(3)   state the names and addresses of the claimants and of the landlord of the property, or, if the landlord cannot be found or his identity ascertained, the steps taken to find him or ascertain his identity;

(4)   state the name and address of:

(a)   the person nominated by the claimants for the purposes of Part III of the 1987 Act; and

(b)   every person known to the claimants who is likely to be affected by the application, including (but not limited to), the other tenants of flats contained in the property (whether or not they could have made a claim), any mortgagee or superior landlord of the landlord, and any tenants' association (within the meaning of section 29 of the 1985 Act); and

(5)   state the grounds of the claim.

Notice under section 27

8.3   A copy of the notice served on the landlord under section 27 of the 1987 Act must accompany the claim form unless the court has dispensed with the requirement to serve a notice under section 27(3) of the 1987 Act.

Defendants

8.4   The landlord of the property (and the nominated person, if he is not a claimant) must be defendants.

Service

8.5   A copy of the claim form must be served on each of the persons named by the claimant under paragraph 8.2(4)(b) together with a notice that he may apply to be made a party.

Payment into court by nominated person

8.6   If the nominated person pays money into court in accordance with an order under section 33(1) of the 1987 Act, he must file a copy of the certificate of the surveyor selected under section 33(2)(a) of that Act.

CLAIM FOR AN ORDER VARYING LEASES UNDER THE 1987 ACT

9.1 This paragraph applies to a claim for an order under section 38 or section 40 of the 1987 Act.

Claim form

9.2 The claim form must state:

(1) the name and address of the claimant and of the other current parties to the lease or leases to which the claim relates;

(2) the date of the lease or leases, the property to which they relate, any relevant terms and the variation sought;

(3) the name and address of every person known to the claimant who is likely to be affected by the claim, including (but not limited to), the other tenants of flats contained in premises of which the relevant property forms a part, any previous parties to the lease, any mortgagee or superior landlord of the landlord, any mortgagee of the claimant and any tenants' association (within the meaning of section 29 of the 1985 Act); and

(4) the grounds of the claim.

Defendants

9.3 The other current parties to the lease must be defendants.

Service

9.4 A copy of the claim form must be served on each of the persons named under paragraph 9.2(3).

9.5 If the defendant knows of or has reason to believe that another person or persons are likely to be affected by the variation, he must serve a copy of the claim form on those persons, together with a notice that they may apply to be made a party.

Defendant's application to vary other leases

9.6 If a defendant wishes to apply to vary other leases under section 36 of the 1987 Act:

(1) he must make the application in his acknowledgment of service;

(2) paragraphs 9.2 to 9.5 apply as if the defendant were the claimant; and

(3) Part 20 does not apply.

(Paragraphs 9.1 – 9.6 no longer apply to proceedings in England but continue to apply to proceedings in Wales)

SERVICE OF DOCUMENTS IN CLAIMS UNDER THE 1987 ACT

10.1 All documents must be served by the parties.

10.2 If a notice is to be served in or before a claim under the 1987 Act, it must be served –

(1) in accordance with section 54, and

(2) in the case of service on a landlord, at the address given under section 48(1).

SECTION II – MISCELLANEOUS PROVISIONS ABOUT LAND

ACCESS TO NEIGHBOURING LAND ACT 1992

11.1   The claimant must use the Part 8 procedure.

11.2   The claim form must set out:

(1) details of the dominant and servient land involved and whether the dominant land includes or consists of residential property;
(2) the work required;
(3) why entry to the servient land is required with plans (if applicable);
(4) the names and addresses of the persons who will carry out the work;
(5) the proposed date when the work will be carried out; and
(6) what (if any) provision has been made by way of insurance in the event of possible injury to persons or damage to property arising out of the proposed work.

11.3   The owner and occupier of the servient land must be defendants to the claim.

CHANCEL REPAIRS ACT 1932

12.1   The claimant in a claim to recover the sum required to put a chancel in proper repair must use the Part 8 procedure.

12.2   A notice to repair under section 2 of the Chancel Repairs Act 1932 must –

(1) state –
   (a) the responsible authority by whom the notice is given;
   (b) the chancel alleged to be in need of repair;
   (c) the repairs alleged to be necessary; and
   (d) the grounds on which the person to whom the notice is addressed is alleged to be liable to repair the chancel; and
(2) call upon the person to whom the notice is addressed to put the chancel in proper repair.

12.3   The notice must be served in accordance with Part 6.

LEASEHOLD REFORM ACT 1967

13.1   In this paragraph a section or schedule referred to by number means the section or schedule so numbered in the Leasehold Reform Act 1967.

13.2   If a tenant of a house and premises wishes to pay money into court under sections 11(4), 13(1) or 13(3) –

(1) he must file in the office of the appropriate court an application notice containing or accompanied by evidence stating –
   (a) the reasons for the payment into court,
   (b) the house and premises to which the payment relates;
   (c) the name and address of the landlord; and
   (d) so far as they are known to the tenant, the name and address of every person who is or may be interested in or entitled to the money;
(2) on the filing of the witness statement the tenant must pay the money into court and the court will send notice of the payment to the landlord and every person whose name and address are given in the witness statement;

(3) any subsequent payment into court by the landlord under section 11(4) must be made to the credit of the same account as the payment into court by the tenant and sub-paragraphs (1) and (2) will apply to the landlord as if he were a tenant; and

(4) the appropriate court for the purposes of paragraph (a) is the county court for the district in which the property is situated or, if the payment into court is made by reason of a notice under section 13(3), any other county court as specified in the notice.

13.3 If an order is made transferring an application to a leasehold valuation tribunal under section 21(3), the court will:

(1) send notice of the transfer to all parties to the application; and

(2) send to the tribunal copies of the order of transfer and all documents filed in the proceedings.

(Paragraph 13.3 no longer applies to proceedings in England but continues to apply to proceedings in Wales)

13.4 A claim under section 17 or 18 for an order for possession of a house and premises must be made in accordance with Part 55.

13.5 In a claim under section 17 or 18, the defendant must:

(1) immediately after being served with the claim form, serve on every person in occupation of the property or part of it under an immediate or derivative sub-tenancy, a notice informing him of the claim and of his right under paragraph 3(4) of Schedule 2 take part in the hearing of the claim with the permission of the court; and

(2) within 14 days after being served with the claim form, file a defence stating the ground, if any, on which he intends to oppose the claim and giving particulars of every such sub-tenancy.

13.6 An application made to the High Court under section 19 or 27 shall be assigned to the Chancery Division.

LEASEHOLD REFORM, HOUSING AND URBAN DEVELOPMENT ACT 1993

14.1 In this paragraph:

(1) 'the 1993 Act' means the Leasehold Reform, Housing and Urban Development Act 1993; and

(2) a section or schedule referred to by number means the section or schedule so numbered in the 1993 Act.

14.2 If a claim is made under section 23(1) by a person other than the reversioner:

(1) on the issue of the claim form in accordance with Part 8, the claimant must send a copy to the reversioner; and

(2) the claimant must promptly inform the reversioner either:

(a) of the court's decision; or

(b) that the claim has been withdrawn.

14.3 Where an application is made under section 26(1) or (2) or section 50(1) or (2):

(1) it must be made by the issue of a claim form in accordance with the Part 8 procedure which need not be served on any other party; and

(2) the court may grant or refuse the application or give directions for its future conduct, including the addition as defendants of such persons as appear to have an interest in it.

14.4 An application under section 26(3) must be made by the issue of a claim form in accordance with the Part 8 procedure and:

(1) the claimants must serve the claim form on any person who they know or have reason to believe is a relevant landlord, giving particulars of the claim and the hearing date and informing that person of his right to be joined as a party to the claim;

(2) the landlord whom it is sought to appoint as the reversioner must be a defendant, and must file an acknowledgment of service;

(3) a person on whom notice is served under paragraph (1) must be joined as a defendant to the claim if he gives notice in writing to the court of his wish to be added as a party, and the court will notify all other parties of the addition.

14.5 If a person wishes to pay money into court under section 27(3), section 51(3) or paragraph 4 of Schedule 8 –

(1) he must file in the office of the appropriate court an application notice containing or accompanied by evidence stating –

(a) the reasons for the payment into court,

(b) the interest or interests in the property to which the payment relates or where the payment into court is made under section 51(3), the flat to which it relates;

(c) details of any vesting order;

(d) the name and address of the landlord; and

(e) so far as they are known to the tenant, the name and address of every person who is or may be interested in or entitled to the money;

(2) on the filing of the witness statement the money must be paid into court and the court will send notice of the payment to the landlord and every person whose name and address are given in the witness statement;

(3) any subsequent payment into court by the landlord must be made to the credit of the same account as the earlier payment into court;

(4) the appropriate court for the purposes of paragraph (1) is –

(a) where a vesting order has been made, the county court that made the order; or

(b) where no such order has been made, the county court in whose district the property is situated.

14.6 If an order is made transferring an application to a leasehold valuation tribunal under section 91(4), the court will:

(1) send notice of the transfer to all parties to the application; and

(2) send to the tribunal copies of the order of transfer and all documents filed in the proceedings.

(Paragraph 14.6 no longer applies to proceedings in England but continues to apply to proceedings in Wales)

14.7 If a relevant landlord acts independently under Schedule 1, paragraph 7, he is entitled to require any party to claims under the 1993 Act (as described in paragraph 7(1)(b) of Schedule 1) to supply him, on payment of the reasonable costs of copying, with copies of all documents which that party has served on the other parties to the claim.

TRANSFER TO LEASEHOLD VALUATION TRIBUNAL UNDER THE COMMONHOLD AND LEASEHOLD REFORM ACT 2002

15.1 If a question is ordered to be transferred to a leasehold valuation tribunal for determination under paragraph 3 of Schedule 12 to the Commonhold and Leasehold Reform Act 2002 the court will –

(1) send notice of the transfer to all parties to the claim; and
(2) send to the leasehold valuation tribunal –
    (a) the order of transfer; and
    (b) all documents filed in the claim relating to the question.

(Paragraph 15.1 applies to proceedings in England but does not apply to proceedings in Wales)

Forms and notices prescribed by the Regulatory Reform (Business Tenancies) (England and Wales) Order 2003, Schedules 1–4

SCHEDULE 1

Article 22(2) Form of notice that sections 24 to 28 of the Landlord and Tenant Act 1954 are not to apply to a business tenancy

To:

_____

_____

[Name and address of tenant]

From:

_____

_____

[Name and address of landlord]

IMPORTANT NOTICE

You are being offered a lease without security of tenure. Do not commit yourself to the lease unless you have read this message carefully and have discussed it with a professional adviser.

Business tenants normally have security of tenure – the right to stay in their business premises when the lease ends.

If you commit yourself to the lease you will be giving up these important legal rights.

- You will have **no right** to stay in the premises when the lease ends.
- Unless the landlord chooses to offer you another lease, you will need to leave the premises.
- You will be unable to claim compensation for the loss of your business premises, unless the lease specifically gives you this right.
- If the landlord offers you another lease, you will have no right to ask the court to fix the rent.

It is therefore important to get professional advice – from a qualified surveyor, lawyer or accountant – before agreeing to give up these rights.

If you want to ensure that you can stay in the same business premises when the lease ends, you should consult your adviser about another form of lease that does not exclude the protection of the Landlord and Tenant Act 1954.

If you receive this notice at least 14 days before committing yourself to the lease, you will need to sign a simple declaration that you have received this notice and have accepted its consequences, before signing the lease.

But if you do not receive at least 14 days notice, you will need to sign a 'statutory' declaration. To do so, you will need to visit an independent solicitor (or someone else empowered to administer oaths).

Unless there is a special reason for committing yourself to the lease sooner, you may want to ask the landlord to let you have at least 14 days to consider whether you wish to give up your statutory rights. If you then decided to go ahead with the agreement to exclude the protection of the Landlord and Tenant Act 1954, you would only need to make a simple declaration, and so you would not need to make a separate visit to an independent solicitor.

SCHEDULE 2

**Article 22(2) Requirements for a valid agreement that sections 24 to 28 of the Landlord
and Tenant Act 1954 are not to apply to a business tenancy**

1. The following are the requirements referred to in section 38A(3)(b) of the Act.
2. Subject to paragraph 4, the notice referred to in section 38A(3)(a) of the Act
must be served on the tenant not less than 14 days before the tenant enters into
the tenancy to which it applies, or (if earlier) becomes contractually bound to
do so.
3. If the requirement in paragraph 2 is met, the tenant, or a person duly authorised by him to do so, must, before the tenant enters into the tenancy to which
the notice applies, or (if earlier) becomes contractually bound to do so, make a
declaration in the form, or substantially in the form, set out in paragraph 7.
4. If the requirement in paragraph 2 is not met, the notice referred to in section
38A(3)(a) of the Act must be served on the tenant before the tenant enters into
the tenancy to which it applies, or (if earlier) becomes contractually bound to
do so, and the tenant, or a person duly authorised by him to do so, must before
that time make a statutory declaration in the form, or substantially in the form,
set out in paragraph 8.
5. A reference to the notice and, where paragraph 3 applies, the declaration or,
where paragraph 4 applies, the statutory declaration must be contained in or
endorsed on the instrument creating the tenancy.
6. The agreement under section 38A(1) of the Act, or a reference to the agreement, must be contained in or endorsed upon the instrument creating the
tenancy.
7. The form of declaration referred to in paragraph 3 is as follows: –
I

_____

(*name of declarant*) of

_____

(*address*) declare that –
1. I/

_____

(*name of tenant*) propose(s) to enter into a tenancy of premises at

_____

(*address of premises*) for a term commencing on

_____

2. I/The tenant propose(s) to enter into an agreement with

_____

(*name of landlord*) that the provisions of sections 24 to 28 of the Landlord
and Tenant Act 1954 (security of tenure) shall be excluded in relation to
the tenancy.
3. The landlord has, not less than 14 days before I/the tenant enter(s) into the
tenancy, or (if earlier) become(s) contractually bound to do so served on
me/the tenant a notice in the form, or substantially in the form, set out in
Schedule 1 to the Regulatory Reform (Business Tenancies) (England and
Wales) Order 2003. The form of notice set out in that Schedule is reproduced
below.

285

4. I have/The tenant has read the notice referred to in paragraph 3 above and accept(s) the consequences of entering into the agreement referred to in paragraph 2 above.

5. (*as appropriate*) I am duly authorised by the tenant to make this declaration.

DECLARED this

_____

day of

_____

To:

_____

_____

_____

[Name and address of tenant]

From:

_____

_____

_____

[Name and address of landlord]

IMPORTANT NOTICE

You are being offered a lease without security of tenure. Do not commit yourself to the lease unless you have read this message carefully and have discussed it with a professional adviser.

Business tenants normally have security of tenure – the right to stay in their business premises when the lease ends.

If you commit yourself to the lease you will be giving up these important legal rights.

- You will have **no right** to stay in the premises when the lease ends.
- Unless the landlord chooses to offer you another lease, you will need to leave the premises.
- You will be unable to claim compensation for the loss of your business premises, unless the lease specifically gives you this right.
- If the landlord offers you another lease, you will have no right to ask the court to fix the rent.

It is therefore important to get professional advice – from a qualified surveyor, lawyer or accountant – before agreeing to give up these rights.

If you want to ensure that you can stay in the same business premises when the lease ends, you should consult your adviser about another form of lease that does not exclude the protection of the Landlord and Tenant Act 1954.

If you receive this notice at least 14 days before committing yourself to the lease, you will need to sign a simple declaration that you have received this notice and have accepted its consequences, before signing the lease.

But if you do not receive at least 14 days notice, you will need to sign a 'statutory' declaration. To do so, you will need to visit an independent solicitor (or someone else empowered to administer oaths).

Unless there is a special reason for committing yourself to the lease sooner, you may want to ask the landlord to let you have at least 14 days to consider whether you wish to give up your statutory rights. If you then decided to go ahead with the agreement to exclude the protection of the Landlord and Tenant Act 1954, you would only need to make a simple declaration, and so you would not need to make a separate visit to an independent solicitor.

8.   The form of statutory declaration referred to in paragraph 4 is as follows: –

I

_____

(*name of declarant*) of

_____

(*address*) do solemnly and sincerely declare that –

1.   I

_____

(*name of tenant*) propose(s) to enter into a tenancy of premises at

_____

(*address of premises*) for a term commencing on

2.   I/The tenant propose(s) to enter into an agreement with (name of landlord) that the provisions of sections 24 to 28 of the Landlord and Tenant Act 1954 (security of tenure) shall be excluded in relation to the tenancy.

3.   The landlord has served on me/the tenant a notice in the form, or substantially in the form, set out in Schedule 1 to the Regulatory Reform (Business Tenancies) (England and Wales) Order 2003. The form of notice set out in that Schedule is reproduced below.

4.   I have/The tenant has read the notice referred to in paragraph 3 above and accept(s) the consequences of entering into the agreement referred to in paragraph 2 above.

5.   (*as appropriate*) I am duly authorised by the tenant to make this declaration.

To:

_____

_____

_____

[*Name and address of tenant*]

From:

_____

_____

_____

[*Name and address of landlord*]

IMPORTANT NOTICE

You are being offered a lease without security of tenure. Do not commit yourself to the lease unless you have read this message carefully and have discussed it with a professional adviser.

Business tenants normally have security of tenure – the right to stay in their business premises when the lease ends.

If you commit yourself to the lease you will be giving up these important legal rights.

- You will have **no right** to stay in the premises when the lease ends.
- Unless the landlord chooses to offer you another lease, you will need to leave the premises.
- You will be unable to claim compensation for the loss of your business premises, unless the lease specifically gives you this right.
- If the landlord offers you another lease, you will have no right to ask the court to fix the rent.

It is therefore important to get professional advice – from a qualified surveyor, lawyer or accountant – before agreeing to give up these rights.

If you want to ensure that you can stay in the same business premises when the lease ends, you should consult your adviser about another form of lease that does not exclude the protection of the Landlord and Tenant Act 1954.

If you receive this notice at least 14 days before committing yourself to the lease, you will need to sign a simple declaration that you have received this notice and have accepted its consequences, before signing the lease.

But if you do not receive at least 14 days notice, you will need to sign a 'statutory' declaration. To do so, you will need to visit an independent solicitor (or someone else empowered to administer oaths).

Unless there is a special reason for committing yourself to the lease sooner, you may want to ask the landlord to let you have at least 14 days to consider whether you wish to give up your statutory rights. If you then decided to go ahead with the agreement to exclude the protection of the Landlord and Tenant Act 1954, you would only need to make a simple declaration, and so you would not need to make a separate visit to an independent solicitor.

AND I make this solemn declaration conscientiously believing the same to be true and by virtue of the Statutory Declaration Act 1835.

DECLARED at

_____

this

_____

day of

_____

Before me

(signature of person before whom declaration is made)
A commissioner for oaths *or* A solicitor empowered to administer oaths *or* (*as appropriate*)

SCHEDULE 3

**Article 22(2) Form of notice that an agreement to surrender a business tenancy is to be
made**

To:

_____

_____

_____

[Name and address of tenant]

From:

_____

_____

_____

[Name and address of landlord]

IMPORTANT NOTICE FOR TENANT

*Do not commit yourself to any agreement to surrender your lease unless you have
read this message carefully and discussed it with a professional adviser.*

Normally, you have the right to renew your lease when it expires. By committing
yourself to an agreement to surrender, *you will be giving up this important statutory
right.*

- You will **not** be able to continue occupying the premises beyond the date
  provided for under the agreement for surrender, **unless** the landlord chooses to
  offer you a further term (in which case you would lose the right to ask the court
  to determine the new rent). You will need to leave the premises.
- You will be unable to claim compensation for the loss of your premises, unless
  the lease or agreement for surrender gives you this right.

A qualified surveyor, lawyer or accountant would be able to offer you professional
advice on your options.

**You do not have to commit yourself to the agreement to surrender your lease unless
you want to.**

If you receive this notice at least 14 days before committing yourself to the agreement to surrender, you will need to sign a simple declaration that you have received
this notice and have accepted its consequences, before signing the agreement to
surrender.

*But if you do not receive at least 14 days notice, you will need to sign a 'statutory'
declaration. To do so, you will need to visit an independent solicitor (or someone else
empowered to administer oaths).*

Unless there is a special reason for committing yourself to the agreement to
surrender sooner, you may want to ask the landlord to let you have at least 14
days to consider whether you wish to give up your statutory rights. If you then
decided to go ahead with the agreement to end your lease, you would only need
to make a simple declaration, and so you would not need to make a separate visit
to an independent solicitor.

SCHEDULE 4

Article 22(2) Requirements for a valid agreement to surrender a business tenancy

1. The following are the requirements referred to in section 38A(4)(b) of the Act.
2. Subject to paragraph 4, the notice referred to in section 38A(4)(a) of the Act must be served on the tenant not less than 14 days before the tenant enters into the agreement under section 38A(2) of the Act, or (if earlier) becomes contractually bound to do so.
3. If the requirement in paragraph 2 is met, the tenant or a person duly authorised by him to do so, must, before the tenant enters into the agreement under section 38A(2) of the Act, or (if earlier) becomes contractually bound to do so, make a declaration in the form, or substantially in the form, set out in paragraph 6.
4. If the requirement in paragraph 2 is not met, the notice referred to in section 38A(4)(a) of the Act must be served on the tenant before the tenant enters into the agreement under section 38A(2) of the Act, or (if earlier) becomes contractually bound to do so, and the tenant, or a person duly authorised by him to do so, must before that time make a statutory declaration in the form, or substantially in the form, set out in paragraph 7.
5. A reference to the notice and, where paragraph 3 applies, the declaration or, where paragraph 4 applies, the statutory declaration must be contained in or endorsed on the instrument creating the agreement under section 38A(2).
6. The form of declaration referred to in paragraph 3 is as follows: –

I

_____

(*name of declarant*) of

_____

(*address*) declare that –

1. I have/

_____

(*name of tenant*) has a tenancy of premises at

_____

(*address of premises*) for a term commencing on

_____

2. I/The tenant propose(s) to enter into an agreement with

_____

(*name of landlord*) to surrender the tenancy on a date or in circumstances specified in the agreement.

3. The landlord has not less than 14 days before I/the tenant enter(s) into the agreement referred to in paragraph 2 above, or (if earlier) become(s) contractually bound to do so, served on me/the tenant a notice in the form, or substantially in the form, set out in Schedule 3 to Regulatory Reform (Business Tenancies) (England and Wales) Order 2003. The form of notice set out in that Schedule is reproduced below.

4. I have/The tenant has read the notice referred to in paragraph 3 above and accept(s) the consequences of entering into the agreement referred to in paragraph 2 above.

5. (*as appropriate*) I am duly authorised by the tenant to make this declaration.

DECLARED this

_____

day of

_____

To:

_____

_____

[*Name and address of tenant*]

From:

_____

_____

[*Name and address of landlord*]

IMPORTANT NOTICE FOR TENANT

Do not commit yourself to any agreement to surrender your lease unless you have read this message carefully and discussed it with a professional adviser.

Normally, you have the right to renew your lease when it expires. By committing yourself to an agreement to surrender, *you will be giving up this important statutory right.*

- You will **not** be able to continue occupying the premises beyond the date provided for under the agreement for surrender, **unless** the landlord chooses to offer you a further term (in which case you would lose the right to ask the court to determine the new rent). You will need to leave the premises.
- You will be unable to claim compensation for the loss of your premises, unless the lease or agreement for surrender gives you this right.

A qualified surveyor, lawyer or accountant would be able to offer you professional advice on your options.

You do not have to commit yourself to the agreement to surrender your lease unless you want to.

If you receive this notice at least 14 days before committing yourself to the agreement to surrender, you will need to sign a simple declaration that you have received this notice and have accepted its consequences, before signing the agreement to surrender.

But if you do not receive at least 14 days notice, you will need to sign a 'statutory' declaration. To do so, you will need to visit an independent solicitor (or someone else empowered to administer oaths).

Unless there is a special reason for committing yourself to the agreement to surrender sooner, you may want to ask the landlord to let you have at least 14 days to consider whether you wish to give up your statutory rights. If you then decided to go ahead with the agreement to end your lease, you would only need to make a simple declaration, and so you would not need to make a separate visit to an independent solicitor.

7. The form of statutory declaration referred to in paragraph 4 is as follows: –

I

_____

(*name of declarant*) of

_____

(*address*) do solemnly and sincerely declare that –

1. I have/

_____

(*name of tenant*) has a tenancy of premises at

_____

(*address of premises*) for a term commencing on

2. I/The tenant propose(s) to enter into an agreement with

_____

(*name of landlord*) to surrender the tenancy on a date or in circumstances specified in the agreement.

3. The landlord has served on me/the tenant a notice in the form, or substantially in the form, set out in Schedule 3 to the Regulatory Reform (Business Tenancies) (England and Wales) Order 2003. The form of notice set out in that Schedule is reproduced below.

4. I have/The tenant has read the notice referred to in paragraph 3 above and accept(s) the consequences of entering into the agreement referred to in paragraph 2 above.

5. (*as appropriate*) I am duly authorised by the tenant to make this declaration.

To:

_____

_____

_____

                                    [*Name and address of tenant*]

From:

_____

_____

_____

                                    [*Name and address of landlord*]

IMPORTANT NOTICE FOR TENANT

Do not commit yourself to any agreement to surrender your lease unless you have read this message carefully and discussed it with a professional adviser.

Normally, you have the right to renew your lease when it expires. By committing yourself to an agreement to surrender, *you will be giving up this important statutory right.*

- You will **not** be able to continue occupying the premises beyond the date provided for under the agreement for surrender, **unless** the landlord chooses to offer you a further term (in which case you would lose the right to ask the court to determine the new rent). You will need to leave the premises.
- You will be unable to claim compensation for the loss of your premises, unless the lease or agreement for surrender gives you this right.

A qualified surveyor, lawyer or accountant would be able to offer you professional advice on your options.

You do not have to commit yourself to the agreement to surrender your lease unless you want to.

If you receive this notice at least 14 days before committing yourself to agreement to surrender, you will need to sign a simple declaration that you have received this notice and have accepted its consequences, before signing the agreement to surrender.

But if you do not receive at least 14 days notice, you will need to sign a 'statutory' declaration. To do so, you will need to visit an independent solicitor (or someone else empowered to administer oaths).

Unless there is a special reason for committing yourself to the agreement to surrender sooner, you may want to ask the landlord to let you have at least 14 days to consider whether you wish to give up your statutory rights. If you then decided to go ahead with the agreement to end your lease, you would only need to make a simple declaration, and so you would not need to make a separate visit to an independent solicitor.

AND I make this solemn declaration conscientiously believing the same to be true and by virtue of the Statutory Declaration Act 1835.

DECLARED at

_____

this

_____

day of

_____

Before me

(*signature of person before whom declaration is made*)
A commissioner for oaths *or* A solicitor empowered to administer oaths *or* (*as appropriate*)

293

APPENDIX E

Forms and notices prescribed by the Landlord and Tenant Act 1954, Part 2 (Notices) Regulations 2004, Schedule 2

FORM 1   LANDLORD'S NOTICE ENDING A BUSINESS TENANCY WITH PROPOSALS FOR A NEW ONE (SECTION 25 OF THE LANDLORD AND TENANT ACT 1954)

> IMPORTANT NOTE FOR THE LANDLORD: If you are willing to grant a new tenancy, complete this form and send it to the tenant. If you wish to oppose the grant of a new tenancy, use form 2 in Schedule 2 to the Landlord and Tenant Act 1954, Part 2 (Notices) Regulations 2004 or, where the tenant may be entitled to acquire the freehold or an extended lease, form 7 in that Schedule, instead of this form.

To: (*insert name and address of tenant*)

From: (*insert name and address of landlord*)

1.   This notice applies to the following property: (*insert address or description of property*).
2.   I am giving you notice under section 25 of the Landlord and Tenant Act 1954 to end your tenancy on (*insert date*).
3.   I am not opposed to granting you a new tenancy. You will find my proposals for the new tenancy, which we can discuss, in the Schedule to this notice.
4.   If we cannot agree on all the terms of a new tenancy, either you or I may ask the court to order the grant of a new tenancy and settle the terms on which we cannot agree.
5.   If you wish to ask the court for a new tenancy you must do so by the date in paragraph 2, unless we agree in writing to a later date and do so before the date in paragraph 2.
6.   Please send all correspondence about this notice to:

Name:

Address:

Signed: Date:

*[Landlord] *[On behalf of the landlord] *[Mortgagee] *[On behalf of the mortgagee]

*(*delete if inapplicable*)

SCHEDULE

LANDLORD'S PROPOSALS FOR A NEW TENANCY

(attach or insert proposed terms of the new tenancy)

IMPORTANT NOTE FOR THE TENANT

This Notice is intended to bring your tenancy to an end. If you want to continue to occupy your property after the date specified in paragraph 2 you must act quickly. If you are in any doubt about the action that you should take, get advice immediately from a solicitor or a surveyor.

The landlord is prepared to offer you a new tenancy and has set out proposed terms in the Schedule to this notice. You are not bound to accept these terms. They are merely suggestions as a basis for negotiation. In the event of disagreement, ultimately the court would settle the terms of the new tenancy.

It would be wise to seek professional advice before agreeing to accept the landlord's terms or putting forward your own proposals.

NOTES

The sections mentioned below are sections of the Landlord and Tenant Act 1954, as amended, (most recently by the Regulatory Reform (Business Tenancies) (England and Wales) Order 2003).

Ending of tenancy and grant of new tenancy

This notice is intended to bring your tenancy to an end on the date given in paragraph 2. Section 25 contains rules about the date that the landlord can put in that paragraph.

However, your landlord is prepared to offer you a new tenancy and has set out proposals for it in the Schedule to this notice (section 25(8)). You are not obliged to accept these proposals and may put forward your own.

If you and your landlord are unable to agree terms either one of you may apply to the court. You may not apply to the court if your landlord has already done so (section 24(2A)). If you wish to apply to the court you must do so by the date given in paragraph 2 of this notice, unless you and your landlord have agreed in writing to extend the deadline (sections 29A and 29B).

The court will settle the rent and other terms of the new tenancy or those on which you and your landlord cannot agree (sections 34 and 35). If you apply to the court your tenancy will continue after the date shown in paragraph 2 of this notice while your application is being considered (section 24).

If you are in any doubt about what action you should take, get advice immediately from a solicitor or a surveyor.

Negotiating a new tenancy

Most tenancies are renewed by negotiation. You and your landlord may agree in writing to extend the deadline for making an application to the court while negotiations continue. Either you or your landlord can ask the court to fix the rent that you will have to pay while the tenancy continues (sections 24A to 24D).

You may only stay in the property after the date in paragraph 2 (or if we have agreed in writing to a later date, that date), if by then you or the landlord has asked the court to order the grant of a new tenancy.

If you do try to agree a new tenancy with your landlord remember:

- that your present tenancy will not continue after the date in paragraph 2 of this notice without the agreement in writing mentioned above, unless you have applied to the court or your landlord has done so, and
- that you will lose your right to apply to the court once the deadline in paragraph 2 of this notice has passed, unless there is a written agreement extending the deadline.

Validity of this notice

The landlord who has given you this notice may not be the landlord to whom you pay your rent (sections 44 and 67). This does not necessarily mean that the notice is invalid.

If you have any doubts about whether this notice is valid, get advice immediately from a solicitor or a surveyor.

Further information

An explanation of the main points to consider when renewing or ending a business tenancy, 'Renewing and Ending Business Leases: a Guide for Tenants and Landlords', can be found at **www.odpm.gov.uk**. Printed copies of the explanation, but not of this form, are available from 1st June 2004 from Free Literature, PO Box 236, Wetherby, West Yorkshire, LS23 7NB (0870 1226 236).

FORM 2   LANDLORD'S NOTICE ENDING A BUSINESS TENANCY AND REASONS FOR REFUSING A NEW ONE (SECTION 25 OF THE LANDLORD AND TENANT ACT 1954)

IMPORTANT NOTE FOR THE LANDLORD: If you wish to oppose the grant of a new tenancy on any of the grounds in section 30(1) of the Landlord and Tenant Act 1954, complete this form and send it to the tenant. If the tenant may be entitled to acquire the freehold or an extended lease, use form 7 in Schedule 2 to the Landlord and Tenant Act 1954, Part 2 (Notices) Regulations 2004 instead of this form.

To: (*insert name and address of tenant*)

From: (*insert name and address of landlord*)

1. This notice relates to the following property: (*insert address or description of property*)
2. I am giving you notice under section 25 of the Landlord and Tenant Act 1954 to end your tenancy on (*insert date*).
3. I am opposed to the grant of a new tenancy.
4. You may ask the court to order the grant of a new tenancy. If you do, I will oppose your application on the ground(s) mentioned in paragraph(s)* of section 30(1) of that Act. I draw your attention to the Table in the Notes below, which sets out all the grounds of opposition.
   *(*insert letter(s) of the paragraph(s) relied on*)
5. If you wish to ask the court for a new tenancy you must do so before the date in paragraph 2 unless, before that date, we agree in writing to a later date.
6. I can ask the court to order the ending of your tenancy without granting you a new tenancy. I may have to pay you compensation if I have relied only on one or more of the grounds mentioned in paragraphs (e), (f) and (g) of section 30(1). If I ask the court to end your tenancy, you can challenge my application.
7. Please send all correspondence about this notice to:

Name:

Address:

Signed: Date:

*[Landlord] *[On behalf of the landlord] *[Mortgagee] *[On behalf of the mortgagee]

(*delete if inapplicable*)

IMPORTANT NOTE FOR THE TENANT

This notice is intended to bring your tenancy to an end on the date specified in paragraph 2.

Your landlord is not prepared to offer you a new tenancy. You will not get a new tenancy unless you successfully challenge in court the grounds on which your landlord opposes the grant of a new tenancy.

If you want to continue to occupy your property you must act quickly. The notes below should help you to decide what action you now need to take. If you want to challenge your landlord's refusal to renew your tenancy, get advice immediately from a solicitor or a surveyor.

NOTES

The sections mentioned below are sections of the Landlord and Tenant Act 1954, as amended, (most recently by the Regulatory Reform (Business Tenancies) (England and Wales) Order 2003).

Ending of your tenancy

This notice is intended to bring your tenancy to an end on the date given in paragraph 2. Section 25 contains rules about the date that the landlord can put in that paragraph.

Your landlord is not prepared to offer you a new tenancy. If you want a new tenancy you will need to apply to the court for a new tenancy and successfully challenge the landlord's grounds for opposition (see the section below headed '*Landlord's opposition to new tenancy*'). If you wish to apply to the court you must do so before the date given in paragraph 2 of this notice, unless you and your landlord have agreed in writing, before that date, to extend the deadline (sections 29A and 29B).

If you apply to the court your tenancy will continue after the date given in paragraph 2 of this notice while your application is being considered (section 24). You may not apply to the court if your landlord has already done so (section 24(2A) and (2B)).

You may only stay in the property after the date given in paragraph 2 (or such later date as you and the landlord may have agreed in writing) if before that date you have asked the court to order the grant of a new tenancy or the landlord has asked the court to order the ending of your tenancy without granting you a new one.

If you are in any doubt about what action you should take, get advice immediately from a solicitor or a surveyor.

Landlord's opposition to new tenancy

If you apply to the court for a new tenancy, the landlord can only oppose your application on one or more of the grounds set out in section 30(1). If you match the letter(s) specified in paragraph 4 of this notice with those in the first column in the Table below, you can see from the second column the ground(s) on which the landlord relies.

Paragraph of section 30(1)	Grounds
(a)	Where under the current tenancy the tenant has any obligations as respects the repair and maintenance of the holding, that the tenant ought not to be granted a new tenancy in view of the state of repair of the holding, being a state resulting from the tenant's failure to comply with the said obligations.
(b)	That the tenant ought not to be granted a new tenancy in view of his persistent delay in paying rent which has become due.
(c)	That the tenant ought not to be granted a new tenancy in view of other substantial breaches by him of his obligations under the current tenancy, or for any other reason connected with the tenant's use or management of the holding.
(d)	That the landlord has offered and is willing to provide or secure the provision of alternative accommodation for the tenant, that the terms on which the alternative accommodation is available are reasonable having regard to the terms of the current tenancy and to all other relevant circumstances, and that the accommodation and the time at which it will be available are suitable for the tenant's requirements (including the requirement to preserve goodwill) having regard to the nature and class of his business and to the situation and extent of, and facilities afforded by, the holding.
(e)	Where the current tenancy was created by the sub-letting of part only of the property comprised in a superior tenancy and the landlord is the owner of an interest in reversion expectant on the termination of that superior tenancy, that the aggregate of the rents reasonably obtainable on separate lettings of the holding and the remainder of that property would be substantially less than the rent reasonably obtainable on a letting of that property as a whole, that on the termination of the current tenancy the landlord requires possession of the holding for the purposes of letting or otherwise disposing of the said property as a whole, and that in view thereof the tenant ought not to be granted a new tenancy.
(f)	That on the termination of the current tenancy the landlord intends to demolish or reconstruct the premises comprised in the holding or a substantial part of those premises or to carry out substantial work of construction on the holding or part thereof and that he could not reasonably do so without obtaining possession of the holding.
(g)	On the termination of the current tenancy the landlord intends to occupy the holding for the purposes, or partly for the purposes, of a business to be carried on by him therein, or as his residence.

In this Table 'the holding' means the property that is the subject of the tenancy.

In ground (e), 'the landlord is the owner of an interest in reversion expectant on the termination of that superior tenancy' means that the landlord has an interest in the property that will entitle him or her, when your immediate landlord's tenancy comes to an end, to exercise certain rights and obligations in relation to the property that are currently exercisable by your immediate landlord.

If the landlord relies on ground (f), the court can sometimes still grant a new tenancy if certain conditions set out in section 31A are met.

If the landlord relies on ground (g), please note that 'the landlord' may have an extended meaning. Where a landlord has a controlling interest in a company then either the landlord or the company can rely on ground (g). Where the landlord is a company and a person has a controlling interest in that company then either of them can rely on ground (g) (section 30(1A) and (1B)). A person has a 'controlling interest' in a company if, had he been a company, the other company would have been its subsidiary (section 46(2)).

The landlord must normally have been the landlord for at least five years before he or she can rely on ground (g).

Compensation

If you cannot get a new tenancy solely because one or more of grounds (e), (f) and (g) applies, you may be entitled to compensation under section 37. If your landlord has opposed your application on any of the other grounds as well as (e), (f) or (g) you can only get compensation if the court's refusal to grant a new tenancy is based solely on one or more of grounds (e), (f) and (g). In other words, you cannot get compensation under section 37 if the court has refused your tenancy on *other* grounds, even if one or more of grounds (e), (f) and (g) also applies.

If your landlord is an authority possessing compulsory purchase powers (such as a local authority) you may be entitled to a disturbance payment under Part 3 of the Land Compensation Act 1973.

Validity of this notice

The landlord who has given you this notice may not be the landlord to whom you pay your rent (sections 44 and 67). This does not necessarily mean that the notice is invalid.

If you have any doubts about whether this notice is valid, get advice immediately from a solicitor or a surveyor.

Further information

An explanation of the main points to consider when renewing or ending a business tenancy, 'Renewing and Ending Business Leases: a Guide for Tenants and Landlords', can be found at **www.odpm.gov.uk**. Printed copies of the explanation, but not of this form, are available from 1st June 2004 from Free Literature, PO Box 236, Wetherby, West Yorkshire, LS23 7NB (0870 1226 236).

**FORM 3   TENANT'S REQUEST FOR A NEW BUSINESS TENANCY
(SECTION 26 OF THE LANDLORD AND TENANT ACT 1954)**

To (*insert name and address of landlord*):

From (*insert name and address of tenant*):

1.   This notice relates to the following property: (*insert address or description of property*).
2.   I am giving you notice under section 26 of the Landlord and Tenant Act 1954 that I request a new tenancy beginning on (*insert date*).
3.   You will find my proposals for the new tenancy, which we can discuss, in the Schedule to this notice.
4.   If we cannot agree on all the terms of a new tenancy, either you or I may ask the court to order the grant of a new tenancy and settle the terms on which we cannot agree.
5.   If you wish to ask the court to order the grant of a new tenancy you must do so by the date in paragraph 2, unless we agree in writing to a later date and do so before the date in paragraph 2.
6.   You may oppose my request for a new tenancy only on one or more of the grounds set out in section 30(1) of the Landlord and Tenant Act 1954. You must tell me what your grounds are within two months of receiving this notice. If you miss this deadline you will not be able to oppose renewal of my tenancy and you will have to grant me a new tenancy.
7.   Please send all correspondence about this notice to:

Name:

Address:

Signed: Date:

*[Tenant] *[On behalf of the tenant] (*delete whichever is inapplicable*)

SCHEDULE

TENANT'S PROPOSALS FOR A NEW TENANCY

(attach or insert proposed terms of the new tenancy)

IMPORTANT NOTE FOR THE LANDLORD

This notice requests a new tenancy of your property or part of it. If you want to oppose this request you must act quickly.

Read the notice and all the Notes carefully. It would be wise to seek professional advice.

NOTES

The sections mentioned below are sections of the Landlord and Tenant Act 1954, as amended, (most recently by the Regulatory Reform (Business Tenancies) (England and Wales) Order 2003).

Tenant's request for a new tenancy

This request by your tenant for a new tenancy brings his or her current tenancy to an end on the day before the date mentioned in paragraph 2 of this notice. Section 26 contains rules about the date that the tenant can put in paragraph 2 of this notice.

Your tenant can apply to the court under section 24 for a new tenancy. You may apply for a new tenancy yourself, under the same section, but not if your tenant has already served an application. Once an application has been made to the court, your tenant's current tenancy will continue after the date mentioned in paragraph 2 while the application is being considered by the court. Either you or your tenant can ask the court to fix the rent which your tenant will have to pay whilst the tenancy continues (sections 24A to 24D). The court will settle any terms of a new tenancy on which you and your tenant disagree (sections 34 and 35).

Time limit for opposing your tenant's request

If you do not want to grant a new tenancy, you have two months from the making of your tenant's request in which to notify him or her that you will oppose any application made to the court for a new tenancy. You do not need a special form to do this, but the notice must be in writing and it must state on which of the grounds set out in section 30(1) you will oppose the application. If you do not use the same wording of the ground (or grounds), as set out below, your notice may be ineffective.

If there has been any delay in your seeing this notice, you may need to act very quickly. If you are in any doubt about what action you should take, get advice immediately from a solicitor or a surveyor.

Grounds for opposing tenant's application

If you wish to oppose the renewal of the tenancy, you can do so by opposing your tenant's application to the court, or by making your own application to the court for termination without renewal. However, you can only oppose your tenant's application, or apply for termination without renewal, on one or more of the grounds set out in section 30(1). These grounds are set out below. You will only be able to rely on the ground(s) of opposition that you have mentioned in your written notice to your tenant.

In this Table 'the holding' means the property that is the subject of the tenancy.

Paragraph of section 30(1)	Grounds
(a)	Where under the current tenancy the tenant has any obligations as respects the repair and maintenance of the holding, that the tenant ought not to be granted a new tenancy in view of the state of repair of the holding, being a state resulting from the tenant's failure to comply with the said obligations.
(b)	That the tenant ought not to be granted a new tenancy in view of his persistent delay in paying rent which has become due.
(c)	That the tenant ought not to be granted a new tenancy in view of other substantial breaches by him of his obligations under the current tenancy, or for any other reason connected with the tenant's use or management of the holding.
(d)	That the landlord has offered and is willing to provide or secure the provision of alternative accommodation for the tenant, that the terms on which the alternative accommodation is available are reasonable having regard to the terms of the current tenancy and to all other relevant circumstances, and that the accommodation and the time at which it will be available are suitable for the tenant's requirements (including the requirement to preserve goodwill) having regard to the nature and class of his business and to the situation and extent of, and facilities afforded by, the holding.
(e)	Where the current tenancy was created by the sub-letting of part only of the property comprised in a superior tenancy and the landlord is the owner of an interest in reversion expectant on the termination of that superior tenancy, that the aggregate of the rents reasonably obtainable on separate lettings of the holding and the remainder of that property would be substantially less than the rent reasonably obtainable on a letting of that property as a whole, that on the termination of the current tenancy the landlord requires possession of the holding for the purposes of letting or otherwise disposing of the said property as a whole, and that in view thereof the tenant ought not to be granted a new tenancy.
(f)	That on the termination of the current tenancy the landlord intends to demolish or reconstruct the premises comprised in the holding or a substantial part of those premises or to carry out substantial work of construction on the holding or part thereof and that he could not reasonably do so without obtaining possession of the holding.
(g)	On the termination of the current tenancy the landlord intends to occupy the holding for the purposes, or partly for the purposes, of a business to be carried on by him therein, or as his residence.

Compensation

If your tenant cannot get a new tenancy solely because one or more of grounds (e), (f) and (g) applies, he or she is entitled to compensation under section 37. If you have opposed your tenant's application on any of the other grounds mentioned in section 30(1), as well as on one or more of grounds (e), (f) and (g), your tenant can only get compensation if the court's refusal to grant a new tenancy is based solely on ground (e), (f) or (g). In other words, your tenant cannot get compensation under section 37 if the court has refused the tenancy on *other* grounds, even if one or more of grounds (e), (f) and (g) also applies.

If you are an authority possessing compulsory purchase powers (such as a local authority), your tenant may be entitled to a disturbance payment under Part 3 of the Land Compensation Act 1973.

Negotiating a new tenancy

Most tenancies are renewed by negotiation and your tenant has set out proposals for the new tenancy in paragraph 3 of this notice. You are not obliged to accept these proposals and may put forward your own. You and your tenant may agree in writing to extend the deadline for making an application to the court while negotiations continue. Your tenant may not apply to the court for a new tenancy until two months have passed from the date of the making of the request contained in this notice, unless you have already given notice opposing your tenant's request as mentioned in paragraph 6 of this notice (section 29A(3)).

If you try to agree a new tenancy with your tenant, remember:

- that one of you will need to apply to the court before the date in paragraph 2 of this notice, unless you both agree to extend the period for making an application.
- that any such agreement must be in writing and must be made before the date in paragraph 2 (sections 29A and 29B).

Validity of this notice

The tenant who has given you this notice may not be the person from whom you receive rent (sections 44 and 67). This does not necessarily mean that the notice is invalid.

If you have any doubts about whether this notice is valid, get advice immediately from a solicitor or a surveyor.

Further information

An explanation of the main points to consider when renewing or ending a business tenancy, 'Renewing and Ending Business Leases: a Guide for Tenants and Landlords', can be found at **www.odpm.gov.uk**. Printed copies of the explanation, but not of this form, are available from 1st June 2004 from Free Literature, PO Box 236, Wetherby, West Yorkshire, LS23 7NB (0870 1226 236).

FORM 4   LANDLORD'S REQUEST FOR INFORMATION ABOUT OCCUPATION AND SUB-TENANCIES (SECTION 40(1) OF THE LANDLORD AND TENANT ACT 1954)

To: (*insert name and address of tenant*)

From: (*insert name and address of landlord*)

1.   This notice relates to the following premises: (*insert address or description of premises*)

2.   I give you notice under section 40(1) of the Landlord and Tenant Act 1954 that I require you to provide information –

    (a) by answering questions (1) to (3) in the Table below;

    (b) if you answer 'yes' to question (2), by giving me the name and address of the person or persons concerned;

    (c) if you answer 'yes' to question (3), by also answering questions (4) to (10) in the Table below;

    (d) if you answer 'no' to question (8), by giving me the name and address of the sub-tenant; and

    (e) if you answer 'yes' to question (10), by giving me details of the notice or request.

TABLE

(1)	Do you occupy the premises or any part of them wholly or partly for the purposes of a business that is carried on by you?
(2)	To the best of your knowledge and belief, does any other person own an interest in reversion in any part of the premises?
(3)	Does your tenancy have effect subject to any sub-tenancy on which your tenancy is immediately expectant?
(4)	What premises are comprised in the sub-tenancy?
(5)	For what term does it have effect or, if it is terminable by notice, by what notice can it be terminated?
(6)	What is the rent payable under it?
(7)	Who is the sub-tenant?
(8)	To the best of your knowledge and belief, is the sub-tenant in occupation of the premises or of part of the premises comprised in the sub-tenancy?
(9)	Is an agreement in force excluding, in relation to the sub-tenancy, the provisions of sections 24 to 28 of the Landlord and Tenant Act 1954?
(10)	Has a notice been given under section 25 or 26(6) of that Act, or has a request been made under section 26 of that Act, in relation to the sub-tenancy?

3.   You must give the information concerned in writing and within the period of one month beginning with the date of service of this notice.

4.   Please send all correspondence about this notice to:

Name:

Address:

Signed: Date:

*[Landlord] *[on behalf of the landlord] *delete whichever is inapplicable*

IMPORTANT NOTE FOR THE TENANT

This notice contains some words and phrases that you may not understand. The Notes below should help you, but it would be wise to seek professional advice, for example, from a solicitor or surveyor, before responding to this notice.

Once you have provided the information required by this notice, you must correct it if you realise that it is not, or is no longer, correct. This obligation lasts for six months from the date of service of this notice, but an exception is explained in the next paragraph. If you need to correct information already given, you must do so within one month of becoming aware that the information is incorrect.

The obligation will cease if, after transferring your tenancy, you notify the landlord of the transfer and of the name and address of the person to whom your tenancy has been transferred.

If you fail to comply with the requirements of this notice, or the obligation mentioned above, you may face civil proceedings for breach of the statutory duty that arises under section 40 of the Landlord and Tenant Act 1954. In any such proceedings a court may order you to comply with that duty and may make an award of damages.

NOTES

The sections mentioned below are sections of the Landlord and Tenant Act 1954, as amended, (most recently by the Regulatory Reform (Business Tenancies) (England and Wales) Order 2003).

Purpose of this notice

Your landlord (or, if he or she is a tenant, possibly your landlord's landlord) has sent you this notice in order to obtain information about your occupation and that of any sub-tenants. This information may be relevant to the taking of steps to end or renew your business tenancy.

Time limit for replying

You must provide the relevant information within one month of the date of service of this notice (section 40(1), (2) and (5)).

Information required

You do not have to give your answers on this form; you may use a separate sheet for this purpose. The notice requires you to provide, in writing, information in the form of answers to questions (1) to (3) in the Table above and, if you answer 'yes' to question (3), also to provide information in the form of answers to questions (4) to (10) in that Table. Depending on your answer to question (2) and, if applicable in your case, questions (8) and (10), you must also provide the information referred to in paragraph 2(b), (d) and (e) of this notice. Question (2) refers to a person who owns an interest in reversion. You should answer 'yes' to this question if you know or believe that there is a person who receives, or is entitled to receive, rent in respect of any part of the premises (other than the landlord who served this notice).

When you answer questions about sub-tenants, please bear in mind that, for these purposes, a sub-tenant includes a person retaining possession of premises by virtue of the Rent (Agriculture) Act 1976 or the Rent Act 1977 after the coming to an end of a sub-tenancy, and 'sub-tenancy' includes a right so to retain possession (section 40(8)).

You should keep a copy of your answers and of any other information provided in response to questions (2), (8) or (10) above.

If, once you have given this information, you realise that it is not, or is no longer, correct, you must give the correct information within one month of becoming aware that the previous information is incorrect. Subject to the next paragraph, your duty to correct any information that you have already given continues for six months after you receive this notice (section 40(5)). You should give the correct information to the land-lord who gave you this notice unless you receive notice of the transfer of his or her interest, and of the name and address of the person to whom that interest has been transferred. In that case, the correct information must be given to that person.

If you transfer your tenancy within the period of six months referred to above, your duty to correct information already given will cease if you notify the landlord of the transfer and of the name and address of the person to whom your tenancy has been transferred.

If you do not provide the information requested, or fail to correct information that you have provided earlier, after realising that it is not, or is no longer, correct, proceed-ings may be taken against you and you may have to pay damages (section 40B).

If you are in any doubt about the information that you should give, get immediate advice from a solicitor or a surveyor.

Validity of this notice

The landlord who has given you this notice may not be the landlord to whom you pay your rent (sections 44 and 67). This does not necessarily mean that the notice is invalid.

If you have any doubts about whether this notice is valid, get advice immediately from a solicitor or a surveyor.

Further information

An explanation of the main points to consider when renewing or ending a business tenancy, 'Renewing and Ending Business Leases: a Guide for Tenants and Landlords', can be found at **www.odpm.gov.uk**. Printed copies of the explanation, but not of this form, are available from 1st June 2004 from Free Literature, PO Box 236, Wetherby, West Yorkshire, LS23 7NB (0870 1226 236).

FORM 5   TENANT'S REQUEST FOR INFORMATION FROM LANDLORD OR LANDLORD'S MORTGAGEE ABOUT LANDLORD'S INTEREST (SECTION 40(3) OF THE LANDLORD AND TENANT ACT 1954)

To: (*insert name and address of reversioner or reversioner's mortgagee in possession [see the first note below]*)

From: (*insert name and address of tenant*)

1. This notice relates to the following premises: (*insert address or description of premises*)
2. In accordance with section 40(3) of the Landlord and Tenant Act 1954 I require you –

(a) to state in writing whether you are the owner of the fee simple in respect of the premises or any part of them or the mortgagee in possession of such an owner,

(b) if you answer 'no' to (a), to state in writing, to the best of your knowledge and belief –

(i) the name and address of the person who is your or, as the case may be, your mortgagor's immediate landlord in respect of the premises or of the part in respect of which you are not, or your mortgagor is not, the owner in fee simple;

(ii) for what term your or your mortgagor's tenancy has effect and what is the earliest date (if any) at which that tenancy is terminable by notice to quit given by the landlord; and

(iii) whether a notice has been given under section 25 or 26(6) of the Landlord and Tenant Act 1954, or a request has been made under section 26 of that Act, in relation to the tenancy and, if so, details of the notice or request;

(c) to state in writing, to the best of your knowledge and belief, the name and address of any other person who owns an interest in reversion in any part of the premises;

(d) if you are a reversioner, to state in writing whether there is a mortgagee in possession of your interest in the premises; and

(e) if you answer 'yes' to (d), to state in writing, to the best of your knowledge and belief, the name and address of the mortgagee in possession.

3. You must give the information concerned within the period of one month beginning with the date of service of this notice.
4. Please send all correspondence about this notice to:

Name:

Address:

Signed: Date:

*[Tenant] *[on behalf of the tenant] (*delete whichever is inapplicable*)

IMPORTANT NOTE FOR LANDLORD OR LANDLORD'S MORTGAGEE

This notice contains some words and phrases that you may not understand. The Notes below should help you, but it would be wise to seek professional advice, for example, from a solicitor or surveyor, before responding to this notice.

Once you have provided the information required by this notice, you must correct it if you realise that it is not, or is no longer, correct. This obligation lasts for six months from the date of service of this notice, but an exception is explained in the next paragraph. If you need to correct information already given, you must do so within one month of becoming aware that the information is incorrect.

The obligation will cease if, after transferring your interest, you notify the tenant of the transfer and of the name and address of the person to whom your interest has been transferred.

If you fail to comply with the requirements of this notice, or the obligation mentioned above, you may face civil proceedings for breach of the statutory duty that arises under section 40 of the Landlord and Tenant Act 1954. In any such proceedings a court may order you to comply with that duty and may make an award of damages.

NOTES

The sections mentioned below are sections of the Landlord and Tenant Act 1954, as amended, (most recently by the Regulatory Reform (Business Tenancies) (England and Wales) Order 2003).

Terms used in this notice

The following terms, which are used in paragraph 2 of this notice, are defined in section 40(8):

> 'mortgagee in possession' includes a receiver appointed by the mortgagee or by the court who is in receipt of the rents and profits;
> 'reversioner' means any person having an interest in the premises, being an interest in reversion expectant (whether immediately or not) on the tenancy; and
> 'reversioner's mortgagee in possession' means any person being a mortgagee in possession in respect of such an interest.

Section 40(8) requires the reference in paragraph 2(b) of this notice to your mortgagor to be read in the light of the definition of 'mortgagee in possession'.

A mortgagee (mortgage lender) will be 'in possession' if the mortgagor (the person who owes money to the mortgage lender) has failed to comply with the terms of the mortgage. The mortgagee may then be entitled to receive rent that would normally have been paid to the mortgagor.

The term 'the owner of the fee simple' means the freehold owner.

The term 'reversioner' includes the freehold owner and any intermediate landlord as well as the immediate landlord of the tenant who served this notice.

Purpose of this notice and information required

This notice requires you to provide, in writing, the information requested in paragraph 2(a) and (c) of the notice and, if applicable in your case, in paragraph 2(b), (d) and (e). You do not need to use a special form for this purpose.

If, once you have given this information, you realise that it is not, or is no longer, correct, you must give the correct information within one month of becoming aware that the previous information is incorrect. Subject to the last paragraph in this section of these Notes, your duty to correct any information that you have already given continues for six months after you receive this notice (section 40(5)).

You should give the correct information to the tenant who gave you this notice unless you receive notice of the transfer of his or her interest, and of the name and address of the person to whom that interest has been transferred. In that case, the correct information must be given to that person.

If you do not provide the information requested, or fail to correct information that you have provided earlier, after realising that it is not, or is no longer, correct, proceedings may be taken against you and you may have to pay damages (section 40B).

If you are in any doubt as to the information that you should give, get advice immediately from a solicitor or a surveyor.

If you transfer your interest within the period of six months referred to above, your duty to correct information already given will cease if you notify the tenant of that transfer and of the name and address of the person to whom your interest has been transferred.

Time limit for replying

You must provide the relevant information within one month of the date of service of this notice (section 40(3), (4) and (5)).

Validity of this notice

The tenant who has given you this notice may not be the person from whom you receive rent (sections 44 and 67). This does not necessarily mean that the notice is invalid.

If you have any doubts about the validity of the notice, get advice immediately from a solicitor or a surveyor.

Further information

An explanation of the main points to consider when renewing or ending a business tenancy, 'Renewing and Ending Business Leases: a Guide for Tenants and Landlords', can be found at **www.odpm.gov.uk**. Printed copies of the explanation, but not of this form, are available from 1st June 2004 from Free Literature, PO Box 236, Wetherby, West Yorkshire, LS23 7NB (0870 1226 236).

FORM 6   LANDLORD'S WITHDRAWAL OF NOTICE TERMINATING TENANCY (SECTION 44 OF, AND PARAGRAPH 6 OF SCHEDULE 6 TO, THE LANDLORD AND TENANT ACT 1954)

To: (*insert name and address of tenant*)

From: (*insert name and address of landlord*)

1. This notice is given under section 44 of, and paragraph 6 of Schedule 6 to, the Landlord and Tenant Act 1954 ('the 1954 Act').
2. It relates to the following property: (*insert address or description of property*)
3. 1 have become your landlord for the purposes of the 1954 Act.
4. I withdraw the notice given to you by (*insert name of former landlord*), terminating your tenancy on (*insert date*).
5. Please send any correspondence about this notice to:

Name:

Address:

Signed: Date:

*[Landlord] *[on behalf of the landlord] (**delete whichever is inapplicable*)

IMPORTANT NOTE FOR THE TENANT

If you have any doubts about the validity of this notice, get advice immediately from a solicitor or a surveyor.

NOTES

The sections and Schedule mentioned below are sections of, and a Schedule to, the Landlord and Tenant Act 1954, as amended, (most recently by the Regulatory Reform (Business Tenancies) (England and Wales) Order 2003).

Purpose of this notice

You were earlier given a notice bringing your tenancy to an end, but there has now been a change of landlord. This new notice is given to you by your new landlord and withdraws the earlier notice, which now has no effect. However, the new landlord can, if he or she wishes, give you a fresh notice with the intention of bringing your tenancy to an end (section 44 and paragraph 6 of Schedule 6).

Validity of this notice

The landlord who has given you this notice may not be the landlord to whom you pay your rent (sections 44 and 67). This does not necessarily mean that the notice is invalid.

If you have any doubts about whether this notice is valid, get advice immediately from a solicitor or a surveyor. If this notice is not valid, the original notice will have effect.

Your tenancy will end on the date given in that notice (stated in paragraph 4 of this notice).

Further information

An explanation of the main points to consider when renewing or ending a business tenancy, 'Renewing and Ending Business Leases: a Guide for Tenants and Landlords', can be found at **www.odpm.gov.uk**. Printed copies of the explanation, but not of this form, are available from 1st June 2004 from Free Literature, PO Box 236, Wetherby, West Yorkshire, LS23 7NB (0870 1226 236).

Index